The Interregnum:
The Quest for Settlement 1646–1660

Each volume in this series is designed to make available to students important new work on key historical problems and periods that they encounter in their courses. Every volume is devoted to a central topic or theme, and the most important aspects of this are dealt with by specially commissioned essays from specialists in the relevant field. The editorial Introduction reviews the problem or period as a whole, and each essay provides an assessment of the particular aspect, pointing out the areas of development and controversy and indicating where conclusions can be drawn or where further work is necessary. An annotated bibliography serves as an up-to-date guide to further reading.

PROBLEMS IN FOCUS SERIES

Britain after the Glorious Revolution 1689–1714
edited by Geoffrey Holmes

*Britain Pre-eminent: Studies of British world
influence in the nineteenth century*
edited by C. J. Bartlett

Popular Movements c. 1830–1850   edited by J. T. Ward

The Republic and the Civil War in Spain
edited by Raymond Carr

Financing Development in Latin America
edited by Keith Griffin

The Hundred Years War   edited by Kenneth Fowler

The Interregnum: The Quest for Settlement 1646–1660
edited by G. E. Aylmer

FORTHCOMING TITLES

The Reign of James VI and I   edited by A. G. R. Smith

The Origins of the English Civil War
edited by Conrad Russell

Industrial Revolutions   edited by R. M. Hartwell

The Conservative Leadership 1831–1937
edited by Donald Southgate

The Interregnum:
The Quest for Settlement 1646-1660

EDITED BY
G. E. AYLMER

Archon Books · 1972

Library of Congress Cataloging in Publication Data
Main entry under title:

Interregnum.

  Bibliography: p.
  1. Great Britain—Politics and government—1642–1660
Addresses, essays, lectures.   I. Aylmer, G. E. ed.
DA405.I57   1972   942.06'3   72–5375
ISBN 0–208–01305–9

Published 1972 by THE MACMILLAN PRESS, LTD
London and Basingstoke
and in the United States of America as an Archon Book
by THE SHOE STRING PRESS, INC
Hamden, Connecticut

Printed in Great Britain

Contents

Acknowledgements   vii

Note on Dating   vii

Introduction: The Quest for Settlement 1646–1660   1

1   London's Counter-Revolution   29
      VALERIE PEARL

2   The Levellers and the Franchise   57
      KEITH THOMAS

3   Conquest and Consent: Thomas Hobbes and the Engagement
      Controversy   79
      QUENTIN SKINNER

4   The Church in England 1646–1660   99
      CLAIRE CROSS

5   Social and Economic Policies under the Commonwealth   121
      J. P. COOPER

6   Cromwell's Ordinances: The Early Legislation of the
      Protectorate   143
      IVAN ROOTS

7   Settlement in the Counties 1653–1658   165
      DAVID UNDERDOWN

8   Last Quests for a Settlement 1657–1660   183
      AUSTIN WOOLRYCH

List of Abbreviations in Bibliography and References   205

Bibliography   206

References and Notes on Text   214

Notes on Contributors   235

Index   236

46627

Acknowledgements

I AM grateful to my fellow contributors for their co-operation and forbearance, and particularly to Mr J. P. Cooper for making valuable suggestions about my Introduction, although I am, of course, responsible for such mistakes and misjudgements as it still contains. In checking references and other items I have been greatly assisted by the staffs of the Borthwick Institute and of the City, the Minster and the J. B. Morrell (University) Libraries in York. I am grateful to Mrs Muriel Farrow and Miss Angela Cooper for their skilful typing; and to Mr Derick Mirfin of the Macmillan Press for his help in the preparation of this volume. Most of all, I wish to thank my wife for her help at all stages.

G. E. A.

Note on Dating

·

THE year is taken to begin on 1 January, but in other respects the 'Old Style' is used. For example, Charles I was executed on 30 January 1649, not on 30 January 1648 (contemporary usage) nor on 9 February 1649 (according to the reformed calendar, then already used in much of Europe).

Introduction: The Quest for Settlement 1646–1660

G. E. AYLMER

'Settlement I fear is not in some men's minds, nor ever will be.'
Thurloe to Henry Cromwell (3 March 1657)

I

As long as English history is studied, historians will continue to debate the nature and significance of the Civil War and its aftermath. It is certainly not because there is any lack of good books on the subject that interpretation of the events of 1640–60 remains so controversial. Rather the opposite; in part at least this is just because there are works by such historians as Clarendon, Ludlow, Hume, Guizot, Macaulay, Ranke, Gardiner, Firth, Trevelyan, and among the living Veronica Wedgwood, Maurice Ashley, Christopher Hill and Hugh Trevor-Roper, whose approaches to the subject have differed and continue to differ so completely. Recently we have seen a new wave of interpretations, or revisions. At one extreme Professor Lawrence Stone has offered an explanation of the revolution in demographic terms – as having been in part at least the consequence of population growth coupled with the frustrated ambitions of men educated above their stations. At the other Professor Geoffrey Elton, with as robust an iconoclasm as befits an admirer of Thomas Cromwell, has asserted that the emperor is wearing no clothes. For he argues that there was no revolution in seventeenth-century England, and that it is therefore otiose to spend time arguing about how to explain it. And from a very different standpoint, if also from Cambridge, Mr Peter Laslett's definition of a revolution would exclude the events of 1640–60, along with a good deal else. 'Social revolution,' he writes, 'meaning an irreversible changing of the pattern of social relationships, never happened in traditional patriarchal, pre-industrial human society. It was almost impossible to contemplate.' Not surprisingly he concludes that the violent upheavals in seventeenth-century England fail to meet the requirements of this definition.[1] No doubt the contributors to this volume are as widely divided in their interpretations as any other more or less representative group of seventeenth-century historians. The reader will notice that the title of Dr Pearl's chapter, 'London's Counter-Revolution', implies the existence of a revolution for London to counter; Mr Skinner writes of the revolution staged by the Independent Party (in 1648–9), while Dr Cross refers to the Puritan Revolution. Probably, like the story about the religion of all wise men, my fellow authors would not wish to tell exactly what sort of revolution they believed that they were writing about. Moreover, although we hope that it may help to illuminate these great issues, the immediate aims of this volume are more modest.

Whatever the origins and nature of the Civil War, we must take for granted here that Parliament, or at least the armed forces raised by Parliament, had won it. Whatever else had been happening since 1640–2, in a military sense the king and his adherents had been well and truly defeated by 1646. And at the other end of the period with which we are concerned, the English republic collapsed in 1659–60, when the monarchy returned carrying back with it the House of Lords and the episcopal Anglican Church. Some contemporaries maintained from the start that the king's military defeat would in itself create insoluble political difficulties for Parliament. The earl of Manchester, who was Oliver Cromwell's superior as commander-in-chief of the army of the Eastern Association, was reported to have said in the autumn of 1644: 'If we beat the King ninety and nine times, yet he is king still, and so will his posterity be after him; but if the King beat us once we shall all be hanged, and our posterity made slaves.' And the king's veteran commander Lord Astley remarked more cynically to his captors in 1646: 'You have now done your work, boys, and may go to play, unless you fall out among yourselves.' Here indeed is the essence of the Cavalier–conservative view of the revolution: that it was a 'great rebellion', an unfortunate aberration from the mainstream of English history, but of which the eventual happy outcome (in 1660) was only a matter of time and God's dispensation. On that view, of course, the problem is not why the victors in the Civil War failed to attain a more lasting settlement, but how on earth such a hopelessly divided, aberrant – one is tempted to say un-English – collection of deviants and misfits managed to defeat the king in the first place and then to postpone the return of his son and heir for a decade after his father's execution. So what we ought to be explaining is not the temporariness of the Puritan–parliament-arian–republican victory, but its very existence, however transient. In a sense this is the theme of Clarendon's great *History of the Rebellion*, the fullest and finest contemporary account of what happened and why. Nor is this far removed from being the assumption of some eminent historians today, such as Professor Trevor-Roper. There is a renewed fashion for books and essays with the phrase 'Great Rebellion' in the title. And when Professor Kenyon, editor of the latest authoritative collection of constitutional documents for this period, writes that 'In a sense, from August 1641 until May 1660 the constitution just marked time,' he too is coming very near to the notion of temporary aberrance. It may therefore be that we are all on the wrong track. Not that any of the writers represented here is concerned to put forward a complete interpretation of the revolution in terms of any particular explanation. The best recent generalised statements of the case for the events of 1640–60 having constituted a revolution and so deserving the name are to be found in the writings of Christopher Hill, Lawrence Stone and Perez Zagorin. Not that these historians are all in agreement as to its nature and significance. While Stone emphasises the underlying social and economic (as well as other) causes of the Civil War, he sees its consequences as less revolutionary. So far from being checked, the trend towards oligarchy was accentuated after 1660, when English society became less mobile, less educated, less fertile, and above all (in part due to these other changes) less revolutionary, than it had been before 1640.[2] We therefore need to distinguish between two partly conflicting interpretations. On Hill's view, the revolution did usher in a more bourgeois, capitalist society, whose coming would have been seriously delayed but for the Civil War and its results. On Stone's, however, the Civil War was itself rather the culminating point of a period of ferment, tension and upheaval, being followed by an age of consolidation if not reaction.

Similarly there are differences among those who would deny that a revolution took place at all. But these may amount to variations of emphasis and presentation more than to logically conflicting interpre-tations. On Laslett's view there was indeed an 'English Revolution', which took place between about 1640 and 1689, but it was essentially of a political and ecclesiastical nature and did not constitute a social revolution. This is to be contrasted with the implication that what happened was no more than a prolonged and temporarily successful insurrection – to be described by de Gaulle's terse if crude term for the events of May 1968 in Paris. More seriously, Mr Laslett would seem to share with Professor Everitt, and perhaps Professor Kenyon, the view that any important changes, especially of a social and economic kind, that did occur took place over the century as a whole, and were neither the cause nor the effect of the upheavals of 1640–60. A variant of this is Professor Wilson's suggestion that, while the Great Rebellion did have momentous economic consequences, this was not because it was a bourgeois-capitalist revolution; its effects were, on his view, more truly 'revolutionary' than its causes or its nature. Dr Hill's most recent major work, his biography of Oliver Cromwell, rehearses his earlier beliefs: there was indeed a revolution in mid-seventeenth-century England, but it failed because it did not go far enough, because constitutional and ecclesiastical changes were not matched by equally thorough-going political and social changes. If one pursues this line of thought, the key elements in the events leading to the Restoration then become the points at which the revolution turned back in a conservative direction. There seem to be three candidates for an English *thermidor* (or, *mutatis mutandis*, for the English equivalent of Trotsky's defeat by Stalin). The date 15 November 1647 saw the crushing of the incipient pro-Leveller outbreak in the army, on Corkbush Field in Hertfordshire. On 14 May 1649 the renewed and more serious Leveller mutiny was decisively put down, at Burford in Oxfordshire. And on 12 December 1653 the conservative majority in the Barebone's Parliament abdicated their powers to Cromwell as Lord General and the man who had summoned them to meet. That the radicals of 1653 were in any case very different from those of 1647–9 and that their revolution, if it had taken place, would have led in an almost contrary direction, are not in themselves decisive objections to this view. But let us for the time being lower our sights and attempt a more modest order of explanation.

Valerie Pearl's study of London in 1647 illustrates one aspect of a wider problem. Why was no peace treaty, no constitutional compromise reached between the spring of 1646 and the end of 1648? The obvious, traditional and still the most cogent answer would be: King Charles I. The king had long appreciated the serious possibilities behind Jacob Astley's flippancy. Indeed his final tragedy was due largely to his overestimate of his own capacity to delay agreement. By playing off the different parties or factions among his opponents he hoped to bring political victory out of military defeat. It was a narrow miscalculation, not a wild or hopeless one. As late as December 1648, even after the Second Civil War, approximately three-fifths of the parliamentarian M.P.s were still prepared to go on trying for a settlement with Charles, essentially on the terms first offered in 1646. If this parliamentarian majority, whether we should call them Presbyterians or moderates or the Peace Party is a continuing matter of disagreement, had been dealing with the king in isolation, agreement of a sort would almost certainly have been reached. This might well have broken down again later, if and when Charles had used his prerogatives to restore Anglicans in the Church and to regain control of the armed forces. And it is arguable whether the men of 1640–2, without the leadership of Bedford, Essex, Pym and Hampden, but under that of Denzil Holles in the Commons and with Northumberland, Warwick, Saye and Manchester in the Lords, had the ability to sustain such a settlement once made. They would have had to face continuing enemies on both Left and Right, unless that is there had been a mass blood-bath to eliminate both the civil and military leaders of the radical or War Party. Even this would have left them with the irreconcilable wing of the Royalist Party – Papists, high Anglicans and others – to contend with. It would have been touch and go. If and in so far as the king had wanted to make such a settlement work, then it might have endured. There were some able new men – John Swinfen is an example – who had entered Parliament among the 'recruiters' (those elected to the seats of expelled Royalists and to replace deceased members) and had already emerged among the leaders of Holles's party.[3] The 'Presbyterian' majority should not be judged by that egregious pair Clement Walker and William Prynne. But this is all theoretical and beside the point. Charles and Holles were not confronting each other in a vacuum, or with everyone else massed in support behind one or other of them.

By 1647 the political struggle, and so the quest for settlement, involved at least three other distinct elements. Generally speaking the Scots were allied to the moderate parliamentarians, but they cannot by any means be identified with them. Furthermore, when we speak of the Scots we mean the dominant faction in the Scottish government and those who controlled the army of the Covenant. The years 1647–8 saw a decisive change here. For Scotland had its own limited but dramatic counter-revolution. With the glamorous but destructive Montrose a defeated exile, the radical convenanting leaders – notably Argyll and Johnston of Warriston – gradually lost control to the Royalist Hamiltonians. A number of influential moderate covenanters, such as the able but unattractive Lauderdale, were converted to the idea of a Royalist alliance; and so – though Lauderdale always had his private doubts – to the ultimate folly of invading England in the king's interest. The Scots disagreed with most of their English allies about the right kind of church settlement, but a general mistrust – and perhaps an element of racial feeling on both sides – affected political and military co-operation too. So theirs was not a united front, even before the victory of Hamilton and the Scottish alliance with the king.

The radical or War Party parliamentarians, alias the Independents, were not – save in the person of Cromwell – identical with the generals of the New Model Army. The younger Sir Henry Vane, the most brilliant if also the most volatile of them, was essentially a civilian and was as much concerned with naval and diplomatic business as with the army. Sir Arthur Hesilrige was a garrison commander in the north-east, but he was first and last a parliament man, a parliamentarian almost in the modern sense. In the army, Sir Thomas Fairfax, the Lord General, not yet an M.P., was neither an Independent in denominational terms, nor a radical in any sense, although he was a Puritan and a sincere servant of the parliamentary cause. Philip Skippon, Major-General of the Infantry, was to go along with the radicals but was hardly one of them. When we refer to the army leaders as being identified with the parliamentary radicals in their political standpoint, we therefore really mean the Lieutenant-General of Horse, the Commissary-General (Cromwell's son-in-law Henry Ireton), the obscure but not at this time insignificant Lieutenant-General of the Artillery (Thomas Hammond) and several of the colonels. We must also remember that at least two of the future republican activists in the House (Edmund Ludlow and Henry Marten) were well to the left of the so-called radicals or War Party on many issues. And at least two colonels in the field army (William Ayres and Thomas Rainsborough) became supporters of the popular movement. So terms like 'army leadership' and 'parliamentary radicals' are convenient shorthand labels, not exact descriptions of neatly packaged entities.

In so far as the so-called War Party had a constructive policy for a political settlement, this was embodied in the famous Heads of Proposals, of July 1647. Ever since Gardiner, historians have rightly praised the pragmatic good sense of this document. Given the king's basic goodwill, but allowing too for his slipperiness, his belief in the divine right of kings to double-cross their rebellious subjects, the Heads provided an altogether more realistic, as well as more generous basis for settlement than the Newcastle Propositions, presented to the king by the parliamentary majority or so-called Peace Party in 1646.[4] But it would be a mistake to see the Heads as the official platform of the radicals or Independents in Parliament. They were actually drafted by Ireton, who was not at this time at all a prominent figure in the House, and the gifted young Yorkshire Colonel, John Lambert, who was not an M.P. at all. The Heads were revised, possibly in a radical direction, at the General Council of the Army, which by then included representatives of the other ranks as well as of the regimental officers. But the text was allegedly altered and made more conservative as a result of private negotiations with the king. There is no firm evidence that the civilian leaders of the War Party had had any hand in them before their publication on 1 August. (As Dr Pearl's chapter shows, a large bloc of radical members withdrew from London on 30 July, but they could hardly have collaborated in a pamphlet published two days later.)

At one stage in these tortuous comings and goings Charles did get so far as to indicate his preference for the Heads over the Propositions. But he never gave even that qualified acceptance of them that could have formed the basis for further, more detailed and constructive discussions. Mrs Pearl's chapter ends with the military occupation of London in August 1647, and the consequent withdrawal of Holles and most of his leading colleagues under threat of impeachment. There was, however, a remarkably buoyant parliamentary majority for the programme of the moderates, or Peace Party. Before the end of the month the House of Commons had decided in favour of presenting the king, not, as might have been expected, with the Heads of Proposals, but with an only slightly modified version of the Newcastle Propositions, sometimes confusingly called the Hampton Proposals (because Charles was by then at Hampton Court). All negotiations were broken off in January 1648, when news filtered through of the king's secret agreement with the Scots; perhaps for the only time before Pride's Purge, the hardliners of the War Party had the upper hand in the House (although even then not in the Lords). But during the course of the Second Civil War (March–October 1648), several of the eleven impeached Peace Party leaders resumed their seats, and they appear rapidly to have recovered their majority. The draft text for the abortive Treaty of Newport (Charles having fled to the Isle of Wight the previous winter) was yet again only a revised version of the familiar 1646 Propositions. It was the king's equivocal reply to part of this, in effect rejecting the crucial clauses on future church government, that led to the celebrated vote of 5 December in favour (by 129 to 83) of carrying on the negotiations – and so to Pride's Purge the next day.

Much that is at present unknown, or tentative speculation, will be clearer when we have Mrs Pearl's sequel to her earlier book on London and her edition of the unprinted parliamentary diaries for the mid- and later 1640s.

The issues and divisions in Parliament both before and after the critical winter of 1648–9 are more firmly established, with full supporting detail, in Professor Underdown's *Pride's Purge* (1971).

The final element in the fluid political situation of 1646–9 was of course the popular movement. Because this was unprecedented it helps to give a special character to the developments during these years. Thanks to the 1647 crisis between Parliament and army, and to the men's mistrust of their own commanders, the soldiers had elected 'agitators' (two representatives, or 'agents' as they were often called) from each regiment. The combination of this basis for a kind of military soviet before its time with the civilian Leveller Party organisation in London provided, for the first time in English history, something like a coherent democratic movement. But, as Mr Thomas's chapter abundantly demonstrates, there were deep divisions – of personality, interest and belief – within the Levellers' ranks. Colonel Rainsborough, who took the most democratic line of anyone in the famous Putney Debates (October–November 1647) and was potentially the movement's most effective military leader, was not a member of the Leveller Party at all. The differences between the civilians and the soldiers – the more and less democratic, the 'hard-liners' and the soft-centred (alias hawks and doves) – all strained such unity as the movement possessed. The eloquence and popularity of 'Free-born John' (Lieutenant-Colonel Lilburne), the only authentic popular hero of the revolution, would have been as inadequate to hold these disparate elements together in the unlikely event of their victory, as they proved to be in defeat. He lacked the sustained energy and organising capacity to be a successful revolutionary leader. Even in what can only seem the exceedingly unlikely event of a Leveller victory and seizure of power, it is hard to imagine how their schemes for constitutional settlement could have been implemented, against what would have been the ferocious opposition of the whole of the traditional ruling class, both parliamentarian and Royalist, without instituting a repressive, even if 'popular', dictatorship.

The Digger movement of 1649–50 posed, it may be argued, an even more fundamental social challenge to the existing social order – and perhaps, at the level of the rural peasant community, more of an actual danger. But as a political threat it was negligible. And whatever interest and attraction the Diggers and their extraordinary leader, Gerrard Winstanley, may have for us today, in their historical context they offered no conceivable basis for settlement. By frightening the more conservative-minded of the propertied parliamentarians, their very existence may well have made any radical or even partially demo-cratic settlement less likely.

The Levellers had two opportunities to stage a popular revolt; they failed both times, which is not surprising if we consider the forces against them. This was especially true in 1649, when their political leaders were all either imprisoned or dead, or else had quit in disillusion-ment before the actual military mutiny began. Much more remarkable are the very fact of their existence as an articulate mass movement and the undoubted influence that they did exert in pushing the army leader-ship and its parliamentary allies in a radical direction. What role in-deed could the Levellers and their allies have played other than as the radical, popular wing of the parliamentary War Party and the army 'grandees'? The notion of a Leveller-Scots or a Leveller-Presbyterian alliance is self-evidently preposterous. Toleration for all Protestant sects was one of their cornerstones; many of them went much further than this towards full religious liberty. In the 1650s, it is true, some Levellers did try to make an alliance with the Royalists. But this was mainly a reflection of their unhappy demoralisation after earlier de-feats; it was as much a move into political Cloud-cuckoo-land as the converse Presbyterian denunciations of them for being crypto-Jesuits. The assassination of Cromwell (at any time from 1653 to his death) might conceivably have given such an alliance its opportunity. More likely, this would simply have led to the closing of republican ranks against the 'common enemy'. Military victory was more dangerous to the political unity of the parliamentarian-republican cause at all times during these years than the threat of defeat.

After the winter of 1648–9 the Gordian knot had been cut. A prag-matic, conservative revolution had taken place. The king had been tried and executed and monarchy abolished; sole legislative power had been voted to reside in the Commons alone, and then the House of Lords had been abolished too. Under the purged, or 'Rump', House of Commons and the Council of State which it then proceeded to elect (almost entirely from its own membership), a form of republican government took shape. A little later the people of England and its dominions were declared a Commonwealth and – to the derision of the

Levellers and Diggers – a 'Free State'. But this was not a settlement made to last, and few even of the Rump saw it, or were prepared to describe it, as such. The new rulers were not identical with the radical War Party (military and parliamentary) of the later 1640s, but substantially overlapped in membership with that party and were certainly its political heirs. Had they any constructive ideas as to what to do with their victory?

Part of what the republicans of the new Commonwealth did – and failed to do – with their power, may be seen in the chapters by Mr Skinner and Mr Cooper and in one section of that by Dr Cross. But these aspects are, unavoidably, far from constituting the whole story; nor would their authors claim otherwise. During the years 1649–52 the whole of the British Isles and the English overseas colonies were either brought directly under the Commonwealth's rule or at least forced to recognise the new regime. Any revolutionary government, which comes to power by extra-constitutional means, has to win recognition of its own authority. This was particularly so with revolutionaries who were most reluctant to admit that they had ever acted illegally, or unconstitutionally. Mr Skinner shows that even the greatest – and superficially the most abstract and least directly committed – political theorist of the time was not exempt from these preoccupations. There has been much argument too about the Rump's economic policy. If a bourgeois-commercial capitalist revolution had by then taken place in England, would one not expect this to be reflected in the programme and attitude of the new government? Hence the importance of Mr Cooper's theme, in addition to its interest for the history of economic and social policy in its own right. The victory of the political allies and associates of the religious Independents in the winter of 1648–9 may be said to have outflanked, or overtaken, the religious settlement of the preceding three years. For this had been a series of qualified but distinct victories for a modified, Erastian Presbyterianism, over high clerical Presbyterianism, episcopalianism and congregational independency alike. While Dr Cross has mapped out, in a pioneering study, a larger area of ecclesiastical history – all the way from the king's defeat to his son's return – her discussion of the practical changes that followed the political upheaval of 1648–9, even though unaccompanied by major legislative enactment until 1654, is of especial interest here.

All this may be thought by some to take 'settlement' in too narrowly political and institutional a sense. Where, it may be asked, are the underlying economic and social realities of these years? Where are the re-

ligious passions and convulsions, and most notably the rise of millenarian
fervour among the Baptists and the emergence of the Fifth Monarchy
Men as a distinct and revolutionary sect? What room is there in this
approach for the role of such men as George Fox and John Bunyan in
the life of republican England; for the poetry of Milton and Marvell;
for the oil-paintings of Lely and the miniatures of Samuel Cooper;
for the music of Locke and Davenant; for the new science that was
shortly to usher in the age of Newton? Certainly the life of a whole
society, of the inhabitants of a relatively small and homogeneous country,
over one quite short spell of time, is – in one sense – a unity, all of a
piece. How easy, one is tempted to say glib, it is to assert this! But it is
often a very different story when we come to try to describe and analyse
more exactly what the relations were between the different parts of
human endeavour, even within such an apparently limited community.
To take one area of stormy controversy among historians: let the interested student follow the arguments and counter-arguments about the
origins of the Royal Society, and the connection (if any) between the
mathematical and scientific advances of the period and the political,
religious and social conflicts.[5] Even the most distinguished historians
have found it easier to demolish the theses of others than to sustain
a positive interpretation of their own.

The demand for a more thorough-going integration of political
with economic and socio-demographic history is easy to applaud. But
it is well to remember the modest limits of our knowledge in those
areas. We can perhaps estimate the total population of England and
Wales in the mid-seventeenth century to within 10 per cent either
way (that is, on either side of about five millions). But we have very
little idea of how fast, if at all, it was growing, and in what ways. And
because our quantitative evidence in economic matters is so heavily
weighted towards external, seaborne trade, we can only guess at
national income, gross national product, output and income per head
and the rate of growth – all regarded as basic vital statistics for understanding any society's economy today. Some historians write of 'Asian
poverty' to describe the lot of the poorer sections of seventeenth-
century English society. And in the 1690s Gregory King was to reckon
that about half the families in the kingdom depended in some measure
upon private charity or public relief for their survival.[6] We know that
food prices were very high in the late 1640s. And it is obvious that this
had some connection with the temperature of popular discontent. But
whether the poverty of half the population in Stuart England was really

at the level of present-day Bengal may fairly be doubted. There are contemporary descriptions of the normal diet of the poor; and except in very bad years foreign visitors and others do not describe people as starving to death in the streets. There were occasional food riots, but except in years like 1647–9 they were not an endemic feature of the social scene. This need not lead us to indulge in any nonsensical counter-mythology about the 'good old days' of pre-industrial merrie England!

In so far as the army played a large part in the popular movement, we must remember too that the soldiers had their own special grievances. Compared with other wage-earners they were not ill paid. The trouble arose when their pay did not come through. But thanks to the land sales under the Commonwealth [7] the army's arrears were much less of a grievance after 1649 than they had been earlier; and this may be another element in the Levellers' decline. It is also possible, though a more open question, that conditions for the people generally became a little easier from about 1650. Population growth had probably flattened out and real wages may – for the first time in a century and a half – have been more or less stable, except for short-term fluctuations due to harvest failures and trade recessions.

As we have already seen, religion did indeed impinge on the problem of a political settlement. Thanks to the work of Christopher Hill and others, most historians would today agree that the fear of popular sectarian enthusiasm, both as a threat to strictly ecclesiastical order and decency of worship, and for social reasons, made a political *détente* more difficult to achieve. And ultimately these fears contributed to the mentality of 1660, though – as Professor Woolrych's chapter shows – they did not in any direct sense 'cause' the Restoration.

The Puritan notion of 'waiting on Providence' often seems near to a belief in justification by results. In practice, moreover, it led different Puritans to draw very different conclusions, and so to act in contrary ways. Some of the most religious of the Rump's civilian members would seem to have felt that their own embodiment of republican virtue was a signal part of God's handiwork; and that it should there-fore be preserved by whatever constitutionally dubious means. Crom-well, however, was to come to feel about the Rump by April 1653, as he had done about the Presbyterians in 1647, about the king by 1648, about the Levellers by 1649, about the Scots in 1650: that the time for treating with the incorrigible was past, and that God's purpose must now be served by decisive action. Hence this pervasive belief could divide more than it unified. For many contemporaries it was perhaps an idiom of speech and thought, rather than a specific political precept. And it could, of course, sometimes slide into sheer complacency and hypocrisy, as readers of Samuel Butler's *Hudibras* will know was alleged by the Puritans' enemies.

Much has been written recently about the challenge of religious millenarianism, which culminated in the Barebone's Parliament of 1653. Close studies have been made of the two most 'far-out' groups: the militant Fifth Monarchy Men, and the professedly quietist but allegedly orgiastic Ranters. Very properly, the most serious and remarkable of all the radical sects, the early Quakers, continue to receive detailed attention, and to arouse some disagreement as to their social origins.[8] Whatever intolerance did disfigure Cromwellian England (but far less so than Cromwellian Ireland), the episode of the Protector's conversations with George Fox is not the least remarkable example of its – and his – tolerance: it is almost as if the U.S. President were to invite the Yippie leaders to the White House!

The relationship between Puritan-republican rule and developments in literature and the arts is a live topic too. Use of the printed word as a political weapon in the 1640s may have done more for English prose than the King James Bible. And it is hard to see, at this distance in time, that English drama was seriously damaged by the closure of the theatres from 1642 to 1660. Not that this makes it a laudable act: it was bigoted, intolerant and – looking ahead to the Restoration stage of 1660–90 – counter-productive even on its own narrow moralistic terms.

II

But when all this has been said (and far more, naturally, could be said on these and related topics), our theme is political settlement and the failure to achieve it. Here the big question with the Commonwealth (1649–53) is whether the Rump House of Commons could – and so should – have done better than it did. In the matters of a constitutional settlement (for the calling of a new and reformed parliament), law reform, fiscal reform and church organisation, it is hard to acquit the Rumpers of dilatoriness. Instead of taking a periodic recess for a holiday, in August 1649 they began the disastrous habit of having long weekends off, and going over to a four-day working week. This was only to be interrupted in times of crisis – threatened invasion like 1650 and 1651 – or when the army's pressure for speedier reform became acute – as at times in 1651–3.

It is tempting to make a division in the Commonwealth's short history at the autumn of 1651. This date marked the return of the army to politics [9] after the 'crowning mercy' of Worcester. Up to that date the Rump could have pleaded a series of military emergencies, and its preoccupation with the problem of its own security and the very survival of the infant republic, as the reason for not getting on faster with domestic reorganisation. After that, the over-close and distracting presence of the army, plus the renewed financial stringency due to the outbreak of the Dutch War, could be adduced in their defence. In his *Pride's Purge* Professor Underdown emphasises the internal divisions within the House, while a further study of the Rump, now in progress, may suggest how far the distinctions between sincere reformers and deliberate procrastinators, altruistic republicans and self-interested oligarchs lining their own pockets correspond to any coherent and consistent political groupings.[10] The Rumpers were not wholly, perhaps not even predominantly corrupt and self-seeking; nor were they bent simply on perpetuating their own power and lining their own pockets. If some spectacular cases of corruption were revealed, and in some instances punished, this argues the imposition of higher standards of official conduct rather than providing proof of general dishonesty.[11] But the members were excessively tender of their own, often quite legitimate, financial interests and those of their collaborators, especially in the City (where they had few enough wealthy allies to risk alienating!). They spent an inordinate amount of time on such business, and morality apart showed thereby a poor sense of financial priorities. They also took far too long going over the details of punitive legislation against Royalists: whose land was to be sold and whose exempted from sale; too long, that is, in relation either to the monetary yield, or to the justice of the cases. Procedurally the Rump desperately lacked consistent front-bench management or, in the technical sense, a 'leader of the House'. The Long Parliament's members had failed to learn some of the lessons from their own past. The way in which they united in their own persons legislative, executive and judicial power, together with all the profits and advantages of office, had already proved a vulnerable target for hostile pamphleteers. The Self-Denying Ordinance of 1645 was still on their statute-book, unrepealed yet flouted; it provided a standing invitation for renewals of the attacks on their high-handedness and self-interest. Ex-parliamentarian peers and their dependants might mourn the loss of the House of Lords as much as that of the monarchy, and the alleged system of checks and balances provided by having the traditional tripartite structure. But for most people outside the narrow ruling circle it was their character as an overlapping, omnicompetent oligarchy that made the rulers of the Commonwealth so unattractive – and so open to criticism.[12] Under the Protectorate, some republicans were to argue that the constitutional arrangements of the Commonwealth had been altogether superior. In extolling its undoubted achievements, they seem to have wholly lost sight of their own regime's constitutionally makeshift character.

At a more fundamental level, the Rump's worst failing was the fact of its being responsible to no one. It seemed intent on self-perpetuation without electoral appeal; even as late as November 1651 the House voted only to dissolve not later than November 1654, which would have marked the Parliament's fourteenth birthday! There was no free and organised opposition, and no expression of any free 'public opinion' save through the now muzzled pamphleteers and the army officers. Writing of the winter of 1648–9 but before Pride's Purge (if I have understood her rightly) Dame Veronica Wedgwood has argued that the army was a truer embodiment of the national will than the Long Parliament.[13] I agree. Yet this seems a dangerous line of argument if one thinks of Robespierrian or twentieth-century parallels. But that apart, at this time the army still included numerous Levellers and other radicals; the grandees were even working out a compromise constitution with Leveller representatives, radical M.P.s and leading Congregationalist divines.[14] But, whatever had been true in 1648–9, by 1651–3 both Parliament and army had become grossly less representative of any meaningful national will. Some striking examples of the Rump's dilatoriness appear in Mr Cooper's chapter. But the most fundamental of all was the question of their own future and the calling of the next Parliament.

A committee was first appointed, to produce a scheme, in May 1649. This included Ireton, the principal author of the compromise Agreement of the People, drawn up a few months before. In January 1650, when Ireton was safely out of the way in Ireland, the younger Vane reported to the House from this committee. He presented a full draft for electoral redistribution; it was probably the boldest measure of its kind to be read in the House of Commons until the 1780s, if not before the nineteenth century. A grand committee (that is, a committee of the whole house) was then appointed to meet weekly and work on the details of this plan, and add to it as necessary. This body lapsed in the late summer, but was revived in the following winter (1650–1), and again disappeared from the April to August after that. In September 1651 the Cromwellian Party in the House began to press for a new (that is, different) bill for a new parliament. The preparation of this was now entrusted to a select committee. But the result was not a new piece of legislation so much as a series of resolutions, culminating in the vote (already referred to) for the present parliament's termination by November 1654. Then very little more happened for some months, except that the House again toyed with the alternative scheme for making up their numbers by 'recruiter-style' by-elections, presumably in the interim until dissolution. After the army officers' hortatory petition to the House, of August 1652, a semblance of acceleration appears. The bill for a new parliament was recommitted in September. In January following, Major-General Thomas Harrison, the most impatient of the Cromwellians in the House and the patron of the millenarian radicals outside it, was put in charge of the bill's progress. Either because of his other preoccupations or because Harrison was somehow outmanoeuvred, it was however Hesilrige who acted as reporter from the committee to the House in February. Several amendments to what looks like a resurrected version of Vane's original draft bill of three years earlier were agreed in March and April. Ostensibly it was on the issue of a genuine dissolution versus a guarantee of permanent seats for the existing members in any new parliament that Cromwell finally lost patience and dissolved the House on 20 April 1653. In fact, as Mr Worden shows,[15] the truth was more complicated, and in some ways less to Cromwell's credit and the Rump's discredit than the standard accounts of this episode would suggest.

The Rump's failure is worth dwelling on here, because we do not have a chapter directly concerned with the political history of the Commonwealth. Also there are different ways of assessing the significance of this failure. For all its unilateral assumption of sole legislative, most executive and even some judicial power, the purged House of Commons remained the last legally constituted link with traditional forms of government. It is fatally easy to try to be too wise after the event. But a little retrospective wisdom is not something that the historian should invariably deny himself. Pride's Purge can be seen to have failed to purify the House, except in the most rigidly ideological sense. The consequent abolition of monarchy and Upper House may have simplified the construction of a new constitution by reducing the number of vested interests that had to be satisfied, compared to the problems of settlement in 1646–8. But this did little, if anything, to advance the likelihood of any more positive basis for agreement. As Milton had already decided some few years earlier, when writing on the 'character of the Long Parliament' in his *History of England*, the members of the House – despite the undoubted talents, idealism and public spirit of several individuals among them – had collectively become incorrigible; and they were to remain so. On this view, with which many of the best critics will disagree, Cromwell and Ireton would have done better to dissolve the House in 1649, and to call elections on the basis of the revised Agreement of the People. This did in fact demand that the Long Parliament should dissolve itself by the end of April. In other respects it embodied a reasonably balanced and enlightened programme. It provided for drastic electoral redistribution in favour of the wealthier counties and some of the new towns, and away from the 'rotten' boroughs; for biennial parliaments with six-monthly sessions; for something very close to a male householder suffrage (such as obtained from 1885 to 1918), active Royalists being excluded from voting and standing for election for seven and fourteen years respectively; for the separation of powers – office-holders were not to be councillors of state or M.P.s, nor were practising lawyers. There was to be no conscription except for home defence; there was to be an end of all special legal privileges, but no levelling of men's estates, or enforced communism. A wide measure of religious toleration was insisted upon, the public profession of popery and prelacy only being excluded; the maintenance of ministers and teachers was guaranteed, but was not to be by the compulsory payment of tithes; other clauses, such as those to do with indemnity and the satisfaction of Parliament's existing creditors (many of whom, it must be remembered, were men and women of small substance who had lent very modest amounts), were common to this and other schemes for settlement, and need not concern us here. Sensibly, the articles of the Agreement were classified according to whether they were 'fundamental to our common right, liberty, and safety', or merely 'useful and good for the public; and . . . not fundamental'. Now it may be objected that there is much here that is visionary or unpractical, though the Leveller leaders were soon to renounce their acceptance of it and denounce the document as far too conservative. But the answer, surely, is that any constitution – written or unwritten – is workable, other than by force and fraud, only if enough people want to make it work sufficiently strongly. On that score, it is at least arguable that given the circumstances of 1649, this scheme had a better chance of satisfying those requirements than any of the others on offer, or which could have been put forward around that time.

The various attempts at settlement from December 1653 to 1659 are fully discussed below, in the chapters by Professors Roots, Underdown and Woolrych. For the possibilities at that other alleged highwater mark of radicalism, the Barebone's Parliament (of July–December 1653), and its plans for settlement, the reader should consult some of Professor Woolrych's other writings.[16] Without reviving other controversies, such as whether Cromwell was taken in by Harrison and his militant Puritan allies, we need only consider what the Barebone's had to offer by way of political settlement. The answer, it may fairly be said, is very little. When he opened what is sometimes rather pedantically called the Nominated Assembly, Cromwell referred to an 'Instrument' (the text of which has not survived) under which they were to act. This apparently devolved supreme authority on them. They were not to sit beyond 3 November 1654 (an obsessive date in these schemes!) and were meanwhile to choose – how is not clear – their successors, who were in turn to act for a maximum of twelve months, and to provide for the future government before then. But, having declared itself a parliament on its first day of business, the Barebone's spent so much of its time on religion, the law and money matters, that there is scanty evidence of any constitutional proposals. Some may have thought of annual or biennial conventions of the same kind, repeated indefinitely; others probably saw the 1653 assembly as being more like a constitutional convention, rather than as a substitute for a normal parliament. There is no evidence that the radicals of the Barebone's were particularly interested in electoral reform or the franchise. They made no move to prevent John Lilburne being tried for his life (for the second time under the Republic). If it has to be characterised summarily, their brand of radical Puritanism was of an exclusive, élitist nature. The 'Rule of the Saints' implies the exclusion of the unregenerate, a sectarian oligarchy, and perhaps a dictatorship in the name of virtue and godliness. The difference between the Levellers in 1649 and the Harrisonians in 1653, despite their agreement on issues like law and church reform, is analogous to that between a democratic mass political party and a monolithic totalitarian one today: almost to that between the British Labour Movement and Lenin's Bolsheviks.

Moving forward to the Protectorate, there may seem little to choose – as bases for lasting settlement – between the 'Instrument of Government' (December 1653) and the 'Humble Petition and Advice' (1657).

But it is perhaps worth considering the respective merits of these two protectorial constitutions a little more closely. If the whole Cromwellian Protectorate (1653–9) is seen as a trend in an essentially conservative direction, towards the restoration of the traditional order in all but name, then the Humble Petition is the more realistic of the two. It certainly had wider and warmer support from members of the traditional governing class. If, however, we accept that at least for a longish interim period any Cromwellian regime would have meant minority rule, and that in this the army had to be accommodated as a kind of additional estate of the realm, then the Instrument was the better-founded of the two. Although the Humble Petition contained fundamental ambiguities, some of them perhaps deliberate, it would be idle to pretend that this was the primary cause of its failure. As Professor Woolrych's chapter shows, the split between the military and civilian wings of the Cromwellian Party, almost corresponding to one between republicans and monarchists among them, together with the personal inadequacies of the leading figures after Oliver Cromwell's death, provides sufficient explanation for the disintegration that followed.

There are other influences that should be considered in a comprehensive survey of the quest for settlement. One is the continuing problem of security against external enemies and internal subversion, and the effect that this in turn had on plans to scale down the army and so to reduce expenditure. For the various Royalist conspiracies, which in some cases were linked to Leveller schemes, recourse should be had to Professor Underdown's earlier book on this subject. Despite the argument developed in his chapter in this volume, about the rule of the major-generals having been a severe setback to schemes for wider conciliation, it is arguable that time was on the republicans' side. More often than not, the longer that an *émigré* regime remains in exile the more unrealistic and out-of-touch it becomes, and the more its chances of getting back diminish.

The part played by public opinion in the 1650s is hard to assess. Except for resentment at the tax burden, notably opposition to paying the excise, the evidence is thin. The brief revival of radical pamphleteering in 1659, described by Professor Woolrych, was not – as far as can be seen – accompanied by any renewal of mass interest in political issues. It could indeed be argued that the Royalists and Anglicans got back in 1660 thanks to popular apathy as well as republican divisions. The populace was ready enough to turn out and cheer for King Charles II in May 1660. But there is no sign, since the crowds who had turned out to cheer John Lilburne's acquittals in 1649 and 1653, of any massive popular participation either way in between. Nothing suggests that the masses would have fought for the king any more than for the republic.

Linked to the question of security, because it too involves the armed forces and so the tax burden, is that of the Protector's foreign and trade policies. The debate about these[17] is tangential to our main concern here. It could be said that a policy of strict neutrality, if less glorious than that which was followed, would have meant greater prosperity and lower taxes and so a better chance of settlement at home. The influence of Irish and Scottish affairs on England is of more obvious and direct relevance. This deserves to be discussed at greater length than is possible here. Much important work, some of a distinctly 're-visionist' character, has recently been produced and more is in progress on both Irish and Scottish history in this period.[18] Not that this, even when more of it has been published, will quite answer our questions for us, as regards the influence exerted on developments in England. In one sense the infant republic could not rest securely until Ireland had been resubjugated and Scotland conquered. Each provided too dangerous and tempting a base for Royalist invasion and counter-revolution. Yet the Commonwealth's very successes in both countries involved additional military commitments and so more expenditure. In Ireland it meant in addition the *damnosa hereditas* of racial and religious hatreds, cultural genocide and colonialist exploitation. It would be doctrinaire to assert that this made a lasting settlement at home impossible, but the expense of military rule and consequent importance given to ambitious soldiers certainly did not make one any easier. Again, we can try our luck at using the privilege of hindsight. The swift elimination of the Royalist bases in both countries could have been followed not by complete conquest and permanent occupation, but by the maintenance of strong naval (perhaps also amphibious) forces to prevent any large-scale repetition of the threats posed in 1649–51. This would have proved less damaging to the republic's prospects in England, as well as being more compatible with its professed ideals of freedom and justice.

III

As the reader will discern, the towering figure of Oliver Cromwell dominates several of the chapters in this book. Indeed he looms large in all of them except perhaps Mr Skinner's and Mr Cooper's. It would be tempting to end by discarding any grandiose social or ideological theories about the English revolution, and to describe it instead in terms simply of his career and then his disappearance from the scene. Whether settlement became impossible and the Restoration inevitable at his death, we may leave to a close reading of Professor Woolrych's chapter to decide. C. H. Firth's study, first published in 1901, remains the classic biography of Cromwell, while two present-day historians, Maurice Ashley and Christopher Hill, have written with great distinction on his life and character. But it would be wrong to suppose that no more remains to be said, or investigated, about him, either as Lord Protector or earlier in his career. The publication of the remaining parliamentary diaries for 1641–8, part of which Mrs Pearl has in hand, may well do more than anything else to effect some revision, at least of the way his political evolution is seen. For the later 1640s and 1650s there is some unexciting but useful archival material (minutes and warrants of committees, and accounts) from which a few additional details can be gleaned; but no new sources of significance are likely to be uncovered. On the other hand, much work remains to be done on the men around Cromwell, both in the army and in civilian life, and on the movements with which he was associated. Among these desiderata we may include: investigation of what was happening in more of the counties, cities and regions of England and Wales, along the lines marked out by Professors Alan Everitt and Roger Howell and others; an extension of the researches of Professor Nuttall, Dr Surman, Dr Cross and others into more aspects of the religious life and church organisation of the time; and a better understanding of the relationship between political theory and constitutional practice.[19]

How far these advances in our knowledge and understanding of the period – and others that cannot be foreseen – will help to explain the theme of this book is less sure. The two dominant extreme interpretations at present seem to be what we may crudely call the social-determinist and the political-circumstantial. Not, one hopes, that every student is obliged to choose tamely between them; nor that, except in their purest, least adulterated forms, they are logically incompatible with each other and mutually exclusive. The former, of which Christopher Hill is the most learned and persuasive protagonist, would in the last resort suggest that the parliamentarians, republicans and Cromwellians of these years all failed to establish a lasting settlement because it was impossible for them to do so. Although a kind of bourgeois-capitalist revolution had taken place, it was only a partial one. The

newly risen capitalist class and the victors in the Civil War then became
so frightened of the masses, of the threat from King Demos – or the
'Many-Headed Monster', as Dr Hill sometimes prefers to call it – that
they retreated and failed to carry their own revolution through to completion, and eventually went back into alliance with the less reactionary
sections of the old ruling class. This begins to be discernible from
Cromwell's and the Independents' breach with the Levellers (1647–9),
and becomes more patent after the fall of the Barebone's, more marked
still with the Humble Petition, and reaches its logical (and seemingly
inevitable) conclusion at the Restoration and after.

It is not always clear whether we are to suppose that the stage of
economic development that England had by then attained, in itself,
made all this inevitable. If so, the political, military, social, religious
and intellectual history of the period is all reduced to mere epi-
phenomena. And in his later writings Dr Hill himself allows for inter-
action both ways: for the possibility that military or political action
could have some effect on the economy and the social structure, and
that these were not solely determined by the relations of the means of
production. But this is not quite the same as saying how and why
particular political happenings came about. And the implication remains that only very limited possibilities were open. The defeat of the
Levellers, the easy crushing of the Diggers, the failure of the radical
republicans – whether secular in 1649 and 1659, or religious in 1653,
the overthrow of the Lambertian Instrument by the second Protectorate Parliament, are all thus a part of an ineluctable process. This raises
some logical as well as historical difficulties. Precisely at what point
did the tide turn and why? If the revolution continued to get more
radical until 1647 (or 1649, or 1653, whichever is the preferred highwater mark), what forces and circumstances caused the revolutionary,
Puritan-parliamentarian section of the upper and middle classes to
turn about in this way? It would presumably have to be shown that it
was the bourgeois–capitalist elements which forced the pace in a radical
direction down to 1647, and also then took alarm at the popular movement and went into reverse gear. Now Dr Pearl's chapter here suggests
that for certain sections of the London business community, this has
some validity. However, as she herself and Professor Robert Ashton have
convincingly demonstrated, the London business community was not
all hewn of one rock.[20] Some of the biggest operators – financiers and
export merchants – had collaborated with Charles I's government back
in the 1630s and remained Royalists into the 1640s. Other elements in

the City's economic life were in opposition by 1640 but had already drawn back from radicalism before the winter of 1641-2. There were indeed pacemakers for radicalism in London, but they cannot be identified with the business community, or even with some hypothetically ultra-capitalist section of it. Even if we exclude those in London who later supported the Puritan sects and the Levellers, the adherents of militant Presbyterianism seem a socially and economically mixed bag. The defeat of these groups in 1647 – the climax and immediate sequel to Dr Pearl's chapter – raises further difficulties for the determinist interpretation. We then have to suppose that further bourgeois–capitalist elements, perhaps now more rural and provincial in provenance, having defeated the Presbyterians and carried the revolution a stage further, in turn took alarm at the subversive tendencies of their own allies. And so, by the autumn of 1647, more decisively by the early months of 1649, they were themselves back-pedalling. Once again, there is a certain plausibility in this, but the difficulties remain.

One problem is that the men who led the opposition to the Levellers in 1647, and again those who brought about their final defeat in 1649, were largely drawn from the landowning class, though from varying sections of it. This was true of Fairfax, Cromwell, Ireton and most of the colonels. At the level of military command and parliamentary leadership, members of that class continued to dominate the scene throughout the years that followed. Nor does it solve the problem simply to assert, as may well be true, that many of their followers were drawn from lower social levels, including what we should now call the middle class. Some of the Rump's leaders had undoubted business connections (e.g. Hesilrige with the north-eastern coal trade). But this was no novelty among English landowners and parliamentarians. Moreover one could point to Royalists as well as Presbyterians and Independents of whom it was equally true.

In the Barebone's, one of the radical leaders, Samuel Moyer, was indeed a wealthy London business man. But this raises further difficulties. It was mainly landowners who led the conservative opposition in this assembly, both from outside the House (Lambert) and from inside it (Rous, Wolsley, Sydenham, Ashley Cooper, Pickering, Strickland). Moreover the London members, if they are to be thought of as representatives of the capitalist classes, were themselves equally divided between moderates and radicals, according to the most quoted contemporary source. The radical millenarian leader, Harrison, fits uneasily into this classification. More to the point, as Professor Trevor-

Roper and others have emphasised, five out of the six Welsh members were Harrisonians; this was thanks to good organisation and the use of old-fashioned patronage.

Under the Protectorate it is much the same story. Any attempt to identify capitalists with conservatives drawing back towards the traditional order is hard to sustain. On the other hand, it may well be maintained that by this time the business and the landed classes (anyway the economically progressive section of the latter) had ceased to be distinct, distinguishable entities. In short, it was a landowner-commercial capitalist merger, or coalition, that won the Civil War, got rid of the monarchy and the House of Lords, experimented with various republican constitutions, restored an upper house and hereditary succession (in 1657) and finally brought about the return of the full traditional order in 1660. And at a certain level of generality, this is unexceptionable. Unfortunately, like the role of Divine Providence in history, it is of more use as a first cause, explaining everything, than as a proximate cause, explaining things in particular. What had determined which landowners were parliamentarians in the first place? The argument presumably requires it to be shown that the most capitalist among them were. This would take us too far back into an analysis of the two sides in 1642, which we cannot pursue here. Royalist landowners were proportionately heavier borrowers, were more in debt than their parliamentarian opposites.[21] This apart, historians other than Dr Hill and Dr Manning[22] have had the greatest difficulty in distinguishing within the landowning class along these lines. Nor is it likely to prove any easier to transfer the argument forward to 1660. This would seem to require us to believe that the more capitalist of the landowners, plus the commercial bourgeoisie, were both the pacemakers for radical policies down to 1647–49–53, or to a certain stage regardless of date, but also sequentially or simultaneously, were the main instruments in forging the alliance with the less unprogressive sections of the ex-Royalist upper class, an alliance which was then consummated in 1660.

It is not that most of those who disagree, or find this unsatisfactory, would want to deny that social and economic issues were involved in the Civil War, or in the so-called 'Interregnum' that followed its conclusion. Few, if any, historians would now see the events of the 1640s and 1650s solely in terms of religious and constitutional disagreements, or the clash of incompatible personalities. Even if one comes out with a sneaking regard for Professor Elton's denial that it was a revolution at all, this is still likely to be so.

The belief that economic interests, social divisions and class feelings played a large part in these events has, as Christopher Hill himself has often reminded us, a long and almost alarmingly respectable pedigree. Such was the view of Clarendon and Hobbes in the seventeenth century, of Guizot and Gardiner in the nineteenth. Nor is it the specifically Marxist, or neo-Marxist, version of this with which other historians necessarily disagree, so much as with its excessively rigid and schematic formulation. The categories are wrong, and words are too often taken for things. This can be briefly illustrated. The dichotomy between court and country was of great importance before 1641 and again from 1653 to 1659. This cuts across the supposed feudal–bourgeois or landowning–business polarities; nor does it at all closely correspond, incidentally, to the moderate-radical political antithesis either. The church-sect antithesis, at which Dr Cross hints in her chapter, is surely one of the keys to the ambivalent role of the Independents. In so far as they were, in denominational terms, Congregationalists, they present the classic spectacle of a sect taking over the national church, and then having very uncertain, anyway very mixed ideas about what to do with it. Lastly one may suggest the concept of conflict between different strata within a class, which can sometimes be as acute, and as influential, as that between classes. The Civil War and the republic undoubtedly saw a shift within the landowning class. Whether because most of them had been Cavaliers or neutrals in the war itself, the aristocracy and the greater gentry landowners were eclipsed in these years. At the top, even the Cromwellian Council of 1657–9 – on the eve of its final merger with the old order according to the Hill view – was less aristocratic in composition than any cabinet until 1906. Likewise at the local level: despite the undoubted tendencies described by Professor Underdown,[23] the 1650s did not see a complete reversal of that shift towards what Professor Everitt, in his study of Kent, has so suggestively called the 'parochial gentry'. This in turn can be seen as one aspect of a wider process, which could be described as radicalisation by practical necessity. This is to emphasise that it was due at least as much to the practical needs of winning the Civil War and then maintaining a viable regime after victory, as to any radical, let alone consciously revolutionary policy or ideology. This tendency can be seen operating in several areas of the country's life: in local administration through county committees, commissions of the peace, municipal corporations, and their various subordinate staffs; through the new fiscal system, notably penal taxation, the weekly pay

B

(later monthly assessment) for the army and above all the excise; at
the military level both of the officer corps of the New Model Army
and its successor, and locally in the officers of county and city militias;
in another way through the connections built up and the new patronage
exercised via the congregations or 'gathered churches' of prominent
sectarian divines; and even at the parliamentary level, in the recruiters
to the Long Parliament and in the members returned in the various
parliaments of 1653–9. Are we to call this shift away from the aristocracy and greater gentry towards the lesser gentry and the 'middling
sort' (Clarendon's term for the middle class) a social revolution or not?
Whether these men were necessarily more capitalist than those whom
they replaced seems to me an unanswerable question, but not decisive
in this context. For if we think more in terms of social status, that is in
a way more familiar to people in the mid-seventeenth century, then it
was – by any standards – a momentous change, and one to which only
a verbal pedant would deny the word revolutionary. The most serious
limitation in the approach of the great historians of the later nineteenth century and the early twentieth, Gardiner and Firth, may not
have been their alleged lack of interest in economics, still less any
unawareness of class as a force in history, but their relative neglect of
the court–country tensions in early modern society, and of the importance – to contemporaries – of rank, style and status.

If we are then dealing with a revolution, albeit a partial, uncompleted
and ultimately unsuccessful one, when did its defeat become unavoidable? Here the role of contingent circumstances does become crucial.
An unconditional Restoration, that is without terms except those to
which Charles II voluntarily submitted himself, was not in the normal
sense of the word unavoidable until February–March, perhaps even
April 1660. On the other hand, the likelihood of a stable alternative
to Stuart monarchy was vastly diminished well before that. One of the
best constitutional settlements on offer during these years, best that is
in the sense of looking the most potentially viable, the 'Heads of Proposals', had been torpedoed by Charles I way back in 1647 before it had
even been launched. The 'Instrument of Government', a kind of
blend of the Heads brought up to date with the compromise Agreement
of January 1649 and the Rump's various drafts of 1650–3, proved more
viable, in that it endured for three and a half years. Patience, restraint
and good luck could have made it more durable than that. But it must
remain in the realm of pure speculation whether an elective protectorate
could have lasted indefinitely, without developing in practice into

something like hereditary monarchy, on the lines of the Dutch stad-tholderate. The role of the Protector under this constitution, even under the Humble Petition, was sufficiently akin to that of King William III after the Revolution Settlement of 1689 for it to remain within the bounds of practicality. So we can hardly hope to settle here whether the fruitlessness of the quest was inevitable. For the editor and probably for most of the contributors to this volume, the answer would be, No, not as the word is generally understood. But given all the circumstances and personalities, including such contingencies as the death of Ireton at the age of forty and the survival of Richard Cromwell as Oliver's eldest son, it is not difficult to see why it was so, and far from easy to imagine how in the end this could have been otherwise.

Did any of those involved have a sense of missed opportunities after the event? Of the leading actors who survived in 1660, the best died defiant – on the scaffold or in exile; others died silently in prison or in obscure retirement. Among those who have left us any record of their feelings – in memoirs, speeches, or correspondence (even in poems if we include Milton and Marvell as leading actors) – scarcely any display any overt sense of realising their own inadequacies. Or rather they see the fall of the republic and the return of the Stuarts as evidence of God's displeasure with them and with their country, but almost exclusively in moral terms, as a punishment for wickedness and vice, not a retribution for vanity, stupidity and ineptitude. The only exception to this is perhaps the feeling that they ought to have seen through Monck sooner than they did, but that was well past the eleventh hour, and hardly meets the burden of the charge.

From widely differing standpoints Cromwell's biographers agree that his fundamental dilemma was how to reconcile minority rule with constitutional government. But it will not do simply to say that the Saints, the Godly Party, were only a small minority of the total population. They were indeed. According to W. K. Jordan, there may have been only around 50,000 Congregationalists and perhaps about the same number of Baptists in the whole country; and within both groups there were divisions – particularly deep in the case of the Baptists. The total strength of the army varied between about 42,000 and 68,000 from 1649 to 1659, including the forces stationed in Ireland and Scotland, and overseas.[24] Yet before the coming of democracy and a mass electorate all governments, elected or otherwise, rested on a basis of minority rule. What matters here surely is not the size of the minority, but its morale and coherence, and the degree of acceptance accorded it by the rest of the population. Judged by these simple, it may even seem platitudinous, but often neglected tests, the English republic never really got off the ground. The traditional upper or ruling class of pre-1642 and post-1660 likewise constituted only a small fraction of the total population, but it enjoyed the tacit acquiescence, not to say the deferential acceptance, of the rest. Whether this was due to the magic of monarchy and inbred respect for social betters, or more to fear of the lash and the rope, there was no serious opposition to this kind of minority rule, except for local outbursts, from 1381 to the 1640s, nor thereafter until the late eighteenth century. It may seem paradoxical, but is not really surprising, that the governments of the years 1646–60, though less aristocratic, up to a point more plebeian even, than their predecessors and successors, in some ways enjoyed less popular, mass acceptance. Their other fundamental weakness arose from what is perhaps a more generic feature of the sectarian mind, and especially of the radical intellectual in politics: a reluctance to compromise, or to settle for half a loaf. A very much smaller fraction than that is sometimes a great deal better than nothing at all.

1. London's Counter-Revolution

VALERIE PEARL

THE abortive attempt to establish a 'high' or 'rigid' Presbyterian Church settlement is a dominant theme of the later 1640s. This powerful movement – backed in 1645 and early 1646 by the Assembly of Divines, Sion College, the city clergy and the municipality – was hardly touched upon by S. R. Gardiner in his *History*; a fuller knowledge will modify our understanding of the religious settlement, the political attitudes of members of Parliament, and relations between the Long Parliament and the Scots. Similarly the story told in this chapter of Holles's attempt to build a counter-revolutionary army in London adds an additional dimension to the conflict between the New Model and Parliament. The sources that are providing new evidence include the 30,000 tracts now housed in the British Museum and collected by George Thomason, the London bookseller; the unpublished parliamentary diaries, particularly those of Walter Yonge which are partly in shorthand; and the records of the City of London preserved at the Guildhall Library and at the Corporation Record Office.

I

Most historical writing on the Puritan Revolution assumes that 'Presbyterianism' was a phenomenon of the 'Right'. It was, of course, a many-sided coalition but its leadership in the Long Parliament seems at first sight to bear out the judgement. At times Denzil Holles, the earl of Essex, Sir Philip Stapleton, each as socially conservative as any Royalist, were prepared, in face of the menace from the army, to accept peace on surrender conditions. Holles and his Presbyterian colleagues were prepared to make greater concessions to Charles in 1645 and 1646 than they were ready to do after December 1646, when they won control of the Commons. The Presbyterian 'Party' was however larger than its parliamentary leadership. If we look at its supporters outside as well as inside Parliament, in particular, at its clerical allies and at its citizen supporters in London, we see at once a different picture, a scene made up of numerous tableaux that belies the neat description and the party label. On the one wing of the movement there is the aristocratic leadership composed of moderate men socially indistinguishable from the Royalist gentry. On the other, there are its 'populist' allies. The Presbyterian 'Party' enjoyed a wider basis of power than historians have allowed and it is these allies whom I will consider. The most prominent were, naturally, the ministers and citizens of London. Clarendon pointed to this strange coalescence of men of different outlook when he tried to explain the victory of the Independents, despite the powerful parliamentary and city support enjoyed by their opponents. 'Their councils,' he wrote, 'were most distracted and divided, being made up of many men whose humours and nature must be observed and complied with.' His judgement is borne out by the evidence of the political events of these years, although as a theme it has hardly been developed in our histories. His second explanation, again a considered judgement on the party, has also been overlooked: 'The Presbyterians,' he wrote, 'formed all their inclinations on the affections of the people,' which made them 'submit to their senseless and wretched clergy, whose infectious breath corrupted and governed the people.'

By 'Presbyterians' Clarendon meant the Scots but his remark applies equally to their allies in the City of London. The 'populism' of Presbyterianism which so distressed Clarendon did not extend very far down the social scale. Yet I shall show that it would be an important element in the attempted counter-revolutionary seizure of power by the city Presbyterians in 1647. Their coup was plotted in alliance with Royalists but it is false to imagine that they were deeply conservative or neo-Royalist in the early days of the conflict in 1642. From the outbreak of the war until Naseby, men of both religious groups, Presbyterian and Independent, had striven for ecclesiastical reform and for an active prosecution of the war. This common effort that cuts across subsequently imposed party labels contraverts a simplistic political division into radicals and conservatives, or into protagonists of peace or war. Similarly it rebuts the formulation that for these early years equates a political view with a particular religious denomination.

The way in which Presbyterian religious views could coexist with politics of a seemingly radical kind is well brought out in the careers of leading city merchants. Throughout these early years of the Civil War the terms 'Presbyterian' and 'Independent' are useless to describe the political divisions within the city councils since the majority of solid citizens who sat in the Court of Aldermen and Common Council were in favour of some kind of Presbyterian Church: few attended independent congregations. Historians who have assumed that political Independents, that is, men who supported the army in 1647 and 1648, were also necessarily independent in religion, would be quite unable to make sense of the careers of London's radical leaders, Aldermen Penington and Fowke. Two of the directors of the political revolution of 1641 and 1642, they would also support the republic. Yet both men were undeniably Presbyterian in religion. Penington would help to eject the Independent John Goodwin from the vicarage of St Stephen's Coleman Street and install in his place the High Presbyterian William Taylor. Fowke would lead his ward in a Presbyterian petition in December 1645. Even Alderman John Warner, the army's nominee as Lord Mayor after the capitulation of the City in August 1647, was a locally elected ruling elder and a patron of Christopher Love, one of the most extreme of the clerical party who met his fate on the gallows, convicted of plotting with the Scots.[1]

Few congregational Independents appeared among the substantial citizens. To Thomas Edwards the tag 'Independent' was as good as an admission ticket to his gallery of public enemies. The small number who could be branded in this way served conveniently as a dire example, their very scarcity making them easy to attack. Abused, their numbers and influence grossly exaggerated, they were guilty by association and could be reviled as carriers of the socially dangerous doctrines of the sects. Contrary to Edwards's propaganda, Independents were not a homogeneous group. Nor were Presbyterians. There were rigid or High Presbyterians after the Scottish fashion and there were others of an Erastian and more tolerant temper. Here the citizens were divided: they would agree on the need for discipline and uniformity in the Church but they might differ on whether there should be any toleration for 'tender consciences' and on whether ministers should have the sole right of excommunication.

As we shall see, the citizens of London would go much further than the gentry along the road to a Presbyterian form of church government during the years from 1645 to 1647. The growth of the sects and the disruption of parochial organisation undermined the traditional ecclesiastical system and presented a threat to the stability of city rule. To the supporters of sound municipal government and to those who cherished the partnership of precinct and Church it seemed as if the twin pillars of the temple were about to be pulled down. But salvation was at hand in the Kirk. The Presbyterian system with its strict discipline and lay participation through the eldership offered the road to deliverance. Some churchwardens might be discomfited but the parish order would be preserved. The citizens approved. Although they were not aware of the paradox, they found purpose and comfort in a regime which seems to us to have conflicting characteristics – an authoritarian order with democratic forms.

Their particular attraction to the idea of discipline and of rule by 'elected' elders, the men of substance in the parish, drew them to that extremist wing known to contemporaries as 'High Presbyterianism'. Its activities reveal clearly the juxtaposition of radical and regressive demands, a characteristic true also of the wider Presbyterian movement. It would be radical as it impelled the citizens into godly reform in Church and State, and in attempting to transfer control of the Church from the gentry to middle-rank citizens and clergy. Such a programme would naturally appeal to the ministers and the middling merchants. It would be a strangely ambivalent movement in politics: in favour of limited reforms in the City and in the State, such as those achieved between 1642 and 1645, and yet joining strongly with political con-servatives from 1645 to 1647 when under pressure from the army and the sects. When London Presbyterianism became associated with political reaction in 1646 and 1647, the movement appeared to be wholly conservative, thus helping to explain the view of historians that it was entirely regressive.

Yet if we are to understand the City's counter-revolution in 1647, it is not sufficient to look only at its politically conservative face. The mili-tant Puritan wing of the Presbyterian movement was active both on religious issues and on questions of municipal reform. On religious reform, there is evidence that in some parishes where Presbyterian support was strong there were far-reaching changes in parochial organisation even before the formal parliamentary establishment of the new church: such were the opening up of the vestry and the involve-ment of laymen in the spiritual life of the parish – now given the power to test the fitness of communicants.[2] Likewise, in municipal affairs we see what would appear to be a striking refutation of the old hypothesis that identified 'Presbyterianism' with political reaction and 'Inde-pendency' with radicalism. The movement to extend the legislative power of Common Council was supported by a small minority of alder-men who were divided on church affairs but shared a distinguishing feature – strong religious affiliation: two of them were 'Presbyterian' in religion (James Bunce and John Warner) and two 'Independent' (Thomas Andrews and Samuel Warner). The alliance of 'godly' men is revealing in its demonstration that denominational differences could sometimes be subordinated to a desire for moderate reform, whatever opposing aims there might be on larger issues. One of the men who led the movement to extend the powers of Common Council typifies the city Presbyterian Party. He was the wealthy bookseller and printer John Bellamy, a man who was not an overseas merchant or one of the ruling élite of the City. He was a prosperous domestic trader who had been a leading reformer in 1641 and 1642; he had also joined the rebel party inside the Stationers' Company with the aim of overthrowing the small clique who monopolised the general stock. In 1646 Bellamy would write, print and publish for the cause of religious Presbyterianism as well as for the political movement. Unlike most of his closest allies in the Presbyterian struggles of 1647, however, he would compromise with the army and remain on Common Council during the first year of the Rump.[3]

The wing of the movement known as the 'High Presbyterian Party' has found no notice in our histories. Yet for a brief time it recruited the city ministers in Sion College, and captured the municipality, including the Court of Aldermen and Common Council, a body some 250 strong composed of some of the most substantial men in the City.[4] It would take us too far afield to describe here the unchronicled events of autumn 1645 when the City challenged Parliament itself and threatened to force it to its will. In the House, M.P.s expressed their fear of popular pressure but as yet the streets remained quiet, perhaps because of the unanimity of the city councils, which gave them the illusion that they might win without force – perhaps also because of the identification of the High Presbyterian movement with substantial citizens rather than with the smaller tradesmen or the labouring classes. As we shall see, by the end of 1646 threatening 'Kirk and king' mobs would come into existence. Then they would be composed partly of middling domestic traders, shopkeepers and apprentices who would stage the kind of 'controlled' demonstration that Professor Rudé has described in eighteenth-century London; in part they would consist of more violent crowds recruited from demobilised soldiers and from the labouring population of the city streets, docks and river, perhaps reflecting the economic pressure of bad harvests and the steep bread prices which characterised the years after the autumn of 1646.

The movement in the City to set up an unalterable uniform church established by divine law and clerically controlled was undoubtedly in part the responsibility of Robert Baillie and what I have called his Scottish 'fifth column' in London. We can trace their influence among the city laymen from vestry to vestry, among the London clergy in Sion College, their metropolitan club, and in the Westminster Assembly of Divines. Even such a powerful organising centre as the Scottish headquarters however could hardly have captured the City if the atmosphere in London had not been favourable. The attraction of the Presbyterian system with its combination of strict discipline, lay participation and genuine concern with moral reform and godliness found a particularly receptive audience among the second rank of London citizens, men who had challenged and displaced the aldermanic élite in 1641 and 1642 and now wished to preserve their own established position in city government threatened from below by the sects and lower-class radicals. We know some of their names from an analysis of the membership of Common Council committees in the years of Presbyterian power from 1645 and 1647; and we can check their religious affiliations by studying the records of London's Provincial Assembly and of Sion College.[5] From a study of these sources we discover that a substantial group among those who dominated the city councils in these years were also fervent religious Presbyterians taking the lead in the London *classes* and Provincial Assembly and continuing to do so into the 1650s, when the victory of the army would have permitted them to desert the Kirk if they had wished. Some leading names appear on the Committee of the Militia as remodelled by the Presbyterians in April 1647.[6]

The trades of the party leaders reveal that they belonged to a single roughly defined socio-economic group. They were not part of the select ruling merchant circle who dominated city councils before 1641. The majority was engaged in domestic trades, either in provisioning food, clothes and arms or in other domestic production such as printing, bookselling and the metal trades.[7] A few of the leading aldermen involved, like John Langham and Simon Edmonds, played their part in the Levant trades or in the Merchant Adventurers' Company, although even among the aldermanic group domestic trades predominated.[8] One could dwell further on the relatively local flavour of Presbyterian business interests, and contrast it with the cosmopolitan experience of an earlier generation of the City's élite. Perhaps it produced a certain narrowing of vision that made them neglect the wider world in favour of their own parish pump. Hugh Peter may have been suggesting something of the sort when he described the prevailing city party as men 'that never lived beyond the view of the smoke of their own Chimnies, that measure States and Kingdomes with their interests, by their private shopwards'.

The High Presbyterian Party in the City, having petitioned Parliament for its programme in November 1645, in January 1646 and again in March, was rebuked and finally rejected by the House of Commons.[9] Rather than contemplate a struggle with Parliament the city government ignominiously climbed down. Perhaps the Presbyterian Party's role as the 'party of order' in the City weakened the resolve to continue their struggle, as we shall see that it would in 1647. Baillie described them now as 'mute as fisch' and was aghast at their surrender. The city ministers continued to fight against the shortcomings of the Presbyterian Church settlement into the summer of 1646, when a compromise settlement was patched up. In the city government however more moderate and less aggressive views prevailed and Alderman Fowke persuaded the City not to challenge Parliament further.[10] When the City tangled again with the House in May 1646, the programme of the municipality would be organised on a broader base incorporating a conservative political policy as well as religious Presbyterianism.

Robert Baillie, the Scottish envoy, was so put out by the City's 'earlier fainting' as he put it that at first he could not believe the news that another petition was going forward from the City in April. The movement was clearly an alliance between religious Presbyterianism and a wholly conservative Peace Party.[11] Now the City was openly marshalled behind the policy of the parliamentary Peace Party led by Denzil Holles and the earl of Essex, and behind the Scots. The first four of the petition's seventeen clauses were devoted to a defence of Presbyterian church government. They protested against the 'swarm of sectaries' who filled the pulpits and occupied places of profit: no one disaffected to the established church, they said, should be allowed to hold any public office. Their political demands figured next: they wanted a speedy settlement with the king and a close union with their Scottish brethren. Then there were financial grievances: they asked that their loans should be repaid from delinquents' estates and that the most hated of the money-raising committees, Haberdashers' Hall, should be either dissolved or regulated.[12] Such committees, staffed as they sometimes were by a socially inferior and newly risen bureaucracy, radical and frighteningly powerful, were especially disliked by the solid citizens. The Haberdashers' Hall committee, in particular, became one such agency of government and to judge from the hostility it aroused it might today be thought to be a *comite révolutionnaire* of Paris in 1793 and not an Office for the Advance of Money in London. It is notable that the more extreme clericalist claims have been dropped: the

omission probably reflected the more cautious attitude towards High
Presbyterianism now gaining ground in the City. This new petition to
Parliament, the London Remonstrance of May 1646, circulated for at
least a month before its presentation. When it finally reached Common
Council it sparked off three whole days of debate. Support for it went
deep among the upper ranks of citizens. Over 8000 people signed a
supporting petition in June 1646 and, according to an opponent, 20,000
copies were printed and distributed as propaganda.[13]

The reaction to this powerful political machine came swiftly:
the Independents prepared a counter-manifesto, the enemies of the
Presbyterian Peace Party petitioned the city government against the
Remonstrance even *before* it was presented and the wards and parishes
rang loud with debate as a minor pamphlet war was waged. We can get
some idea of the relative strengths of the two sides by comparing the
number of signers each was able to muster. The Independents claimed
to have the signatures of many well-affected citizens, but George
Thomason, the Presbyterian bookseller, scornfully announced the
names on one petition to be a mere ninety-three. Even allowing for his
prejudice, we can assume that the Independents were nothing like so
numerous among substantial citizens at this time as were the Presbyterians. Thomason preserved these petitions and on one of them he
wrote, 'I having a hand in it, both in composing and promoting it'.[14]
He was a fairly well-to-do man and the active involvement of other
middle-rank citizens in the movement emerges strongly from the
evidence. From now on the merging of the religious Presbyterians and
Peace Party becomes clear. Perhaps we should consider it as a three-
stranded alliance rather than two. Besides the Presbyterians, it is natural
that Royalists should also have taken a hand in what was becoming a
conservatively based movement. Their presence would become more
evident in 1647. But even in 1646, the allegations were made that the
Presbyterians had taken into their cause Royalist 'yoke-fellows' or,
as we should say, 'fellow-travellers'. Like all such alliances in politics
this was a weakness as well as a strength. As Clarendon observed, it
gave the Presbyterian movement less coherence than their independent
army opponents. Apart from Royalists, the movement was now also
divided between its clerical and lay sections.

The City's complaint against Parliament, as evidenced by the
'Humble Remonstrance and Petition', of 26 May 1646, provoked
another major clash between the city government and the Commons,
although the Lords, now moving towards the Peace Party, voted by

a majority of one to accept the petition and authorised John Bellamy to print it.[15] The web of Presbyterian activists was far-flung and tightly spun. This is the Bellamy whom we have already met as a leading spokesman for the Presbyterians in the City. In contrast to the close vote in the Lords, the Commons forcefully showed its disapproval and Bulstrode Whitelocke recorded the annoyance of the House that once again the City should presume to command them.[16] Even the more moderate M.P.s found their irritation with the City turning to something far stronger when the nascent Leveller movement took a leaf out of the Presbyterian book and produced *their* 'Remonstrance of many Thousands', as they called it, to attack the City's stand and launch their own political programme. Thus the Presbyterians by their politicising stimulated the very radicalism that they feared. Others besides the Levellers saw the 'City Remonstrance' as a political challenge. Hugh Peter, looking back to this period, saw the petition and the Presbyterian organisation that preceded and followed it as 'the first force ever put upon the Parliament' and he asked, 'Did not the City *Remonstrance* hang like a petard upon the *Parliament* doore, weeke after weeke, and every ward in [their] course to attend and fire it?' The representatives of the city wards who thus agitated and lobbied prefigured the later more famous and much more radical agitators in the army. They also foreshadowed the events of 1647 when, as Hugh Peter said, the City would exert such pressure on the House that it would be forced to speak 'pure London'.

It is impossible to understand what historians have called the Presbyterian movement of 1646 and 1647 (but which is also really a conservative peace movement), without an appreciation of both the great fear of the army and the hearty dislike of taxation, the latter an unprecedented burden that seemed to grow more onerous as time passed. Hobbes expressed this dislike of taxes, linking it with urban discontent and a business ethos, when he wrote in *Behemoth* that great cities will always be of the rebel party because 'Grievances are but taxes, to which Citizens, that is, Merchants (whose Profession is their private Gain) are naturally mortal Enemies'. But property was menaced in an even more frightening way. The fear of plunder and fire, the peril of losing all one's possessions at the hands of mutinous soldiers or a marauding army, the dread of pillage, arson and violence by a brutal soldiery, all run like a nightmare refrain in diaries of the time. In Whitelocke's unprinted annals, for example, we find expressed a horror of billeting and a mounting anxiety about the destruction of property.

Besides the threat of violence, there was the more insidious threat of revolutionary and radical opinions. Such views were found not only among the soldiers but among the Levellers and some of London's religious sects.

The alliance of conservative-minded men in Parliament and the City, together with Royalists and High Presbyterians, was brought about from November 1644. The Peace Party in the Commons, which was forging close links with the city Presbyterians, was led by Denzil Holles and Sir Philip Stapleton. Its figurehead was the earl of Essex, the popular, pacific and wavering parliamentary general. On his death Baillie wrote, 'Essex was the head of our partie here [he] keeped all together.' The close links between this party and the City were publicly acknowledged from at least the time of Baillie's attempt in the summer of 1645 to expose a Royalist-Independent 'plot' to surrender Oxford. After the summer of 1646 the City Party should be seen as a coalition of three rather than two parties – because we should include the Royalists. In September the election of Sir John Gayre as lord mayor showed how far the swing towards Charles had gone. Right and Left were perturbed. Baillie because his candidate, Alderman John Langham, one on whom the Scots could rely, was defeated, and because the new lord mayor was more of a malignant than a sectary.[17] Lilburne because he recognised that Gayre's sympathies had never really been with Parliament – a fact so well known that the City had deliberately passed him over in earlier years because of his political views. It was left to the Independent minister, Henry Burton, to portray the Royalist and Peace Party machinations in a sermon that he preached in October. With a mixture of presumption and irony, he dedicated it to the lord mayor and aldermen. They must have found little comfort in his description of their intrigues in the aldermanic chamber and the chief magistrate's house.[18]

Of the many complex factors that produced so strong a counter-revolutionary movement in London, one was the burden of taxes; another, which has largely escaped notice, was the behaviour of the finance committees responsible for their collection. In the early days of the war Parliament had financed itself by loans pledging the security of the state, the 'Public Faith' as it was called amid some derision, and by fines on delinquents. *Ad hoc* and piecemeal methods were quickly replaced by a system of weekly assessments on all who owned property and movables worth more than £100 a year. In addition, all those who had failed, voluntarily or otherwise, to contribute to parliamentary loans were to be individually assessed at a maximum of one-twentieth of their real estate and one-fifth of their personal possessions. This heavy separate burden on non-contributors with its threat of an inquisitorial, discriminatory wealth or income tax aroused particular hostility. The main work of organising and collecting these special assessments fell on the parliamentary committee set up at Haberdashers' Hall. It in turn elected a sub-committee which met at Weavers' Hall and was made responsible for an area of Greater London extending twenty miles into the countryside. The Weavers' Hall sub-committee spawned another tribe of officials, the collectors and overseers of the tax in the city wards and in the surrounding out-parishes and villages. There were at least 110 in the City, for this is the number named in a single list, but there were probably more whom we cannot now identify. That the total was large is evident from one ward alone, Farringdon Within, where there were twenty-five. The office was unpopular, the posts were new and demanding of a peculiar hard-skinned talent: sometimes they attracted the kind of careerist, the petty functionary, who rides in the wake of every revolution. How doubly irritating then to find such jacks-in-office gathering more and more power into their hands. It was not an irritation confined to rank-conscious Royalists. Even the widow of Alderman John Towse, a faithful Puritan supporter of the parliamentary cause, found herself forced to pay over to the collectors the final twentieth part of her estate, although the alderman, as treasurer of the weekly assessment and other parliamentary loans, had spent most of his substance in the parliamentary cause. Nothing could hide the ingrained dislike of traders called upon to finance governments. As early as March 1643 the collector for the parish of St James Garlickhithe returned the news to Haberdashers' Hall, 'Not one man that will subscribe for a penny in this parish.' In that year, too, there is evidence of citizens shutting up houses to avoid payment, to the chagrin of collectors who were ordered to put assessment slips under the door or through the keyhole. By September assessors in London were being instructed to let the houses of those who had fled to avoid taxation. The operations of Haberdashers' and Weavers' Hall and of their various sub-committees remained a constant grievance. Denunciations against their activities appeared in all city petitions from the end of 1645 to 1647 and forced the Commons to appoint a special commission of its own to 'consider the Proceedings of the Under-Officers'.[19]

The excise-tax that Pym had also imposed in 1643 fell much more heavily on the poor than on substantial citizens. It covered a wide range of goods, including essential foods like meat (although not bread), ale and some imported commodities. The tax was paid by the manufacturer but it was widely believed that he passed it on to the consumer and used it as an excuse to put up prices. There are continual complaints that the real hardship was borne by the poor. But the opposition to the tax was much more widely diffused and frequently wore a radical guise. Some of the tracts published in the Civil War denouncing it would be republished by the opposition to Walpole in 1733 and the tax was long associated in the popular mind with the standing armies and with tyranny. Indeed the opposition to it and the memory of its origin persisted so long that one is tempted to employ that dubious term 'folk-memory' to account for its survival. How else can we attribute the appeal to the labourers and the radicals of England made by William Cobbett in 1834 when he denounced 'Cromwell and his vile associates' for imposing the tax? In 1643, new and monstrous, the tax appeared as an infringement of personal liberty (to be compared with the French *gabelle*); the methods and organisation of the collectors enhanced its unpopularity. One of the objections to excise, as to the sprouting of committees in the Civil War, was the bureaucratic organisation on which it rested. The resentment against all committees and excise officers is well brought out in Samuel Shephard's satire entitled *A Committee-man curried*. The pejorative names of the characters reveal the drift: Common-curse, an excise man, and Shallow-braine, his clerk, Suck-dry, a committeeman and Sneak, his clerk. The humour is coarse but it has not faded, and it has a modern ring in its references to the nuisance of form-filling and the practice of tax evasion. It reveals also that popular distaste was not merely against taxes but against the whole gang of officials responsible for collecting them. It is expressed in a line whose content is often repeated in the literature: 'None can rise Without they'r' o' th' Committees or the Excise'. Perhaps the threat to a man's ability to rise, the hint of an obstructive state power coming in a period of heightened middle-class assertiveness, expresses yet a deeper cause of dissatisfaction against what was abusively called, from that time to William Cobbett's, the 'Dutch Tax'.

The attempted coup of July 1647 was foreshadowed in 1645, but its course was already anticipated in detail in the events of December 1646. Although the High Presbyterian Party had lost its struggle with Parliament over an extreme clericalist settlement, the cause of religious Presbyterianism of an intolerant and theocratic variety was still powerful. Not all of its supporters would be High Presbyterians. Some who had supported religious Presbyterianism, and continued to support it, would not join the political movement (Alderman Penington was perhaps the most prominent). Others would go with the tide without fully understanding its import. Henry Burton summed up the political innocents when he said, 'I put a difference between Sion College and Common Counsell, as between Seers and not Seers, between the leaders, and the led.'

Before the Scottish army left the north of England in December 1646, another High Presbyterian petition was circulating in the City and was being advanced by the same group of laymen. According to the newspapers, it resembled an earlier one, the forerunner to the City Remonstrance, in its formulation of the High Presbyterian programme. The Commons, as in 1645, acted swiftly against its promoters: three citizens, all prominent in the movement and responsible for distributing printed copies in the City, were arrested by warrant of the House. The Presbyterian city government, in open defiance, adopted the petition and, after slight modification, presented it to Parliament.[20] It had been supported in Common Council by Colonel William Barton, one of the signers of the laymen's High Presbyterian petition of November 1645. Barton was a wealthy clothier and a clothing contractor to the parliamentary armies, a man of whom it was said that he employed one hundred people. Even if he was not hard-faced, plainly he had done well out of the war. Typical of the movement, he combined substance in business with adherence to rigid Presbyterianism and active participation in the Kirk. He was also one of that small group of committed men who kept close links with the Scots, and his own parish minister was a close friend of Robert Baillie. Later, in 1651, he would be involved in Love's plot. The petition had served as a kind of party manifesto at the Common Council elections of 21 December 1646, at which an even greater Presbyterian majority was returned. Notable for the prominence given to religious grievances, it demanded an altogether stricter church, and called for the outlawing of separatist congregations, punishment for heresy, and exclusion from office not only of those who refused the Covenant but of all who were 'manifestly disaffected to its ends therein expressed'. It would have set up an inquisition into men's consciences both in political and in religious matters. The Presbyterians were not above appealing demagogically to the economic interests of the middling and smaller tradesmen: the petition complained of 'the doubling ordinance' on the security of bishops' lands – a proposal by which wealthy lenders could double their loans to the government in return for ecclesiastical land on advantageous terms. They protested that this left the smaller lenders who could not 'double' in a position where they could be bought out at less than the value of their loan. Then they rehearsed the political programme which was now the main platform of Holles and the Peace Party: the disbandment of the army – the arm of revolutionary Independency – the issue of writs for free elections to Parliament, the reform of county committees, and the dissolution of the hated money-raising committee of Haberdashers' Hall. Some minor modifications were made before it was presented to Parliament. It was pressed again by the municipality in January and March 1647. Political grievances were now more prominent, although the demands for a strict intolerant kirk and the suppression of all sects (demands which were also put forward fiercely in supporting petitions from Sion College) also had a place.[21]

In other ways also the December 1646 petition prefigured later events. On its second presentation to the House in January, the aldermen and Common Council were pressed to elect an official roster of men who would solicit Parliament every week until action was taken. Two aldermen and two common councilmen were to go each week from every ward to beard M.P.s, perhaps the earliest example of a modern type of organised lobbying.[22] Popular pressure from the Presbyterian Party, which was exercised earlier in the campaign in the vestries in 1645 and over the City Remonstrance in May 1646, was now demonstrated again in an open struggle to bend Parliament to its will. It was a striking reversal of roles not uncommon in the history of revolution. The Civil War had ended and some of the men who had led the City in rebellion in 1641 and 1642, half-satisfied with its gains, gave their support to a conservative programme that had the appearance if not the reality of a continuation of the revolution: a strict ecclesiastical programme for the Church, citizen pressure on Parliament and a 'Kirk and king' mob in the streets.

This mob pressure, so noticeable from December 1646 in the memoirs, pamphlets and newspapers of the time, has not been given prominence by historians who have isolated later events and have ignored the mounting wave of agitation and violence that foreshadowed them. I stress this violence because it greatly affected the attitude of the parliamentary leaders and rank and file M.P.s, whose actions, now and later, were much influenced by fear of the mob. Some of the contemporary accounts give a poignant picture of tumult and the threat of disorder in London that is missing from our political histories.

Partly it was caused by disbanded soldiers (both Royalist and New Model Army men) known as Reformadoes, who drifted to the capital to collect their arrears of pay and to lobby M.P.s about their grievances. But the crowds were also composed of respectable citizens. The Londoners were so insistent and clamorous in December 1646 that a moderate Independent M.P., Sir John Evelyn of Wiltshire, threatened to bring in the army to quell the 'mechanick citizens', as he was alleged to have called them.[23] Nothing expresses better than this epithet the inappropriateness of a simple class label affixed to either of the contending parties. Evelyn, a wealthy country gentleman, reacted violently against social inferiors, artisans and traders, stirred up by prominent Presbyterian merchants. For good measure he saw them alike – the lower and middle classes possessed of these dangerous notions were all labouring men to him. The menace of the crowd frightened others too. On the last day of 1646, when part of the City's petition was under discussion, Whitelocke said that the House was 'awed' by the great multitude of citizens assembled outside. The fear of the crowd revealed also in Harington's diary was one reason why the Commons was so sensitive about the excise riots that took place in London in February 1647. As a result of the butchers' strike and the disturbances to which it gave rise (including the burning of the offices at Smithfield), the administration of the tax was reformed. The concessions served only to whet the appetite. Demands for the complete abolition of excise would follow from all the radical parties – the army, the Levellers and later the Fifth Monarchists – and formed part of the moderate 'Heads of Proposals' in June 1647.[24]

The events leading up to the crisis and counter-revolution of the summer are very confusing because of the welter of diplomatic bargaining between the various parties and the king amid a multitude of rumours and speculation, many of the stories contradicting each other. It is, however, clear that from December 1646 Parliament was dominated by Holles and his Presbyterian Peace Party. Some of his followers wanted to settle with the king on minimum terms: the token establishment of Presbyterianism for three years and the parliamentary control of the militia for ten. Others, including Holles himself, wanted solid commitment to religious Presbyterianism, partly to satisfy the Scots. On the whole Holles tried to pursue as firm a religious Presbyterian policy in Parliament as was consistent with attempts to come to terms with the king. Thus he went ahead with the sale of bishops' lands, even at a time when some of his allies among the peers, together with a few leading conservative citizens, were proposing, in secret negotiation with Charles, to preserve the episcopalian church. Meanwhile, Lords and Commons pursued a policy designed to protect Presbyterianism. On 8 February, under city pressure, the Lords voted that anyone refusing the Covenant should be barred from both civil and military posts. Five weeks later the City showed that it meant this ruling to apply to the highest in the land: it petitioned that now that the king had moved nearer London, he should immediately take the Covenant and sign whatever propositions Parliament should place before him.[25]

II

Holles's chief design in these months is well known – his attempt and that of his supporters to disband the New Model Army. It was this plan that, in part, caused the famous confrontation between Parliament and army in the summer of 1647. What has not been pointed out, however, is that Holles's schemes for the New Model were only part of a larger strategy: to create an alternative army that would, if necessary, defeat and supplant Cromwell's Ironsides. The Presbyterian M.P. William Strode had the alternative plan in mind when he was alleged to say that an army of 40,000 could be raised in London and, with the help of deserters and the Scots, could destroy their opponents. Their official policy, as declared in the House, was to reduce the New Model Army to 5400 foot and 1000 dragoons and to cut down drastically the size of local garrisons. When the soldiers protested (partly because their pay was in arrears), Holles embarked on the second and secret phase of his plans: the building of a counter-revolutionary force and the seizure of power. As for the protesting New Model soldiers, they were branded in the House on 29 March as 'Enemies of the State and Disturbers of the Public Peace'.[26]

The stage was now set for the creation of a powerful army. It was to consist of three elements: Reformadoes (that is, disbanded officers and soldiers), such regiments of the New Model as were still commanded by safe 'Peace Party' men, and the Presbyterian Trained Bands of London, themselves remodelled as Cromwell and others had remodelled the old parliamentary forces. The political leadership of the Militia Committee was the first target. Out must go all those like Alderman Penington and Alderman Fowke, John Estwicke and Colonel Player who leaned in politics towards the parliamentary Independents. In their place must be put sound men, committed to the cause of the High

Presbyterians, the conservative Peace Party and the Scots. The first stage of the campaign was achieved. In April, the Old Guard of the Revolution in London were voted off the committees and replaced by a group who were closely bound to the Presbyterians and deeply involved in plans for the seizure of power; like their predecessors they were drawn from the ranks of the city government and most were serving officers of the Trained Bands. At its highest point this force with its auxiliaries had numbered 18,000 men. In 1647, with the disbandment of the auxiliary troops it had been reduced to 12,000. But, as we have seen, the secret plans envisaged the recruitment of Reformadoes who could be enticed to the capital with the offer of the payment of their arrears. First, however, the Trained Bands of London were to be made ready for expansion. Their new-modelling was quickly undertaken by the freshly appointed Committee of Militia and through their friends in Parliament they got the power to create an additional troop of 500 horse, a force in which the City had always been weak. London had prided itself on the valour of its defenders, the pikemen and musketeers of the infantry, and on its long line of fortifications. An arm of cavalry suggests an aggressive war of movement and the possibility of an encounter with Cromwell's victorious army. Meanwhile the City's control of its fortifications was reinforced by the reduction of the New Model guards, who were replaced by one of London's Trained Bands. Also in order, presumably, to safeguard one of the approaches to the City and, nominally, to encourage the military ardour of the inhabitants of Westminster, £500 was voted in May 1647 to the Middlesex Artillery Company and their training-ground was restored to them.[27]

The second step in their plans was to put sound Presbyterian Peace Party citizens in control of the financial committees charged with disbursing the arrears of pay owing to soldiers of the New Model Army. In May 1647 a loan of £200,000 was negotiated from the City for this purpose. Three men who would play leading roles in the counter-revolutionary movement of July 1647 were installed as treasurers, Alderman James Bunce, Colonel Lawrence Bromfield and Common Councilman Richard Glyde. They were all members of the new Militia Committee and they were given authority to pay the arrears. Certain army auditors were also empowered to disburse the large sum of £10,000 which was allocated for immediate payment of the Reformadoes by ordinance of 3 June. One of the places occupied for this purpose was Christ Church, Newgate, Thomas Edwards's domain where he rehearsed his _Gangraena_.[28] Rarely can pulpit, party headquarters, army pay centre and recruiting office have been so effectively combined in one place as they were here, where the funds were distributed to likely supporters ready to bear arms, the citizens were organised and edified, and prayers were offered for the success of king and kirk. In his *Mysterie of the Two Juntoes* Clement Walker summed up the strategy of the Presbyterians when he said that the City was their bastion. It is 'their cheife foundation', he wrote, 'with which they keepe a strict correspondencie, and dayly communication of Counsells. Upon this consideration, they have lately put the Parliament's Purse into the Cities Pocket . . . and setled and inlarged the City Militia.'

The army was not passive while the Presbyterians openly prepared for war. They struck back – or rather Cornet Joyce and the agitators struck by capturing the king on 3 June 1647. It was an act of defiance that drove Holles and his supporters in Parliament to retaliation. Compelled into the open by events, they established a parliamentary Committee of Safety to act with the now remodelled London Militia Committee, from which the political Independents had been purged. They also empowered the Committee for Irish Affairs, whose task it had been to select the forces to be sent to Ireland, to raise troops; discontented Reformadoes were encouraged to return under their old leaders, safe conservative men like Colonel Richard Graves and Colonel Robert Pye. From 3 June to 12 June Holles and his party were blatant in the openness of their preparations for war. A sum of £10,000 was ordered to be paid out by Alderman Bunce and the treasurers at Weavers' Hall to sound Presbyterian officers, and the soldiers were given quarter by the Committee for Irish Affairs. These same soldiers, joined by apprentices, were meanwhile exerting mob pressure on Parliament, besieging it clamorously for pay. John Harington records in his diary that the House was again 'over-awed' on 4, 5 and 6 June by Reformadoes, and on 7 June his diary has the single terse entry: 'We [are] kept prisoners, [and] threatened.' He was probably too disgusted or frightened to say more because there is no further entry until 26 July. On 8 June Whitelocke tells us that soldiers blocked the doors of the Commons for two hours, refusing to allow members to pass unless they granted them further sums for arrears – which the House promptly did, thus strengthening the weapons which it had already placed in the hands of the City's Presbyterian treasurers.[29]

At the level of city government and of Parliament, the Presbyterian and Peace Party were within an ace of success. There was one difficulty. How could they recruit a mass army? Presbyterian and moderate though the substantial citizens were, they were not necessarily prepared to risk life and property in a mortal struggle with the highly renowned New Model Army, particularly since there were leading men in Parliament, the City and the army leadership who were clearly seeking a compromise, rather than a head-on collision. News circulating in London that the army leaders were putting forward a moderate programme of their own to be submitted to the king had its effect. When Cromwell and the army started their march south, the Committee for the Militia called out the Trained Bands but found, in the words of an army supporter, that they 'would not budge, not ten of some Companies appeared, and many Companies none at all but the officers'. We are told that the call to arms sounded by drum in the city streets was answered only by the jeers of boys. The lord mayor was very active in person trying to shut up the shops and although he managed to get the wealthy shopkeepers of Exchange to comply, the rest preferred to wait and see. The conciliatory tone of the army's letter and the unwillingness of the citizens to fight caused the moderate party to win power temporarily in Common Council and a pacific letter was sent to General Fairfax. The action of the City and the advance of the army southwards brought about the collapse of Holles's party in the Commons. Immediately an order was passed in the House to annul the enlisting of Reformadoes and the activities of the Committee of Safety were repudiated. The army was mollified by the dispatch of £40,000 to pay their arrears. In his *Memoirs* Holles singled out the payment of '£49,000' (as he wrongly remembered it) to the New Model as the greatest blow to his cause, 'for it served to keep the soldiers together, and unite them for marching up, whereas before there were high discontents among them'.[30]

The refusal of the ordinary citizens and members of the Trained Bands to take the offensive against the army should have been a warning to the Presbyterian leaders. As we shall see, it went unheeded. Conspirators often suffer from a form of political intoxication and it is not difficult to imagine that they thought that next time it would go better. After all, on the surface things were encouraging: thousands of unemployed demobilised soldiers, a restive army troubled by Left versus Right dissensions, the backing of the city bigwigs and the knowledge that no one could so effectively fill a petition sheet as their supporters. But more is required for a successful revolution and we must ask why the Londoners refused to rise. Thomas Hobbes had one answer: the traditional timidity of citizens and merchants who were always 'bad at venturing'. Half a century before John Stow, from a different standpoint, had said that London was never the author of rebellion. Both would have agreed that the rich City feared sack and plunder as the devil holy water. But these reasons do not satisfy. The citizens had shown heroism enough in enlisting in the Trained Bands and had fought in large numbers in the New Model Army (as an indignant vindication claimed – for who would sack a city 'having their wives and children therein?'). They had not lacked enthusiasm either or courage in 1643 when they had prepared to defy Royalist marauders and, almost as though on festival, great sections of the population had marched out to dig fortifications. Perhaps this last action gives us a clue to understand their behaviour. Their collective action was basically and traditionally defensive, a reflection of deep-seated civic patriotism. A new aggressive military coup was a different matter. Then life, liberty and property might fail in a cause that was not completely theirs.

Let us look at that cause. The policy of the Presbyterian and Peace Party as it drew on Reformadoes and made 'yoke-fellow' with Royalists was becoming openly 'counter-revolutionary'. The soldiers who intimidated Parliament and terrified the shopkeepers were the 'White Guard' of the revolution, many of them ex-Royalists. Their destructive impulses might endanger life and property as soon as, or sooner than the army. The terms of settlement with the king would, if conducted with such a force, result in few if any guarantees for the future – and the wealthy aldermen who acted as financiers of Parliament stood to lose the money they had invested in the parliamentary war. As the 'White Guard' of the revolution frightened the Londoners, so the army leaders deliberately strengthened their own cause by the moderation of their policy and their seeming willingness to make an immediate settlement with the king. These, then, were some of the reasons why a party among the leading aldermen and common councilmen deserted Holles at a critical moment and prepared to negotiate with the army. Obviously, it happened only after a struggle. The leaders of the party of compromise are known to us – they were Aldermen Fowke, Gibbs, Warner and Viner, some of the leading financiers of the Long Parliament. Gibbs and Viner shared more than Fowke and Warner, a position of waiting on events, veering from one alternative to another under the pressures of the time, choosing always the lesser of evils rather than allowing themselves to be swayed by ideological or political passion.[31]

As the City swung into neutrality, so did Parliament. Until the end of June there were many attempts in both the Commons and the municipality to make some kind of *rapprochement* between the political parties. But in July, as their Scottish allies intrigued for invasion of England, the counter-revolutionary plans of Holles and his allies were gradually exposed by their opponents. Parliament began to look more sympathetically towards the army. A series of liberal proposals from Fairfax and his council of officers started to win supporters. It culminated in the 'Heads of the Proposals' which would have restored the king, put a limit to the Parliament, permitted some measure of religious toleration and brought about a modified episcopacy. These proposals struck a deep well of sympathy among parliamentarians. They were called on, however, to pay a price: the exclusion from Parliament of Holles and his ten leading supporters and an investigation into the activities of their city allies – in particular into the enlisting of soldiers and the payments made by the city treasurers to the Reformadoes and to the city militia in the attempt to build a rival army in the city.[32]

When Parliament accepted the army's demands for the removal of the M.P.s and followed it by submitting to the army's insistence that the City's militia be remodelled, the Presbyterian and Peace Party and their allies in Parliament decided to act. Holles's supporters had fought on there until they were defeated over the Militia Bill. The very next day (20 July) they asked for and obtained permission to leave England. At this point their City allies struck. They determined to get by force what had been denied to them constitutionally. On 20 July great crowds of citizens and soldiers flocked to Westminster to protest against Parliament's action in dismantling the Presbyterian Militia Committee. The disturbance was so great that a hundred troopers had to be brought in to guard the House. Two days later a meeting was held in the City at Skinners' Hall, where a great number of people signed a statement known as the 'Solemn Engagement', pledging themselves to maintain the Covenant and to procure the king's presence in London and his restoration to power. It is important to see who they were, because their action sparked off violent demonstrations that threatened Parliament with mob terror and forced it to adopt their programme. The 'Solemn Engagement' was entitled 'The humble petition of the citizens, commanders, officers and souldiers of the Trained Bands and Auxiliaries, the young men and apprentices of the cities of London and Westminster, sea commanders, seamen, watermen, together with divers other commanders, officers and souldiers within the lines of communication'. The document was to be circulated in the wards by officers, styled 'agitators' in imitation of the Levellers, and petition forms were attached. Even so, in spite of so much organisation, there was division at the top: some of the leading men in the City were reported to be party to it; others ostentatiously stood aside. The 'Solemn Engagement' was printed by the same Colonel John Bellamy whom we have found to be so active in the Presbyterian cause throughout these years – the man who had led the movement to extend the powers of Common Council, who printed and published in favour of the City Remonstrance and who, as a member of the Presbyterian Militia Committee, would take a leading part in the counter-revolutionary attempt about to be launched.[33]

Parliament passed the Militia Act on 23 July, reinstating the political Independents into the city militia and removing the leaders of the Presbyterian and Peace Party. Immediately, two petitions were sent to Common Council urging the city government to protest. The petitions were accepted and it was decided that the Sheriffs and the whole Common Council should attend their presentation to the Commons on the following day, 26 July. That day witnessed a unique and astonishing scene. A great crowd of citizens accompanied the city officials to Westminster. When the Sheriffs had said their piece and departed, the crowds swept into the Palace of Westminster. First they went into the Lords and stood menacingly at the door, refusing to go away until they had compelled the peers to recall their declaration against the city; they forced the clerk to read the order publicly in the Painted Chamber, standing on a table. Then they swept on to the Commons. Here they were not content with remaining at the door but rushed into the chamber, where they kept the House prisoner and, further to insult the Commons, kept their hats on, shouting 'Vote! Vote!'. When the members hesitated, they forced the speaker to put the question, and the clerk to write out the necessary order; dominating the House, they obtained the repeal of the militia ordinance. Some of the members tried to send for help, but Colonel Nathaniel Campfield, of the London Trained Bands, a Presbyterian, refused to release them, saying that 'the carriage of the apprentices was more warrantable than the House's'. This outrageous violence, which caused about sixty M.P.s to flee to the army for protection, was recounted in a thanksgiving sermon by Stephen Marshall. After describing the action of the mob, he called it, 'that most horrid rape and violence' offered to Parliament 'wherein the most loathsome filth and dirt was thrown in the faces of our nobles and our senators'. Nothing like it, he said, had ever before been done in England. Whitelocke's comment for his children was: 'Here . . . you may observe an instance of the highest insolence in the rabble and of popular madness that you can meet with in any other story.' John Harington gives us the vivid account of an eye-witness: the climax came when the intruders refused to allow a division. 'They that imprisond us,' he wrote, 'beat and cry out at the dore and would not p[er]mit us to divide, the votes beeing doubtful. After[wards] wee weare forced to be a howse with them, [they] being within [the Chamber] with us, and to vote the king's pr[e]sent coming to Parl[iamen]t.'[34]

This event was excused by members of the Presbyterian Peace Party as an affair of the apprentices, as though it were an example of student-like high spirits, not at all supported by, or connived at, by the grave city fathers. This was what the City would afterwards say in its own defence. Nothing could be further from the truth. The mob rushed into Westminster Hall after the sheriffs had left, but their programme was the same as that of the city government. Observers were in no doubt that the municipality had a hand in the affair. Viscount Lisle remarked that the city rulers were clearly behind the mob because as soon as they had got what they wanted the organisers 'dismissed the multitude and sent them away to theyr homes'. Subsequent events also confirm the complicity of some of the leading citizens.[35]

Having won back the militia, the City started again to recruit an army to counter the New Model. They began on 28 July with a Day of Humiliation at Guildhall, in which Simeon Ashe, Edmund Calamy and Anthony Burges preached.[36] It is notable that Calamy, who would shortly, at the height of the crisis, desert the Presbyterian and Peace Party, should still at this point act with them. Thomas Edwards and William Jenkin were meanwhile stirring up the people from the pulpits. Common Council met on 29 July and voted £20,000 for defence purposes. On the same day the city walls were again plastered with bills urging the apprentices and the crowd to appear at Westminster. When Parliament sat on 30 July the speaker and many of the members failed to appear, having taken refuge with the army. Since the serjeant-at-arms was also absent and with him the mace, it seemed at first that the House would be unable to sit. So the city government intervened and offered its own mace.[37] Only thus could Parliament sit at all. The City's willingness to supply even the mace, the outward symbol of legality, reveals its deep implication in the counter-revolution. The House or what was left of it now voted to invest new powers on the Militia Committee, giving it authority to seize all horses in London and its suburbs and to appoint a Commander-in-chief of its army. Prompted by the City, it also sent to Fairfax asking him not to move nearer London.

Although in his *Memoirs* Holles denied any direct complicity in the events of these tumultuous days, there can be no doubt that he and the other ten members worked closely in harness with their citizen allies. We know that on 26 July, the day of violence in Westminster, Holles himself, Sir William Waller and John Clotworthy met together at the Bell Tavern in King Street, Westminster; the evidence suggests that this was their headquarters or command post from which all was directed. The appointment of one of the eleven M.P.s to be Commander-in-chief of the city forces, Waller's own involvement with the apprentices and with the enlisting of men, and Holles's account of the affair, all point to the complicity of this parliamentary group. Whitelocke, who had been so close to Holles (although now, the typical trimmer, he was trying hard to ingratiate himself with St John), wrote in his diary that 'all this part of the action [i.e. from 29 July] was contrived and directed by the eleven members and their friends'.[38]

The rest of the story is easily told. As Fairfax and his troops moved inexorably nearer, the party that had asserted itself in the City in June in favour of a *rapprochement* with the army and the Independents began to win support. On 2 August there was a day of agonising debate in the city chamber as the army came closer to London. The Common Council and the City Militia Committee sat all day. The newspapers gave breathless excited accounts of the City's dilemma and of its dramatic changes of mood. When a scout came in and brought news that the army had made a halt, or other cheerful accounts, the Common Council would be filled with courage and shout, 'One and all!'. Alas, it is the duty of intelligence to give a true report. When the scout brought information that the army was advancing, their courage ebbed and there were equally loud shouts of 'Treat, treat, treat!'. In this hopeless state of indecision they spent most of the night.[39]

Ironically, the final collapse was brought about by some of the city clergy – the very men who had supported the High Presbyterian Party in London in 1645 and 1646 and had played so big a part in their sermons and among their parishioners in creating the movement that they were now to desert. On 2 August a petition went from the Assembly of Divines to the City, begging them to negotiate with the army leaders, and it contained signatures of some like Calamy who had played their part in the High Presbyterian Party. Robert Baillie was aghast at the mindless treachery of his own friends and agents when 'one stout look more' would have saved all. If only, he would lament, Parliament had seized the heads of the Independent Party, had stopped their flight to the army, if Massey and Waller had doubled their rate of enlisting – then Stephen Marshall and his 'seventeen servants of the synod' would never have been able to offer that destructive petition to Common Council which 'without any capitulation, put presently in the armie's power, both Parliament, City and all England, without the least contradiction'. Such an example of treachery, cowardice and childish improvidence had never been seen. From that moment, he thought, the army was absolute 'master of all'.[40]

The final blow came that evening while the ministers were inducing aldermen and common councilmen to submit. Disbrowe's troop of horse coming up through Kent persuaded the city regiment in Southwark to let them in and to deliver up the bridge. The commander of the regiment, Colonel John Hardwicke (whom the Presbyterians had taken to be one of their own), betrayed his party and handed over the bridge. Thereafter, his name was a byword for perfidy. 'That Trecherous base Skellum Hardwicke', they called him, who 'after that he had vowed by the Honour of a Souldier, the Faith of a Christian, the Reputation of a Man, that he would resist all Armed men whatever who would endeavour to enter the lyne',[41] invited in the army and betrayed all. The ballad-mongers, scribblers and pamphleteers made merry with the ludicrous collapse of the City after so much bustle and preparation for war. The acts of defiance followed by such base cowardice and treachery, the desertion of allies and the complete surrender to the army produced a rich vein of satirical ballads and rhymes.

On 3 August Fairfax marched into London. He took possession of the Tower, restored control of the city militia to the previous command, removed the suburban areas from city control and ordered the demolition of the lines of fortification. All London's power was gone in one night. As Denzil Holles complained, the City made no effort to rescue anything from the disaster; no bargain was attempted to preserve the eleven members; they did not even provide for the safety of their own commander-in-chief, Colonel Massey; instead, they left all in the lurch – in Holles's words, 'Like Isacher [Issacher] bow'd under the Burden, betray'd themselves and all that had to do with them'.

Why did they desert? Not, superficially, for lack of trained and organised soldiers. Sir William Waller, who took part in organising the city forces, claimed that London in July 1647 had no less than eighteen regiments of foot (some of them 2000 strong – though others were incomplete, none were less than 800). An army sympathiser thought that 10,000 auxiliaries had been enlisted in the City besides the Trained Bands.[42] Moreover, the counter-revolutionaries could expect support from between 4000 and 5000 horse officered by Reformadoes. The threat was real. Fairfax, at the time, had less than this number of infantry under his command and only a quarter of these were properly armed, while his horse, although strong in numbers, were also badly equipped. Waller was probably exaggerating the strength of the counter-revolutionary army and we have already seen that rank-and-file citizens were not easily prevailed upon to serve. Nevertheless, one cannot dismiss them simply as lacking in military strength. To discover the reasons for their collapse we must look first at the nature of the Presbyterian and Peace Party alliance and its composition.

Who planned this counter-revolution that ended so disastrously for its authors? We know some of the men involved merely from looking at those singled out for punishment by Parliament. They were the leading members of the Militia Committee and of the Trained Bands, who were responsible either for mustering the military forces in June and July 1647, or for organising mob riots and violence against the two houses of Parliament. Apart from the apprentices, leaders of the seamen, the Reformado soldiers and the watermen who were mentioned as actors in the affair, the chief culprits were certain prominent members of the Militia Committee, common councilmen and militia captains who had also been associated with the High Presbyterian campaign since 1645 and with the political Presbyterian Party. Some of them were local ruling elders and were also delegates from their *classes* to the London Provincial Assembly.[43] This argues a considerable commitment to the Presbyterian Church. The political wing of the movement was even more strongly represented. Prominent among them was Colonel Lawrence Bromfield. He does not appear to have been an elder (but since our records are incomplete, we cannot be certain) and he was not a delegate to the London Provincial Assembly. His role in these events was crucial. *A Paire of Spectacles for the Citie*, in describing the purge of Presbyterians from the City Militia Committee conducted by the army and Parliament after the July days, says that Bromfield was a leader of his party. He would play the same role as a political Presbyterian spokesman in 1659 and he would be knighted for his services by Charles II. The anonymous author says that Bromfield was a gentleman of 'unquestionable faithfulnesse and integrity', who 'muted those Apostates Fowks, Estwicke, Player and countermined their designes'. This was his crime and this is why he was dismissed from his office and impeached for high treason.

The part played by Bromfield emphasised the important role of political Presbyterians among the city leaders. Parliament took particularly strong action against them. They included the five aldermen who were impeached by both Houses and were as a group much less involved with religious than with political Presbyterianism. Sir John Gayre was, as we have seen, probably a Royalist – and his predecessor as lord mayor Thomas Adams probably had similar leanings. Alderman Adams and Alderman John Langham had nevertheless both worked very closely with the Scots, and Baillie had hoped that Langham might have been elected lord mayor in 1646. Alderman James Bunce was the only alderman who was closely involved with the Kirk. Bunce was imprisoned until 1648 and left England on his release – we do not know whether he would have continued to support the Presbyterian Church – but he was associated with Love's plot and the designs of Royalists and Scottish Presbyterians throughout the 1650s.[44]

Parliament chose to punish the political members of the group rather than the clericalists. It was expedient, it was good propaganda, it provided easy and identifiable victims. Can we also show that, besides the political culprits arraigned by Parliament, leading religious Presbyterians in the city government were involved in the counter-revolution? We can. A chance survival of documents in the Public Record Office Exchequer Papers reveals their complicity. A bundle of militia warrants, dating from June and July 1647, shows payments made to officers in the Trained Bands and authorises the collection and organisation of troops, horses and ammunition. The aldermanic signatories of the warrants are the same men as Parliament impeached – the political incorrigibles of the counter-revolution. The Common Council signatories however are nearly all men actively engaged for the Kirk. Of the seven (sometimes eight) names of the non-aldermanic members of the Militia Committee, all were ruling elders of their parishes, were active delegates to the London Provincial Assembly, and continued their support into the 1650s when they could, if they wished, withdraw into other congregations. Some of the men can also be identified as supporters of the High Presbyterian campaign in the City or as close allies of Baillie.[45]

There is therefore no doubt about the important part played by Presbyterian laymen in this revolutionary *putsch*. When it was all over,

Anthony Nicoll, one of the eleven M.P.s, told Hugh Peter that the city ministers had set them on foot against the army and without them it would not have happened.[46] Nicoll was exaggerating. The conservative political wing of the alliance was also very powerful. It was just because it was an alliance of dissimilar groups that it broke asunder. Although, as I have shown, Presbyterianism had some popular roots in the City, it appealed essentially to the middle strata of merchants. When they called out the *menu peuple* in July 1647 the City trembled on the brink of anarchy. The seamen and watermen may have acted at the behest of highly placed merchants (the Watermens' Company, for instance, was closely controlled by the Court of Aldermen who selected its officials). But popular agitation can easily overreach its organisers, burst the bonds of control and develop dimensions undreamed of by its instigators. The Royalist Sir Lewis Dyve wrote to Charles I on 1 August that the City was reduced to anarchy with the apprentices, watermen and seamen 'governing all' by their 'agitators'. The radical Leveller movement and popular fury against the excise conjured up visions of social revolution. One pamphleteer thought that the City drew back in 1647 because if the king were restored without guarantees, the people would simply refuse to pay any taxes or excise. In that event, how would the public faith debts be discharged? As he said, 'Money was the bottome of the businesse.' Hobbes was perhaps saying the same thing more elegantly when he likened London to a creature that 'hath a great belly; but no palate, nor taste of Right and Wrong'. In their last surrender to the army, the city money-bags were swayed not by ideologies or political passion but simply by the desire to survive.[47]

In times of revolution, men do not simply argue about principles and then act on their ideas. They are also pushed by events. The political Independents of the Long Parliament were driven to support the army as the lesser evil. For the citizens of London, the alternatives were very similar. It is not therefore surprising that they finally made the same choice.

2. The Levellers and the Franchise

KEITH THOMAS

I

A DISCUSSION of the Levellers which concentrates solely on their proposals for a new parliamentary franchise calls for some justification.
These proposals formed only one part of the Leveller programme, and
not necessarily the most important part at that. In the history of political
theory the Levellers are important for many other reasons. They
proclaimed that men were born equal and that government could be
founded only on consent. They stood for religious toleration and equality before the law. Their concern for civil liberties led them into making
the first-known attempt at writing down a law paramount which not even
the legislature could alter. Their successive manifestoes, the 'Agreements of the People', were the earliest English approximations to a
written constitution. They also gave early expression to the doctrine of
the separation of powers. If to these achievements we add their advocacy
of numerous specific reforms, from the abolition of tithes to the reform
of the law, we can recognise that the Levellers have an importance in the
history of social and political thought which far transcends any plans
they had for remodelling the franchise.

We can also see that their influence as an active political party did not
depend upon their views on the suffrage. The Levellers are immediately
recognisable as a crucial pressure group who, by their influence in
London and the army, did much to determine the course of events
during the critical years, 1647 and 1648. Through their links with the
'agitators' (elected representatives of the regiments) the Levellers
forced Cromwell and the army 'grandees' into increasingly radical
postures. They engineered the seizure of the king in June 1647, the
march on London, and the staging of the remarkable debates at Putney
in October–November when officers, agitators and civilian Levellers
thrashed out the principles on which the new political order was to rest.
In 1648 the Levellers continued to press for the removal of the king
and the implementation of their social and political reforms. In the

C

autumn of that year they held the balance between the manoeuvring parties of king, Parliament and army grandees. For a time they collaborated with representatives of Parliament and the army in an attempt to draw up a new 'Agreement of the People' on which all might agree. But with Pride's Purge and the execution of Charles I the Levellers ceased to hold the balance. Their support in the army melted away when the new government paid off the soldiers' arrears and raised their pay. In 1649 the Leveller leaders were imprisoned and their adherents crushed by military force. But by then the Levellers had exerted an influence out of all proportion to their numbers; and they had pioneered techniques of agitation by petition, pamphlet, party organisation and public demonstration that were to have a long subsequent history.

In these events the Leveller proposals for the franchise had played a part, but only a small one. It is true that regular parliaments, of short duration and of limited powers, were basic to the Leveller programme. So was the redistribution of constituencies. But less prominence was given to the question of who was actually to have the vote. It was known that the Levellers stood for a wide popular franchise, but the subject was not mentioned in the first 'Agreement of the People' (October 1647), and when the details were spelled out in the later 'Agreements', they were not entirely consistent.

Nevertheless, there are two good reasons for concentrating on this one aspect of the Leveller programme. The first is that the Putney debates reveal the franchise issue to have been the one that most obviously divided Levellers from army grandees. However inconspicuous in the Leveller documents, it was quickly seized upon by politicians of the time. The second is that the Levellers' franchise proposals have recently been subjected to a penetrating if controversial analysis. In fifty compellingly lucid pages in his *The Political Theory of Possessive Individualism* (Oxford, 1962) Professor C. B. Macpherson has put forward a striking interpretation.* The Levellers, he tells us, were not the champions of universal manhood suffrage that many earlier historians took them to be. On the contrary, they 'consistently excluded from their franchise proposals two substantial categories of men, namely, servants or wage-earners, and those in receipt of alms or beggars' (p. 107). Even when the Levellers appeared to talk in terms of universal manhood suffrage they were in fact assuming such exclusions. They 'always intended . . . a franchise excluding servants and alms-takers; and . . . they saw no inconsistency between this exclusion

* Page references henceforward are given in brackets in the text.

and their assertion of the natural right of every man to a vote.' This, says Professor Macpherson, was 'because of certain assumptions they made about the nature of freedom' (p. 111). The Levellers deemed wage-earners and alms-takers to have forfeited that birthright or equal natural right upon which each man's claim to vote was based. They held that everyone was entitled to civil liberties, but they confined political rights to those who had not 'lost the property in their own labour' (p. 145).

On this interpretation the Levellers can no longer be regarded as the forbears of modern democrats. On the contrary, it seems that they unwittingly paved the way for Locke and the Whig tradition by making freedom a function of proprietorship, though in the Levellers' case it was proprietorship in a man's own capacities rather than in land. It also appears that the gap between their proposals and those of the army leaders at Putney was much less than is usually assumed. For on Professor Macpherson's calculations (p. 292) universal suffrage in 1648 would have involved enfranchising 1,170,400 people, whereas the Levellers would have given the vote to 416,700 at most; that is to say they would have doubled the then existing electorate (estimated by Professor Macpherson at 212,100), but would have still left voteless nearly two-thirds of the adult male population. The army leaders on the other hand had been prepared to make some concessions. At Putney, Cromwell was ready to give votes to copyholders by inheritance.[1] And in the second 'Agreement of the People' (December 1648–January 1649) the grandees even accepted a ratepayer franchise (estimated by Professor Macpherson at 373,000, and thus only 41,000 votes short of the full Leveller proposals; or even fewer if, as seems likely, the grandees were also prepared to admit to the franchise those serving soldiers who did not otherwise qualify).

Professor Macpherson was not the first to portray the Levellers as anything other than unqualified adherents of universal manhood suffrage. Most previous historians had noticed that the later versions of the 'Agreement' excluded servants and alms-takers. But most of them had also tended to regard these exclusions as compromises or shifts of policy.[2] Professor Macpherson's originality is to detect an 'underlying consistency in the Levellers' franchise ideas' (p. 110), by denying that they *ever* wanted manhood suffrage, and by suggesting that their views were based upon a consistent theory in which the right to political participation depended upon retaining property in one's own labour.

The distinction with which Professor Macpherson argued his case has won him many converts. But his interpretation has also been subjected to a good deal of criticism. In particular, it has been urged that the Levellers were not the homogeneous political group his argument requires, but that they differed among themselves, some being in favour of manhood suffrage, others not; that the later exclusions of servants and alms-takers represented tactical compromises in the face of changing political circumstances rather than adherence to a fixed political principle; and that the 'servants' thus excluded were not the whole wage-earning class but only a section of it, so that Professor Macpherson's numerical calculations greatly exaggerate the actual number of individuals the Levellers wished to shut out from the franchise.

The aim of this chapter is to reassess the merits of Professor Macpherson's interpretation in the light of these and other possible objections. But an attempt will also be made to place the Leveller proposals in a wider context. In particular it is hoped that by relating them to previous seventeenth-century discussions of the franchise it will be possible to throw more light upon their distinctive significance.

II

The Leveller demand for wider popular participation in the election of members of Parliament is normally seen as the result of two main influences. The first was the Protestant doctrine of the spiritual equality of all believers. This generated the model of the sectarian congregation, whose members, having joined together by compact, participated equally in the choice of ministers and the making of collective decisions. The second was the collapse of the old political order under the pressure of civil war. This left the way open for the construction of a new society and justified the members of the victorious New Model Army in laying claim to a greater share of political power.

But the Leveller proposals were not simply the outcome of sectarianism and civil war. Their roots lay deep in the traditional political structure. For one of the distinguishing features of Tudor and Stuart England, by comparison with most continental countries, was the wide degree of participation in local government enjoyed by men of humble status. The Elizabethan commentator Sir Thomas Smith is often quoted for remarking of 'day labourers, poor husbandmen, yea merchants or retailers which have no free land, copyholders and all artificers, as tailors, shoemakers, carpenters, brickmakers, masons, etc.', that 'these have no authority in our commonwealth, and no account is made of them but only to be ruled'. But he went on to say of these classes that 'they be not altogether neglected. For in cities and corporate towns, for default of yeomen, inquests and juries are impanelled of such manner of people. And in villages they be commonly made churchwardens, ale-conners, and many times constables, which office toucheth more the commonwealth' (*De Republica Anglorum*).

Since the Middle Ages there had existed a bewildering mass of local institutions – parish vestries, courts baron, courts leet, town meetings – which were accustomed to making their own rules, appointing their own officers, and levying rates and fines upon their own members. Professor W. O. Ault has drawn attention to village meetings in which most if not all inhabitants came together to make bye-laws about such matters as gleaning or the use of the commons. 'Anyone who reads the manorial records,' remarks Carl Bridenbaugh, 'cannot fail to be astonished at the extensive participation of nearly every adult male in local affairs.' It is true that such participation was justified on grounds of status rather than of natural right, but its practical implications were considerable. It was in contexts like this that Englishmen became used to such democratic concepts as that of decision by majority (found in the fifteenth-century village meeting at Harlestone, Northampton-shire) or of voting by ballot (used in the election of municipal officers in some sixteenth-century towns). It was possible for labourers to be churchwardens; and in Devonshire the Stannary Parliament was elect-ed by all the tinners, labourers included.[3]

But it would be an exaggeration to say with one historian of the Level-lers that 'their ideas were formed in the communities in which they lived and worked, and the democracy which they advocated for the nation was still a working reality in their own local communities'.[4] For in fact many local communities were oligarchic in the extreme. Village meetings of the kind chronicled by Professor Ault were rare and it would be wrong to romanticise the democracy of the localities. Nevertheless it can be confidently presumed that at the village level the participation of every social group in the making of semi-political decisions was a familiar enough experience to make its extension to the parliamentary sphere seem by no means unreasonable.

The parliamentary franchise also offered some encouraging pre-cedents. It is true that at the county level the electorate had been limited since 1430 to freeholders worth 40s a year. But steady inflation must have done something to widen this franchise, though little seems to be known about this process. There were also counties where the minimum qualification was not strictly observed.[5]

In the boroughs the franchise varied. Most boroughs came into one of five categories: those where the franchise was confined to members of the ruling corporation; those where it depended on freemanship of the town; those where it required possession of a burgage property; those where the vote was exercised by all the ratepayers ('scot and lot'); and, widest of all, those where it was enjoyed by the whole 'commonalty', i.e. all the householders or even all the 'potwallers' (men with their own hearths). At its most extensive, therefore, the borough franchise could include wage-earners and labourers of all kinds.

The borough situation, moreover, was very fluid. 'The popular movement for a wider franchise was never at rest in the constituencies from the time of James I to the coming of William III,' declare the historians of the unreformed parliament.[6] In many towns there was genuine uncertainty as to exactly who possessed the right to vote, and every general election gave rise to numerous electoral disputes.

After 1604 these disputes were adjudicated upon by the House of Commons and in the 1620s the Commons showed a pronounced (though not invariable) tendency whenever the franchise was in doubt to declare in favour of a wider electorate. This bias may have reflected a desire to reduce electoral corruption and to counteract the influence of the court rather than any prejudice in favour of popular participation as such. Whatever the reason, parliamentary committees of 1621, 1624, 1625 and 1628 opened the franchise to 'the commonalty' in a series of disputed constituencies. Sometimes the vote was said to lie in 'all the inhabitants', as at Bletchingley (1624) or Lewes (1628); sometimes in all the 'resiants', as at Cirencester (1624). In the case of Pontefract (1624) the Commons committed themselves to the general principle that 'where no constant and certain custom appeareth who should be the electors in a parliamentary borough, there recourse must be had to the common law, or common right', and that 'of common right, all the inhabitants, householders, and residents within the borough, ought to have voice in the election, and not the freeholders there only'. In the case of Boston (1628) the committee asserted that the election of burgesses, in *all* boroughs, did, of common right, belong to the commoners; and that nothing could take it from them but a prescription, and 'a constant usage beyond all memory'.[7]

In addition to these decisions in individual cases there were attempts to standardise the franchise by legislation. Bills to regulate elections were brought forward in the parliaments of 1621, 1623, 1625, 1628 and 1640, though none was successful. The 1621 bill proposed a county electorate of £4 freeholders and £10 copyholders of inheritance, and a borough electorate of resident freemen or, if the freemen were fewer than twenty-four in number, of all the inhabitants not in receipt of alms.[8]

At the opening of the Long Parliament the franchise was still a central problem. Its precise extent was a major issue in at least ten of the disputed election cases and in another ten it was *the* issue. 'One cannot study the Long Parliament elections,' writes Mrs Keeler, 'without becoming aware of an under-current, genuinely democratic and apparently quite independent of the question of the royal prerogative, which was moving townsmen to demand extensions of the voting privilege.'[9] Moreover, an influential section of M.P.s was in favour of franchise reform. In a debate on an election petition from Great Marlow on 11 November 1640 the question was raised 'whether the poor should have a voice or no'. Sir Simonds D'Ewes 'moved that the poorest man ought to have a voice; that it was the birthright of the subjects of England'. At least five other members spoke in defence of this position. A bill to regulate elections was brought in. It had got as far as a second reading by 30 March 1641, when D'Ewes 'moved that I liked the bill well and would not retard the committing of it. Only I desired that whereas it was provided in the bill that none who took alms should have voices in elections, which I well allowed, we would likewise provide that no more monopolizing elections might be in cities and boroughs, but that all men resiants there might have voices.' The first bill seems to have been scrapped and replaced by a new one that received a second reading on 28 April, and then got lost under the pressure of other business.[10]

The Levellers, therefore, had been preceded by several decades of intermittent agitation for a wider parliamentary franchise. Successive parliaments had shown a preference for a wide borough franchise, for all scot and lot payers, if not for all inhabitants; and there had been an attempt to widen the county franchise to include some copyholders. In practice the electorate had grown substantially, running into thousands of voters in most counties and some of the boroughs. As Professor Plumb remarks, 'the fact of the emerging electorate, both in the boroughs and in the counties, helped to create the issue of representation and the debates about it. . . . When the Levellers demanded a vote for all inhabitants, this arose from their experience of county elections, from what they had seen and heard, not from abstract theory.'[11]

But the pre-Civil War parliaments had also provided the Levellers with a theory. For it was widely (and correctly) held that the statute of 1430 had taken away the vote from persons who had previously had it. 'Anciently all the communalty had voice,' declared William Noy in 1621, 'but because such a multitude made the election tumultuous it was after reduced to freeholders.' 'Anciently all the freeholders had voices,' agreed D'Ewes in 1641: oligarchic elections were 'against the hereditary right of the subjects of England'. The same theory of the lost voting rights was reiterated by William Prynne: 'Before this Petition and Act [8 Hen. VI c. 7] every inhabitant and commoner in each county had a voice in the election of knights, whether he were a freeholder or not, or had a freehold only of one penny, six pence or twelve pence by the year, as they now claim of late in most cities and boroughs where popular elections are admitted.' In the later eighteenth century it was to be revived by Major John Cartwright as part of his case for manhood suffrage.[12]

For the Levellers this argument was central. In *Londons Liberty in Chains* (1646) John Lilburne complained of the disfranchising of 'thousands of people' by the 'restrictive and unjust statute of the 8 H. 6' and urged that steps be taken to 'restore every free-man of England, to his native, and legal rights and freedoms'. At Putney Commissary Cowling commented on the restrictive intentions of the 1430 statute, while the authors of the 'Earnest Petition' (January 1648) claimed that the Act had abridged their birthright: 'It hath been the ancient liberty of this nation that all the free-born people have freely elected their representers in Parliament.'[13] The Levellers, we know, had already begun to shift their claim from historic right to natural right; but for the original historical argument they were indebted to the parliamentarians of the early seventeenth century.

To trace Leveller ideas to this ancestry is not necessarily to confirm Professor Macpherson's argument that the Levellers assumed the exclusion of servants and alms-takers from the franchise. It is true that alms-takers were explicitly excluded in the Long Parliament's bill, and D'Ewes seems to have approved this step, despite his plea for the rights of 'the poorest man'. When parliamentary committees ruled that the vote in any particular borough lay 'in the inhabitants' it seems clear that apprentices, alms-takers and criminals were tacitly excluded. But in practice the situation was very confused. In the boroughs it was easy for a qualified voter to fall on hard times; and in some election disputes it was revealed that persons in receipt of public relief had voted. A striking case occurred at Great Marlow in 1640, when no fewer than

77 of the 245 voters were said to have been alms-takers, nine of them being actual inmates of the alms-house. Alms-takers also voted at Bedford. Usually the right of such persons to vote would be defended by the interested candidate and rejected by the parliamentary committee; by the end of the century a long list of decisions against alms-men-voters had been accumulated. But there were some notable exceptions. In 1640 it was claimed that the right of inmates to vote had been upheld at Bramber. In 1662 it was testified that at St Albans the alms-men 'had had voices time out of mind'; and their right to vote was upheld by the House of Commons. The same thing happened at Sandwich in 1690, when the parliamentary committee resolved 'that the freemen of the port of Sandwich, inhabiting within the said borough (although they receive alms) have a right to vote in electing barons to serve in Parliament'. In 1711 a witness declared that in Grantham freemen in receipt of weekly relief had voted in parliamentary elections for the past forty or fifty years. By the later eighteenth century it was said to be a 'commonly received doctrine, that servants, and those who receive alms, have no right to vote for members of Parliament'.[14] But in the days of the Levellers and for some time afterwards the position of alms-takers was a good deal less clear. It was by no means axiomatic that they were automatically disqualified from voting.

Servants and wage-earners also played some part in seventeenth-century elections. 'Labourers and handicraftsmen' were said to have intervened at Wigan in 1640. Many wage-earners voted legitimately in the potwaller or householder boroughs: in constituencies like Wootton Bassett, Tregony or Honiton it was quite usual, even in the eighteenth century, for poor labourers to take part in elections. Resident household servants, however, could participate only irregularly. 'Servants' were said to have voted in the Worcestershire county election of 1604; and five certainly did so at Sandwich in 1690. But no spokesman defended their rights. On the other hand it should be remembered that in Virginia all male inhabitants, indentured or covenanted servants included, were allowed to participate in elections to the General Assembly from 1619 until 1655. This concession was said to have been secured by the English parliamentarian Sir Edwin Sandys, who, it was alleged, 'aimed at nothing more than to make a free popular state there'. Since 1557, moreover, when two servants voted in the adoption of the *Book of Discipline* by the Frankfurt group of Marian exiles, there had been precedents for the exercise of voting rights by servant members of sectarian congregations.[15]

It is clear, therefore, that by the mid-seventeenth century the idea of allowing the vote to alms-takers, wage-earners and even household servants was by no means inconceivable. We also know that the Diggers accepted universal manhood suffrage (delinquents and criminals apart), while the Fifth Monarchy Men included labourers and servants among their élite. Other contemporary radicals also saw lowliness of status as no bar to political participation.[16] Where, then, did the Levellers stand on this important issue?

In his attempt to prove the underlying consistency of Leveller ideas Professor Macpherson fastens upon Maximilian Petty's statement at Putney that 'we would exclude apprentices, or servants, or those that take alms'. He declares that this dictum shows 'the Levellers had been assuming the exclusion of "servants" all along', and uses it to explain away any previous or subsequent statement to the contrary. Colonel Rainsborough's insistence upon the rights of 'the poorest he that is in England', 'any man that is born in England', or 'the meanest man in the kingdom', is, therefore, not to be taken literally, since 'in their contexts these terms may equally be assumed to have been understood as "all free-born men who have not lost their birthright"'.[17] Only, Professor Macpherson explains, in that sense could they be 'consistent' with Petty's utterances (pp. 122–3, 125–6). But there is of course no reason to look for any such consistency. The Levellers we know to have been a heterogeneous party. There was a radical wing which shaded off into 'Diggers' (or 'True Levellers'), and there were more conservative figures who subsequently made their peace with the Commonwealth regime. The much-quoted statement in Henry Denne's *The Levellers Designe Discovered* (1649), 'We were a heterogenial body, consisting of parts very diverse from another, settled upon principles inconsistent one with another,' referred to the whole parliamentary party, not to the Levellers. But the very varied subsequent careers of the Leveller leaders clearly show how mixed was the character of the temporary alliance of soldiers and civilians that went under the name of the Leveller party.

It is to establish a quite unnecessary consistency that Professor Macpherson (pp. 126–8) has to explain away the statements of Rainsborough, Captain Clarke and Captain Audley. He also has to treat the allegations of Cromwell and Ireton that the Levellers wanted manhood suffrage as mere hyperbole; and he has to dodge the problem of Rainsborough's failure to repudiate Colonel Rich's suggestion that the Levellers would make 'master and servant . . . equal electors'.[18] All this is necessary if every Leveller statement at Putney is to be forced into line with the isolated utterance of Maximilian Petty, one of the more obscure Leveller spokesman, but significantly one of those whom we know to have been prominent in hatching the compromise second 'Agreement of the People', and later to have become a member of Harrington's Rota Club, whose aristocratic republican tone was very different from that of the Leveller movement. There seems no reason why he should be taken as a more representative Leveller than Rainsborough. For it was Rainsborough who was said to have had 'the greatest interest' among the agitators. We know him to have been dissatisfied with the outcome of Putney, and his untimely death in October 1648 robbed the Levellers of one of their more radical spokesmen.[19]

The pressure of debate at Putney, therefore, revealed internal divisions and uncertainties over a programme which had clearly not been worked out in all details. Afterwards the General Council of the Army voted 'that all soldiers and others, if they be not servants or beggars, ought to have voices in electing those which shall represent them in Parliament'.[20] But there is no way of proving that for many Levellers this was not a compromise.

If we go back to Leveller declarations before Putney we find no reference to any exclusions from the franchise at all, Royalists apart. Professor Macpherson has to admit that the Levellers at times 'appeared to be speaking for manhood franchise' (p. 115), but he prefers to reinterpret everything they said earlier in the light of Petty's remarks at Putney. In *The Charters of London* (1646) Lilburne had declared that 'the poorest that lives, hath as true a right to give a vote, as well as the richest and greatest'. This, says Professor Macpherson, cannot mean what it seems to mean 'in view of the position we have seen the Levellers to have taken in the Putney debate' (p. 134). The same method is employed to deal with all other apparent assertions of manhood suffrage during the pre-Putney period. It involves flying in the face of some contemporary opinion, for, as a pamphlet of July 1647 observed, 'the new doctrine of the people's sovereignty extends to give power to all servants and children grown up, as well as to their parents and masters'. It also comes up against the *Case of the Army truly Stated* (October 1647). For this demanded unambiguously 'that all the freeborn at the age of 21 years and upwards, be the electors, excepting those that have or shall deprive themselves of that their freedom, either for some years, or wholly by delinquency'.[21]

When he first considered the *Case of the Army truly Stated* in 1945

Professor Macpherson was prepared to recognise it as 'the only clear claim for manhood suffrage',[22] but in his book he has to force it into conformity with his general theory by arguing that it was servants and alms-takers who were here assumed to have deprived themselves of their freedom 'for some years'. This would mean, of course, that the 'Case' proposed to disfranchise delinquents (i.e. Royalists) 'wholly', and that, Professor Macpherson tells us, would be consistent with 'the harsh tone of "The Case of the Army" towards delinquents' (p. 130). In fact the 'Case' was notable for urging merciful treatment for Royalists. The Levellers had always stood for the healing of past differences and in their final 'Agreement of the People' they excluded Royalists from Parliament for ten years only. It is quite improbable that the authors of *The Case of the Army* wished to disqualify all delinquents for ever; and it is much more likely that, along with the parliamentary seques- trators, they envisaged 'degrees' of delinquency, some Royalists being only temporarily disabled, while those unprepared to submit were permanently excluded.[23] It is also possible that the temporary depriva- tion of freedom referred to apprentices. Professor Macpherson dismisses this possibility on the grounds that apprentices were 'mainly under 21, and so excluded by the age clause' (p. 130). In fact, the legal age at which apprentices might gain their freedom was not twenty-one but twenty-four. So a special provision would have been necessary to dis- franchise them.

After Putney Professor Macpherson has plainer sailing. The second 'Agreement' explicitly confined the franchise to its subscribers, 'not persons receiving alms, but such as are assessed ordinarily towards the relief of the poor; not servants to, or receiving wages from, any parti- cular person'. The third 'Agreement' (May 1649) was somewhat wider: 'all men of the age of one and twenty years and upwards (not being servants, or receiving alms, or having served the late King in arms or voluntary contributions)'. But both these exclusions came late in the day. The Levellers were displaying more political realism. They had learned the need to compromise: Wildman tells us of *The Earnest Petition of Many Freeborn People* (January 1648) (which excluded criminals, minors, 'servants' and 'beggars') that its authors wisely 'inserted no such particular grievances as might disengage any consider- able party, and so continue our distractions . . . the removal of such a particular grievance is not worth blood, or the hazarding of a war'. The second 'Agreement' is well known to have been a compromise with the army leaders and others; Professor Macpherson does not argue that the

Levellers ideally wanted the ratepayer franchise it asked for. The third 'Agreement', however, though not without its compromises, was a more independent document and its exclusion of servants and alms-takers can be reasonably taken as the final position of what remained of the Leveller party. Yet later in 1649 *The Remonstrance of Many Thousands of the Free-People of England* offered votes to 'all that come unto us'; and in 1653 *A Charge of High Treason exhibited against Oliver Cromwell* summoned all the people of England to the polls, 'as well masters, sons, as servants'.[24]

The extant evidence, therefore, is consistent with more than one interpretation. It can be argued, with Professor Macpherson, that when the Levellers appeared to be saying one thing they really meant something else; but it can also be argued that they were a heterogeneous party, divided among themselves, and forced to make a series of tactical compromises as they went along. Until new evidence appears both possibilities must be allowed for.

There is also room for debate about the meaning of the 'servants' and 'receivers of alms' whom the Levellers ultimately agreed to exclude. So far as alms-men are concerned, it should be noted that until the second 'Agreement' it was only 'beggars' who were mentioned as candidates for exclusion. It was 'beggars' who were formally voted out in the resolution passed after the Putney Debates. It was 'beggars' who were mentioned by John Harris in *The Grand Designe* (December 1647); and it was 'beggars' who were excluded in *The Earnest Petition*. Even the recipients of alms excluded in the third 'Agreement' were taken by an informed contemporary, Marchamont Nedham, to be synonymous with 'vagabonds'. At Putney, Petty was the only person to mention 'those that take alms'. The passage is ambiguous, for, as J. C. Davis points out, it is possible that Petty regarded the exclusion of alms-takers as Cromwell's proposal rather than his own. But in any case it is notable that Petty should have explained that the exclusion envisaged was of 'those that receive alms from door to door'. This was surely a reference to beggars rather than to regular recipients of parish relief. Petty's view thus contrasted sharply with the practice in contemporary election cases, where haggling about what was meant by 'receiving alms' usually ended up with the disqualification from the franchise of all those in regular receipt of parochial relief.[25] Such persons were emphatically not synonymous with the 'beggars' whom the Levellers had primarily in mind. The statistical difference between the two classes is enormous, for Professor Macpherson estimates that in 1648 there were 343,000 male adult alms-takers, as compared with a mere 10,000 beggars (p. 287).

The impression that the Levellers originally excluded not alms-takers but only beggars is confirmed by a piece of evidence unavailable to Professor Macpherson, namely the report in John Boys's parliamentary diary of how Cromwell told the Commons on 23 November 1647 that the agitators 'would exclude children and servants, yet such as received alms they insisted on as persons competent for electors'. We know that the Levellers had every sympathy with those who had been temporarily impoverished by the effects of civil war and this may explain why they did not initially contemplate their exclusion from the franchise. We also know that they regarded alms-men as capable of taking their own decisions. For in *The Earnest Petition* they demanded that 'the Poor be enabled to choose their trustees' – a desire which was by no means utopian so long as there were alms-houses in England like the one at Sherborne, where under the terms of the fifteenth-century foundation deed the inhabitants customarily elected their own prior or ruler.[26]

III

The excluded 'servants' pose even greater problems. For in the seventeenth century the word 'servant' could have many meanings. 'There is scarce any general name of a calling,' wrote Richard Mayo in his *Present for Servants* (1693), 'that contains under it such different kinds of persons, as this of servant.' Professor Macpherson makes short shrift of any such ambiguities. 'In seventeenth-century usage,' he tells us, 'servants meant wage-earners, anyone who worked for an employer for wages' (p. 107n). Acting on this comprehensive definition, he is able to give statistical meaning to the Levellers' exclusions. Using Gregory King's estimates for England in 1688 he calculates that there were 509,000 adult male 'servants' (comprising 130,000 in-servants and 379,000 out-servants). Allowing for a population growth of 10 per cent in the intervening forty years, he reduces this to a figure of 458,100 for 1648. So that on this reckoning the 'servants' to whom the Levellers would have refused the vote were no less than 39 per cent of the adult male population of 1,170,400. This percentage is only slightly diminished if allowance is made for the soldiers whom the Levellers would have enfranchised, even though they had been servants in civilian life (pp. 282–6, 290–2).

There are various objections to these calculations. First of all, it must be remembered that Gregory King set no great store by his own figures; his notes show that his estimates of the size of the different social classes varied wildly.[27] Secondly, it does not follow that the proportionate size of the different classes in 1688, even if properly estimated by King, was the same as it had been in 1648. On the contrary, there is every reason to believe that the number of wage-earners had risen sharply during the intervening years, with the growth of industrial and agricultural capitalism. To apply King's figures to 1648 is to read backwards into the mid-seventeenth century a situation that had not yet come about. Professor Macpherson thus exaggerates the proportion of the population who in 1648 were wholly or partly dependent upon wages. Besides the Levellers did not have access to anyone's social statistics. Like all men who live in a changing society they had a conception of their own age that was out of date. They probably thought that there were even fewer wage-earners than there actually were.

But most serious of all is the lack of evidence to show that when the Levellers spoke of 'servants' they meant all wage-earners. It is true that this is what some contemporary writers meant when they used the term – though not the ones cited by Professor Macpherson. Of the three economic writers whom Macpherson cites (p. 282n), neither Andrew Yarranton nor John Cary equates day-labourers with 'servants', while Thomas Firmin actually contrasts single persons who earn money by spinning with the 'servants' who are apprenticed or go into domestic service. But there is an overwhelming volume of evidence to suggest that in the mid-seventeenth century the term 'servant' normally had a more restricted meaning. Its 'most usual' usage, thought Richard Mayo, was in respect of 'such as . . . have voluntarily submitted themselves, by contract, for a certain time, to the disposal of others, according to the Word of God, and laws of the realm'.[28] The Statute of Artificers (1563) was the law of the realm most relevant here. It distinguished 'servants', who covenanted to serve by the year or similar period, from 'artificers and labourers being hired for wages by the day or week'. The former were 'servants'; the latter were usually described as 'day-labourers'. Their relationship with their employer differed, for whereas the servant entered into a firm covenant which could be unilaterally broken only with the consent of a J.P., the day-labourer was on a more casual basis. He might frequently change employers; he might be on a piece-work basis; and he could be dismissed at will. In the wage assessments issued by the J.P.s the wages of 'servants' are almost always given by the year; those of labourers by the week or day. The Suffolk assessment for 1630 quoted by Macpherson (p. 282n) is one of the very few extant exceptions to this rule. This distinction between servants and day-labourers was preserved in later labour legislation and is found in the literary sources.[29]

The other great difference between the two categories was that the servant often lived in as a member of his master's family, whereas the labourer lived out. In the assessments made under the fiscal Act of 1694 it was the unmarried resident employees who were normally described as 'servants'.[30] They were subject to their master's discipline and they were the ones to whom the traditional teaching about master and servant most obviously applied.

Contemporary usage of the term 'servant' was inconsistent. It reflected the semantic confusion arising from an attempt to apply a social vocabulary inherited from a feudal and patriarchal past to the needs of a society in which the relationship of master and servant was steadily yielding to that of employer and wage-earner. There was a time-lag between the development of new social relationships and the invention of a vocabulary adequate to describe them, just as there was a time-lag in the development of a social ethic appropriate to these new relationships. Late seventeenth-century clerical teaching, for example, was 'based upon the assumption that employees were in fact members of the family, living under the same roof with the master's wife and children'. Despite the growth of the wage-earner, moralists 'clung to the traditional teachings about master and servant'.[31]

Similar anachronisms underlay Leveller thinking. It cannot be definitely proved that when they spoke of 'servants' they meant only resident, covenanted servants, rather than the whole wage-earning class. But there are two reasons for thinking that this is what they did mean. The first is that whereas previous political thinkers had had little if anything to say about wage-earners they were fully accustomed to excluding household servants from political participation. For if political freedom required independence then it was the independence enjoyed by heads of households. 'All men understand that where the election is most freest and most general,' wrote the Elizabethan Puritan, Thomas Cartwright, 'yet only they have to do which are heads of families.' The 1646 Ordinance on Church Government allowed the vote in the election of parochial and congregational elders to those who 'have taken the National Covenant, and are not persons under age, nor servants that have no families'. Similarly John Eliot, the apostle of the American Indians, declared in his *Christian Commonwealth* (1659, but written earlier) that 'servants, or sons living with their parents as in the condition of servants . . . may not explicitly, politically, personally, choose public rulers, while they live under the authority of family-government. . . . But if they marry, or live in the state of allowed public freemen, then are they capable of . . . the choice of their public rulers'. As Mr Schochet has well put it, 'The crucial fact that seems to have set servants and beggars off from the rest of society and deprived them of political significance was not so much the alienation of their labour . . . as it was their lack of familial headship.'[32]

The second indication that the Levellers did not equate 'servants' with wage-earners is to be found in their own manifestoes. For the fact that the second 'Agreement' excluded both 'servants' and persons 'receiving wages from any particular person' strongly suggests that the two categories were thought of as different ones. The third 'Agreement' by contrast excluded only 'servants'. Even the second 'Agreement', with its emphasis on wages 'from any particular person', suggests uneasiness about the dependence that sprang from subjection to an individual master rather than that deriving from the alienation of one's labour as such (to a large corporation, for example, or to the state).

We may therefore conclude that the servants whom the Levellers ultimately agreed to exclude were not identical with the whole body of wage-earners. In Gregory King's tables resident servants form little more than a quarter of the wage-earning classes. Moreover in-service was usually a temporary state, appropriate to young unmarried persons who would in due course move on, either to a new employer or to a new status as independent wage-earners or even proprietors. In late seventeenth-century Bristol over half the 'servants' listed under the 1694 Act were in fact apprentices who would shortly attain their freedom. In the present state of our knowledge figures can mean little. But if we assume that by excluding 'servants' the Levellers were temporarily denying the vote to at most 15 per cent of the population we shall not be far out. The figure would be increased by 0·1 per cent if we added the beggars.[33]

Can we find a theory behind these exclusions? Professor Macpherson suggests that the Levellers spoke only for the 'freeborn' and that they considered servants and wage-earners to have 'lost their birth-right'. It is certainly true that the Levellers usually claimed political rights upon behalf of the 'freeborn', the 'freeman' or the 'free com-moners'. Although such terminology was part of the general rhetoric of contemporary discourse and in no way peculiar to the Levellers, they

were particularly associated with this appeal to 'native freedoms'.
Dr Hill quotes a piece of contemporary verse in which 'freeborn
birth' is contrasted with 'peasant blood', but there does not normally
seem to have been anything socially exclusive about the term 'freeborn'.
The word had originally distinguished those who were born free from
those who were unfree, namely villeins and slaves; thus a seventeenth-
century clergyman thanked God for making him 'a man, not a beast;
civil, not barbarous; freeborn, not a slave'. Slavery had long disappeared, but villeinage was a more recent memory and had survived
as a legal disability into the early seventeenth century. What the
Levellers were emphasising by their use of the term 'freeborn' was that
Englishmen were now free. 'All slaves have bought their freedoms,'
said Cowling at Putney. England was 'too pure an air for slaves to dwell
in', thought Lilburne. He was alluding to the already established tradition that a foreign slave brought into England became *ipso facto* free.[34]
But the main Leveller theme was the end of villeinage. For them bondage had been a tyrannical Norman innovation. According to the author
of *Vox Plebis* (1646) – possibly Lilburne himself[35]:

> As God created every man free in Adam, so by nature all are alike
> freemen born; and are since made free in grace by Christ; no guilt of
> the parent being of sufficiency to deprive the child of this freedom.
> And although there was that wicked and unchristian-like custom of
> villeiny introduced by the Norman Conqueror; yet was it but a
> violent usurpation upon the law of our creation, nature, and the
> ancient laws of this kingdom; and is now, since the clear light of the
> Gospel hath shined forth, quite abolished as a thing odious both to
> God and man in this our Christian commonwealth.

This was to invoke the language of the sixteenth-century charters of
manumission in which serfdom was conventionally described as being
against the laws of God and nature.

For the Levellers, therefore, all men were doubly freeborn. Slavery
and villeinage were intrinsically contrary to nature and reason.[36] They
had also been abolished in England by legal means. So every man was
free, whatever his social position. 'Albeit these labourers be of the most
inferior in degree,' wrote the Elizabethan John Hooker of the Devonshire day-labourers, 'yet they be *liberi homines* and of a free condition,
no villeins, no bond slaves.' 'Servants or serving men and women,'
said another Elizabethan, Sir Thomas Smith, 'be for other matters in
liberty as full free men and women.' The law was 'the common birth-

right and inheritance of every particular individual freeman of England,'
declared Lilburne, 'yea of the meanest cobbler and tinker, as well as of
the greatest gentleman or nobleman'. 'This word, *liber homo*, or free
man, extends to all manner of English people,' explained *Vox Plebis*;
the *liber homo* of Magna Carta was 'every man born in the realm'. 'Let
not the greatest Peers in the land be more respected with you,' thun-
dered Overton, 'than so many old bellows-menders, broom-men,
cobblers, tinkers or chimney-sweepers, who are all equally free born.'[37]

It was precisely because all Englishmen were now 'free' that the
Leveller slogan became so irritating to their opponents. 'Why "many
freeborn people of this nation"?' asked a hostile commentator on the
'Earnest Petition of Many Freeborn People'. 'Are there any Englishmen that are not freeborn? Why do you distinguish yourselves? What
need of that epithet?' In ancient Rome, said Roger Coke, only the
civitate donati were free. 'But in England the case is much otherwise; for
with us there is no *civitate donatus* in one more than another, but all
men are alike born free; and so by consequence every man as a freeborn
man of England has as much right to his freedom one man as another.
. . . Two parts of three have not forty shillings a year, yet are as freeborn
as they who have.' This was why the Levellers demanded popular
suffrage, and it was why they so frequently denounced all infringements
of their liberties as treatment fit only for 'bondmen and bondwomen',
or for slaves with holes bored through their ears, or for those who held
by 'tenure in villeinage'.[38]

Professor Macpherson, however, argues that the Levellers considered
wage-earners and alms-takers to have forfeited this native birthright
(pp. 122, 124). They had 'lost a crucial part of their native freedom or
property, namely the property in their own capacities or labour' (p. 144).
They were entitled to civil rights, but political participation depended
on 'retention of the property in one's labour' (p. 146). His texts in
support of this argument, however, are noticeably thin. The key ones
seem to be Petty's two separate assertions at Putney, that 'all inhabitants
that have not lost their birth-right' should vote, and that servants,
apprentices and alms-takers should not vote. But the reason Petty gives
for their exclusion is the traditional one: such persons 'depend upon the
will of other men and should be afraid to displease them'.[39] There is
nothing here about the alienation of their labour.

This is not to say that the Levellers did not consider that birthright
could not be forfeited. On the contrary, like many of their contemporaries they considered that crimes against the state might justify such

a forfeiture. 'I am a freeborn Englishman,' declares Lilburne in one of his pamphlets, 'and have lived a legal man thereof all my days, being never yet convicted of an attempt or design undertaken or countenanced by me that did tend to the subversion of the fundamental laws and constitution thereof.' Overton proposed that thieves convicted thrice should be made into bondmen, and he also argued that 'enemies' of the state had forfeited their political rights. The Levellers therefore countenanced the temporary or permanent exclusion of delinquents from the franchise, for they had drawn their swords against freedom.[40]

The temporary exclusion of apprentices could also be justified, since apprenticeship was commonly regarded as 'another kind of servitude or bondage'. Edmund Bolton, in *The Cities Advocate* (1629), had vigorously denied that apprenticeship was 'in any sort of bondage'. But forty years later Edward Chamberlayne could still assert the older view: apprentices, being subject to their master's authority in all respects, were 'a sort of servants that carry the marks of pure villeins or bondslaves'. This was perhaps the 'voluntary servitude' mentioned by Lieutenant-Colonel Reade at Putney. But apprenticeship was only a temporary state and involved no permanent disqualification. Apprentices played a prominent part in Leveller agitation; and Lilburne, though himself an ex-apprentice (as were also Petty, Sexby and Walwyn), could nevertheless declare himself to be a 'freeman of England, who to his knowledge never did any act that deserveth the forfeiting of his birthright'.[41]

Criminal delinquency and apprenticeship apart, there is little indication in the Leveller writings of other circumstances under which birthright could be forfeited. On one occasion Overton, charged with being 'one of Lilburne's bastards', retorted that he was 'free-born'.[42] But to infer from this that he regarded illegitimacy as incompatible with free birth would be to build too much on a passing remark.

It is therefore hard to extract from Leveller writings any theory that the loss of birthright followed from the alienation of one's labour. In any case such a theory would not explain the position the Levellers took up, even the position Professor Macpherson attributes to them. It would not explain why ex-soldiers were to have the vote, even though they were wage-earners or alms-takers in civilian life. And it would not explain why all women were to be excluded, even though they were widows or single women with independent means. For, as Filmer pointed out, if individuals were born free and equal, as the Levellers held, then 'women, especially virgins', had by 'birth as much natural freedom as any other, and therefore ought not to lose their liberty without their own consent'.[43]

Professor Macpherson has rightly been praised for the courage and ingenuity with which he has attempted to impart intellectual consistency to the Leveller manifestoes. But it is doubtful whether any single theory can adequately rationalise the Leveller position. What can, however, be seen is a faith in human equality and natural right, modified by traditional patriarchal assumptions about the place of women, apprentices and household servants, and further tempered by a specifically Leveller desire to eliminate clientage and dependence on great persons. John Harris commented on the old county franchise that 'the persons choosing are commonly more swayed by favour than reason in their choice, being tenants either to the persons chosen or their friends; which hath been one main reason that the lost liberties of the Kingdom have been . . . no better . . . preserved.'

This theme frequently recurs in Leveller writings.[44] Their eagerness to improve popular education also suggests that the Levellers were worried as much by the illiteracy and ignorance of the lowest classes as by their economic dependence.[45] The political experience of the boroughs certainly shows that a wide franchise was not necessarily accompanied by an increase in political self-consciousness on the part of the labouring poor. On the contrary, the very poor frequently regarded their vote as a marketable commodity. Such considerations may help to explain why the Levellers ultimately agreed to exclude both servants and alms-takers from the franchise. We cannot be sure. But at least we can avoid endowing the Levellers with views that we feel they ought to have held, even though there is little evidence that they did.

For the Levellers are implausible as prophets of the new age of capitalism and wage-labour. However 'advanced' their constitutional notions, their economic ideas were backward-looking. They wanted to preserve (or rather to create) a world in which every man was an independent proprietor. Hence their attempt to ensure the widest possible distribution of private property by abolishing monopolies, banning primogeniture and throwing open the commons. Hence Lilburne's scheme for distributing inalienable lands to the soldiers and the poor, in order to set them up as private owners. The Levellers did not aim to bring riches to everyone, but at least there were to be 'no beggars, or any that want necessaries'. They wished to bring things 'to such a pass that every man may with as much security as may be enjoy his propriety'.[46] Whether they would have excluded wage-labourers and alms-takers from the franchise will long remain debatable. What is certain is that they hoped that these classes would wither away to the absolute minimum. In such circumstances the only adult males denied the vote would have been apprentices, temporary household servants and, possibly but not certainly, elderly or impotent persons dependent on public relief. Otherwise all men would enjoy a modest self-sufficiency. This would enable them to exercise political choice and to enjoy their birthright as freeborn Englishmen.

3. Conquest and Consent: Thomas Hobbes and the Engagement Controversy

QUENTIN SKINNER

I

THE opening months of 1649 saw the climax of the revolution staged by the Independent Party. The king was executed, the House of Lords abolished, the Commonwealth of England proclaimed. This outcome, however, was far more radical than most of the moderates in the Presbyterian Party had wanted, and far more revolutionary than the instinctive royalism of most Englishmen could readily countenance. One of the most immediate tasks of the new government was thus to persuade such moderate and hostile groups that the revolution was really over. They had to be given reasons for obeying and submitting to the newly established Commonwealth rather than trying to continue the fight. There was a need, in short, for a theory of political obligation in terms of which the new government might be legitimated. And it was clear that any such theory would in turn need to satisfy two contrasting conditions. It would need to be couched in a sufficiently familiar form to be acceptable to Presbyterian and even Royalist opinion. But it also needed to be capable of performing the revolutionary task of justifying the duty to obey a merely *de facto* and usurping political power.

The Council of State itself was plainly aware of this need, which it tried to meet in March 1649 with its own 'Declaration', 'expressing the grounds of their late proceedings, and of settling the present government in the way of a free state'. The arguments of the 'Declaration' were immediately taken up by several government propagandists, notably by John Milton in his *Tenure of Kings and Magistrates*. The basic contention of this propaganda reflected the most characteristic political belief of the Independents: that the origin of any lawful government must lie in a decision by the people to consent to its establishment. The execution of Charles I was thus vindicated with the claim that it represented the removal of a tyrant and the reassertion of the people's right to set limits to the power of governments.[1]

This type of justification, however, was of very limited value outside the ranks of the Independent Party. It could scarcely be expected to persuade any former Royalists, since most of their views on political obligation derived simply from the assumption that the king had a God-given right to rule. And there was a special reason for doubting whether it could be expected even to persuade many of the Presbyterians. They had admittedly supported the revolution at least up to the time of Pride's purge of Parliament, and many of them would have been prepared to accept the premises of the Independents' political arguments. But the Presbyterians had also sworn the Solemn League and Covenant, which had included an oath binding them to protect the life and person of the king. All the Presbyterian writers were insistent that any new oaths of allegiance must be consistent with the Solemn League and Covenant. It was thus difficult to see how any but the most cynical could now justify taking oaths of paying allegiance to the Commonwealth, the very power which had deprived the king of his life.

It was at this juncture that a quite different line of defence of the new government began to be urged by a studiously moderate (though mainly Presbyterian) group of political writers. These are often called the 'Engagers', but I shall call them 'the *de facto* theorists', because it was possible to agree to engage with the Commonwealth for reasons quite different from those offered by the writers with whom I am here concerned. The basic claim made by these *de facto* theorists of obligation was that the Pauline injunction to obey the powers that be as ordained of God could validly be argued even in the case of usurping powers. This claim is historically important, and worth examining in some detail, for it was their defence of *de facto* powers which in the event supplied exactly the type of argument most needed to persuade the Presbyterians and even the Royalists of their duty to obey the new government. They thus provided an essential ideological contribution to the quest for settlement at this most anxious stage of the English revolution. This chapter seeks to evaluate their contribution, the importance of which has been unrecognised until recently.[2] A further reason for studying them is that their theories, and the conditions out of which these were generated, can be shown to provide the context within which the main aims and several of the most characteristic doctrines of Hobbes's political philosophy can best be understood. In Hobbes's intellectual house there are of course many mansions. The main thesis of the following analysis, however, is that one of Hobbes's main aims in *Leviathan* was to contribute to precisely this debate about the rights of *de facto* powers at this stage of the English revolution.

II

One justification for remaining passively obedient to the Commonwealth government, even if one disapproved of it, was provided simply by invoking the authority of Calvin. The *Institutes* had frequently reiterated the duty of private citizens not to meddle in affairs of state. This sentiment was in turn reiterated by many of the more religiose *de facto* theorists. The most indefatigable of these was John Dury, a Presbyterian divine who spent much of his time travelling abroad in the interests of Protestant reunion. He returned to England in 1645, changed sides, took the Covenant, and remained in England until 1654. Dury limited himself exclusively to Calvin's argument in publishing what was in fact the first *de facto* defence of the Commonwealth government, *A Case of Conscience Resolved*, which originally appeared in March 1649. This simply insisted that even if questions arise about the legitimacy of one's governors, one 'ought not to apply' oneself 'to intermeddle in their affairs' (p. 4). All Dury's later contributions to the debate continue to insist on the same essentially Calvinist point. 'All private men,' he insists, 'ought to walk unblameably under the superior powers of the world', since 'it doth not belong to us to judge definitely of the rights which the superior powers over us in the world pretend to have unto their places.' The whole lesson, in short, which Dury puts with characteristic repetition, is that it is simply 'no part of our Christian profession to become judges of the great ones of the world'.[3]

There was also a more secular version of this contention which consisted, equally simply, of pointing out that there had already been far too many disputes over matters of government, that they had led only to chaos, and that the time had come to settle for peace at any price. This argument was of course particularly attractive to the surviving Royalists, who later tended to insist that their own non-intervention in the affairs of the Commonwealth represented the badge and guarantee of their political innocence.[4] Something of the same attitude can be seen reflected in the obsession of the Royalist poets in the 1650s with the innocent pleasures of pastoral retreat (as in Waller, Cowley and

Vaughan), and in the popularity of such encouragements to rustic withdrawal as Walton's *Compleat Angler*, first published in 1653. The same attitude can be found in several of the *de facto* defenders of the Commonwealth. Anthony Ascham closes one of his pamphlets with the earnest hope that his countrymen will now prevent anyone from 'coming on the stage to act our late tragedy over again'. Marchamont Nedham in his *Case of the Commonwealth* is concerned to vindicate not just the 'necessity and equity' of submission to the new government, but its 'utility and benefit' as well. And the major benefit which he insists would result if everyone were now to 'submit and settle' and 'close cordially in affection' would be that the Commonwealth would 'have leave to take breath a little in the possession of a firm peace'. And the same desire above all for 'the preservation of a firm and lasting peace', the same hope for a 'unity of minds' and 'a restraining of the hands' provides a typical and recurrent theme of *de facto* theory.[5]

There are many elements of the same temperament to be found in Hobbes's political works. He frequently cites the ambitions of men excluded from political power who try to gain it for themselves as a major cause of the dissolution of states. He also stresses the value of being able to leave political matters for others to decide, while one gets on with one's own life. He thus treats it as one of the disadvantages of democracy that 'all men have a hand in public business', for this serves to encourage us 'to neglect the affairs of our own family' for more public but less genuine duties. Conversely, he treats it as a special virtue of monarchies that one can 'lead a retired life' and be 'out of danger' whoever is in control. He speaks of large towns with suspicion, and regards them as the natural centres of sedition. And most insistently of all, he claims that the highest aim in any political society must be to hold fast to whatever security has been attained, and to prevent men from acting – even out of the highest motives – in such a way as to endanger that security. It is an axiom in *Leviathan* that if you 'take away in any kind of state the obedience and consequently the concord of the people', then 'they shall not only not flourish, but in short time be dissolved'.[6]

Such demands for submission simply in the name of peace doubtless had some effect. They could scarcely be said to offer any new arguments, however, to anyone who remained in doubt as to either the godliness or merely the legality of taking oaths and paying allegiance to the new government. The problem of persuading these men of tender conscience remained the same. They needed to be presented with an argument in terms of which it might be shown not merely to be beneficial to submit but in some way compatible with their loyalty to their existing oaths and obligations.

The credit for originating the main argument in terms of which this difficulty was in fact overcome seems to be owed to Francis Rous, who published in April 1649 a brief pamphlet entitled *The Lawfulness of Obeying the Present Government*. Rous, a Presbyterian, had sat in the 1625 and 1628-9 parliaments, as well as in the Long Parliament. He took the Covenant in 1644, and went over to the Independent Party (like several other 'engagers') only at the very end of the war. His pamphlet sought to show 'that though the change of a government were believed not to be lawful, yet it may lawfully be obeyed'. Rous thus began by making a prudent and very important concession: he did not attempt to deny that the new government was unlawful, but sought to prove only that it was not unlawful to obey such an unlawful power. His argument proceeded in three simple stages. He began by taking his stand squarely on 'the duty of submission and obedience to authority' laid down by St Paul in the opening verses of Chapter 13 of his Epistle to the Romans. This was, of course, the most quoted of all texts on the question of political obligation throughout the seventeenth century. It represented an inescapable authority, which no Presbyterian or even Royalist opponent of the new regime could possibly fail to accept. The second stage of Rous's argument then consisted of examining historically just *what* powers had been accepted by St Paul, and throughout English history, as having a title to be obeyed. He claimed to discover that even though 'in this Nation many persons have been settled in supreme power and authority by mere force, without title of inheritance', yet this had never been regarded hitherto as a sufficient reason for refusing them the obedience which the apostle commands (p. 4). The conclusion of the argument then readily followed. St Paul's injunctions to obey the powers that be must be taken literally: we must obey *whatever* powers are in a position to command our obedience. And the reason is that their capacity to rule is in itself a sufficient sign of God's will and providence. Thus

... when a question is made, Whom we should obey? it must not be looked at what he is that exerciseth the power, or by what right or wrong he hath invaded the power, or in what manner he doth dispense it, but only if he have power. For if any man do excel in power, it is now out of doubt that he received that power of God. Wherefore without all exception thou must yield thyself up to him and heartily obey him (p. 7).

Rous's argument was to be of the utmost importance throughout the ensuing debate over the legality of obeying the Commonwealth government, and many obviously accepted it immediately and with relief. To the most tender conscience, however, this ingenious transformation of passive obedience into a defence of the revolution was far more shocking than persuasive, and no sooner had Rous published his pamphlet than a series of counter-attacks began to appear. All Rous's critics focused on the same two vulnerable points in his argument. They first of all fixed on his interpretation of the Pauline injunctions. All of them insisted that Rous had merely confused the authority of a political office with the power exercised by the person holding the office. The anonymous author of *The Grand Case of Conscience Stated*, an attack on Rous published within two months of his pamphlet, put the point particularly clearly. 'The authority was ordained by God' but 'not the rulers' who 'are constituted by men' and at most have 'God's permission', not his ordinance. Obedience to the powers that be is therefore due not for anything they may do, but only for the things they do by that authority. 'Men in authority' are 'to be obeyed no further than acting according to that authority.' A large number of other Presbyterian opponents of Rous immediately took up the same point. They all agreed that the crucial text from Romans 13 would yield the right answer 'if clearly opened and rightly understood'. But they all insisted that the correct interpretation could only be that the apostle intended to refer exclusively to 'lawfully invested' authority. It is this alone which is *ordained* of God, though God may well *permit* many forms of tyranny to exist. And while 'The Apostle requires' us 'not to resist their power', he does not require us 'not to resist their tyranny'.

The second point made by all Rous's critics was that the reason St Paul must have intended to make this precise distinction between power and authority was that there could otherwise be no justifiable resistance to tyrannous government. Again the author of the *Grand Case* particularly insisted on the point. If we grant 'that men assuming themselves the place and power of magistrates, by what right or means soever they came by it, must be obeyed, surely it would be the greatest inlet to tyranny in the world, and the speediest means of destroying states that could be invented.' And again the same point was made by all Rous's other critics. His doctrine would 'open too wide a gap to rebels' powers and loyal subjects' misery', and would merely encourage 'intrusion into the seat of authority'.[7]

For any but the most cynical Presbyterian, it was impossible not to concede that this counter-attack completely demolished Rous's case. Once the distinction between powers ordained and powers merely permitted by God was established, the way was open first to point out that God never ordains but often permits the wicked to rule, and then to insist that the rule of the Commonwealth was just such a wicked power, sent to vex but also to test sinful men. And the Royalists of course reached the same conclusion as Rous's Presbyterian opponents. One well-known and rather touching example is provided by the Royalist John Wenlock, who records his reply to a soldier who had assured him that the victories of the Parliament over the king were directly a sign of God's providence: 'Alas, friend, that is no good argument on your side, for we know that God doth many times permit wicked men to prosper in their ways, to their own destruction; and if you were an historian, you would know that God hath suffered the Turks so to prevail against the Christians for many hundred years because of their sins.'[8]

At the same time, however, that Rous's position was being dismantled during the summer of 1649, the need for some such justification of the new government was becoming more urgent. The authority of the Rump Parliament was being increasingly called in question by a strange but predictable coalition of Royalist and Leveller arguments. The Levellers turned against the new government the arguments which they had themselves used against the king: that their rule was a tyranny that ignored the will of the people. This was John Lilburne's claim as early as February 1649, in his pamphlet *England's New Chains Discovered*. Meanwhile the Royalists had already begun to fan the hatred of the Rump with their celebrations of the mythological but appealing figure of 'Charles, king and martyr', exhibited notably in the *Eikon Basilike* (1649). They had also begun to mount their highly emotive attacks on the impiety, as well as the illegality of the new regime.[9] By the end of the summer, moreover, the need for a convincing defence of the government had been made more urgent by its own actions. For the government took the crucial step, in October, of requiring that an oath of 'engagement' to its authority should be sworn by virtually every literate member of society, and in January 1650 this was extended to the entire adult male population.[10] The question of political obligation was thus turned into a formal test of citizenship.

It was, of course, possible in this situation simply to continue reiterating the purely providentialist argument in favour of 'engagement' that Rous had originally presented. Many of the defenders of the new government and its oath of allegiance did continue throughout the next two years to insist simply that God's providence required submission. And it is arguable that this straightforward invocation of providence remained the most basic argument in favour of 'engagement' throughout the ensuing controversy. As the anonymous author of *The Engagement Vindicated* was to put it, writing in the first week of the new year, 'every change' in 'the great bodies politic' must be seen as 'a signal act of providence' and must for that reason be seen as a reflection of God's will (p. 3). Or as William Jenkin was still claiming, in his *Recantation* of November 1651, *all* alterations of civil government reflect 'the wise and righteous providence of God', so that 'a refusal to be subject to the present authority' is equivalent to 'a refusal to acquiesce in the wise and righteous pleasure of God' (p. 3). Other pamphleteers likewise defended 'engagement' in purely providentialist terms.

The difficulty was, however, that Rous's original opponents had made it impossible to regard this form of argument as a sufficient reason for accepting the duty to 'engage' with the Commonwealth government. Just as these invocations of providence continued, so the attacks continued on the interpretation of the Pauline injunctions upon which they depended.[11] The polemical situation at this level was thus one of stalemate. If it was to be claimed that there were any good arguments in favour of submitting in conscience to the rule of the Rump, they would now have to be new arguments as well.

One such new argument defended 'engagement' by the principles of radical Independency. This was the government's own form of defence, and continued throughout the debate about political obligation to provide an alternative defence of *de facto* powers. Henry Parker and Henry Robinson both argued for 'engagement' by claiming that the new government reflected the will of the people. The reissue of Milton's *Tenure of Kings and Magistrates* at the start of 1650 suggests that this more radical line of argument had continuing force. The extent to which even the most radical political writers were thus persuaded to argue in favour of the new oaths can be gauged from the fact that even Winstanley the Digger felt able to write in support of 'engagement'.[12]

The real ideological need, however, was for a more conservative defence of 'engagement'. And it was clear what form such an argument would have to take. The vulnerable point of Rous's argument had been his dangerous interpretation of the Pauline injunctions. It followed that the need was for an argument in which the emphasis was shifted away from the question of God's providence, so that a different, less vulnerable kind of defence might then be offered of obeying merely *de facto* political powers. There was already available an existing tradition of political argument – deriving particularly from Grotius – in which the rights of *de facto* powers (especially of conquerors) had already been discussed, and in which the obligation to obey such powers had been vindicated less by citing God's providence than by stressing the needs of political society, and specifically man's paramount need for protection from himself and his fellow men.[13] I wish to show that this type of argument was now exploited and applied by a group of lay defenders of 'engagement' whose specific concern was to rescue the purely providentialist defence of *de facto* powers from the vulnerable position in which Rous had left it, and to defend the same position with this new, more secular, less vulnerable form of argument.

III

The first writer who recognised and supplied this increasing need for new arguments in favour of obeying *de facto* powers was Anthony Ascham.[14] He had already published a *Discourse*, in 1648, treating the rights of conquerors in the manner of Grotius. He now turned, in two anonymous but important attacks specifically directed against the Presbyterians who had attacked Rous, to show how this type of argument could be deployed to rescue Rous's position. The first of these counterblasts was a brief anonymous pamphlet of July 1649 called *A Combat Between Two Seconds*. This was immediately followed by the much longer essay (also anonymous), *The Bounds and Bonds of Public Obedience*.[15] And by November Ascham had added nine new chapters to his original *Discourse* and reissued it, in a much more polemical and topical form, with the title *Of the Confusions and Revolutions of Governments*.

All these defences of *de facto* powers appear to make the same basic concession as Rous had made, to the effect that the new government may lawfully be obeyed even though it may not be a lawful power. All of them, moreover, still contain something – though not perhaps very much – of Rous's invocation of God's providence as the touchstone for obedience.[16] But they also contain two new and quite different emphases. The first is that the grounds of obligation are now lodged not merely

– or even mainly – in a discussion of providence, but rather in a discussion of political society and its needs. It is first laid down that the highest end in political society must be the maintenance of what the *Combat* calls 'public peace and quietness' and 'the preservation of the commonwealth from destruction' (p. 13). 'The soul of a state', according to the *Bounds and Bonds*, itself consists of 'the administration of public justice and protection' (p. 27). For 'the end of all law and government' is said in this account to be essentially concerned, not so much with consent and the maintenance of rights, as with the need 'to preserve our persons and estates' (p. 31). The same assumption is repeated in the *Confusions*, in perhaps the most important of its additional chapters. The 'chief end' of government is 'security and protection', and it is essential that we should yield up 'much of our general rights' in the name of attaining this 'security for our persons' (p. 109).

Ascham corroborated this assumption by considering the alternative to this yielding up of one's rights in the name of protection. The sole alternative, as the *Combat* puts it, is to abandon 'all justice and order, give up all to power, and so bring confusion upon the whole' (p. 14). The *Bounds and Bonds* emphatically draws the same conclusion. Unless we submit, we are resolving in effect that 'the commonwealth were dead, and each man were left in his naturals, to subsist of himself and to cast how he could in such a state of war, defend himself from all the rest of the world, every man in this state having an equal right to everything' (p. 27). And the *Confusions*, in another of its additional chapters, again endorses the same claim. 'He who would keep his natural liberty without relation to a state shall lose that and everything else; and he who will resolve to lose that liberty may conserve to himself the enjoyment of all necessary things' (p. 138).

The upshot is that Ascham is prepared to insist on the duty to obey whatever power exists, simply on the grounds that it is maintaining our protection – which is taken to be its essential duty – and that the sole alternative to accepting such protection will be a *bellum omnium contra omnes*. As the *Combat* puts it, there is already a duty to obey if peace is being protected, simply 'in regard of common good' (p. 15). Again the *Bounds and Bonds* takes up and extends the same point. As our present situation is that of 'the whole kingdom now receiving all laws, protection and subordinate magistracy' from the existing government, so we ought to obey it simply because 'we receive necessary protection' from it (p. 24). And again the *Confusions*, in its final additional chapter, endorses the same claim in completely secular tones. 'It is but reasonable, just and necessary that we obey those who in good and convenient things command and plenarily possess us' (p. 157).

The first crucial development that Ascham thus introduces into the *de facto* argument consists of the special stress that he lays on the needs of political society in his discussion of obligation. The vulnerable interpretation of the Pauline injunctions, on which Rous's whole case had rested, is thus effectively bypassed. The other change of emphasis that Ascham introduces is that he begins in consequence at least to wobble somewhat over the question of whether it is really necessary to concede (as Rous had done) that such a protecting power need be called an unjust power at all. But this is at least to call in question the relevance of the distinction on which the whole Presbyterian counter-attack on Rous had relied. And so Ascham begins to hint at the possibility of bypassing in turn the argument by which the Presbyterians had demolished Rous's original defence of *de facto* powers.

There is no suggestion of such a *démarche* in the *Combat*. But there seems to be a distinct hint of it in the *Bounds and Bonds*, with its claim that to say that those 'who have us in their power may be obeyed in no lawful thing' is tantamount to saying that no man has ever lived under a lawful political power, since 'we and our forefathers for the most part have lived under no better title than plenary possession' (p. 15). And by the time we reach the additional chapters of the *Confusions*, Ascham seems near to the brink of claiming that since the present government might be considered 'equitable if not lawful' (p. 111), it might actually be denied that it is an unlawful power. Why may we not regard a govern-ment as lawful, he asks, even if it may not have been founded upon a 'formal succession of persons', provided that it maintains 'the same law and equity which the excluded magistrates ought to have done, if they had succeeded' (p. 137).

This highly original attempt by Ascham to suggest a line of argument by which Rous's original defence of *de facto* powers might be rescued and restated was not at first taken up in the controversy about 'engage-ment'. It is true that John Dury in his next pamphlet, his *Considera-tions Concerning the Present Engagement* of December 1649, took up Ascham's claim that 'we are bound to show fidelity unto those of whom we desire protection' (p. 16). But Dury was something of an opportunist in his exploitation of all available arguments in favour of 'engagement'. And though he mentioned this view he still continued to rely for his major argument on the purely Calvinistic claim that 'it is not possible that any can attain to the height of power without God's disposal of it

D

into his hands' (p. 13). It is also true that a markedly secular tone, very similar in spirit to Ascham's account, was immediately taken up by Albertus Warren in *The Royalist Reformed*, published within a month of the *Confusions*. But Warren's defence of the duty to 'engage' was a genially cynical affair, with none of Ascham's careful attempt to meet the remaining doubts of the moderates with new arguments. Warren defended *de facto* powers simply on the grounds that to 'persevere in screwing rigour of general laws up to the height of injury' is merely to make yourself 'a burden unto our fellow subjects' and to 'weaken the esteem of the Commonwealth's wholesome constitution' (p. 44).

Ascham had not quite finished, however, for when his own position was in turn attacked, notably by the great Anglican casuist Sanderson, Ascham completed his contribution to the discussion of *de facto* powers with a *Reply* to Sanderson, published in January of the new year. Here the two new emphases introduced by Ascham into the discussion are now quite distinctly reiterated. First, the whole question of providence is side-stepped at the outset, with the claim that although governments may have been 'ordained some times and in some places extraordinarily by God', yet they are 'ordinarily now' set up 'by man in his public necessities', in order 'that nations may be conserved from confusions and private injuries' (p. 2). And secondly, Ascham now comes even closer to withdrawing Rous's original concession that the new government is an unlawful power. Ascham's claim is that if an action or situation can be called equitable, then even if it is not legal, it may be considered lawful. On the one hand, he understands by the concept of 'lawfulness' something that is not so much legal as equitable. And on the other hand he believes that 'in this confused state of the world' the idea of providing 'an original and legal assurance' of the right to govern is probably 'a moral impossibility' (p. 4).

Ascham's secular mode of argument, concerned less with the immediate 'case of conscience' in the approved casuistic mode than with an abstract account of political obligation, never commended itself to the casuists or the Presbyterian divines who mainly kept up the argument over 'engagement' during the next two years. Among a group of lay theorists, however, it is clear that Ascham's new mode of defending the rights of *de facto* powers had an immediate impact. The earliest defender of 'engagement' to take up this more secular line seems to have been the anonymous author of *A Discourse Concerning the Engagement*, published within a month of Ascham's final pamphlet, at the end of January 1650. The same new emphases were then taken up first by

Marchamont Nedham in his book, *The Case of the Commonwealth of England, Stated*; next in the anonymous *Memorandums* of a conference held in London during February and March 1650 to discuss the engagement; next in George Wither's *Respublica Anglicana*; and then in 1651 in John Drew's important pamphlet *The Northern Subscribers' Plea Vindicated*; and at the start of 1652 in Francis Osborne's *Persuasive to a Mutual Compliance*.

All these lay defenders of engagement took up the two forms of argument that had particularly marked Ascham's contributions to the debate. First, they all managed, at least to some extent, to avoid questions about providence by focusing instead on the question of what political society is *for*, and answering that it is essentially a product of necessity and a means to secure peace and protection. This is first hinted at by the anonymous author of the *Discourse*, with his stress on the 'dismal confusion' that must 'unavoidably follow' any refusal of allegiance (p. 5). The same point is very strongly emphasised in Nedham's account, which begins its discussion of political obligation by claiming that the reason why 'there is a necessity of some government at all times' is 'for the maintenance of civil conversation and to avoid confusion' (p. 30). It is similarly insisted in the *Memorandums* reporting the conference about the engagement that the basic point of government is to provide 'a mutual relation for safety', a means to ensure 'that the public may be preserved in peace', that 'assurance may be gained of mutual safety between subject and subject', and that the otherwise unavoidable 'ruin of all' is avoided (pp. 12–13). And the same note is struck in all the later pamphlets that take up this line of argument.

This view of government can be vindicated, according to several of these writers, by considering the political nature of man. Again this takes up a form of argument particularly characteristic of Ascham's original account. Nedham insists at the start of his discussion about the origins of government that it was only when the world 'grew more populous and more exceeding vicious, being inclined to rapine, ambition etc.' that there arose the 'need of someone more potent than the rest that might restrain them by force' and prevent the 'grand enormities' of human behaviour that would otherwise have developed (p. 15). The same pessimistic assumption is echoed in the *Memorandums*, in which it is insisted that men in political societies must be ruled 'without intermission', since the existence of a power to restrain them is 'absolutely necessary for the preservation of human societies' (p. 7). And the same assumption appears at the start of Osborne's account, in which the 'foul beginnings' of all governments are traced, and the 'strong necessity' which compels all men to accept government is emphasised (pp. 2–3). The implication – as Sanderson had already pointed out in shocked tones in his attack on Ascham – was that self-preservation was being taken to be the origin of government, the first law of nature, and 'the first and chiefest obligation in the world'. (A well-known example of political advice based on the Hobbesian principle which Sanderson is attacking occurs in a letter of December 1650 from the Duke of Buckingham to the Marquis of Newcastle.)[17]

The most notable feature, however, of these discussions about the necessity of subjection and the corresponding need for absolute power is that all these writers corroborated these claims by developing and making fully explicit the two further arguments that Ascham had barely suggested. The view of political obligation at which Ascham had in effect arrived was that the capacity of any government to offer protection to its citizens constituted in itself a sufficient title to be paid allegiance. Whereas Ascham had scarcely stated this conclusion in explicit terms, however, it was now cited by all these writers as the essence of their view of political obligation. The claim that there is simply a 'mutual relation of protection and allegiance' is already stated quite explicitly by the author of the *Discourse* (p. 11), and is explicitly distinguished in his account as a 'second argument' in favour of *de facto* powers, apart from any arguments that might be derived from the Scriptures (p. 11). The same explicit claim is then taken up by Nedham, who cites as his first contention about political obligation the claim that 'protection implies a return of obedience' (p. 30). And thereafter this conclusion, at which Ascham had only hinted, reaches the status of an axiom with all these writers. The *Memorandums* conclude with the claim that 'protection and allegiance are relatives' (p. 8). Wither begins his preface with the claim that we cannot in conscience 'receive protection and not return subjection' (Sig. A, 3a). Drew similarly insists that 'the mutual relation of protection and allegiance presseth us to an owning and realliance with them (our present powers) as our actual protectors' (p. 23). And Osborne, too, has no doubts that a government 'having the only power of protection cannot in duty be denied the duty of obedience' (p. 10).

The other argument at which Ascham had only hinted, but which is now made fully explicit by all these writers, is that since the capacity to protect is said to constitute a sufficient reason for political obligation, so the original concession that Rous had made could now be simply

withdrawn. All these writers now deny quite explicitly that the distinction between powers ordained and powers merely permitted by God
has any force at all. All of them are in consequence able to reject the
counter-attack mounted by Rous's opponents, by insisting that the
present government not only has a just title, but no less a just title than
any other government. This conclusion is already reached, though in a
somewhat hesitant way, by the anonymous author of the *Discourse*. It is
objected, he admits, that only 'lawful powers, or powers of right' are
ordained of God and ought to be obeyed. But it may be, he suggests,
that 'our present powers may fall within that compass' (p. 8). Nedham
has no such hesitation. 'It is undeniably evident,' he insists (p. 40),
'that the present prevailing party in England have a right and just
title to be our governors.' And this new note of confidence is then struck
by all the later lay theorists. In the *Memorandums* there is said to be no
doubt that 'a full possession of the place of government doth give a title
to govern' (p. 12). And in Wither's account there is said to be no reason
to deny that the existing government of England is for this reason just
as much 'a just and lawful power' as that of many other states whose
legality has never been doubted (pp. 42-3). And so the case for the
justice, and not merely the utility, of submission to the Commonwealth
of England was completed.

IV

During the years 1650 and 1651, when the debate about politica
obligation reached its height, the insights that Anthony Ascham had
first offered in his defence of *de facto* powers were thus converted into
a full-scale secular defence of the Commonwealth government. The
development of Ascham's argument, however, was not perhaps quite
such a clear-cut process as the above account may tend to suggest.
Although all the lay defenders of 'engagement' did explicitly state this
new *de facto* theory of obligation, none of them argued for it in a very
systematic way, and few of them even stated, except in a very frag-
mentary manner, the pessimistic view of man's political nature upon
which the theory depended. And although all these theorists made use
of these purely secular arguments, most of them continued at the same
time to invoke the original discussion of God's Providence at least as a
supplementary argument – and sometimes as a very prominent argument – in favour of the same conclusion. This is true even of Nedham
and Osborne, and is true to an even greater extent with the other

theorists who followed Ascham's perhaps somewhat equivocal lead.[18] Only one, in fact, of all the theorists who contributed to this discussion about the rights of *de facto* powers managed to eliminate all invocations of God's providence, and to predicate a *de facto* theory of political obligation entirely on an account of the political nature of man. And this one genius at large in the discussion was, of course, Thomas Hobbes.

It was exactly at this time that Hobbes published – for the first time in England, and for the first time in English – his major works on political obligation. The *Elements of Law*, the manuscript of which had been completed some time before 1640, was now published for the first time, the epistemological sections in February 1650 under the title *Humane Nature*, the political sections three months later as *De Corpore Politico*. Next Hobbes proceeded to translate the one work on politics he had already published, his *De Cive*, which had appeared abroad in a very small edition in 1642, and again in 1647. This was now reissued, in March 1651, under the title *Philosophical Rudiments concerning Government and Society*. Finally, within a few months of this, there appeared the masterpiece on which Hobbes was known to have been working intensively throughout the previous two years, his *Leviathan*.[19]

As soon as Hobbes's remarkable series of works appeared, moreover, at the height of the controversy over 'engagement', they were immediately recognised by the other lay defenders of *de facto* powers as giving the most authoritative presentation of a view of political obligation at which they had all independently arrived. This was explicitly pointed out by Ascham, by Warren, by Nedham and by Osborne. This is not to say, however, that they were thus acknowledging anything that can meaningfully be called an *influence* of Hobbes upon their own political works. Ascham, Warren and Nedham all published their defences of *de facto* powers before they could possibly have read *De Corpore Politico*, and there is good evidence that none of them, at the time when they originally wrote, had ever read *De Cive*, Hobbes's one published political work. The much more striking fact is that all these lay defenders of 'engagement' appear to have come upon Hobbes's works *after* they had already published their own markedly similar conclusions. It was at this point that they recognised, and took the opportunity to say, that Hobbes had articulated their own view of political obligation in a uniquely systematic and comprehensive way. Ascham read *De Cive* between publishing the first and the second versions of his *Discourse*. He then included in the second version (the

Confusions) a new chapter on the state of nature and political obligation, in which Hobbes's views are cited in corroboration of Ascham's own conclusions, and Hobbes is quoted (along with Grotius) as one of Ascham's major authorities. Nedham never seems to have read *De Cive*, but he read *De Corpore Politico* immediately after he published his own *Case of the Commonwealth*. (The two works were, in fact, published in the same week.) When the *Case* reached a second edition later in 1650, Nedham then added an appendix in which Hobbes's similar views are extensively quoted and used to corroborate the position Nedham had already taken up. Both Osborne and Warren evidently read *Leviathan* soon after it came out in the following year. Neither of them cites Hobbes as an authority in their 'engagement' pamphlets. But both of them cite him in later works as an authority on exactly the theory of political obligation at which, in their 'engagement' writings, they had arrived independently of reading him.[20]

There can be no doubt, moreover, that all these defenders of *de facto* powers were correct in seeing in *De Corpore Politico* and in *Leviathan* a theory of obligation which corroborated their own conclusions. Hobbes first of all endorses, both in *De Corpore Politico* and in *Leviathan*, the basic assumption of these *de facto* theorists that political society is a product of natural necessity and has as its essential aim the securing simply of peace and the protection of its citizens.[21] And in both these accounts, of course, Hobbes deduces these conclusions from a characteristically *de facto*-ist (though uniquely systematic) account of man's basically anti-social nature.[22] Political society is thus seen, in Hobbes's account just as in the accounts of the *de facto* theorists, both as the sole alternative to anarchy and as the indispensable means by which men can protect themselves from themselves and each other. The need for obedience is thus justified, in Hobbes's account just as with the *de facto* theorists, on the grounds that 'the consequence of the want of it, which is perpetual war of every man against his neighbour', is much worse than the apparent 'inconveniences' of submission (*Leviathan*, ed. Macpherson, p. 260).

Hobbes is thus led to endorse all the most characteristic claims of the *de facto* theorists. He agrees that conquest gives a valid title to allegiance. He even systematises this claim, made by all the lay defenders of 'engagement', by deriving all political power from the 'natural force' of conquest when it is not derived from 'institution'.[23] He also agrees in consequence that a citizen is released from all existing oaths and obligations when he is conquered by some new political power. When an existing sovereign power is 'subdued by war', then its subjects are automatically 'delivered from their former obligations, and become obliged to the victor'.[24] He is thus led in turn to endorse one of the most important polemical claims made by the lay defenders of 'engagement', to the effect that no valid distinction can be made between powers 'ordained' and powers merely 'permitted'. For he insists that any political power with the capacity to protect its citizens is for that reason a justifiable political authority, and so is entitled to their obedience. It is an axiom in *Leviathan* that in discussions about government 'the present ought always to be preferred, maintained and accounted best' (p. 577). And in the additional 'Review and Conclusion', Hobbes adds to this – very much in the spirit of the 'engagers' – that to ground political obligation on supposed rights rather than on possession would mean that 'there would perhaps be no tie of the subject's obedience to the sovereign at this day in all the world' (p. 721).

The basis of all these contentions, moreover, in Hobbes's account, just as with the other lay theorists of *de facto* powers, lies in the claim that there is a mutual relation between the duty of the sovereign to protect his subjects and the duty of his subjects to obey. And in Hobbes's account, just as with the other *de facto* theorists, this is encapsulated in the claim that 'the end of obedience is protection' (p. 272). For 'the obligation of subjects to sovereigns is understood to last as long and no longer than the power lasteth by which he is able to protect them (p. 272). On the one hand any citizen who has protection 'is obliged, without fraudulent pretence of having submitted himself out of fear, to protect his protector as long as he is able' (p. 375). But on the other hand, when 'there is no further protection of subjects in their loyalty, then is the commonwealth DISSOLVED, and every man at liberty to protect himself by such courses as his own discretion shall suggest unto him' (p. 375). The essential doctrine, as Hobbes summarises it himself in the 'Review and Conclusion' of *Leviathan* is that if a man should submit to the powers that be, and 'live under their protection openly', then 'he is understood to submit himself to the government' (p. 721).

The doctrines of Hobbes's main political works can thus be represented as a somewhat belated though highly important contribution to the lay defence of 'engagement'. It might still be doubted, however, how far this conclusion gives an accurate reflection of Hobbes's *intentions* in writing these works. But there can be no doubt that it does. When Hobbes replied some years later to the attacks that John Wallis had made upon his loyalty during the revolution, it was his proudest boast about *Leviathan* that it had 'framed the minds of a thousand gentlemen to a conscientious obedience to present government, which otherwise would have wavered in that point'.[25] And at the time of publishing *Leviathan* Hobbes made it quite clear that he both saw and intended his great work precisely as a contribution to the existing debate about the rights of *de facto* powers. It goes without saying that *Leviathan* is much else besides. But when Hobbes concluded by pointing out what he was trying to do in the work, it was this intention which he emphasised himself. The book, he said, was 'occasioned by the disorders of the present time' (p. 728). It was motivated by the discovery 'that the civil wars have not yet sufficiently taught men in what point of time it is that a subject becomes obliged to the conqueror; nor what is conquest; nor how it comes about, that it obliges men to obey his laws' (p. 719). And the basic aim, as Hobbes himself put it, was the same as the basic aim which all the lay defenders of 'engagement' had tried to fulfil: it was written 'without other design than to set before men's eyes the mutual relation between protection and obedience' (p. 728).

It can be shown, moreover, that Hobbes actually adapted his own earlier presentations of his theory to bring it into line with these other theorists of *de facto* powers. The formula of 'mutual relation' might be said to be implied by the doctrine of *De Cive*. But it is nowhere explicitly stated in that work and although it virtually surfaces in the 1650 version of the *Elements of Law*, it is not stated absolutely explicitly until the Review and Conclusion of *Leviathan* in 1651.[26]

These very strong family resemblances between Hobbes's account of political obligation and the views of the other theorists of *de facto* powers suggest two important conclusions about the place of Hobbes's political theory within the ideological debates of the English revolution. First, it is clearly a mistake to suppose (as most of Hobbes's commentators have done) that Hobbes's theory was an isolated phenomenon in the political world of its time. It is clear, on the contrary, that there is nothing unusual or even particularly original about Hobbes's most characteristic political beliefs. The second conclusion, which follows from this, is that we shall misunderstand Hobbes (as his commentators consistently do) if we try to give an account of his special status as a political writer mainly in terms of these doctrines. Hobbes's originality and his special claims upon our attention can scarcely be vindicated in terms of his actual political beliefs if there was nothing particularly novel or original about them. His real claims to originality must lie rather at the epistemological level, in the reasons he gave for holding his political beliefs, rather than in the beliefs themselves. It was in his predication of his political system upon a comprehensive account of man's political nature, and in his unique emancipation from the confines of the providentialist vocabulary, that Hobbes made his most original contributions to political theory. It was this achievement that was barely hinted at by the other lay defenders of the rights of *de facto* powers, even though many of them, independently of Hobbes, articulated the political doctrines that have usually been associated exclusively with Hobbes's name.

4. The Church in England 1646–1660

CLAIRE CROSS

For religion was not the thing at first contended for, but God brought it to that issue at last, and gave it unto us by way of redundancy; and at last it proved that which was most dear to us. And wherein consisted this, more than in obtaining that liberty from the tyranny of the bishops to all species of Protestants to worship God according to their own light and consciences?

Oliver Cromwell, 1655

THE period from the defeat of the Royalists to the restoration of Charles II saw the failure of the plan to create a system of rigid Protestant uniformity in England, and then the temporarily successful evolution of a very broad Protestant Church with toleration in practice for all peaceable Christians who could not accommodate themselves within it. In retrospect Cromwell considered this the great achievement of the Civil War and certainly he, more than any other single man, must be held responsible for it. His critics both then and later have regarded his grand scheme for toleration as mere religious anarchy and have denied that a church in any organised form existed in England between 1646 and 1660. Yet there may well have been more order in the diversity than they would concede, for although Parliament abolished episcopacy, at no time during this period did it disestablish the Church. The sequence of legislation which led from the abolition of the old episcopal system to this wide and diffuse Cromwellian Church has often been rehearsed: it will be necessary to retrace the sequence here in order to set this experiment in toleration in context. Historians, however, are only just beginning to examine in critical detail church life as it was actually lived in England at this time. This chapter attempts, in a very provisional and impressionistic way, to summarise recent research on the national church that resulted from the Puritan Revolution and on the peripheral churches and congregations that grew up partly or entirely outside its boundaries.

Looking back after fifteen years Cromwell recognised that religious grievances had not forced Charles to call first the Short and then the Long Parliament which brought about the final collision between king and Parliament and led to the Civil War. Nevertheless, once the Long Parliament had met its members very soon demanded reforms in religion. They attacked with passion the hierarchy fashioned by Laud. They hated the innovations in ceremonies he had introduced with their underlying Catholic implications; they hated the resurgence of clericalism symbolised by ecclesiastics holding high offices in the state for the first time since the Reformation; above all they hated the close alliance between the Crown and the bishops by which it seemed that the king and the Church might succeed permanently in making ordinances and raising clerical taxation independently of Parliament. Laymen in the Long Parliament knew very clearly what they wished to cast down but their agreement ended when they came to consider the form of the new church to be built where the old one had stood.

The Long Parliament made rapid progress in its proposed destruction of the organisation of the old church. In November 1640 it set up a grand committee for religion, later divided into several subcommittees, which the following month received the first petition from London for the abolition of episcopacy root and branch. The House of Commons in February 1641 read a bill for suppressing Arminian innovations and in December that year the House of Lords consented to the exclusion of bishops from Parliament. Yet Parliament soon began to take more constructive action by summoning an assembly of divines commissioned to devise a scheme of church government to replace Laudian prelacy. The members of the Westminster Assembly first came together in July 1643; by this date, however, Parliament no longer retained the power to authorise a form of church government free from external political pressure, since through military weakness it had been driven to seek Scottish help against the king. The bringing of the English Church into uniformity with the Church in Scotland was a condition of Scottish aid which Parliament could not afford to refuse, and when the Westminster Assembly met it contained, in addition to 120 English ecclesiastics (not all of whom obeyed the summons to attend) and thirty lay assessors from the Lords and Commons, eight commissioners from Scotland. In September 1643 both Houses of Parliament ratified the Solemn League and Covenant with the Scots.

From its first meeting, therefore, the Westminster Assembly felt constrained to produce a system of church government acceptable not

4663̅7̅

only to Parliament but also to the Presbyterian Scots, and the completed plan it submitted to the Commons in July 1645 was largely an adaptation of the Scottish form of organisation. In theory the Commons did not oppose the idea that the English Church should be governed through congregational, classical and synodical assemblies but it had absolutely no intention of substituting for one form of clerical government, prelacy, another, Presbyterianism, even less susceptible to lay control. Backed by the Scots, the majority of divines in the Westminster Assembly wished to keep the new church free from state interference; Parliament refused to countenance any form of church organisation not in the last resort answerable to itself. Only in June 1646 when the members of the Westminster Assembly reluctantly conceded a right of appeal from the hierarchy of clerical courts to a committee of Parliament did the Commons authorise the erection of a form of Presbyterianism in England. The Scot, Robert Baillie, referred in disgust to this English version of Presbyterianism as 'but a lame Erastian Presbytery'.

Once they had made it abundantly clear that the final power in church matters rested with themselves, then the governing classes as represented in Parliament seem to have been eager that a Protestant uniformity should be re-established throughout England. A small group of highly articulate Puritan ministers backed by more radical and more diffuse lay support thwarted their intentions. Not all the clergy who attended the Westminster Assembly had favoured a Presbyterian form of church government, and particularly ministers who had spent time in exile during Laud's supremacy among English congregations in Holland and New England questioned the claims of Presbyterianism to be the one form of church government laid down in the New Testament. They placed far more importance upon the independence of the individual congregation, reacting against an 'authoritative presbyterial government in all the subordinations and proceedings of it.'[1] Five ministers, Thomas Goodwin, Philip Nye, Sidrach Simpson, Jeremiah Burroughes and William Bridge, led the opposition within the Westminster Assembly, and when they realised that they could not deflect that body from producing some form of Presbyterian government they appealed to the nation at large in 'An Apologeticall Narration' in which they asked for a limited toleration for orthodox Calvinist ministers to gather their own congregations at least partially outside a state system. Had the Independent clergy protested alone they might very well have been overwhelmed by the significantly greater majority of their colleagues who wanted no such latitude, but their opposition, in combination with a vociferous lay demand for religious liberty expressed mainly outside Parliament, in the event considerably modified the full implementation of Parliament's legislation to set up a Presbyterian Church in England.

Parliament's decision to establish Presbyterianism in 1646 came too late to stand much chance of success. Since the breakdown of effective episcopal authority in 1640 English zealots had enjoyed in practice a religious liberty which they would not now willingly forgo. In different parts of England gathered churches had already appeared: to name but three examples, the Church at Bristol drew up its covenant in 1640; two years later the combined Norwich and Yarmouth church came into being, while the Church in Stepney formed around William Greenhill in 1644. In addition, the parliamentary army, removed from all parochial confines, provided ideal conditions in which sectarian movements could flourish. Soldiers, frequently encouraged by their officers, met in prayer meetings which often developed into gathered churches entirely separate from the parochial churches and parochial ministers of the area where they might happen to be stationed. Sometimes, as at Nottingham when Colonel John Hutchinson commanded the garrison there, some of the soldiers in the castle deliberately set themselves against the parish clergy of the town and defied their authority.[2] After the parliamentarian victory of Marston Moor in July 1644 and especially after the overwhelming defeat of the Royalists at Naseby a year later, Parliament no longer depended so heavily upon the Scots; instead, it had to take into account the forcibly expressed wishes of its own victorious army.

Fresh from his triumph in Yorkshire, Cromwell made a decisive intervention on behalf of the army in the politics of the religious settlement in September 1644, when he succeeded in persuading the Commons to accept a motion that the committee of the Lords and Commons appointed to treat with the Scottish commissioners and the committee of the Westminster Assembly 'endeavour the finding out some ways how far tender consciences, who cannot in all things submit to the common rule which shall be established, may be borne with, according to the Word, and as may stand with the public peace . . .'.[3] Time and again the army repeated this demand for liberty for tender consciences. The army leaders gave it a prominent place in their negotiations with the king after the Scots had handed him over into English custody in January 1647. When the army representatives brought out manifestoes like the 'Heads of the Proposals' again they emphasised the principle of religious liberty. Parliament had little choice but to give way to the agitation, and in its plan for an agreement with Charles in December 1647 for the establishment of Presbyterianism it included the provision 'that all such persons as shall not conform to the said form of government and divine service shall have liberty to meet for the service and worship of God, and for the exercise of religious duties and ordinances . . . so as nothing be done by them to the disturbance of the peace of the kingdom.'[4]

Since Parliament had allowed such major inroads to be made upon the ideal of a narrow Protestant uniformity by the end of 1647, it could not withold further concessions after the Second Civil War when the alliance between Charles I and the Scots had further discredited Presbyterianism with many Englishmen. Once Parliament had been purged of elements most hostile to the army, once the king had been executed, little prevented the implementation of the army's desire for some form of religious toleration for Protestants. In September 1650 the Rump, in the Act for the relief of religious and peaceable people, repealed the Elizabethan Act of uniformity and the Act for the punishing of persons obstinately refusing to come to Church, and so, in this negative way, relieved citizens from the legal obligation of attending their parish churches.

The somewhat grudging withdrawal by the Rump of compulsory attendance at the state Church contrasts markedly with Cromwell's attitude towards the Church in England after the army had proclaimed him Protector. Cromwell had a vision of the English Church as a multitude of congregations seeking truth in diversity and he looked upon toleration as a necessary condition of the search.

Therefore, I beseech you, [he exhorted the Barebone's Parliament] . . . have a care of the whole flock! Love the sheep, love the lambs; love all, tender all, cherish and countenance all, in all things that are good. And if the poorest Christian, the most mistaken Christian, shall desire to live peaceably and quietly under you – I say, if any shall desire to lead a life of godliness and honesty, let him be protected.[5]

More soberly, after the failure of the Barebone's Parliament and after the waning of many hopes for the immediate realisation of the kingdom of God on earth, the 'Instrument of Government' laid down a declaration of the extent of religious toleration in England which Cromwell permitted none of his subsequent parliaments to limit:

That such as profess faith in God by Jesus Christ (though differing
in judgement from the doctrine, worship, or discipline publicly held
forth) shall not be restrained from, but shall be protected in, the
profession of the faith, and exercise of their religion; so as they abuse
not this liberty to the civil liberty of others, and to the actual disturbance of the public peace on their parts. Provided this liberty
be not extended to Popery nor Prelacy, nor to such as, under the
profession of Christ, hold forth and practice licentiousness.[6]

In his pessimistic moments, when he realised how few others understood his vision of the English Church, or if they understood it, would
share it with him, Cromwell described himself as a mere parish constable charged to maintain the peace between warring factions. Yet the
Church that emerged during the Protectorate was far more of a positive,
planned creation than this negative comparison suggests. Cromwell
constantly strove to promote unity, and never tired of trying to bring
Presbyterian, Independent and Baptist clerics together to discuss
matters of common religious concern. He also held decided views on
the duty of the State to provide adequate maintenance for its clergy.
From early in the Civil War, with the setting up of the Committee for
Plundered Ministers, Parliament had taken pains that loyal ministers
should receive adequate remuneration and, when from 1649 the State
began to sell episcopal and capitular lands, had set aside certain income to produce a considerable fund to augment poorer livings. A
Commonwealth parish minister could hope to obtain grants to bring his
annual income to about £100 a year; one incumbent who recorded the
payment of his augmentation was the diarist Ralph Josselin, of Earls
Colne in Essex. In addition the government authorised the creation of
cathedral lectureships out of the same fund, and at York, to mention
only one cathedral city, the four ministers attached to the Minster
each received £150 annually. With its appointment of trustees for the
maintenance of ministers in 1649 the Rump followed the example that
the Long Parliament had already set. Cromwell ensured that this
financial support of the clergy continued and refused to allow the
Barebone's Parliament to abolish tithes until a new form of public
maintenance could be devised for the parochial ministry, which no
Parliament subsequently ever succeeded in doing.

Apart from the maintenance of the clergy by the State, two other
Cromwellian innovations, the 'tryers' and the 'ejectors', both of which
developed from suggestions first made by members of the Rump in

1652, provided a bare framework in a loosely organised church.[7] These commissioners, the tryers who met in London to examine all men seeking to enter the ministry of the national church, and the ejectors, organised on a county basis to remove unworthy ministers still in possession of livings, carried on, probably more effectively than before, the work of earlier parliamentary committees. Characteristically Cromwell persuaded Presbyterians, Independents and Baptists to act on his board of tryers, and even Baxter, an unconcealed opponent of Cromwell, acknowledged the extent and value of their activities.

> They saved many a congregation from ignorant, ungodly, drunken teachers . . . [he confessed] so that, though they were many of them somewhat partial for the Independents, Separatists, Fifth Monarchy men and Anabaptists, and against the Prelatists and Arminians, yet so great was the benefit above the hurt which they brought to the church, that many thousands of souls blessed God for the faithful ministers whom they let in, and grieved when the Prelatists afterward cast them out again . . . .[8]

Cromwell's Church, therefore, although it had no articles of religion approved by the State and no common liturgy, established institutions to oversee the maintenance and the conduct of the clergy. It went further and commissioned a new *Valor Ecclesiasticus* in the form of parliamentary surveys of all parochial livings. With the ordinance of 1654 which authorised the uniting of the many small parishes in some towns and country districts and the division of huge parishes in other areas, a scheme existed through which an ecclesiastical framework dating from the early Middle Ages could have been adapted radically to meet the requirements of seventeenth-century England. The weakness of this Church lay in the fact that it depended overmuch upon the initiative and the continuing protection of one man. Even Cromwell, in return for the greater political stability he hoped it would introduce, accepted in 1657 in the 'Humble Petition and Advice' some limitation to the toleration granted in the 'Instrument of Government'. He formally agreed to the exclusion from toleration of Socinians and Quakers and other socially disruptive sectaries and consented to the drawing up of a national confession of faith, although little was done to carry out either proposal while he lived.[9] After his death, Richard Cromwell proved unable to preserve his father's Church and in 1659 his Parliament set to work to confine toleration further and re-establish Calvinist orthodoxy. Once again the army succeeded temporarily in intervening to save liberty of conscience, but as soon as Monck had restored the Long Parliament it endeavoured to revert to the state of religion as it had been in 1646. It declared the Westminster Confession to be the faith of the nation, renewed the Covenant and tried to revive the classical organisation throughout the country. So before Charles II returned Parliament had done its best to bring the dangerous experiment in toleration to an end.

Although during the Protectorate the State in this way undertook partial responsibility for the payment of the clergy, nominated commissioners to scrutinise the ministers appointed to livings and made proposals for the reorganisation of the administration of the Church, hostile critics have subsequently contended that the Cromwellian Church allowed such a degree of theological licence that it did not merit the description of a national church. Not all contemporary opponents of the state ecclesiastical machinery reacted in this way: the Baptists of Cambridgeshire regularly spoke of the maintained ministers as 'priests of England' and referred to services held in the parochial assemblies between 1646 and 1660 as 'Church of England' worship.[10] Obviously they thought of the national church as a real entity. Nevertheless, these accusations retain considerable force and can be critically assessed only if we turn away from the legislative ordinances and the formal organisation of the Church to an attempt to reconstruct, so far as the imperfect survival of original records permits, religious life within the Church as it was lived in the localities.

Inevitably Parliament's legislation and relaxation of legislation strongly influenced the Church that emerged during the Cromwellian period. Many contemporaries when they described their Church considered it to be an English Presbyterian Church and at least at the parish level their definition may have had a certain validity. Perhaps on a wider scale than has been supposed, after Parliament's endorsement of a Presbyterian form of church government and of a Presbyterian *Directory of Worship* in June 1646, a significant number of incumbents in their parishes voluntarily tried to establish an attenuated variant of Presbyterian discipline. For almost a century Puritan ministers had been calling for greater powers to control their parishioners and few objected now to excluding the unworthy from receiving communion. At Kidderminster Baxter, although he had little love for the full Presbyterian system, regularly catechised and instructed his flock and imposed a moral discipline upon the town seemingly more severe and effective than it had known before. He believed, however,

that the exercise of discipline belonged to the minister alone and refused to countenance the office of lay elders. Many incumbents shared
his objections and probably the greater number of English parishes
never progressed so far as to substitute elders for churchwardens, for
the clergy were not alone in their reluctance to permit an invasion of
their clerical prerogative; many of the laity had equally firm objections
to being considered for the office. Nevertheless, some parishes where
the minister and the leading laymen agreed set up a functioning parochial presbytery. In the large parish of Bolton the two ministers there
worked together with twelve lay elders in examining those fitted to
receive communion and distributed tickets which parishioners had to
surrender to the elders before they could communicate, a practice
which many members of the congregation, including Oliver Heywood's
father, strongly disliked. Some ministers, when they discovered their
congregations refused to accept examination, discontinued celebrating
Holy Communion entirely, rather than permit all promiscuously to
approach the Lord's Table. Others, like Ralph Josselin at Earls Colne
in Essex, found a partial compromise. After a series of admonitions
and examinations attended by the squire he found, to his relief, that
most of his unworthy parishioners excluded themselves: not even all the
committed Christians in the parish dared present themselves to receive
communion.[11]

Conforming ministers differed over the extent to which they wished
to impose discipline upon their parishes and over the extent to which
they would share its exercise with the laity, but on the whole they seem
to have accepted the substitution of the *General Directory of Worship*
for the *Book of Common Prayer* with remarkable equanimity. The
Directory of Worship offered a guide to the form of service to be performed by the incumbent but did not prescribe set forms of prayer.
Few Calvinists could have disagreed with its theology and probably
the majority of English parish ministers who remained in their livings
still were under the domination of Calvin and his popularisers. It may
well be that the regular Sunday services in the parish churches between
1646 and 1660 departed little in substance from the outline of worship
used in non-Laudian parish churches before the Civil War where,
despite the rubric in the prayer book, some ministers contrived to avoid
wearing the surplice and the laity did not kneel for prayer.

Ministers who co-operated with elders in the government of their
particular parish and willingly followed the *Book of Discipline* still
might have doubts, as Adam Martindale did, over the right of one

parish to interfere in the activities of another: 'I had no mind to meddle with the affairs of other congregations, except by way of advice and assistance in some extraordinary cases upon their desire; and for our own I was verily persuaded that if I were once ordained and an elder-ship settled we could do all our business amongst ourselves, or else it would not be done at all . . . .'[12] Yet despite hesitation some form of Presbyterian classical organisation above the parish presbyteries oper-ated in certain parts of England. The minutes of classes which functioned more or less continuously throughout the Commonwealth and Pro-tectorate survive at least for one part of London, for Manchester, for Bury in Lancashire, for part of Nottinghamshire and for Wirksworth in Derbyshire; and from these and other records classes are known to have existed in other areas of the country. Some clergy made a valiant effort to replace the old episcopal organisation with an alternative system.

The Fourth London *Classis*, which first met in November 1646, three months after Parliament had given permission for the setting up of the Presbyterian organisation throughout England, consisted of fourteen parishes in the Cornhill, Eastcheap, Billingsgate part of the city. In spite of many attempts the *classis* never succeeded in getting all its parishes within its boundaries represented, but by January 1647 eleven out of the fourteen parishes had constituted themselves presbyteries by choosing lay elders to act with the minister. The *classis* failed to persuade the parishioners of St Michael, Crooked Lane to elect lay elders, while a prospective incumbent for St Margaret's, Fish Street would not come to the living unless the lay elders there laid down their office. On the whole, however, the *classis* seems to have been reasonably satisfied that some version of Presbyterianism was operating at the parish level. It received occasional reports when an incumbent did not use the *Directory of Worship* and made frequent efforts to encourage catechising in the parishes in its area. After 1649, although some form of general oversight continued, the *classis* increasingly concen-trated upon the business of ordination, and between 1647 and 1659 examined and commissioned a total of ninety men to livings throughout England.[13] Their records no longer exist, but from the minute book of the London Provincial Assembly it is clear that seven other *classes* (out of a possible total of twelve), in addition to the Fourth London *Classis*, functioned in London at some time between 1646 and 1660.

The *classes* of Manchester and Bury, both within the province of Lancashire, resemble the Fourth London *Classis* in that in their first years they gave priority to the erection of the Presbyterian system, though occasionally they sat in judgement upon moral offences. After 1649 these *classes* also largely concerned themselves with ordinations, enquiring into the spiritual aptitude and educational qualifications of candidates probably with considerably more rigour than bishops in the previous hundred years had ever done. Significantly, the Bury *Classis* fairly often called upon local justices of the peace to bring pressure upon ministers who did not observe the ordinances of the *classis*. Throughout their existence these *classes* seem to have contained their complement of lay elders and never became exclusive ministerial gatherings. Historians once assumed that the classical system operated only in London and Lancashire, areas where they considered that Presbyterian ministers were untypically influential, but with the more recent discovery of classical records for other parts of England this can no longer be maintained. A *classis* functioned effectively at Wirksworth in Derbyshire, where in the 1650s it performed a considerable number of ordinations according to the Presbyterian form, and an area of Nottinghamshire also had an active *classis* which included lay elders even though all the ministerial members of the *classis* could not agree to divide their authority with elders in their particular parishes. It also seems likely that some type of *classis* functioned at least in parts of county Durham, Essex, Shropshire and in Yorkshire around Leeds, and further research may well uncover positive evidence of Presbyterian organisation in other areas of England.[14]

According to the scheme authorised by Parliament, provincial assemblies should have been set up in the regions to co-ordinate the activities of the *classes*. Certainly two provincial assemblies, for London and Lancashire, acted throughout the period of the Commonwealth and Protectorate. The provincial assembly of London first sat in May 1647, and continued to meet without any substantial break until 15 August 1660. It also contained its complement of lay members till the end, and indeed the ministers of the provincial assembly took particular pains to maintain the prescribed proportion of double the number of lay to clerical representatives. Formally, the London provincial assembly had a general oversight of the activities of the *classes* in its area, encouraging the setting up of *classes* where they were deficient, urging the *classes* to promote discipline, observe the Sabbath more strictly, increase catechising and perform ordinations in due rotation. Because of its position, and because no national synod was ever convened, the London provincial assembly in addition increasingly became an advisory body for Presbyterians throughout England. It took upon itself the responsibility for defining Presbyterian principles and as an assembly composed several pamphlets: in 1650 it published *A Vindication of the Presbyteriall Government and Ministry*; in 1654 it brought out *Ius Divinum Ministerii Evangelici* and a year later *An Exhortation to Catechising*. The assembly in its later years worked for a limited accommodation between Presbyterians and moderate Independents and moderate episcopalians, and throughout the Protectorate ministers of different theological persuasions and from different parts of Britain sought its advice.[15] In 1654 the ministers of Worcestershire wrote to the assembly about a version of the psalms and in 1655 West Country ministers consulted it about the translation of a theological treatise; Irish Presbyterians repeatedly asked for its ruling upon the divine origin of the office of lay elders. Even as Charles II landed in England to take possession of his throne the assembly commended to the ministers of the nation a project for the translation of the Bible into the language of the New England Indians.

English Presbyterianism differed in an important respect from Scottish Presbyterianism in that virtually throughout its operation it was a voluntary system dependent upon the energy and initiative of the local clergy and laity. Particularly after the purge of the Long Parliament when the civil government no longer gave active support to the establishment of Presbyterian discipline, parish incumbents could not be forced to work with lay elders, or to co-operate with a local *classis* and obey its injunctions. This lack of compulsion undoubtedly attenuated the Presbyterian character of the national Church, but it made it possible for Protestant ministers who were not convinced Presbyterians to work within a nominally Presbyterian Church when a more effective system might have excluded them. Almost three-quarters of the ministers who had been episcopally ordained before the Civil War retained their parochial livings or accepted preferment in the Commonwealth Church.[16] Some ministers positively welcomed the freedom inaugurated by the abolition of episcopacy and rejoiced at being no longer tied to the liturgy of the *Book of Common Prayer*. Baxter typified convinced Puritans of this sort who, while they could not accept the divine-right claims of Presbyterianism, yet held no inflexible views on the matter of church government. Many others, who preferred an episcopal system, considered it their duty to work within the Protestant Church supported by the State. Thomas Fuller wrote a revealing defence of these moderate episcopalians. Openly admitting that he thought the episcopal government to be 'most consonant to the word of God and the practice of the primitive church', he added:

> I know that religion and learning hath flourished under the Pres-byterian government in France, Germany, the Low Countries. I know many worthy champions of the truth, bred and brought up under the same. I know the most learned and moderate English divines (though episcopal in their callings and judgements) have allowed the Reformed Churches under the discipline for sound and perfect in all essentials necessary to salvation. If, therefore, denied my first desire to live under that church government I best affected, I will contentedly conform to the Presbyterian government, and en-deavour to deport myself quietly and comfortably under the same.[17]

Not only the moderate episcopalians among the clergy but also per-haps the majority of those episcopally minded among the laity seem to have succeeded in accommodating themselves to the latitudinarian form of church that developed under Cromwell. Indeed, this church corresponded more closely to demands made by gentlemen in Parlia-ment just before the beginning of the Civil War than Royalists later were willing to admit. The radicals in the Barebone's Parliament failed to alter the rights of the laity in church patronage, and gentlemen, other than Catholics and sequestered Royalists, continued to nominate candidates to livings in their possession. With the various parliamentary committees selected on a county basis, to enquire into the fitness of the clergy and to review parochial boundaries, the Church had become more open to adaptation to regional requirements under parliamentary oversight than ever before. Episcopalian and Royalist though he was, the desire to make the Church more local, more susceptible to the wishes of local gentlemen, had been one inspiration behind Sir Edward Dering's scheme to transform the English Church in 1640.[18] Gentle-men who in the reign of Charles II made extravagant professions of their past loyalty to Anglicanism do not seem as a body to have re-fused to conform to the national church. Even so convinced a Royalist as John Evelyn conscientiously attended his parish church at Deptford Sunday by Sunday, and carefully recorded the topics of his minister's sermons. When later he wrote up his diary for 30 November 1656 he excused his behaviour by explaining 'that though the minister were Presbyterianly affected, he yet was, I understand, duly ordained and preached sound doctrine after their way, and besides was an humble, harmless and peaceable man.' Scruples of this kind concerning conformity to the national church seem not to have occurred at all to laymen lower in the social scale.

Episcopalian ministers and episcopalian gentlemen believed in the necessity of a state church and disagreed with English Presbyterians only over the form this state church should take. The breadth of the Cromwellian Church made possible the inclusion within its bounds of Protestants considerably more radical than these. Certain ministers of separated churches, who in theory had wholly or partly repudiated the idea that the Church and State either could or should be coterminous, felt able to hold office in the national church. Dr Nuttall has discovered some 130 Independent ministers who accepted parochial livings from which they were ejected after the Restoration and they seem to have been particularly numerous in the eastern counties. These men served both the entire parish composed of the regenerate and unregenerate and their gathered church of visible saints. William Greenhill, called by the Independent Church in Stepney to be its minister at its formation in 1644, from the outset combined this work with that of evening lecturer in the parish church; and when in 1653 he became vicar of Stepney, he still contrived to perform his very varied religious duties to the apparent satisfaction of both his parochial and his gathered congregation. The Independent incumbent appointed to the parish of St Bartholomew Exchange in the City of London, John Lodder, showed less tact. His new parishioners reacted in 1657 by withholding their tithes 'because he refused to administer the sacrament and christen children except we would join in communion with his church'. John Tombes, whom Baxter considered to be the most formidable protagonist of the Calvinist Baptists, actively propagated Baptist doctrine and founded Baptist churches in Worcestershire and Herefordshire and still held parochial cures at Bewdley and at Leominster.[19] Perhaps this behaviour can be more easily understood in a pastoral and historical context rather than in a theological one. For more than a century Puritan ministers had tended the godly within a parish who had often met separately from the rest of the parish for religious exercises. In the freer atmosphere of the Commonwealth nothing logically prevented the continuation of this practice, which allowed a minister in his parish congregation greater opportunities for evangelism than he could have had merely in his gathered church. In addition to the holding of parish livings by Independents and an occasional Baptist, many more, although they would not accept parish cures, did recognise the state church in that they accepted preaching or teaching appoint-

ments within it, as lecturers in cathedrals or attached to town corporations or as fellows of colleges at Oxford or Cambridge.

The Cromwellian Church in this way comprehended a very large
sector of the clergy and laity in England, almost certainly a proportionately greater number than the established church ever included subsequently. Nevertheless, some clergy and even more of the laity quite
deliberately excluded themselves from the national church. Cromwell's
government openly tolerated the separatist churches of the more
radical Protestants, and connived at the continuance of the separate
churches of the Roman Catholics and the Laudians; so in practice, on
the periphery of the very broad national church, a collection of churches
existed in a condition of partial or total isolation. Cromwell had no
doubts that all these churches contained true Christians, and, while
few of his contemporaries shared his wide ecumenism, any survey of
the Church that grew up under his protection must contain some
consideration of the separated churches.

The High-Church episcopalian ministers, who refused any form of
co-operation with the state church between 1646 and 1660, probably
formed only a minority of the 2000–3000 Royalist clergy ejected from
their livings during and after the Civil War. Professing episcopacy to
to be the only valid form of church government, fanatically loyal to
the liturgy of the *Book of Common Prayer*, they ignored parliamentary
ordinances against prelacy but can hardly be said to have organised
a church in opposition to the national church.[20] Some bishops, like
Robert Skinner, Brian Duppa, Henry King, Joseph Hall, Ralph
Brownrig and Thomas Morton in retirement in England, went on
ordaining candidates for the priesthood, and other bishops who chose
exile occasionally held ordination services in the chapel of Sir Richard
Browne in Paris and later in the chapel for which Cosin was responsible
at the court of Charles II. Yet in a church which had come to place
such emphasis upon the necessity of episcopacy the Laudian clerics
did remarkably little to perpetuate the apostolic succession. In 1650
Evelyn noted the scarcity of bishops and expressed the fear that the
succession might become extinct; even when urged by Charles II
himself the bishops in England failed to meet to perform conse-
crations. Old age took its toll and by the winter of 1659 only nine
English bishops remained alive; the episcopal succession by the time
of the Restoration had almost failed through inanition.

The passivity of the bishops and the High-Church clergy who stayed in
England cannot be explained by the intensity of persecution. Officially

the Long Parliament had proscribed prelacy, and the 'Instrument of Government' and the 'Humble Petition and Advice' repeated the ban. Yet, except at times of Royalist risings, these prelatist clerics encountered little opposition in conducting their services in private. Throughout the Protectorate whenever Evelyn came to London he succeeded in finding episcopalians celebrating the chief feasts of the Christian year – Christmas, Easter and Whitsun – which the national church no longer observed. On 30 December 1655, just after Penruddock's Rising, he recorded how he went to St Gregory's in London to hear 'the funeral sermon of preaching, this being the last day after which Cromwell's proclamation was to take place, that none of the Church of England should dare either to preach, administer sacraments, teach school etc. on pain of imprisonment or exile.' His apprehension proved to be exaggerated for he did not understand that the government attacked the prelatists for their political and not their specifically religious activities. In fact right until 1660 Evelyn was able to attend worship in London according to the *Book of Common Prayer*, though he bitterly resented that 'the Church of England was reduced to a chamber and conventicle'.[21]

Prelacy during the Commonwealth period shrank into a position much resembling that of Catholicism under Elizabeth I, but episcopalian clergy sheltered in Royalist households had to endure none of the raids by pursuivants, the public trials, the agonising executions suffered by Elizabethan Catholic priests. The appeal of this form of episcopalianism seems to have been confined largely to the Royalist nobility and gentry, much like Elizabethan seigneurial Catholicism, and indeed the meetings for worship at Exeter House chapel in London took on something of the nature of a political demonstration against the government by the excluded members of the governing class. Roman Catholicism, on the other hand, after a century of persecution presented far less of a political threat. No Protestant in the seventeenth century could have contemplated including Catholicism, a totally exclusive form of Christianity, within an English Protestant church; yet, contrary to what might have been predicted when the Puritans came to power, Catholics did succeed in maintaining, even apparently increasing, their church alongside the national church.

The Irish Rebellion raised the spectre of a Catholic counter-rebellion in England and wild fears of a massacre of English Protestants by Irish Catholics. In consequence Parliament intensified efforts against Catholic priests in England and between 1641 and 1646 twenty-one were captured and put to death. In very marked contrast the government authorised the execution of only two priests during the Commonwealth and Protectorate and Cromwell personally tried to spare one of these. As under Cromwell's influence the government allowed greater toleration to different forms of Protestantism, so Catholics began to avail themselves of the same liberty; and the increased numbers of English Catholics attending mass at the chapels of foreign embassies in London provoked the second Protectorate Parliament into passing an act in 1657 which would have required any Catholic on demand to take an oath abjuring the Pope. Cromwell never permitted the act to be enforced. Catholics under his protection probably enjoyed a greater freedom to carry out their own worship in private than they had had under any of the previous monarchs since 1558 and Cromwell could with some justice emphasise to Mazarin his liberal treatment of this minority: 'Truly I have . . . made a difference; and, as Jude speaks, plucked many out of the fire, the raging fire of persecution which did tyrannise over their consciences, and encroached by an arbitrariness of power upon their estates. And herein it is my purpose, as soon as I can remove impediments and some weights that press me down, to make a farther progress, and discharge my promise to your eminency in relation to that.'[22]

Prelacy and Catholicism seem to have attracted only a very small and socially distinct sector of the laity between 1646 and 1660. When, virtually for the first time, the generality of Englishmen had the liberty to choose their own form of Christianity, their overwhelming preference appears to have been for types of Protestantism that allowed a greater degree of lay participation. The abundance of information about the activities of certain lay Protestants at this period may exaggerate their strength and enthusiasm; probably, as in earlier periods rapid religious change, the majority of Englishmen either supported or acquiesced in the policy of their parish incumbent. Yet the determination of a minority of lay Protestant zealots cannot be gainsaid. Whereas the Laudian and Catholic clergy took the initiative in keeping their churches outside the national church, more radical Protestant laymen, sometimes in spite of the inclinations of their ministers, led their gathered churches into open separation.

Contemporary annals and minute books of gathered churches have survived for many parts of England and from these it is possible to build up a more accurate impression of what the godly in very varied levels of society wanted than perhaps at any earlier period of English history. Some lay people quite clearly had a burning desire to set themselves apart to worship with the saints uncontaminated by the unregenerate. At Bristol by a series of logical steps a little group of lay people came to the conclusion that they must leave the national church. Ever since the reign of James some 'awakened souls' in the city had met together for fasts and to bewail the corruptions and blind devotions of the times. In 1640 five of these covenanted together to 'come forth of the world and worship the Lord more purely, presevering therein to their end'. At first they merely contracted out of the formal part of Common Prayer on Sundays and then went into church to hear the sermon of Matthew Hazzard, the incumbent of St Ewins. Soon the conviction came upon them that even this showed too much conformity with the world and they forsook the established church entirely. At first the separatist church had no permanent minister of its own; it relied upon the 'gifted' among its members for inspiration and the occasional services of sympathetic visiting ministers. Yet despite this inauspicious beginning the church had achieved a membership of about 160 before the Civil War broke out. Even after episcopacy had been abolished and the incumbents of the city churches no longer used the *Book of Common Prayer*, the Broadmead church kept itself quite separate, calling its own ministers and, on one occasion, dismissing a minister it did not consider sufficiently scrupulous. Some of the members of the church renounced infant baptism, others did not; they clearly appreciated mutual edification more than uniformity in doctrinal matters. In this they resembled the church founded in Bedford in 1650, where 'the principle upon which they . . . entered into fellowship one with another, and upon which they did afterwards receive those that were added to their body and fellowship, was faith in Christ and holiness of life without respect to this or that circumstance or opinion in outward and circumstantial things . . . .'[23]

Other separatist churches maintained a far greater doctrinal distinctiveness, and members joined them, or decided to leave them, for theological reasons. The elders of Dr Peter Chamberlen's church in London, which held strictly to the tenet of believer's baptism, excommunicated Eleazer Bar Ishai, a converted Jew, for attending other religious assemblies and for permitting his child to be 'sprinkled' by the Presbyterians. Another member, Sister Anne Harriman, threatened to withdraw from the church because Brother Naudin had said he would not walk with such as gave liberty to women to speak in church, and she would not walk where she had not got this right. Untypically on this issue, for in most gathered churches sisters could make their opinions known in public only through brothers, Dr Chamberlen's church decided 'a woman, (maid, wife or widow) being a prophetess (I Cor. 11) may speak, prophesy, pray, with a veil. Others may not.' One Ewin, a watchman, left the Independent church in Stepney in 1657 to join 'a church of Christ that walked according to the ordinances of the gospel which he thought we did not in regard to that ordinance of baptism.' Another member, Mistress Mary Browne of Limehouse, announced she would not attend the church any longer because the pastor, William Greenhill, 'had declared that man hath not power of himself to do anything', and became an enthusiastic member of the church of the Arminian, John Goodwin, a theological rebel among the Independents since he persisted in maintaining that all men might be saved. Perhaps the church at Fenstanton, founded by the Baptist Henry Denne, which drew its members from villages in Huntingdonshire, Bedfordshire, Cambridgeshire and the Isle of Ely, displayed the widest range of independent lay thinking. The church underwent a continued assault in the 1650s from Quakers who, according to the annalist of the Cockermouth church, 'like a mighty torrent, had like to have swept down all the churches in the nation'. Former members of the Fenstanton church declared that they were illumined by God; they refused to try their inspiration by the Scriptures and denied the necessity of sacraments. Some, like Widow Sanders, attained an unusual degree of religious tolerance: when pressed by the Baptist elders to explain why she no longer attended the Longstanton church, she replied 'that she did walk in the ways of God, and so did we; so did those people that did live under episcopal and presbyterial government, and those that walked under no ordinances: they all walk as God would have them'.[24]

This kind of outspokenness by individual church members could lead to schisms and ultimately to the breakdown of all religious organisation. Such tensions built up in Dr Chamberlen's church during the three years for which the records survive that it suffered two secessions of members who objected to the doctor's autocratic behaviour and his interpretation of the Scriptures. Yet the gathered churches early in their existence drew up rules and built up associations in order to prevent fragmentation of this nature. The Baptists especially, perhaps because their churches tended to be founded by the missionary efforts of certain inspired individuals, quickly realised the need for organisation to support the weaker churches and preserve harmony of doctrine. The

General Baptists, so named because they believed that Christ had died for all mankind, were particularly strong in the East Midlands and in Kent. They held a general assembly in London in 1656 at which they considered such common problems as the attitude of the churches to the State, offences meriting excommunication, the tenure of office of elders, and then went on to define some points of theology. The Particular Baptists, who like most Independents derived from the orthodox Calvinist theological tradition and held that only the elect might be saved, concentrated more on regional organisation. Five associations of Particular Baptists, the Welsh Association, the Berkshire Association, the Irish Association, the Western and the Midland Associations all met regularly in the 1650s. Just as the London Provincial Assembly came to be looked upon as the fount of Presbyterian authority, so the leaders of the London Particular Baptist churches acted as advisers to the various regional associations. By 1660 there were well over 200 General and Particular Baptist churches in existence in England.[25]

Independent churches seem always to have been more self-sufficient than Baptist churches of either type, yet they also from the beginning recognised the duty of the eldership of one church to advise another when invited to do so. Mr John Simpson acted in accordance with this belief when in 1656 he asked the Stepney church to send messengers to give advice in a dispute which had resulted in part of his church seceding. Towards the end of the Protectorate Independent churches felt the need of more formal guidance than this type of consultation could provide. In the autumn of 1658 representatives of 120 Independent churches met in London to draw up the Savoy Confession of Faith. Even the far distant church at Cockermouth in Cumberland sent its pastor as its representative and on his return, as the conference had suggested, duly kept a day of thanksgiving for the agreement that the envoys had achieved, for their safety and for the favour given them by those in authority.[26]

In this way between 1646 and 1660 distinctions sharpened between Independents and Baptists, between General Baptists and Particular Baptists, though the period as a whole can be studied meaningfully only if it is seen as the prehistory of the different denominations. In the past some historians have been too eager to divide Commonwealth churches according to later theological distinctions that the churches themselves did not yet make. The churches at Bristol and Bedford refused on principle to pronounce on the lawfulness of infant baptism, but left the issue open to the decision of individual members. A Par-

ticular Baptist minister like John Tombes had far more in common
with a Calvinist Independent minister of the stature of John Owen
than he had with 'mechanic' preachers of his own sect. John Goodwin,
on the other hand, though an Independent and an opponent of believer's
baptism, in matters of theology agreed more nearly with Henry Denne,
the General Baptist apologist, than with Calvinist Independents.
Baptists in their association meetings stressed and restressed the necessity
of their ministers being maintained by the voluntary offerings of church
members, just because some of their ministers still had not fully accepted
this ruling and were willing to receive some form of maintenance from
the State. It is, therefore, less of a paradox than might first appear that
a period that marked the beginning of denominational exclusiveness
saw also a development of co-operation between individual gathered
churches, and between the separated churches and the national church.
Partly this co-operation was forced upon the churches through fear of
what they considered as the social excesses and blasphemous theological
ideas of the Ranters, Quakers and Socinians, but partly it seems to
indicate a genuine growing together after a time of sectarian strife.
Perhaps Cromwell's enforcement of the religious peace between the
factions had begun to take effect. At Yarmouth and at Newcastle-upon-
Tyne Presbyterian and Independent ministers worked together in
harmony. At the foundation of the Independent church in Cockermouth in the winter of 1651-2 the Church took care that George
Larkham should be ordained by three presbyters, 'called to that work,
for fear of offending the godly brethren of the Presbyterial way'. Above
all, this desire for co-operation between the churches began to show
itself in Baxter's concept of voluntary associations of ministers. In his
Worcestershire Association Baxter called for 'unity in things necessary
and liberty in things unnecessary, and charity in all'. His association
attracted seventy-two members, some being of 'no sect or party at all,
though the vulgar call them by the name of Presbyterians'; others
were Independents, conforming episcopalians and at least one a Baptist. At the same time as Baxter was working for unity in Worcestershire, the ministers of Cumberland and Westmorland independently
began to associate, and clerics in Wiltshire, Dorset, Somerset, Hampshire, Essex, Cambridgeshire, Cornwall and Devonshire copied their
example. 'A great desire of concord began to possess all good people
in the land, and our breaches seemed ready to heal.'[27]

Had Cromwell lived for a further decade perhaps many of the Independent churches and some of the Baptist churches on the periphery

of the national church might have been more fully comprehended within it. With the deaths of the remaining Laudian bishops perhaps some modified form of episcopacy, as envisaged by Ussher and Baxter, might possibly have been voluntarily adopted as a means to unity by the national church. These attempts to achieve unity in diversity were halted by the death of Cromwell, whom the Cockermouth annalist apostrophised as 'that eminent servant of the Lord, and nursing father of the churches, Oliver Cromwell'. Even before the Restoration, Parliament tried to restore a far less tolerant form of Presbyterianism; the whole venture came to an end with the reimposition of a form of Anglicanism on St Bartholomew's Day 1662 more narrow and more exclusive than the national church had ever been under Elizabeth or the early Stuarts. Unlike the minister of Cockermouth church, relatively few Protestants at the time appreciated the Church as it existed in England between 1646 and 1660. To convinced Presbyterians and to Puritans of no particular religious party like Baxter, it tolerated far too much, and did not exercise discipline. To Protestant radicals it retained too much of the framework of a national church. Very soon after 1662, however, non-conformists looked at the religious history of the previous twenty years from a very different perspective; the period of Cromwell's dominance became, to congregations such as those at Broadmead, 'those halcyon days of prosperity, liberty and peace'.

5. Social and Economic Policies under the Commonwealth

J. P. COOPER

THERE is no general study yet of the social and economic history of the Interregnum and of what may be distinctive about it.[1] What we have are general accounts which place the Commonwealth within various teleological perspectives – such as the origins and growth of *laissez-faire*, or of the old colonial system, or of truly national economic policies – and there are detailed studies of the Navigation Act.

Some historians have seen the period from 1640 to 1660 as one of decisive changes, symbolised by the decline of regulation in internal trade and industry and of control over policies on poor relief by the central government. Some imply that the Commonwealth contributed to this, either inadvertently by political weakness, or by more conscious encouragement of greater economic freedom. Dr Hill sees the Commonwealth as a militarily strong, highly centralised system of government, preparing fairly coherent and essentially new policies, whose logic underlies future measures and trends from first permitting and then encouraging the export of corn to ending the privileges of chartered companies in overseas trade and of oligarchies at home. Revolution in government was accompanied by revolutions in agriculture and commerce.[2]

Originally this interpretation was mainly an adaptation of widely accepted views from Archdeacon Cunningham's conspectus of English history. In Dr Hill's most recent versions it has been reinforced by Dr Farnell's interpretation of the Navigation Act. This claims that the Rump and its Councils of State and Trade were dominated by the interests of new men, who had made fortunes in the distant trades of the Atlantic and the East Indies, but especially in the West Indies, and were hostile to traditional policies and to chartered companies. There is contemporary warrant for such views. Goddard called the Long Parliament 'an Iron Parliament, a Trading Parliament' and saw 'the country gentlemen' of the first Protectorate Parliament siding

E

'against the citizens and late Parliament men . . .'.[3] Thomas Scot, Slingsby Bethel and the Commonwealthsmen attacked the the Protectorate's foreign policies for neglecting and ruining the trading interest that they and the Rump had successfully cherished.

Hill and Farnell also stress the Venetian ambassador's alleged claim in 1651 that there was economic progress due to government and trade being ruled by the same powers. But the ambassador was in Madrid, not London, and he combined a low opinion of the Rump's competence and probity with the view that 'the facility with which the English increase their fortunes by trade . . . has made great strides for some time past and is now improved by the protection it receives from Parliament, the government of the Commonwealth and that of its trade being exercised by the same individuals'. By implication he invokes the commonly held view that republics were more beneficial for trade than monarchies, a view that some Commonwealthsmen used in their attack on the Protectorate.[4] According to the republican Henry Neville, the Protectorate was created to make peace with the Dutch and war with Spain, while the 'Humble Petition and Advice' made another Dutch war impossible, 'It is not for a hierarchy to maintain that war.' Thomas Violet, who had lavished economic advice on the councils of both the Commonwealth and the Protectorate, assured Charles II '. . . that King that will be happie must alwaies rule the Merchants. . . . This last twenty years many young Merchants and young gentlemen that have studied the forms and moddells of Commonwealths . . . having beyond seas observed that the Government of Commonwealths equally descends upon Merchants and Tradesmen, nay the common sort of people in some Commonwealths, more than on the Nobilitie and Gentrie. These notions have for this twenty years been the oyl that fed the flame of rebellion in London.'[5]

Just as some contemporaries for polemical reasons chose to argue in terms that still attract historians today, there are also historiographical problems inherited from the pioneering days of economic history. Miss Leonard's *Early History of English Poor Relief* (Cambridge, 1900) had a general and enduring influence, since it apparently demonstrated the truth of Cunningham's conceptions, not only that the privy council was the agent of paternalistic social policies, but also that the execution of such policies was decisively defeated after 1641 to be replaced by *laissez-faire* policies. Although Tawney and Unwin both criticised Cunningham, both supported the view that after 1641 the way was cleared for *laissez-faire* in agriculture and industry. Both Cunningham and Unwin saw this in the context of mercantilism as a state-building policy, of which Cunningham approved as the harbinger of nineteenth-century Prussia and which Unwin condemned. Later J. U. Nef argued that the peculiarity of English developments was due not only to long-term constitutional and administrative differences but also to the great expansion of large-scale industry (1575–1620), which made the resistance to state regulation much stronger and more precocious in England. More particularly C. M. Andrews considered that the Commonwealth's Council of Trade was hostile to chartered companies in overseas trade and favoured free trade, though opposed in this by the Rump.[6] This interpretation of the Council of Trade's aims has been taken to be those of the whole regime by Dr Farnell and Dr Hill, though if these aims were so clear and generally accepted it seems puzzling that the Council of Trade lasted for little more than a year. Andrews believed that it continued after December 1651, but this is not so (see below, page 137).

Yet undeniably the Rump had begun with general good intentions towards trade. The fifth article of the act constituting the Council of State instructed it 'to use all good ways and means for the securing advancement and encouragement of the trade of England and Ireland ... to promote the good of all Foreigne plantations and factories'.[7] Whatever their intentions they were faced by what was probably the worst economic crisis of the century. A run of bad harvests had multiplied the effects of civil war – excise had already increased food prices. 'The harvest of 1646 was ... deficient and the next three were very bad, verging on a dearth.' In 1648 there was 'widespread murrain among cattle', and though there were regional variations in food prices these rose continuously until 1650.[8] This reduced home demand for manufactures, while depression in the cloth industry and foreign trade was intensified by Royalist privateering and French hostility, both of which reached a peak in 1649. After 1648 the higher wartime freight rates of Dutch shipping fell and their competitiveness in the carrying trade of English ports must have increased. Assisted by the stimulus to the Baltic grain trade provided by bad harvests in western and southern Europe, Dutch trade was entering on probably its greatest boom of the century.

The reactions to crisis and depression followed the pattern of the 1620s or 1641. Traditionally merchants, and especially the Merchant Adventurers (whose company had a monopoly of the export of cloth to the Netherlands and Germany), had blamed slumps in exports on defective manufacture; clothiers often blamed restrictions on export due to privileges of companies. Yet important groups of clothiers, especially from the new draperies, favoured some form of industrial regulation through corporate bodies. Many of the richer clothiers were hostile to middlemen in the wool trade and demanded that wool should be sold only direct to clothiers. Landowners resisted this as seeking a monopoly that would lower wool prices, although accepting the merchants' and clothiers' proposition for export of wool. The attack on chartered companies in overseas trade and demands for free trade were also often a manifestation of resentment by the provinces and outports at London's predominance (perhaps three-quarters of total foreign trade in 1640), since the important companies were dominated by Londoners. Moreover, between 1600 and 1640 that predominance in the staple export of cloth had increased; the total share of the outports had declined, though Hull, Exeter and to a lesser extent Newcastle remained comparatively flourishing.[9] Traditionally the main export had been expensive, mainly unfinished broadcloth, but its relative importance was declining, as that of the cheaper new draperies grew. The major change in overseas trade between 1640 and 1662 was the growth of re-exports of tobacco and sugar. Very little is known about the exact chronology of this; probably most of it came after 1650, but it was already under way before. Again the chief beneficiary was London; if it ultimately provided new prosperity for Bristol, any such growth before 1650 must have been outweighed by the dislocation of its Irish trade.

Contemporaries saw the seriousness of the immediate crisis and were even more jealous of Dutch success than in the 1620s. Henry Robinson claimed that export trade 'is not one fourth part of what it was ten years ago as will appear by the receipt of Customs' and that 'our woollen manufacture . . . through continuance of this warr and rot of sheepe are reduced to about one quarter of what they were . . .'. But it was essentially traditional grievances and remedies that were presented in pamphlets and to Parliament from 1646. As well as the traditional attacks on privileged companies by outports and interlopers, the Levellers' programmes included what seemed more sweeping demands for freedom of trade, though the chief target was still the Merchant Adventurers, whose privileges had been confirmed by Parliament. Thanks to a multiplicity of conflicting demands and interests, the only remedy on which there was general agreement in 1648, as earlier and later when political distractions were less acute, was the prohibition of the export of wool. The Commons had attempted to lessen their unpopularity by taking off the excise on meat and salt in June 1647, 'then the tumults and ryotts began in the severall counties which hath much obstructed the increase of the receipts ever since'.[10]

From its beginning some had seen the Long Parliament as called to work a general renovation of which the first apostle was to have been Comenius. After his departure the circle round Hartlib and Dury had continued to plan hopefully; Sir Cheney Culpeper was much concerned with economic matters and had parliamentary contacts. From 1646 their activity increased and they were associated with anti-Presbyterians in the struggle for toleration, so that after 1648 they had what seemed hopeful contacts with those in power. Hartlib, as well as planning educational reform, was, like Culpeper, particularly concerned with agricultural and technical improvements. Another of their associates, Henry Robinson, had long- and well-considered plans for economic and social reforms inspired by Dutch examples, and he too seemed to have more opportunities to influence affairs under the Commonwealth.[11]

The Rump also inherited policies and attitudes towards trade and industry adumbrated by the Long Parliament and its committees. Of more immediate importance were the reactions of local leaders to dearth and depression. In most counties by 1648 there had been a political and social break with the groups who had ruled before 1642, but if they were new men they did not necessarily break with the traditional expedients for dealing with such crises. Before considering the new regime's efforts, it may be worth seeking a basis of comparison with the prescriptions of radical opinion represented in the *Moderate*, the pro-Leveller weekly. Its editorials were mainly concerned with constitutional problems such as the need for a new representative, or toleration; it advocated law reform and advertised more Utopian programmes, such as Jubbes's agrarian reforms.

It also reported both general and local reactions to the economic crisis. It published London's petitions, demanding 'some effectual course for the recovery and increasing of the almost lost Trade and Manufacture of this City and Kingdom'. Before and after Pride's Purge a major theme was the oppressiveness of taxation; until February 1649 the main target was the excise, thereafter the monthly assessment. It also publicised abuses from free quarter and billeting. Distress and inability to pay taxes were blamed on lack of trade and resulting unemployment in Dorset and Essex. The reporting of dearth concentrated on the north, especially on Cumberland and Westmorland. Parliament's efforts to encourage imports of grain were discounted, because of the people's poverty. (However, the arrival of cargoes of rye at Hull, causing the price to fall from near £3 a quarter to under £2, was reported.) It noted very briefly the shortage of bullion and coin and printed the army petitions which made abuses of clipped money a major grievance. A great deal of space was given to the army's grievances, but the *Moderate* believed the troops could be paid from the proceeds of crown, delinquents' and church lands and found further common ground with civilians in demands for full investigation of all committee men's accounts.[12] Its basic remedy was political change along Leveller lines. It included in passing exhortations to set the poor on work, so general that no one would have disagreed. What is remarkable is the *Moderate's* silence in 1649 about engrossers, forestallers, badgers, maltsters and alehouses, the traditional targets in times of dearth.

Gardiner long ago pointed out that the Rump's policy towards such distress was the traditional one. This was also what some local authorities had vigorously attempted before 1649. In October and November 1647 the Wiltshire justices regulated maltsters and corn markets to give priority to sales to the poor. In 1648 voluntary agreements, followed by elaborate orders at Quarter Sessions and Assizes, arranged for a proportion of all barley marketed to be sold at cheap rates to the poor and a further proportion to be levied for their use. There was also an offensive against alehouses. The grand jury complained of neglect of these orders and asked for a ban on all buying by maltsters until September. In Cheshire Mr Morrill has shown that there was stringent and probably effective control of maltsters, badgers, corn markets and alehouses in the interests of the poor from 1648 onwards. In Somerset from 1647 J.P.s were active restraining maltsters, badgers and alehouses and more active against vagrants than in Cheshire. The order book for the Assizes shows action against maltsters and alehouses in Cornwall and against alehouses in Devon and testifies to the general revival of local government in the western circuit.[13]

The Long Parliament itself had begun to move towards a general policy for poor relief with the ordinance of December 1647 establishing the London corporation of the poor and offering it as a model for other towns. From 1647 the clothiers had been campaigning against the staplers and all other middlemen in wool trade as engrossers, demanding effective prohibition of the export of wool and regulation of old and new draperies by enforcing apprenticeship and sealing of cloth. The Commons' committee on these problems, despite protests of staplers, broggers and landowners, favoured some restrictions on middlemen and enforcement of apprenticeship on all artificers in the cloth industry. In October 1648 its powers were extended to consider means to remedy abuses in manufacture of old and new draperies and silk and 'the Grounds of the Decay of Trade in General'.[14] The work of this committee was invoked under the Rump, though its report was never presented to the Commons.

More immediately the Rump had to see that the distractions caused by the end of monarchy did not interrupt the general trend of local actions about the dearth. Their solicitor at the king's trial, John Cook, in *Unum Necessarium* (1648) had blamed the dearth on covetousness, engrossers and drunkards and called for regulation of prices and suppression of alehouses. Sergeant Thorp in his charge to the York Assizes in March 1649 was mainly concerned to defend the new form of government, but he also urged the grand jury to enquire into offences 'against the plenty of the Commonwealth' and more particularly 'whatsoever tends to inhance the Price of Victuall for unlawfull increasing particular men's profits by it, this is an offence against the plenty of it'. He defined forestalling and engrossing and the offence of conspiring 'to sell victuals at unreasonable prices' and explained the laws regulating the leather trades, labourers, weights and measures, and overseers of the poor.[15]

Meanwhile the Rump itself had been considering how to keep prices of provisions for the poor 'at reasonable rates'. They were urged on by a petition from London; on 19 March they asked the Common Council to advise how to provide the poor with corn and coal and instructed the speaker to write to the J.P.s to execute the laws against engrossing and 'that the Stock of every Parish be so supplied as the poor . . . may be relieved with corn and other necessaries . . .'. In Somerset a presentment by the grand jury and an order by the assizes were needed in July to put these and other matters into execution. If this argues that the letter was ineffective, we must also note that the other counties of the western circuit did not receive special orders. The Council of State ordered the attorney-general to prosecute a merchant for engrossing corn on the petition of Ipswich, 'to the end the poore people may see that care is taken of them in tyme of dearth'. It eventually adopted an attitude of cautious enquiry towards a riot about taking toll corn for the poor in High Wycombe.[16]

The new regime in London co-operated enthusiastically against engrossers and for the relief of the poor. Urged on by the Common Council, the act of October 1650 controlling the corn and meal trade and prohibiting bolting mills was passed 'being so much of publique concernement and for the generall goode of the poore'. Earlier the Rump had extended the power of London's Corporation of the Poor and endowed it with two houses and £1000 per annum to set the poor on work. The Common Council urged it to set up similar corporations elsewhere and believed it ready to do so. The Rump's 'Committee for setting the Poor on Work' wanted general commissions of charitable uses to enquire into money given for the poor and sale of fabrics of superfluous churches to 'be employed for a stock for use of the Poor'. On 4 April the house resolved that Lichfield Cathedral be used to set the poor on work and that the commissions should be issued. Miss James may well be correct in saying that in the long run London's corporation devoted most energy to repressing vagrants, but she does not mention some more constructive efforts. After the battle of Worcester the assize judge got the grand jury to raise £500 'out of the County for the finding of the poor people of the City materialls to set them on work to releeve themselves . . .'. The Council of State itself set in motion relief for the poor of Bocking. Even when pressure from dearth was less in March 1651, the Rump sweetened the unpopularity of the new import on coal by providing that a proportion should go to relieve the poor. This raised £4190 in 1652–3 and £5500 the next year. Given the small total of local rates, this first national tax for poor relief was not negligible.[17]

Miss James's view 'that during the Interregnum the emphasis was shifted from the employment of the poor to the suppression of the vagrant' seems based on illusions about the 1630s derived from Miss Leonard. The Commonwealth's intentions were at least as good as those of the Privy Council before 1640; in some places the results were better, but there is not yet enough evidence for a general comparison. Probably most local authorities at any time showed more enthusiasm about harassing vagrants than in more constructive efforts.[18]

The dearth cured itself, whatever the government did or failed to do. Its waning helped to delay any general measure for codifying and reforming the poor law and increased the dissatisfaction of reformers with the Rump. By November 1650 William Hickman was urging Cromwell that, without speedy constitutional change, other reforms would fail, while Peter Chamberlen and Samuel Chidley also soon despaired of the Rump. Bills for relief and for setting the poor on work were still being debated in February 1653.[19]

Two other problems, the coinage and the cloth industry, demanded attention in 1649. Domestic trade was hindered by a high proportion of light coins, due to clipping and considerable counterfeiting. No silver came to the Mint, because the mint price was lower than the market price; it was believed that both coin and bullion were being exported. Given the disruption of export trade and the considerable imports of grain, these symptoms were presumably aggravated by a seriously adverse balance of trade. As we have seen, the merchants' traditional remedy for improving exports was regulation of the quality of cloth, which was also advocated by some clothiers in 1649, chiefly those dominant in Leeds, Norwich and Essex. But complaints from Hamburg about frauds in English cloth were the immediate reason for the Council of State's consideration of an act to regulate the manufacture of woollen cloth.[20]

The basic problems seemed much the same as in the early 1620s and one of the first from whom the Council sought advice was Sir Ralph Maddison, who had taken part in the debates of 1622. He remained a fervent disciple of Malynes, advocating strict control of foreign exchange transactions to preserve the par of sterling. For the next couple of years elaborate investigations were made into the true par of English and foreign coins, attempts were made to discover the balance of trade from the customs accounts and information about mint ratios and currency laws in other countries was collected. The desirability of enhancing the coinage, of altering the mint ratio and prices, of controlling trade in bullion, of milling coins and of minting farthings were all debated. As a result of all this, little was done. Counterfeiting and clipping were made treason; another act guaranteed imports of bullion from seizure and allowed re-export, provided one-third was taken to the Mint to be coined. A bill to prevent export of English coin and bullion was introduced, but never passed. As in the 1620s extensive debate and dissatisfaction failed to produce any changes in monetary policies.[21]

Again, as in the 1620s, lowering the rate of interest proved an easier and swifter decision. This appeared to follow the advice of Robinson and many others who believed that low interest rates were fundamental to Dutch success. But the immediate reason for reducing interest to 6 per cent was to promote 'the more ready sale of lands for the Commonwealth', though the act of 1651, like that of 1624, hoped to remedy 'the general fall . . . of the value of land and the prizes of . . .

Merchandize' and to revive trade. It also empowered the Commissioners of the Great Seal 'to moderate Interest incurred' between 1 September 1642 and 1 February 1648 according to circumstances and equity.[22] It had taken the Rump two years and five months to implement its first resolution.

But there were also differences in the approach to economic problems in 1650 as against 1622, quite apart from differences in the political and international situations. The new topics were the need for free ports and for encouraging immigration. The first, discussion of which went back to the 1620s, was undoubtedly assisted by the success of the composition trade at Dover in the 1630s which had made it virtually a free port. Interest in encouraging immigration grew because, like low customs and low interest rates, it was seen as one of the secrets of Dutch success and as a remedy for the emigration of the 1630s. From 1640 a frequent theme had been the loss of skilled workers by emigration, not so much to the colonies, as to Europe. Free ports were the means to build up re-export trade in staple commodities and colonial goods. Immigration was to attract skill and capital by allowing aliens to enjoy the same rights and privileges as Englishmen through naturalisation. The Levellers had claimed that men's rights should not be curtailed by restrictive privileges claimed by corporations, and advocacy of easy general naturalisation often went with hostility to corporate privileges. In 1651 Hugh Peters wanted freedom for all strangers and 'Freedom for all that will (and are capable thereof) to . . . bee free of that Trade without paying anie for freedom either of the Citie or Companie . . .'. The less radical Henry Robinson advocated general naturalisation in order to improve the general level of skill and industry by competition, even though individuals might suffer. Thomas Violet saw naturalisation as a means of attracting Dutch capital. Both believed that free ports should be complemented by general naturalisation.[23]

Throughout the second half of the seventeenth century general naturalisation was fiercely opposed by corporations. In 1649 London was reviving traditional restrictions on foreigners.[24] If the main aim of general naturalisation was to strengthen the economy with Dutch capital and skill, plans for union with the Dutch might hold hopes of doing this with less sacrifice of corporate privileges. The reasons for the English offer of union in 1651 and the Dutch refusal were basically political, but it held prospects of economic advantage to England. Cromwell's offer in 1653 to divide world trade with the Dutch attempted to offer the Dutch an incentive that seems to have been lacking in 1651.[25]

In choosing to seek union and – when that failed – war, the Rump concentrated on mobilising immediate force, rather than on a long-term anti-Dutch strategy of trying to increase material wealth by new policies that might alienate traditional corporate interests.

The Rump never considered general naturalisation, as opposed to that of named individuals. But in December 1649 it instructed the Navy Committee to consult with merchants and others about free ports. In January the Council of State asked for speedy decision on petitions from the East India, Levant and Eastland companies which involved 'some restraint to General Liberty of Trade' and an act was ordered to be prepared 'for settling Commissioners as a Standing Council for ordering and Regulating Trade'. Meanwhile the East India Company's joint stock was confirmed and it was licensed to export bullion and the Council of State was receiving petitions from merchants, companies and shipowners; the Act for the Council of Trade was not passed until 1 August. This attempted to delegate and systematise the functions of diagnosis, collection of information and especially arbitration which the Council of State and committees had attempted, mainly in response to the depression and to lobbying. The instructions owed something to the precedents of the commission of 1622, but were directly influenced by the aspirations of more recent expositors. The second instruction puts long-standing resentment of London's dominance in a form resembling Henry Robinson's pleas for redistribution of trade and industry, 'that one part may not abound with trade and another remain poor . . . for want of the same'. The third, like Robinson and Hartlib, called for consultation to improve river navigation and ports. The information to be collected was to provide 'a perfect Ballance of Trade, establish the intrinsic par of English and foreign coins' and 'the gain or loss that comes to the Commonwealth by the Exchange now used by Merchants' (instructions 6 and 7). The first instruction required them to advise how manufactures could be 'well and truly wrought'. They were to consider how to encourage exports, how to regulate customs and excise to provide revenue without hindering trade, where and how free ports should be established, how to encourage fishing and the management of the plantations so that they alone might supply England's wants. These were all acceptable general aims, however controversial the specific means of attaining them might be. Much more immediately controversial were the ninth instruction, to consider whether 'a more open and free Trade than that of Companies and Societies' was necessary, while ensuring 'that Government and Order in Trade may be preserved', and the tenth to review the orders and constitutions of companies of merchants and craftsmen so that any tendency 'to the hurt of the publique' may be ended as Parliament directs.[26]

The Act named fifteen commissioners, any five of whom could act; unfortunately no records of their meetings and attendance survives, so it seems best to deal with what is certainly known about the Council's actions and then with uncertainties, including inferences from analysing its membership. The most difficult task set the Council was about free trade; in principle almost everyone favoured some kind of regulation of industry. Hugh Peters and Walwyn came nearest to expressing consistent hostility to all forms of corporate regulation, but they are exceptional. Attacks on the privileges of chartered companies were always strongest in times of depression; the Civil War had left a confused legacy. The chartered companies had perforce supported Parliament, while Charles had granted freedom of trade to merchants in Bristol and elsewhere in violation of the privileges of the Merchant Adventurers, the Eastland, Russia and Levant Companies. Interlopers hoped that the Rump might break with the Long Parliament's policies, hence the companies' petitions. Virginia, Maryland and the main West Indian colonies were still controlled by Royalists whose authority in many cases derived from proprietary patents; in this context to support the Rump was to attack chartered privileges.

The narrative of the Council's work shows that it made seven reports to Parliament or the Council of State in its first five months and only eight in its remaining twelve months. In January 1650 the report about encouraging import of bullion produced the only legislation by Parliament, the Act being passed the following day. There is no evidence of doctrinaire hostility to chartered companies; it favoured allowing the East Indian Company its customary export of bullion; the full demands of both the Guinea Company and the free traders were rejected, the company being awarded a fourteen-year monopoly of the coast where it had factories and the rest being left free. For the Greenland Company it confirmed the Long Parliament's grant of exclusive rights to the two most valuable sounds, leaving the others free, each to be fished by a joint stock. This award was for a year, the first step to perfecting 'a Free Trade at Greenland under due Regulation'.[27]

The Council's work on domestic trade and industry resulted in only one report being submitted for regulating the trade of 'dornix weaving' in Norfolk and Suffolk. Others about regulating dyeing, gold and silver thread and Colchester bays were ready but never delivered. They claimed to have made progress in settling differences among various companies, notably the clothworkers, skinners and upholsterers and in 'that great dispute between the clothier, grower, stapler, and brogger and jobber in the buying of wool'. They also produced general reports calling for regulation and inspection of manufactures to prevent frauds and abuses as the means 'to regulate or settle a forraigne Trade'; Parliament was to settle 'some way for the viewing, confirming or rectifying of the By Lawes . . . now in use by the severall Societyes of Merchants and Manufacturers; and for the hearinge . . . and determining' cases in handicraft trades.[28] The aim was regulation through corporate bodies themselves subject to review and regulation; it is possible, but less certain, that their attitude towards chartered companies in foreign trade was the same.

Of the fifteen members of the Council only five were M.P.s, three of whom were members of the Council of State: Sir Henry Vane, Thomas Challoner (whom the godly regarded as a libertine) and (from 1651) Richard Salwey; the other two, John Ash, the great Somerset clothier, and Thomas Boon, an important Dartmouth merchant, were more likely to have time for this Council. Other provincials were Henry Thompson, alderman of York, William Greenwood of Yarmouth and perhaps John Fowles. Londoners were William Methwold, a leading member of the East India Company, with which another member, Alderman Fowke, was at loggerheads and Maurice Thompson, a leading colonial merchant. Sir Ralph Maddison was there as an expert on exchange and mint affairs, as probably was Edward Johnson. Sir Robert Honeywood was Vane's brother-in-law and had resided much in Holland; he and his wife were acquainted with the Hartlib circle, a leading member of which, Sir Cheney Culpeper, was also a member. Thus the membership represented a variety of interests and was not dominated by Londoners, still less by great London companies.[29]

The Council also had close connections with Hartlib's circle through its staff. Its secretary, Benjamin Worsley, had been in lengthy correspondence with Dury and Hartlib on religious, alchemical and technological matters, and in 1649 about plans for setting up a parliamentary commission to govern Virginia. Worsley hoped to become secretary to the new governor and that Hartlib would be secretary to the commissioners. His residence in Holland had made him acutely aware of Dutch dominance of English colonial trade. He expected the important Dorset M.P., John Trenchard, and his son-in-law, John Sadler, to support these plans. He was in correspondence with Lady Honeywood, Vane's [sister. He himself recommended Maurice Thompson, William Pennoyer and Martin Noel as suitable commissioners and was involved with the first two in putting these plans to the Admiralty Committee. Thus Worsley had important connections with Parliament and City before becoming secretary. Hartlib's son was Worsley's clerk and Hartlib himself took a direct interest in the Council's business.[30]

Thomas Violet also claimed to have influenced the Council. He claimed Lord President Bradshaw's patronage and had been much involved in consultations about mint affairs. Worsley was the more important and reputable figure: he influenced the instructions for Charles II's first Council of Trade and became Shaftesbury's chief economic adviser. Both claimed to have helped draft the Navigation Act. Worsley wrote: 'I was the first sollicitour for the Act . . . and putt the first fyle to it and after writt the Advocate in defence of it'. Violet reproduced the official narrative of the Council of Trade's work and added to its reports 'concerning restraint of goods of forraign growth to be imported in forraigne bottomes' to the Council of State of 4 April and 31 July 1651: 'This Act I dayly attended and drew the draft of it, it hath been the bane of Dutch greatness and will reduce them to reason.'[31]

Whatever their contributions may have been, the surviving evidence supports Professor Harper's view that the Council of Trade played an important part in the making of the act. He has also shown that the Act was almost certainly different in principle from the measures proposed by Trinity House, the Levant and Eastland Companies which were considered by the Council of Trade in 1650. The Act's main principle, that imports should be in English ships or those of countries producing them, had been proposed in 1622. Identifying the Act's authors – whether Oliver St John or the merchants Maurice Thompson and James Drax – is less important than its purpose. That it was more hostile to Dutch interests fits in with Worsley's and Violet's claims and those of the Council, if Dr Hinton's suggestion that *The Advocate* may contain one of its memorials is accepted.[32] Nevertheless the earlier proposals were concerned about the competition of Dutch shipping and the dominance of the Dutch entrepôt in Baltic and extra-European commodities. Andrews claimed the Act was in the interest of the chartered companies, Hinton and Farnell that it was against those interests. There is no evidence that any company lobbied for the Act, but this does not show that the act was destructive of the companies' interests, or that it was the work of a group of interlopers and free traders as Farnell suggests.

The leader of this group was Maurice Thompson, 'the non-company, interloping, free merchant par excellence'. He had indeed been an associate of Courteen in his Crown-sponsored violation of the East India Company's charter and had also infringed the Guinea Company's claim to monopolise African trade. By 1649 he was a leading member of the East India Company, wanting to change it from a joint stock to a regulated company, but this scarcely makes him a doctrinaire enemy of chartered companies. Moreover the Act of 1651 was less favourable to merchants like Thompson than the Act of 1650, piloted through the House by his brother, George, since it allowed direct exports from the colonies to other countries even in foreign ships, while allowing imports direct from other countries to the colonies in English ships, or ships of the countries producing those commodities.[33]

In the short run neither Act was enforced effectively enough to exclude the Dutch from the colonial trades. In the long run the 1651 Act may be the beginning of a change to national statutory regulation of foreign trade, instead of regulation through chartered companies supplemented by statutes. More immediately the East India and Levant Companies benefited from it and the Eastland Company approved of it. The traditional target of free-trade agitations, the Merchant Adventurers, had their import trade restricted, but so did their traditional enemies, the interlopers in the entrepôts of Hamburg and the Netherlands. A more extreme form of Dr Hinton's interpretation, that the Act was concerned with power and national interest, is that of Dr J. A. Williamson. He argued that the Act was not 'intended to benefit English trade', but to increase shipping and to ensure 'national safety', not the interest 'of any particular clique'. Yet Trinity House put forward very specific proposals to promote shipping which were apparently ignored in framing the Act.[34] However Hinton rightly argues that for Worsley and perhaps for the Council of Trade free ports were to be the main expedient for increasing trade (Violet, Maddison and Robinson took the same view). Unlike the Restoration Acts, that of 1651 did not provide for an English monopoly in entrepôt trade in colonial wares, and it was during the genesis of the Restoration Acts that plans for free ports were finally abandoned. The most important specific instruction to the Council of Trade was to produce a plan for free ports, yet their report was never even presented, while the Navigation Act, unlike so many bills before the Rump, was enacted. How did this come about?

The Council appointed a committee to deal with free ports.

Unfortunately neither its membership nor the final report is known, but Dr Hinton suggests very plausibly that its views are expressed in Worsley's pamphlet, *Free Ports*. Dr Farnell believes that free ports got sincere support only from the enemies of chartered companies. Faced with the fact that 'aldermanic governors of monopoly trading companies' were members of the committee to petition that London should be a free port, Farnell argues that the real support came from common councilmen associated with the new trades. Yet Chiverton, the Governor of the Eastland Company, a member of the London committee, and three other important members of the Levant and East India Companies, certified to the Council of Trade's committee that free ports without customs on re-exports 'and forbearance of the Custom of the rest until sale be made will increase the Shipping, Navigacon and Trade of this Nacon', especially if all re-exports were in English ships. The Merchant Adventurers, or any others trading to the Dutch and Hamburg entrepôts, would have gained from free ports, if they could have imported goods for re-export that were prohibited by the Navigation Act, as not being of the growth of those countries. This may explain why there were three Merchant Adventurers on the committee to maintain London's claim to the Council of State 'with the best reasons they canne'.[35]

Undoubtedly some advocates of free ports, like Violet, were very hostile to the companies, and this view was strongly put to the Council of Trade: 'Trade being the Bassis and well being of a Commonwealth the way to obtain it is to make it a free trade and not to bind up in-egenious Spiritts by Exemptions and Priviledges . . . granted . . . Companies . . .'.[36] As we have seen, the Council cannot be shown to have followed this line in its known dealings with companies. The fact that it probably approved free ports does not demonstrate its hostility to companies. What is certain is that free ports rallied a variety of contradictory interests in their support. They aroused London's apprehension, because they were seen by the outports as a means to check London's dominance; within London they fed the animosities between advocates of free trade and their opponents. For some they were the complement to general naturalisation, or union with the Dutch. The difficulty of producing a plan that would reconcile all these expectations and interests probably contributed to the ending of the Council of Trade itself.

The Council was first conceived to deal with the problems of depression at the beginning of 1650; by the time it was instituted in August, the

Commonwealth's power was about to be asserted at Dunbar. By the end of 1650 the quest for power and security was producing plans for union with the Dutch, of which several members of the Council, perhaps including Vane, probably approved and of which their plans for free ports were a complement. The failure of the union produced the Navigation Act, consultations about which may have delayed work on proposals for free ports and probably made generally acceptable ones more difficult to achieve. On 22 September 1651 the Council presented its general report on manufacturers, lack of resolutions on which suspended much of their business. Delay in the Rump's decisions was common enough, but they gave a swift and decisive indirect answer: on 26 September they renewed the Council's powers only until 31 December 1651, thus reversing the earlier decision to have a standing commission. This extension may have been in the hope of producing the plan for free ports.[37]

But anxiety about free ports was only one reason for London's resentment against the Council. One of its early reports had been 'about enlarging the number of meal markets for the ease of the inhabitants about London'. The Common Council had just sponsored the act for controlling the meal trade and later violently resisted other proposals to increase the number of markets. As a result of intervention by the Council, tables of rates for garbling, gauging and measuring were to be set up at convenient places. Londoners were in a minority on a body which was a forum for attacks on Londoners. The Merchant Adventurers of York, Hull, Newcastle and Leeds were urged on by a member of the Council, Alderman Thompson of York, to petition against Londoners trading at fairs and markets north of the Trent and for the confirmation and strengthening of the Merchant Adventurers' privileges. Merchants and citizens of York in their petition asked for the same prohibition, as Londoners 'ingrosse . . . all Trade to themselves and hinder all propertion of Trade which of right belongs to other Countries'. They complained of the exclusion of non-Londoners from the Greenland and Muscovy Companies; they demanded regulation and enforcement of apprenticeship in the cloth industry, while demanding that all cloth shipped from Hull and other northern ports should be marketed and sealed at York. Their opinion was that 'Trade bee not left loose but may be regulated by Companies'.[38]

These provincial exponents of corporate regulation and opponents of Londoners' engrossing would not necessarily welcome the Council of Trade's demand for an authority to review all orders and bye-laws by corporations. As we have seen, the Council complained that the failure to act on this report left many suitors in suspense. But another report, completed on 26 September 1651, after lengthy hearings, condemned Newcastle Corporation's assertion of its privileges over navigation in the Tyne in order to extort dues from shipmasters, and to harass craftsmen in North Shields, who were not members of its guilds.[39] Moreover the east coast outports resented the effects of the Navigation Act, for which the Council was presumably blamed, in hindering their imports from the Dutch entrepôt. This was seen as a plot by Londoners to hinder their cloth exports and make them pay high prices for colonial and staple goods at London. More generally provincials complained that the act had 'upon it only a London stamp . . . most of the outports [are] not capable of the foreign Trade to Indies and Turkey, the Londoners having the sole trade, doe set what price they please whereby . . . the outports are undone . . . the Country bought to the Divotion of the Citty'. Not content with this they procured licences for prohibited commodities, just as they had done when French wines were prohibited, which was 'a meer London interest, pretending it would prove a great prejudice to the French'.[40] Thus it seems likely that the Council alienated or threatened a variety of London and provincial interests and provided the Rump with plenty of excuses for procrastination. Even if its existence had been prolonged, the possibilities of effective action would have been overwhelmed by the necessities of the Dutch War.

If the Dutch War distracted the Rump from any clear domestic policy, it did give immediate remedies for some, perhaps the main, problems at which the Navigation Act had been aimed. It checked Dutch trade, and by taking over 1000 Dutch prizes at last provided the English with economical carriers of bulk cargoes, which they had so conspicuously failed to build for themselves. The prize goods temporarily increased entrepôt trade (the object of the plans for free ports) and at last brought some bullion to the Mint. The customs' figures suggest that the volume of trade remained the same. By 1653 London claimed to be so impoverished by 'the great decay and interruption of trade both domestique and forreigne' that a quarter of its inhabitants were too poor to be charged in the assessment.[41] Those outports whose cloth trade had best survived London's competition before 1640 suffered most and soonest. The cloth exports of the east coast ports and Exeter were mainly to the Netherlands. The direct Baltic trade was completely lost, the trades to Hamburg and to the Mediterranean through the

Channel were seriously interrupted and French trade continued to suffer from prohibitions and reprisals. Bristol and the West Country ports, apart from Exeter, probably suffered least and gained most from prizes. Despite a good harvest in 1652 the whole cloth industry was depressed.

The Rump in its last six months was again busy with traditional remedies for depression; it was both spurred on and distracted by the growing discontent of the army. Many of the clothiers' demands, under discussion since 1647, were brought nearer to being met than ever before. After the end of the Council of Trade the disputes between clothiers and middlemen in the wool trade were referred to the Council of State and its committees. In April 1652 another complaint from Hamburg about defective English cloth and the petitions from overseas' trading companies received attention. But it was not until November 1652 that pressure from the clothiers, especially in Essex, began to be effective. The clothiers of Coggeshall, who had petitioned the Council of Trade for authority to regulate and seal manufactures, now complained of the complete stoppage of trade to the Straits 'so that every 20^{li} per ann [was] paying 5^{li} yearly to the poor'. They also complained that the townspeople had lent £6000 on the public faith, much of it borrowed at interest and all still awaiting repayment.[42]

By February 1653 the Council of State had drafted an act to reform abuses in the cloth industry. This covered both old and new draperies and was based on clothiers' petitions so that it is likely to have included provisions for regulation, enforcement of apprenticeship and sealing. Bills 'for further providing for and setting on Work the Poor' and for the public faith debt achieved second readings. It was resolved to take off the excise on woollens. If the Rump had survived, this would not have had to wait until the general reduction of the excises in 1654;[43] it also seems likely that regulation of the cloth industry and perhaps a new poor law would have been enacted.

The Rump's conservatism and reluctance to override corporate privileges or vested interests appear in prolonged failures to act. It failed to abolish the aulnage, a long-standing grievance to clothiers and an obstacle to regulating quality. The army's constantly repeated demand for freedom for ex-soldiers to practise trades without apprenticeship or buying their freedom was not met until the Protectorate. The Council failed to override the moneyers and introduce milling of coins and found its advocacy of a bill to relieve delinquents' tenants unavailing. It might be argued that the tendency to frustrate positive action encouraged *laissez-faire*. But even if the Rump were merely a collection of log-rolling self-seekers, as the Levellers had always claimed and as Violet did after its dissolution, this does not endow them with policies of *laissez-faire*. Collectively they did attack engrossers and middlemen, desired to set the poor on work, set up a company to regulate the cloth industry of Norwich and Norfolk, enacted seven-year apprenticeship in book-printing and approved a privileged corporation of seamen.[44]

If there were views on general economic policies as clear-cut and divisive as those on tithes, commissions for propagating the Gospel or law reform, they are concealed from us. The record suggests lack of persistence in either positive or negative policies. Sometimes this may have been due to clashes of interests or opinions, more often it was probably due to preoccupation with security and war finance and to investing time in interminable proceedings about delinquents' lands. The Dutch War first absolved the regime from pursuing the questions raised by the Council of Trade, then made it necessary to deal with a new depression and at the same time to retain the good will of the great trading companies.

The assumption that political deadlock at the centre was likely to produce rapidly new attitudes and behaviour in local government seems based on false assumptions about the nature of English government before 1640. These imply that only constant intervention and supervision by the Privy Council controlled the selfishness of landowners and traders. Without these they would have ground the faces of the poor in uninhibited pursuit of economic individualism and of free markets for labour and capital. Undoubtedly there were many selfish individuals prepared to profit from the misfortunes of others, but generally they denounced in others what they forgave in themselves. In times of dearth and depression the task of maintaining order was likely to become impossibly difficult for local élites unless they were seen to make efforts to control the corn trade and relieve the poor. Pressures to do this came as much from fears or threats of riots, the acceptance of custom or even the call of conscience, as from orders or threats by the Privy Council – 'The poor will not be famished if they can by any means prevent it.'

John Cook also observed that some of the strongest opposition was not from gentry or townspeople: 'What saies the husbandman, if Corne be deare but one year in seven, then everyone labours to abate the price, but in plentifull years . . . who labours to make it dearer . . . let me sell as the Market goes. . . .'[45] The Essex grand and hundred juries were concerned with much the same kind of presentments under the Commonwealth as in the 1560s under Tudor paternalism.[46] It is yet to be shown that 'the new men' in the local communities in 1649 had new ideas for dealing with dearth and depression. In the 1660s, spurred by decaying rents, the Commons did labour to make corn dearer and had begun to do so in 1654.

The pattern of overseas trade was probably beginning to change fairly quickly after about 1650. Baltic trade became less dominated by Danzig's grain exports, while exports of iron from Sweden and raw materials from her Baltic empire and elsewhere became more important. English trade to the area changed from a favourable to an unfavourable balance as imports of raw materials and iron grew. Neither the Eastland Company nor the Navigation Acts could reverse this trend and create a favourable balance. The growth of colonial trade, especially in sugar, was particularly rapid; the 1651 Navigation Act showed awareness of this, but was much less well designed than its successors after 1660 for creating a colonial monopoly for English merchants. After 1660 the building up of this monopoly proved an acceptable substitute for free ports; the Rump's preference for war with the Dutch to pursuing plans for free ports had proved decisive.

Its quest for security brought the Commonwealth unprecedently strong armed forces to defend its interests at home and abroad. They made feasible the sort of attack on Dutch interests already desired in the 1620s, though the Navigation Act did not satisfy the full demands of English shipowners about exports. They made possible the purging of county committees and borough corporations, but later questions of how far to require taking of the Engagement and how severely to deal with its opponents divided the Rump. Many members, especially those who had resumed their seats after a period of absence, opposed severe measures. Such members were likely to favour a sort of negative permissiveness (negative towards innovations, permissive towards established interests), to prefer procrastination unless it clearly added to immediate dangers, which was seldom the case with economic questions. Such established interests were not necessarily only those of urban oligarchs and wealthy landowners. The range of possible effects is illustrated by the contrast between the completion of the draining of the Great Level by the restored Adventurers under the act of 1649, and the triumph of the commoners over attempts to restore and continue prewar drainage works and schemes in the northern fenland. Thus apart from jealousy about delegating executive power, the setting up of a body to receive complaints about abuses of corporate privilege, let alone one to review all bye-laws, would seem rash. The Council of Trade's proposals for regulating industry and trade resemble the 1622 commission's instructions; although political remodelling of borough corporations flourished down to 1688, plans for general regulation of the cloth industry were as abortive after 1651 as before. Yet regulation by local options continued to flourish and was especially strong in Essex. The only clear example of a conscious acceptance of arguments for *laissez-faire* was the removal of restrictions on exports of bullion after 1660, but the Rump had followed the traditional policy.[47]

More immediately the 'Instrument of Government', by setting up a stronger executive less constantly dependent on fluctuating parliamentary moods and attendances, made more consistent action possible. The main practical effect may have been in encouraging alien immigration in addition to the reception of the Jews. There was more consistency in the intentions of the foreign and especially of the domestic economic policies between Commonwealth and Protectorate than the Commonwealthsmen allowed.[48] Cromwell was the heir of the more constructive efforts of the Rump's last phase in these, as in its plans to reform the law.

6. Cromwell's Ordinances: The Early Legislation of the Protectorate

IVAN ROOTS

BAREBONE'S Parliament dissolved itself on the morning of 12 December 1653: in Sir Arthur Hesilrige's words, 'Some of them ran to Whitehall and returned their power; whence it came, thither it went.' It went to Lord General Oliver Cromwell, who made only a perfunctory gesture of surprise. 'The seeming willingness' of the Assembly to go was, in fact, very welcome. Cromwell and his leading associates, both military and civilian, had been exasperated by the eagerness of radical groups there to sap at both 'ministry and property'. The fact that he could 'not do what he would do' was obvious to all and for weeks past men had been wondering if he would resort to 'the old way of a purge' or to 'the new one of a dissolution'. A voluntary resignation of powers signed by his good friends Sir Charles Wolseley, Sir Gilbert Pickering, Walter Strickland, Sir Anthony Ashley Cooper and a majority of moderates was, indeed, a relief. The embarrassment of being sole constituted authority was dissipated at once by the acceptance of a new constitution, already drawn up into a brief document – or 'instrument' – of government, which had been discussed over the last month or so in the council of officers and no doubt elsewhere. This 'work of darkness', a 'scissors-and-paste' affair, was compiled chiefly from the 'Heads of the Proposals' of 1647, the officers' 'Agreement of the People' of 1649, with snippets of proposals from the Rump and elsewhere.[1]

Major-General John Lambert is generally accepted as its author. He had not been active in Barebone's Parliament or in its Council of State, and his return to London in November suggested to some that 'suddenly a new May-game [was] to be played'. His interventions in later Commons debates on the Instrument betray an author's techiness at criticism. On the other hand the writer of an intercepted letter from Paris on 3 January 1654 n.s. was 'a little surprised' that Lambert had 'so fully concurred in this change' of government. Whoever wrote it, the true contents of the Instrument were slow to make themselves known. On 23 December 1653 illicitly printed and presumably inaccurate 'abstracts' were seized by council order while still in the press. The full version, not completed and engrossed until February 1654, reads more like a miscellany of memories and notions than a coherent 'expression of the ideals' of the men who set up the Protectorate. Professor H. R. Trevor-Roper suggests that to see the Instrument as 'the product of a group chiefly of army officers' is 'to ignore the previous history of the reforms', which 'the independent country gentry' had demanded 'since 1645 (and indeed before)'. But surely the fact that their requirements (or, rather, *some* of them) were put into effect by an army caucus in a particular set of circumstances at the end of 1653 is not irrelevant either.[2] Moreover, from the start the Instrument proved defective. The history of the Protectorate is in great part the history of its deficiencies, some of which can be traced in the early legislation made under its auspices.

By the 'Instrument of Government',[3] the Commonwealth of England, Scotland and Ireland – not yet in fact constituted and to take some months to achieve even on paper – was placed under a single person with the title of Lord Protector and in the indispensable person of Oliver Cromwell, who shared the executive with a nominated Council and the legislative with a single-chamber, triennial parliament, elected on a new franchise and to meet for the first time on 3 September 1654. Control of the armed forces was vested in Protector and Parliament, when it was sitting, and in him and the Council during the intervals. Clause XXX provided that:

> . . . the raising of money for defraying the charge of the present extraordinary forces, both at sea and land, in respect of the present wars, shall be by consent of parliament and not otherwise, save only that the Lord Protector with the consent of the major part of the Council, for the preventing of the disorders and dangers which might otherwise fall out both by sea and land, shall have power, until the meeting of the first parliament, to raise money for the purposes aforesaid. . . .

All this suggests a sense of immediate necessity rather than a cool academic constitutionalism, working from clearly grasped principles. The impression is confirmed by the rest of the clause, which goes on: '. . . and also to make laws and ordinances for the peace and welfare of these nations where it shall be necessary which shall be binding and in force, until order shall be taken in parliament for the same'. (It is not clear whether any distinction was implied between 'laws' and 'ordinances'; in the event none seems to have been made. The Council had originally intended to call its decrees 'acts'.)[4] At any rate, it was under this provision, tacked on as a sort of afterthought to the vital matter of raising money to keep the army quiet, that the early legislation of the Protectorate was issued. It is not surprising that a good deal of that legislation should be financial or devoted to providing for the military and political security of the new regime. That anyone visualised using this clause as an opportunity to bring in a great programme of reform seems doubtful. Nor in the event was there one.

The Lord Protector was impressively installed in the Court of Chancery on 16 December. In the meantime a Council of fifteen members had been named. (Clause 11 of the Instrument provided for a Council of between thirteen and twenty-one members and before the first Parliament met four others were recruited. Most of the members had served in either Barebone's Parliament or its Council of State or both. They included Francis Rous, half-brother to John Pym and Barebone's speaker, Sir Anthony Ashley Cooper, young and articulate, Edward Montague, later Pepys's earl of Sandwich and a leading actor in the Restoration, and Colonel William Sydenham, who had just moved the resignation of the late Parliament. Such men gave a continuity of talent and experience to the new executive. Among the new members were Philip Skippon, commander of the London militia, and Lambert, ready to turn his hand to putting his Instrument to use. Like any other political group got together in this period they were a mixed batch in social origins, age and religious outlook. None was in political terms really radical. Apart from Cromwell himself, none was a regicide. Only Lambert, Disbrowe, Fleetwood, Sydenham and to some extent Skippon may be taken to be representative of the army as it was in 1653–4. Philip Jones was an absentee garrison commander without a regiment; others (Fiennes, Montague, Mackworth) held only honorific military rank. As Gardiner pointed out eighty years ago, they look on the whole like 'men of practical efficiency opposed to further changes in the state . . . [and] . . . content to devote themselves to the tasks of carrying on government without taking into account the theories upon which any special government is founded'. They left the theoretical justification of the Instrument under which they served to the pliant publicist Marchamont Nedham in his *True State of the Case of the Commonwealth*

(February 1654), while they got on quietly with the job in hand.[5] It was not that they were colourless or passionless men – they could on occasion get quite worked up – but they were at this point in time, after the upsets of a hectic year, more concerned with stability and retrenchment than with further experimentation. They would work hard and intelligently but within a deliberately limited context.

Meeting without fuss on the day of Cromwell's installation, the Council took up, much as the Privy Council had done in 1625 on the death of James I, the formalities demanded by the new alteration. A proclamation declaring His Highness Oliver Cromwell Lord Protector of the Commonwealth of England, Scotland and Ireland was read out and ordered to be sent to all sheriffs and others to read out in the cities, boroughs and market towns within their jurisdiction. Similar proclamations went to Ireland and the colonies. Another continued all commissions and so on 'in order to the execution of public justice'.[6] All this was routine but it was vital.

At the next meeting (19 December) Henry Lawrence, experienced, competent and unexciting, was elected to the chair. He got them at once on to essential business. All addresses by petition – many were expected and more came in – were to be directed to the Lord Protector in his full style. Representatives of foreign states were likewise to make their addresses to the Lord Protector as head of the State – an immediate test perhaps of where their governments stood. Other formal measures (taken at the meeting on the following day, 20 December) reinforced the assumption of power and responsibility by the new government – a transition eased by continuity of personnel in council membership, in its secretariat and in every part of the administration and judiciary, both central and local. Where men had acquired vested interests, not all of them venal, they would not willingly let them go. They might have reason, too, to think that the new order meant them the very reverse of harm. Thus the counsel learned who had advised the late Council of State accepted instructions to draft appropriate proclamations for continuing legal proceedings and considered how best to amend the forms of writs and patents. The serjeant-at-arms, and other keepers, held in custody until otherwise ordered all those imprisoned by Barebone's, including John Lilburne. Council officials got on with devising acts for renewing the powers of the Army Committee, the Treasurers at War and the Navy Treasurer. Alderman Tichburne was asked to prepare and bring in an act for continuing payment of the duty for the relief of Algiers prisoners, a measure about to expire.[7]

The meeting on 20 December had been a very busy one. Already men not in the direct employ of the State but who felt their fortunes tied up in its processes were showing anxiety to be reassured. A petition from 'the late farmers of customs' begged for them, together with their creditors, to be satisfied that no alteration was intended by 'the government now established' from the act of the late Parliament for the sale of forest lands. Whereupon the Council ordered them to have a copy of the appropriate clauses in the 'Instrument of Government', which Secretary Thurloe was still preparing for enrolment in Chancery. Cooper and Disbrowe were deputed to draw up a draft act for renewing the Rump's act for 'probate of wills and granting administrations'.[8]

In these early meetings a pattern had already been set, one of assiduous and sensible conciliar effort. Major measures of transition had been achieved. Anticipatory attention had been given to useful legislation about to lapse and moderate men had been encouraged to expect conciliatory gestures. It seems clear that there was no intention, implicit or expressed, for clearing the way for any grandiose schemes of far-reaching reforms, already devised in detail or about to be prepared. There was no discussion of principles, no taking of stock. The new executive, which was in fact very much the old, released from the distractions of the heady minority in the Assembly, would when the time came renew some of the work of Barebone's, implement a few of its agreed intentions, and bring to completion other reformatory work to which it had contributed. What it would not do was to extend the revolution. The key word was 'settlement'. Change, expressed as 'overturn, overturn, overturn', was now anathema.[9] Appeal was to be made not to men who – in Cromwell's words at Putney – had 'but the interest of breathing', nor to those substantial men who had succumbed to the ferment of ideas, either impractical or, worse still, realistic, but to that part of the political nation which might be open to persuasion that the preservation of the traditional social order was high on the priorities of the new regime. If in religion the Instrument and the ordinances that followed it showed some disturbing features – for example a toleration too generous even for some of Cromwell's closest supporters[10] – there was still to be a state church, and tithes, symbol of the sacrosanctity of private property, would survive, even in lay hands.[11] When the second Protectorate Parliament struck at that toleration in the person of the horrid blasphemer, James Nayler, Cromwell enquired by what right they did it – but did not wait for an answer, a hint of his pragmatism.[12] Union of the British Isles might at a glance seem revolutionary, but the Instrument and its Scottish and Irish ordinances merely clinched the work of the Rump and Barebone's and the underlying intentions of English policy for centuries past. Even the legal reforms did not strike deep nor extend into the criminal law. Cromwell indicated to both Protectorate Parliaments his desire for a programme of legal reform. Mr Veall says that after the fall of the Barebone's there were 'no further legislative attempts to relieve debtors'. But in fact, although the Barebone's Act of 5 October 1653 was several times suspended by the Council, an ordinance of 9 June 1654, in which Cromwell took a personal interest – and which 'explained' the original act – can be considered a separate measure; it expired in October 1655.[13]

The procedure for the passage of an ordinance was both formal and regular, though not rigidly so. The decision to set one in motion was taken in full Council in response to a request or petition from interested parties (individuals and groups, whether corporate or *ad hoc*) or at the initiative of members, officials or the Lord Protector himself. A committee, usually of two or three, was appointed to prepare a draft, enlisting the aid of council officials and counsel learned and with power to consult with anyone whose knowledge or opinions might be relevant or otherwise helpful. Papers could be sent for and evidence collected in a variety of ways.[14] It is clear that the procedure was modelled on that of a parliamentary committee. The parliamentary experience of the Council and its secretariat was, of course, considerable and various. Henry Scobell, one of the clerks, for example, had been clerk of the Commons, a life appointment.

Some drafts were prepared by officials alone or even by an outsider. But this was uncommon and hardly applied to major ordinances. All members of the Council except the president and the Lord Protector seem to have been active committee-men at one time or another, though some were certainly much more assiduous and wider ranging in their interests than others, as they were in their attendance at full Council. Examination of committee composition and procedure shows that some members had from the start particular interests and could fairly be considered specialists. Others were more eclectic. On 20 June 1654 the Council divided its members into some informal groupings for specific topics but during most of the nine months before Parliament no really fast line had been drawn. What is certain is that those members who were willing to be hard-worked were encouraged to be so both in full Council and committee, and if they really wanted to be involved in preparing a particular piece of legislation they could be. Among the really vigorous members Lambert, Mackworth and Ashley Cooper were conspicuous.[15]

Draft 'bills' (as they were called) usually had three readings, though there are a few examples of both more and less. Discussion, even debate, could follow on a reading of a bill or on a verbal report from a committee. Drafts that did not meet in substance or in detail with the approval of Council could be referred back. When the Council agreed on the final form – clauses were sometimes added at the very last minute on the third reading – the intended ordinance went to the Protector for his approval. This was given in person either in Council itself (the Protector was of course a member) or more often, since Oliver was not a regular attender, at 'court', where the Lord President of the Council waited upon him. No ordinance could have force without the Protector's assent and he obviously did not regard that as a mere formality. He queried several ordinances which then came back to the Council for revision, and he sometimes offered specific changes. The ordinance for creditors and poor prisoners was presented to the Protector on 26 May 1654. He referred it to counsel and sent their suggested amendments to the Council. 'Upon reading whereof after some alterations and the addition of two provisos, the same was agreed and ordered to be presented' to Cromwell who finally approved it on 9 June. He had similarly amended the cock-fighting ordinance (31 March) and in giving his approval on 10 February to 'the ordinance for the better ordering and disposing the estates under sequestration' he had made 'an amendment by omitting the name of John Reding, thus reducing the commissioners to six'.[16]

Not every suggested or drafted ordinance reached completion. Some were lost because they could not be got through before Parliament met on 3 September, when it would seem, according to the Instrument, that the power of making them must lapse. It is not surprising that on 2 September a large batch of ordinances, some of considerable importance, some long in the pipeline, were rushed through. But one or two were rather trivial and it is odd that these should be given apparent priority.[17] Some ordinances had failed earlier because no agreement could be reached on them, or because the pressures behind them were too slight or fitful.

The Council was an extremely busy institution. Not all of its time could be given over to legislation or even to the semi-legislative process that produced 'personal' or 'private' ordinances, of which there were a great many. There were sixty-two items on the agenda for 31 March

1654. Like the Caroline Privy Council it could be generous in the time and attention devoted to the minutiae of business. The Protector, too, was kept busy giving personal approval to a great many of its mundane orders. Like the Council of Henry VII, this one was perhaps more a civil service than a cabinet. It needed sometimes to be jogged from trivialities into attention to really important matters. A number of ordinances clearly emerged from simple reminders by officials that such and such an act of the Long Parliament or the Nominated Assembly was about to expire, needing to be renewed *in toto* or in a revised version. Some ordinances involved merely routine changes in phraseology to meet the existence of the new regime. Thus the ordinance for 'passing custodies of idiots and lunatics' (20 March 1654) amended the Barebone's Act of 13 October 1653 by providing for the signature of the Lord Protector before they could go under the Great Seal.[18] Other amending ordinances introduced modifications of perhaps more significance, but even most of these can be considered to be basically re-enactments of useful or essential existing legislation rather than new departures.

Examination of the provenance, procedure and passage of the ordinances again establishes that only in a very loose sense can they be taken to represent a firm government programme, let alone the personal policy of the Protector himself. Too much time had been taken in framing the Instrument and coping with the problems, foreign and domestic, of the latter half of 1653 for Oliver and his henchmen to be able to aim at a definite target of legislation to be realised before meeting the new Parliament, whose outlook would remain until the last minute unpredictable. Rough priorities no doubt were in mind. Finance and security, union with Scotland and Ireland, and religion are obvious examples.[19]

There were twenty-odd ordinances on finance, mostly continuing existing taxation. The ordinances of 21 June and 2 September 1654, the one bringing the public revenues into one treasury and the other settling 'several branches of revenue' under the management of the Treasury and Court of Exchequer, might suggest some fully worked-out scheme to move towards an ideal of administrative efficiency. In fact they were the outcome of expediency. The proliferation of financial bodies during the 1640s had encouraged waste, duplication of effort and even downright corruption. To supervise and check the procedures and records of institutions so diverse in origin, function, structure and location was impossible unless they were somehow lumped together.

Moreover there now seemed to be no new major source of revenue to be tapped. Existing ones must be more fully exploited. Thus the steps towards consolidation, inspection and retrenchment were *ad hoc*, though no doubt they also gave expression to a latent conservatism in the Protectorate, contributing to the 'revival of oligarchy' which was a consequence of its establishment.

Security cropped up in about a dozen ordinances including those prohibiting cock-matches, duels and horse-racing, which often led to public disorders, which the regime could afford no more than general risings. Other ordinances chiefly of a social and economic nature were – like the proclamations on poor law and food supply in the 1630s – also concerned with public order. The regulations of hackney-coaches in London (23 June 1654) aimed to minimise the long-standing wrangles between watermen and coachmen. The ordinance was indeed a response to a petition from the Lord Mayor for sensible and effective discipline. Ordinances for the highways (31 March 1654) and for the post office (2 September) were as much for the ease of military movements and the dispatch of intelligence as for the convenience of the public. But they had beneficial, social and economic side-effects, some of which were recalled with nostalgia later in the century.[20]

The six ordinances dealing with religion, including those for the triers and ejectors, the basic State–Church machinery of the Protectorate, provided for the implementation of little more than proposals long aired in the Rump and Barebone's. There is little systematic or adventurous in them, and it is unrealistic to feel that there ought to have been. Taken by and large the items of legislation actually achieved – and the ordinances printed or listed in Scobell and Firth and Rait need here to be supplemented by those very various minor or private ones which can be traced in the state papers and elsewhere – are a very scratch lot, some long anticipated, others quite unforeseen. One or two are clearly postscripts to others. The treason ordinance of 19 January 1654, though drafted by the competent Philip Jones and Ashley Cooper with the assistance of counsel learned, curiously overlooked the fact (quickly pointed out to Thurloe by the Irish Council) that by revising laws it modified the legal nature of the crime of murder in Ireland and allowed 'mean and despicable persons' and their 'commanders' among 'the chiefest of the Irish gentry' to 'escape the hand of Justice'. It was necessary therefore to bring in another ordinance 'declaring that the proceedings in case of murther in Ireland shall be as formerly' (20 March 1654), to meet Fleetwood's *cri de cœur* that 'the high court of justice sits not, nor can they, until we have accompt from you [Thurloe] concerning the business for murder'. The ordinance of 31 March 1654 'for better amending and keeping in repair the common highways within this nation' required by 16 May another one 'of explanation' including 'a proviso relating to the carriage of great guns, timber and other necessaries for the navy and army that where more horses are necessary the persons employed on such draughts are to incur no penalty thereby'.[21] Some of the minor and private ordinances amount to little more than implementing or relaxing other ordinances or clauses within them – a use of a dispensing power of the sort which would cause so much controversy after the Restoration. Like the exercise of that dispensing power (and the more extensive suspending power) under the later Stuarts, this activity of the Council is really as much legislative as administrative and could represent a similar constitutional and political danger, but it is doubtful if it derived from anything more sinister than expediency.

The examination of the whole body of what were called ordinances in these months suggests that the Council itself did not distinguish specifically between major and minor, public and private ordinances. Many of the private ones were later included in the blankest confirmation of legislation by the second Protectorate Parliament of 1656, after the acceptance of the 'Humble Petition and Advice'. When all of these are considered the *ad hoc* appearance of the legislation is intensified. The government is seen seriously, energetically but somewhat incoherently tackling problems as they occurred or demanded closer attention. This pragmatic approach produced ambivalences and inconsistencies which puzzled contemporaries, who often put down to Machiavellian deviousness and subtlety what was in fact the effect of immediate rather than long-term reactions and considerations. Thus the regime was at once conciliatory and oppressive, removing the Engagement – already relaxed by the Barebone's – and yet bringing in the same day tougher treason legislation, appealing to erstwhile enemies to become present friends while at the same time hardening some of the divisions of the Civil War.[22] Like previous governments in England this one lived from hand to mouth.

History, we need to remind ourselves, is the record of processes of change through time. A study of the chronology of the ordinances passed in these nine months may help us to get towards their true inwardness. We need to know about the prehistory of this legislation – i.e. what was done or intended on the topics before 12 December 1653. We must ask when it was introduced, how long it was in gestation (was it delayed or rushed through, pushed along at a steady rate or temporarily dropped and taken up again?) before finally being approved, assented to, printed, published and implemented. Long delays can suggest a lack of interest and sense of urgency. They can also indicate strong conflicts of opinion needing time to be reconciled. It is possible to trace these processes for a good many of the ordinances. A good example is that for reform of Chancery.[23]

The story can begin with the Hale Commission on the reform of the laws of 1652. This produced in January 1653 a series of moderate draft proposals on many legal topics which would have directly or indirectly touched Chancery. These were read in the Rump but nothing had been passed when Oliver dissolved it. Barebone's also set up a law committee which took over and extended some of the Hale proposals. Abolition of Chancery was voted in the Assembly early in August and the law committee was ordered to bring in a bill. On 15 August a motion was passed – barely – for Chancery to be suspended for one month, during which time a new structure for it could be effected. The bill for this was lost two days later by the Speaker's casting vote. The radical reformers came back in October with a further bill for establishing a body of commissioners to hear Chancery cases for a limited period, pending a final disposition of the problem of reform. This, too, was turned down by moderate votes. The radicals took revenge a few days later by obtaining the rejection of a mild reforming measure drafted by interested lawyers. A further bill enabling cases involving less than a couple of pounds to be dealt with summarily – reducing, of course, the costs and delays of existing Chancery procedures – was still under consideration in committee at the time of the Assembly's resignation.[24]

From this it is clear that there existed a great deal of support for some reform of Chancery, though strong conflict of views as to how and how much. That agitation outside Parliament and at least argument within a new Parliament would continue was certain. There was therefore an incentive for the new regime to try to come up with something generally acceptable, and a committee 'for regulating the courts of law and Chancery' was soon set up. Discussions were held with lawyers but little progress was made until on 13 July a draft ordinance from the committee was read twice in Council and referred to a committee consisting of Lambert, Mackworth, Disbrowe, Strickland, Wolseley and Fiennes with 'power to examine fit persons'. Mackworth, at least, of these had legal knowledge, but the composition of the committee suggests an impatience with the lukewarmness, not to say obstructionism,

F

of the legal profession. On 24 July the draft came back to Council and was debated and proceeded on 'by parts'. After further discussions on 27 July the 'penning' of clauses relating to fees and the 'business of the registers in Chancery' was referred to Disbrowe, Mackworth, Wolseley and Sydenham. On 1 August several other clauses were added on report from the committee and the ordinance was read, amended and passed to be printed and published. But early in August the Protector had some observations of his own to make, and on the fifteenth his alterations to Clause VI were agreed in Council. His final approval was given on the nineteenth. The ordinance was finally issued on 21 August. Associated with it were a number of 'private' ordinances nominating various individuals to appointments.[25]

It seems that there was a disposition to get something done about Chancery and that the Protector himself was interested. But the matter did not become in any way urgent until late summer 1654, when arrangements were being contemplated for the elections to the Parliament.[26] On 12 July Fleetwood reminded Thurloe that 'it is much wondered at that the regulation of the law goes so slowly'. 'I know your hands are full' – they always were, of course – 'but the eyes of all men are upon my Lord Protector and if ever these considerations [law and tithes] are before the parliament, where there will be such a diversity of interests, I fear it may prove as fatal as both have been in the last two parliaments.' This sort of prodding and the failure of the lawyers to produce anything positive determined the Cromwellian sponsors of moderate reform to produce a reasonable measure of their own, facing critics from both left and right with (it was hoped) a *fait accompli*. As it eventually emerged the ordinance was very much a mixture, incorporating bits of many old and some new proposals. It is doubtful whether anyone saw it as even a potentially permanent measure, and its later history underlines its inability to be a scheme for all seasons. Much more can be said about it, but the narrative of its production as much as its content surely demonstrates it as little more than a stop-gap measure and as such typical of the early legislation of the Protectorate.

Parliament was certainly an essential part of the machinery of government set in motion by the Instrument. But it would not be one in permanent session and its first meeting was deferred for nine months – for a variety of reasons. One was the desire of the new executive to be free for a while of parliamentary critics or pressures, an urge strengthened by the still raw experience of the Rump and its unamenable successor in sovereignty. No doubt if Cromwell and his closest advisers had been abler politicians and more apt in the arts of parliamentary management they ought to have been sure of dominating a parliament elected on their new franchise. But in December 1653 there was little in the foreign situation, in the affairs of Scotland and Ireland and in attitudes at home to encourage an early confrontation.

Cromwell was determined to end the Dutch War as soon as practicable and to give foreign policy a sharp pro-French and anti-Spanish turn. Religion and traditional patriotism mingled here with mundane considerations of imperialism, trade and security. Negotiations with the States were bound to be difficult and would be hampered if opportunity were given to critics in the City, pushed by radicals smarting from defeats in Barebone's and in the Common Council elections, to put in a parliamentary way their objections to any peace, even one made on the favourable terms upon which the Protector was insisting. It would be safer to meet them in September with a firm-grounded treaty.

The peace actually concluded in April 1654 was a solid achievement for the new regime.[27] Among its clauses was a secret one whereby the States undertook to remove the pro-Stuart House of Orange from its present place, ambiguous but influential, in political life. This ties in with the several ordinances intended to check Royalist hopes. As we have seen some were oppressive, others conciliatory. Between them they should have scared off some and attracted others among the moderates. Time was needed to rehearse these gestures and to estimate their effectiveness. Elections for an immediate parliament would place the aspirations behind them in jeopardy. Royalist conspiracy, though always exaggerated both by those in favour of it and by those against, certainly did exist and worked towards hopeful coups, whether as internal risings or power-backed foreign invasion. The treason ordinance of January 1654 seemed justified when the Vowell–Gerard attempt was uncovered. At his trial by a high court of justice Vowell made a direct appeal against the ordinance. It would have been alarming had in fact a parliament been sitting. The authority given to Protector and Council to make ordinances was, he argued, 'but a temporary power . . . until parliament took further order and by such a temporary law he ought not to be questioned for his life, for if he should die by this law, how could his life be restored if parliament should reverse their ordinance?' The solicitor-general replied that the same objection could well be levelled at any law, 'for no law is in force but till parliament take further order, for any act of parliament may be repealed by parliament'.[28] It is obvious that the framers of the Instrument had had no intention of allowing

Parliament's verdict on the ordinances to be retroactive. Proceedings under the treason ordinance between 19 January 1654 and the date of Parliament's further orders on it would be valid, regardless of the burden of those orders. The same would apply to all the other ordinances. Anything else would have opened a doorway to anarchy.

If foreign relations and internal security argued for deferment of Parliament, so did the problem of the unification of the British Isles. The Instrument spoke of the Commonwealth of England, Scotland and Ireland as if it already existed. In fact it did not. Both the latter countries were being reduced to order but still only with difficulty. Robert Lilburne's letters from Scotland in 1653 are eloquent of his problems, which were intensified by the rapid changes in regime in England. 'Monk's spiritt would doe well amongst them,' he believed, and it was not until the Protector took this hint that the grip on Scotland really tightened. Ireland, where many members of the government, like Ludlow, were sadly out of tune with the 'alteration' of December 1653, the situation was as complicated, except that there would be fewer qualms at home about a ruthless handling of the problem.[29] Looking at Ireland, few Englishmen could be bothered with constitutional niceties even of the rather grudging sort that were applied to Scotland.

A great deal of work had already been done by the Rump towards an Anglo-Scottish union. Negotiations continued under Barebone's, in which there were five members from Scotland. These could hardly be called representatives, but at least they were Scots, whereas five of the six Irish nominees were Englishmen. A bill for union was given a first reading on 4 October 1653, and a second on 11 October. From committee it was reported to the House on 11 November but it was not completed when Parliament resigned. This bill formed the basis of the discussions of a high-powered and very active committee (it included Lambert and Ashley Cooper) to which 'the Scotch business' was confided on 26 December 1653. The first draft of an ordinance had two readings on 20 January 1654 but was much amended in Council. The committee reported again on the twenty-third, having worked over the amendments, and it was agreed to present the revised version to the Protector as the advice of the Council. But though after some further changes it was ordered to be engrossed on 2 February, it was put off until April. The delay can be explained in part by the need to devise a number of other ordinances relevant to 'the affairs of Scotland'. On 12 April a version of the union ordinance was read yet again, 'the blanks filled up at the table', and was passed by the Protector, who assented at the same time to ordinances for pardon and grace to the people of Scotland (drafted at the end of January), for erecting courts baron in Scotland (read for the first time on 26 January) and for leasing the estates of excepted persons there to trustees (first reported on 16 March). On 22 April these were ordered to be published by the commander-in-chief in all the Scottish shires, though not apparently in England, where the matter of a union with an old enemy was surely not a matter of indifference.[30]

On 27 June a further ordinance arranged for elections in Scotland and was accompanied by a very similar one for Ireland. Irish affairs had taken up a lot of the time of the Council and there was in fact a standing committee that produced a number of ordinances, some relating to the affairs of that privileged lobby the Irish Adventurers. Altogether more than a dozen ordinances were specific to Scotland and Ireland, but in addition most of the other major ordinances were relevant, too, notably those for treason and for religion. But in none of them is there much that can be considered a fresh departure, a radical reappraisal of the way things were going, but rather an effort based upon immediate and practical considerations to complete something of what had already been started.[31]

The elections for the Parliament of September 1654 produced a very mixed membership, much of it unwelcome to the government. Many of those chosen, both in counties and boroughs, were flatly inimical to the regime; some were certainly Royalists. It is a criticism of the Council's political sense that, given the opportunity to use their temporary legislative power, they failed to arrange for the registration of voters. As it was, difficulties in deciding on claims to voices gave opportunities, perhaps beyond even the normal, for sharp practice and electoral disputes. Interference as always came both from above and from below. What determined success or failure at the hustings can be determined only by examining particular cases. Local politics, traditional family rivalries or connections could be vital, but the total defeat of the radicals – less than a handful of the extremer groups in Barebone's was returned – suggests that everywhere there was at least a hint of a common reaction in favour of property and a maintained ministry and against what was obviously considered feckless reform. On the face of it this ought to have benefited the government, which stood for precisely these things, but there were other issues, too, to complicate things – as the presence in the House of some staunch Rumpers, even of Republicans, testifies.[32]

But the Protector, confident that there was a reaction in favour of retrenchment, assured of the presence of many 'courtiers' and of the near-certainty of support from the Scottish members and the members for Ireland (who cannot be described as Irish), gave his speech on 4 September an optimistic tone. He ran through the dangers that still existed but appealed expectantly for support for a policy of 'healing and settling' that would be positive as well as deterrent. He took the opportunity to advertise what the government had already done, notably peace with the Dutch and some major stabilising ordinances, among them the religious ones, which lay close to his heart and which of their nature touched upon many aspects of social and political as well as religious life. All this he felt provided a base from which Parliament, Council and Protector could go on together in harmony to provide for 'the interest of these great affairs and of the people of these nations'.[33] What that interest was he assumed was not a matter of controversy. He was, of course, quite wrong.

In inviting the Commons to examine the 'Instrument of Government', he really meant that they should accept it more or less *in toto* as it stood. They should go on quickly to take 'further order' on such matters as the Instrument had laid down for them, including the voting of revenue and the confirmation of the ordinances issued, which had been rushed through on 2 September, taken to be the last day on which Clause XXX of the Instrument operated. (These included one to enable 'such soldiers as have served the Commonwealth in the late wars to exercise any trade', one for the post office, another for the visitation of the universities, and one for 'the recovery and presentation of many thousand acres of ground in Norfolk and Suffolk surrounded by the rage of the sea' – a really random harvest.) But the House, many of whose most vocal members had been waiting patiently for just this occasion, responded literally to his request, preferring the larger task of taking further order about the Instrument itself to trifling with details. The 'Recognition' of 12 September may have got rid of the more adamantine republicans and single-minded advocates of a sovereign parliament, but the rest went on to devise piecemeal a new or 'proposed' parliamentary constitution which paid only grudging respect to Cromwell's fundamentals and made Parliament itself rather than the Council the key to the constitution.[34] No wonder the Protector seized on the shortest possible period allowed in the Instrument to get rid of the unhelpful parliament called under it.

So for five months the work of healing and settling languished and

Parliament only fitfully contemplated taking further order about the ordinances. Even so, it showed how inimical it was to the legislative power claimed by Protector and Council and to the actual exercise of it. As early as 6 September the (so-called) treason ordinance was assailed as a genuine threat to freedom of speech within the House – 'the very heart-strings' of a Parliament. A month later the Chancery ordinance went to a committee, 'there being some things . . . not practicable in it'. Four days later it was resolved that all acts and ordinances made since 2 July 1653, including those of 'the late little convention' should be referred to a sub-committee to consider what were fit to be continued or repealed. Late in November, when the revenue clauses of the Instrument were under fire, someone proposed that the ordinances should be accepted as valid for the time being. Members objected that the very reverse would be more appropriate. 'If we confirm them until the parliament take farther order, and perhaps we shall not sit to take any further order then we have given it our stamp and impression, which is more than it did become us to do.' In the end it was agreed that the ordinances 'shall remain and continue to the end of this parliament and no longer, unless the parliament shall take further order to the contrary or unless the said ordinances shall expire before that time.' Meanwhile the Chancery ordinance was temporarily suspended.[35] If these were devices to ensure the continuance of Parliament they failed badly. For the government to save the Instrument entire was more important than to save some of its parts.

Between January 1655 and September 1656, when the second Parliament assembled, the regime, facing Royalist and a miscellany of other threats, some real, all perhaps exaggerated, undertook activity which in spite of its modest denial to assume a legislative power came very close to the exercise of it. Proclamations, the establishment of a new militia, a decimation tax, instructions to major-generals and local commissioners – all these look like an unacknowledged resort to Clause XXX of the Instrument. At the same time the ordinances that had already been issued were held to be in force. The monthly assessment for the maintenance of the army and navy was renewed on 8 February 1655, and 'an order and declaration' did much the same for the excise.[36] In April the Chancery ordinance was reissued, precipitating a conflict. Bulstrode Whitelocke argued as a commissioner of the Great Seal that he could not implement an ordinance 'when he knew that those who made it had no legal power to make law'. He also had objections to the substance of the ordinance and claimed that many of its proposals were impracticable and that so far from aiding poor plaintiffs it would in fact put them into the hands of well-to-do defendants. Cromwell seems to have been positively in favour of the ordinance but willingly deferred execution until criticisms had been considered. However, by 6 June there seemed to him and the Council no grounds for further delay. Whitelocke and others promptly resigned. Their successors found that in face of the opposition, sometimes violent, of Chancery officials generally they could not in fact operate the new system. It remained little more than a token – an earnest of the good intentions of moderate reformers and a demonstration of the vitality of entrenched interests.[37] To that extent it was an encouragement to conservatism in government circles, contributing to the state of mind which produced and ensured the acceptance of the 'Humble Petition and Advice'.

Other ordinances were also called in question. Sir Peter Wentworth put the old claim that no taxation could be levied without general consent in Parliament but was easily convinced that it were better to hold his tongue. In Yorkshire two judges could not find it in them to apply the treason ordinance in the general round of trials that followed the misjudged Royalist risings of the spring of 1655. They were compelled to resign. A City merchant of an argumentative disposition, George Cony, refused to pay charges on Spanish wines imposed under the excise ordinance. He applied for a writ of *habeas corpus* and in the hearing on the return his counsel, among them Thomas Twisden and John Maynard, who had accepted serjeantcies from the regime, argued that he was wrongfully imprisoned because Protector and Council had in law no power to raise customs and excise by themselves and that 'subjects were not to be imprisoned nor their goods attached but in a legal way', which did not include ordinances. For this dangerous talk they were in their turn committed until they apologised. As Gardiner points out, the revenue ordinances were covered not only by Clause XXX of the Instrument but also by Clause XXVII, which set a constant revenue for the armed forces, not to be 'taken away or diminished, nor the way agreed upon for raising the same altered, but by consent of the Lord Protector and parliament'. Thus to impugn customs and excise was to repudiate the entire constitution provided by the Instrument. Cony's action was in fact suspected by some to be the result of a conspiracy among the merchants 'to obtain judgment of law against the customs and in consequence to overturn the payment of all taxes in like manner not *imposed by common consent in parliament*'. Moreover Cony was prepared to argue that the ordinance was doubly illegal in that it was 'never published nor certified and enrolled in Chancery, nor sent by mittimus unto the upper bench'. No wonder his later withdrawal was a source of relief to the government.[38]

The ordinances continued to be implemented where they were needed, but it was force of arms rather than force of law that backed them. It was obvious that the government, particularly the civilians and officials to whom Cromwell at all stages of his career felt he owed a loyalty, would have been glad to obtain a parliamentary sanction for them. The second Protectorate Parliament eventually passed an act that reviewed not only the ordinances of 1653–4 but all legislation made since the dissolution of the Rump. This legislation, which included many private acts and ordinances, was described as 'not according to the fundamental laws . . . but the actings thereupon tending to the settlement of several persons and families and the peace and quiet of the nation'.[39]

Discussion of the ordinances had already begun even before the defeat of the major-generals on the decimation tax (which even they would have put on a statutory basis) and before Sir Christopher Pack put in 'the paper' out of which emerged the 'Humble Petition and Advice'. On 3 December 1656 a bill for the relief of poor prisoners and creditors was introduced, followed by bills to regularise the Scottish and Irish unions. Next day 'a long bill' for surveying and repairing the highways got a first reading. It seemed at first that what was intended were piece-meal, *ad hoc* reviews, but in the wide-ranging debates on the 'Humble Petition and Advice' – which was, of course, nothing less than a full-scale constitutional revision – opportunity was seized to follow up suggestions put by 'courtier' M.P.s to review all laws and ordinances about which there might be some doubt. Walter Strickland, a Council member, proposed that 'all such as you think fit [should] continue, that they may have your seal of authority upon them'.[40] The discussions which followed are eloquent of the unease in all quarters about legislative machinery that did not at least include Parliament.

When a committee reported a list of acts with a preamble that 'some have been made not according to the fundamental laws and rights of the people', a lively member interjected that 'contrary to' would be nearer the truth. Disbrowe (who had, of course, helped to frame and pass ordinances) stated boldly that 'where the supreme power and authority is there is the legislature and what was done by them [the Protector and Council] are as good laws as any that have been done by us [parliament]'. This was as unpalatable to this Parliament as to any

other and put a bitter tang into the debate. Whitelocke extended his
objections to the Chancery ordinance (where, of course, his professional
interests had been at stake) to a general criticism of the ordinances, in
the making of which he had as ambassador to Sweden fortunately
played no part. Admitting that the Protector and Council had been
genuinely prompted to make 'good laws for the nation' he still could
not accept 'those laws to be equivalent' to acts of Parliament, which
were of a different order. Tactfully he suggested, 'let there be no word
of reproach in the preamble upon any person that in these exigencies
has undertaken for the good and safety of the nation, but only some few
words to vindicate the undoubted right of the people in law making . . .'
He meant, of course, the people in Parliament assembled. Inderwick
suggests that Whitelocke's animosity was 'much accentuated by the
fact that the ordinance was settled during his absence (in Sweden)
and without his opinion having been taken . . .'.[41] Whitelocke com-
pensated himself for the loss of his commissionership of the Great
Seal by accepting from the Protector a salaried post as Treasury Commissioner (summer 1655), an office ironically enough not legalised by
statute.

When the House accepted a preamble stressing the *bona fides* of the
government, Colonel Briscow complained that confirmation of the
ordinances must be tantamount to acquiescence: 'The chief magistrate
hereafter may be apt to think he has the power of making laws.' Other
members objected to confirming the ordinances 'all in a lump'. To do
that was 'to do it at a blind man's bluff' and could only lead to 'such a
scandal upon us as never was'. 'If we swallow such hooks, it will be that
which posterity would never claw off.' (The consciousness of holding
the liberties of the nation as a trust for posterity is characteristic of
the age. In the debates on the case of James Nayler, John Lambert,
whose view of the ordinances was necessarily different from that of the
average member, had nevertheless assailed the alleged sovereignty of
the Commons on very similar grounds.)[42]

Sir Charles Wolseley, another ordinance-framer, tartly reminded
his fellow-members that 'if the legislature had not sometimes been
undertaken by another power than was parliamentary you had hardly
sat here to make this settlement', a crude hit at the dilemma in which
men who would have somewhat to do with politics found themselves.
Thurloe backed him but worked towards a practical accord by stressing
the need to get something done while 'settlement lies in the minds of
men' – and he meant men in government as well as private members of

various outlooks.[43] In the end it was agreed to embody all ordinances to be confirmed in one act mentioning each specifically.

Matters did not stay there. When a list of those intended for confirmation was produced, members showed an inclination to debate every item on it. The Master of the Rolls let himself get indignant. If they went off on that tack, 'I know not how in twelve months you will end'. The new constitution might get lost because of pettifogging details. Still members persisted in looking over some major ordinances, notably that for appointing 'approvers' or 'triers' for church preferments. Some wanted it limited to three years, say, or for his highness's life or 'while he shall be chief magistrate'. It might be of dangerous consequence if the supreme magistrate – king or whatever – should be a Papist or a Fifth Monarchy Man. 'He might change but six names of the approvers and turn out all the godly ministers of the nation' – an anticipation of the threat that could be seen later in James II's Ecclesiastical Commission. The case for 'a probationer' confirmation was backed by one member's proposal that 'we should in making laws always suppose that the executioners will be the worst'. Another pointed out that as the ordinance provided for the single person 'to put in or to put out that of "sitting the parliament" signifies little. There will be no recourse to parliament. All will be filled up in the intervals. The parliament shall never hear of it.'[44]

Distrust of this sort extended the debates into generalisation about the relations of executive and legislative. But some of the ordinances were hardly controversial, and while there could be a flare-up over the ejectors or even the jurisdiction of the admiralty court, others such as that for probate of wills 'went off cleverly without any debate'. Colonel Hewson was heard to give his *yea* to his own ordinance – for arrears of pay – 'which caused a laughter'. Like the framers of the ordinances, Parliament found little distinction between public and private and particular ordinances. Some of the latter raised controversial issues. For example the Windsor almshouses ordinance was described aptly as 'a business of great weight' because it touched upon the whole question of the maintenance of ministers. Tithes always dragged property in with them and property was perhaps the greatest single, though complex, interest in the whole period.[45]

One by one the ordinances were agreed to or cast aside, until on 26 June, a month after the Protector in rejecting kingship had nevertheless gratefully accepted a new constitution in the 'Humble Petition and Advice', 'an act and declaration touching several acts and ordinances' was passed, and the provisions of Clause XXX of the Instrument could now be regarded as fulfilled. Parliament had at length taken further order, sensibly confirming much that was worth confirming and much, especially in the private ordinances, which if undone would have led to unwelcome resentments.[46] The government could take satisfaction in that. But the Act clinched Parliament's legislative supremacy. On the same day, the last of the session, Scobell was ordered to print a collection of acts and ordinances made since 3 November 1640, 'together with such as have been passed and confirmed this parliament'. Ironically it was published in February 1658 as the second Protectorate Parliament came to an abrupt end.

But the 'Instrument of Government' had been cast aside, replaced not by a more radical tool for the maintenance of the machinery of the State and community, but by a more conservative one. In the localities the major-generals had had to give way to more 'natural rulers'. In central government the same trend can be seen. Losing his grip, Cromwell dissolved Parliament in February 1658, lingering on for eight depressing months. His oppressive decrees looked even more like naked tyranny than they would have done in 1654 and were even more hand-to-mouth gestures than the bulk of the earlier ordinances. Just as the 'Instrument of Government' had meant the end of the age of revolution so Cap. X of the Parliament of 1656–8 ensured that government by decree was over. The return of the king in 1660 was only a part, and perhaps not the most important or even a necessary part, of what turned out to be a protracted and piecemeal restoration.

7. Settlement in the Counties, 1653–1658

DAVID UNDERDOWN

I

REVOLUTIONARY governments are usually centralising governments. In all three of the great European revolutions of modern times, determined minorities – English Puritans, French Jacobins, Russian Bolsheviks – having seized the power of the State promptly used it to impose their will on the regions of their still provincially structured nations. In all three cases the conflict between national and provincial loyalties accounts for an important part of the history of the revolution: in none of the three is this more evident than in the revolution of seventeenth-century England.

Historians of that great convulsion, from S. R. Gardiner to G. M. Trevelyan, almost invariably used to write of it from the standpoint of the nation, in terms of issues that were of nationwide concern – the conflict of constitutional liberty with royal absolutism, of Puritanism with Laudianism. Only rarely and in the most cursory fashion did they descend to the local communities in which the protagonists actually lived: to the counties and towns, the manors and parishes of England. Local history was left to the genteel amateur, dabbling harmlessly but unprofitably in genealogy and antiquarianism. But in recent years more and more historians have recognised that the peculiar nature of the English revolution cannot be fully understood unless the tension between the nation and the provinces is properly explored. In a series of provocative essays Hugh Trevor-Roper has argued that the division between court and 'country' was a fundamental cause of the original conflict, that it was indeed part of a general European reaction against the centralising Renaissance monarchy, and that the English revolution was in one sense 'a revolt of the provinces against a century of Tudor centralisation'. More recently, Perez Zagorin's *The Court and the Country* (1969) has made this polarity the theme of a full-scale reinterpretation of the causes of the Civil War. Neither writer has penetrated very deeply, if at all, the actual structure and behaviour of the English counties, contenting himself with a general conceptualisation of the subject. But others, notably T. G. Barnes for Somerset and J. T. Cliffe for Yorkshire, have shown what can be achieved when the social and political structures of particular counties are studied intensively.[1]

The most striking application of the 'grass-roots' approach to the English revolution appeared in 1966, when Alan Everitt's study of Civil-War Kent threw searching new light on the relationship between the local and national communities. Everitt reversed Trevor-Roper's contention that the enemies of centralisation were the radical parliamentarians, the 'Independents'. These were in fact the centralisers, opposition coming mainly from the moderates, 'Presbyterians' and non-party local gentry.[2] To approach the political struggles of the Interregnum, Everitt showed, without appreciating the differences in social composition, in political tradition and outlook, in tone and character, between one county and another was to ignore a crucial part of the historical situation. Even the politically conscious gentleman of the seventeenth century was as much a man of his county – a Yorkshireman, a Devonian – as he was a man of the nation, an Englishman. Except in unusual times of crisis or commotion (and perhaps even then), his horizon was largely confined by the tight bonds of neighbourhood, of kinship, of acquaintance, that formed his county community. An important feature of the Interregnum, Everitt wrote, was 'the gradual merging or submerging of these communities, under the stress of revolution, in the national community of the New Model Army and the Protectorate'. This same development, furthermore, was a major cause of the revolution's failure and of the impermanence of the Cromwellian regime. For the county communities, though politically submerged, did not lose their social cohesion; their gentry leaders suffered temporary eclipse, but they were not destroyed. Years of government from London, of high taxation and military rule, of subjection to the righteous dictates of a small revolutionary élite, simply drove them steadily to the conclusion that only by a Stuart restoration could they regain what seemed to them their natural authority, and an appropriate balance between the nation and the localities.[3]

The Protectorate, according to Everitt, was thus one of a series of centralising governments, doomed to the failure that soon overtook it after Oliver Cromwell's death. There is, of course, much truth in this. But there was another side to the Protectorate, just as there was another side to Cromwell. For the Protectorate was in many respects the kind of conservative regime that so often follows a period of revolution. Cromwell did in fact make a serious effort to reconcile just those gentry leaders who in the end proved irreconcilable; to restore by a policy of 'settlement' at least part of the old independence and integrity of their county communities. Before we examine the nature and limitations of this policy of settlement, however, it is necessary to review briefly first the state of English local government after the Civil War, and secondly Cromwell's own assumptions and intentions towards it.

II

Ever since 1642, as a result of the war and its aftermath, both the independence of the counties and the authority of their gentry hierarchies had been steadily eroded. This was a paradoxical outcome of a parliamentarian movement that had originally been inspired as much by dislike of Stuart centralisation as by anything else. In 1640 there were, to be sure, issues enough to unite the country gentry in opposition to the court: unparliamentary taxation, arbitrary government by Star Chamber and High Commission, fear of a vast, imaginary Romish conspiracy in both Church and State. But a generalised 'country' resentment against excessive government by court and Council was certainly important among such issues. The unity of the country soon disappeared, as other issues arose and men reluctantly had to choose between king and Parliament in the ultimate disaster of civil war. Not all of them found it possible to choose. Strong political views on either side were confined to a minority, and a widespread localist current could produce either abortive neutrality compacts (as in Yorkshire, Devon and other counties), or a massive apathy towards the locally dominant side, as in Kent. Yet almost everywhere outside the Royalist north-west and Wales, Parliament retained the passive loyalty of at least a large minority of the country gentry. When war came there was generally a sufficient cadre of accepted local leaders for Parliament to be able to govern, subject to the inevitable realities of the military situation.

Such men might work and fight for Parliament's victory, but no more than their leaders at Westminster did they want a revolution. Their war aims were essentially conservative: to preserve the constitution, the ancient liberties of Englishmen, from the encroachments of centralising monarchy. Yet the demands of war drove Parliament increasingly towards that anathema of the gentry, rule from London. The Puritan counties of East Anglia merged their forces in the Eastern Association, whose army under Manchester and Cromwell was at first under local control. But by 1645 it was taken out of their hands and, protesting, the counties saw it made part of the nationally based New Model. Such inroads on local independence were not the only wartime developments disliked by the gentry. To run the war efficiently, to administer the complex business of war finance and the sequestration of Royalists' estates, Parliament had to create a new kind of local administration. The old structure of county government by J.P.s and quarter sessions was largely superseded by the soon notorious county committees. The committees were the creatures of Westminster; equally displeasing to the gentry was the fact that they quickly fell into the hands of men chosen more for their religious and military zeal than for their social prominence. Although some of the committees' leaders – county bosses like Kent's Sir Anthony Weldon and Somerset's John Pyne – were men of solid local position, all too often their allies and subordinates were not. To fight the war efficiently meant ruthlessness in overcoming local vested interests, offending men who might be moderates, neutrals or Royalists, but were also often friends and kinsmen. The new men were capable of such single-mindedness: the old gentry leaders were not, and they were thrust aside.[4]

By 1646 the old fabric of local government had been disrupted, the independence of the county communities violated infinitely more savagely than by Charles I himself. This, coupled with high taxes, quartering and all the other unpopular features of military rule, led in 1647 to an attempt, organised in Parliament by the political Presbyterians, to get rid of army and county committees alike. It failed, and with another war threatening from Scotland, in the following spring came the inevitable explosion. The petitions for settlement which touched off the Second Civil War came from the arc of counties to the east and south of London, from Essex to Hampshire. This was not only the wealthiest and most populous region in the kingdom, but also the one outwardly the most securely attached to Parliament. So far had the alienation of the counties proceeded by 1648. The defeat of localism in the Second Civil War, the failure of the moderates' last desperate effort for settlement in the Treaty of Newport, the consequent execution of Charles I and establishment of the Commonwealth, mark the final frustration of the aspirations of the country opposition of 1640. Almost the last act of the moderates in the Commons before they were sent packing by Colonel Pride was the passage of a militia ordinance, which would have restored control of the local forces to the safe hands of the country gentry.

The Commonwealth, however, made less difference to the state of the counties than might have been expected. Two possible solutions to the problem of their control confronted the republic. If the one favoured by the revolutionary minority had been adopted, the institutions of local government – the committees, the commissions of the peace (now gradually regaining their old functions) – would have been staffed even more selectively, by men chosen for their godly zeal and enthusiasm for the revolution, and thus probably even further removed from the old leadership than ever. To make this effective against the passive resistance of the still socially powerful gentry would mean even more unpalatable doses of centralisation and military rule, and still further alienate the old power structures. On the other hand the alternative – a return to the former system, in which the counties ran themselves under men chosen in the traditional way, for social position rather than political reliability – would in effect be to restore local power to the Rump's enemies. No one doubted that the overwhelming majority of the gentry were, to use national political labels, neutrals, Presbyterians or Royalists.

As usual the Rump followed the uneasy path of compromise. The commissions of the peace were purged, none too systematically, of the republic's open enemies, and the survivors required to subscribe the Engagement to be 'true and faithful' to the Commonwealth. But the Engagement was a negative test, not one that demanded really positive enthusiasm for the revolution. And the changes in the commissions of the peace, though they carried the process of excluding the old gentry leaders a stage further, still left a good many in office. In one important respect, indeed, the Rump took a step back towards the 'normal' system. Early in 1650 the county committees were to all intents and purposes abolished. As far as sequestration business was concerned this was, to be sure, a centralising move. Sequestrations were now totally under the control of the Goldsmiths' Hall committee in London, to which all funds had to be returned; the officials in the counties were now no more than sub-commissioners, directly responsible to Goldsmiths' Hall. But in most other ways the change aided the recovery of the quasi-independence of the counties. The J.P.s lost their most dangerous rivals (neither the surviving assessment nor the new militia committees had anything like the wide-ranging powers of the old committees), and were now probably less supervised from Westminster

than ever. Even the more radical Barebone's Parliament, which succeeded the Rump in 1653, produced no drastic solutions to the problems
of local government, beyond a more ruthless tendency to purge the
J.P.s of some particular counties, especially in Wales.[5]

III

When Oliver Cromwell began to rule as Protector late in 1653 the old
structure of local government had thus survived all the revolutionary
changes of the previous ten years. But at the same time the county
élites had been alienated by Parliament's policies of centralisation, high
taxation, military rule and the violation of the accustomed order of
society by the overthrow of monarchy. The counties, therefore, were
still volatile and unstable, and the Protectorate could not rely, as any
government needs to do, on acceptance by the political nation. The
Protectorate seemed as much of a stop-gap regime as its predecessors,
offering no security for a stable future. Cromwell's task was thus to
achieve a settlement that would bind up the wounds in the body
politic, reconcile the traditional governors and provide a convincing
promise of permanence at both local and national levels. The Protectorate aimed to harmonise some of the gains of the revolution – religious toleration, 'godly reformation', a moderate degree of legal and
parliamentary reform – with the existing social fabric. This would mean
reconciling the Presbyterians and the non-party country gentry, and
even holding out an olive branch to the Royalists, if they would abandon
their sentimental attachment to Charles Stuart. It would *not* mean
transforming the structure of society: like all seventeenth-century
regimes, the Protectorate accepted without question the limitation of
political rights to the propertied.

Oliver Cromwell was the right man to attempt all this. Far from
being the committed revolutionary depicted by Royalists and later
popular historians, he was still as much the conservative Huntingdon
squire as he was the Puritan zealot, the exalted New Model commander. His earlier parliamentary connections had been as much with
the old 'middle group' as with the radical Independents. Even in 1648-
9 he had been only a belated convert to the revolution, taking a lead in
the king's trial only after repeated hesitations and efforts at compromise. When he returned to Parliament after Worcester in the autumn of
1651 he promptly began to work for measures that combined moderate
reform with preservation of the traditional order. 'Truly it was then I

thought upon settlement,' he said years later, looking back on 1651.[6]
There would be religious toleration, but within a national church. There
would be parliamentary reform, but not a Leveller democracy or a Fifth
Monarchy theocracy. There would be enough law reform to satisfy
the army, but not enough to upset the lawyers. Cromwell's inability to
get this programme through the Rump's clogged legislative channels in
the end meant the downfall of the Rump itself. The 'Instrument of
Government' gave him another chance.

With almost wearisome repetition, Cromwell's speeches echo the
theme of 'settlement', repeatedly declare his determination to reconcile
the revolution with the old order. 'A nobleman, a gentleman, a yeoman:
that is a good interest of the nation and a great one,' he told Parliament
in September 1654, denouncing the Barebone's alleged tampering with
'the ranks and orders of men, whereby England hath been known for
hundreds of years'. Stability and security, this was the aim, accepting
that people 'hoped for rest after ten years civil wars'. Cromwell liked
to think of himself as the 'good constable to keep the peace of the
parish', and the homely analogy shows how easily his mind could slip
into thinking of England in the old country way. Arguing for the legitimacy of the Protectorate, he made much of the expressions of support
from the counties, the addresses from grand juries at quarter sessions
and assizes. When the 1654 Parliament refused to settle a proper
establishment for the army, thus threatening a resumption of free
quarter, always bitterly resented, Cromwell urged the members to be
more sensitive to local feeling. 'I know not what the Cornishmen or the
Lincolnshiremen may think, or other counties,' he reproved the erring
M.P.s as he dismissed them.[7]

Was the Protector sincere in this talk of settlement? Historians have
by no means been unanimous in thinking him so. Wilbur C. Abbott,
his great editor-biographer, was convinced that it was little more than
rhetoric, verbal smokescreen for the real essence of the Protectorate,
Puritan authoritarianism. Certainly Cromwell had no objection to imposing godly reformation from above. He was quite ready, he told a delega-
tion from the Isle of Ely, to purge the J.P.s if necessary: to have 'men
fearing God put into the commission of the peace in all places, for the
putting down supernumerary alehouses, and for the punishment of
profane oaths, sabbath-breaking and drunkenness, and the advancement
and increase of virtue and piety'.[8] And in fact it is impossible to state
categorically that the Protectorate was either a reformist dictatorship or
a moderate, conservative regime: at different periods it was each in turn.

Three main phases can be distinguished. In the first, in 1654, settlement is indeed the objective. But early in 1655 Cromwell angrily dissolved his first Parliament, having concluded that even his moderate critics were irreconcilable; and then in March came apparent confirmation, in Penruddock's rebellion, that the Cavaliers had rejected his proffered leniency. And so Cromwell swung over to the advocates of Puritan repression, the generals Lambert and Disbrowe, and their uncompromising supporters. In the second phase of the Protectorate the country was divided into military districts, each under a major-general, and in each county a body of commissioners 'for securing the peace of the Commonwealth' regained the police functions of the old county committees. A new militia, officered by loyal partisans rather than by country gentry, was organised, the money to pay for it being extracted from the Royalists by a 'decimation' tax. The major-generals' system, centralised and authoritarian, incensed the country gentry, moderate and Royalist alike. There was widespread resentment at their interference in the 1656 elections, and when Parliament met Edmund Ludlow noted how opposition to them was led 'by the lawyers and country gentlemen'. Cromwell gave way, and in 1657 the Protectorate entered its third phase, as the Protector responded once more to the moderates' pleas for settlement. The 'Humble Petition and Advice' involved a conservative revision of the constitution, and was accompanied by yet another attempt to conciliate the old leaders of the county communities. By the time Cromwell died, even if many of the gentry were still far from being fully assimilated, local government was again being run on more nearly traditional lines. 'We may bless God,' an M.P. cried in February 1658, 'that our constitution is come again to a settlement.'[9]

IV

How was the settlement policy implemented in the counties? The two periods in which it was attempted, separated by the centralising aberration of the major-generals, will be treated in turn. During the first phase it quickly became clear that Cromwell was out to appeal to the moderate gentry. Local officials were immediately confirmed in their posts in December 1653, but this was a routine move, such as would have been taken by any new government. More important was the rapid abolition of the Engagement: there was now no more stringent political test for appointment than the oath of loyalty to the Protector.[10]

For more than a year the local officials were permitted to operate with no greater supervision than had been common under the old monarchy. Special problems, such as the Gloucestershire farmers' stubborn defiance of the laws against tobacco-growing ('the use of it breeds disease,' the Council wisely observed), did indeed provoke pressure, and even the use of troops, by the government. And the Protectorate's middle course in religion could lead to action against J.P.s at both extremes. Those in North Wales, many of them installed by the radical Propagators of the Gospel, were dangerously out of sympathy with the regime, turning a blind eye to the seditious agitation of Vavasor Powell's Fifth Monarchy Men. These had to be, and soon were, weeded out. On the other hand, an occasional J.P., not sharing the official attitude of toleration, also had to be reminded that it was no longer legal to arrest an innocent Baptist or two. But outside Wales there were no drastic changes in the commissions of the peace. A few 'Presbyterians' who had withdrawn from public affairs during the Commonwealth began to reappear: Sir John Palgrave in Norfolk, Sir George Booth in Cheshire, Anthony Nicoll in Cornwall, for example. Even men unwilling to serve in Parliament because of the Protector's purge of the potential opposition could still be active in their counties. Such a man was Thomas Reynell in Devon, of whom the sheriff reported that 'he was ready to act in the country as a justice of the peace, though he could not as a parliament-man'. Leaders of particularly oppressive local regimes, notorious for their rigidity, lost influence. Sir Michael Livesey's power declined in Kent; John Pyne was replaced as local boss in Somerset by the trimmer John Gorges.[11]

The authority of the country gentry increased in other ways. The new church settlement – the system of triers and ejectors – gave a good deal of power to the local men named to the commissions. They were necessarily chosen for their Puritan reliability as much as for their connections, but most were in fact men of solid county position. Cromwell's desire to return to moderate legal courses and his willingness to use whatever elements of the old county establishments he could trust are to be seen in his initial response to Penruddock's rising. Militia forces mustered during the emergency were quickly disbanded to avoid imposing new taxes. 'We wish to ease, not to burden, this nation,' Cromwell told them.[12] And the rebels were tried, not by a special high court of justice, such as had been used after earlier conspiracies, but in the old way by a commission of Oyer and Terminer, whose members included many of the western gentry.[13] Already, under the

Commonwealth, the upper levels of the London-based bureaucracy built up during the war – for sequestrations and the like – had been consolidated and reduced in size. The Protectorate gradually dismantled what was left.[14]

This, then, was a government closer to the hearts of the gentry than any since the Civil War. Men of lower rank – yeomen, husbandmen – sometimes bitterly regretted the new regime's social conservatism. Petitions from the northern counties in 1654 reminded Cromwell of the harshness of landlords who 'aggravate our sorrows by the pretence that you are engaged to maintain their oppressions'. When the Lancashire gentry asked to have their own palatine court restored, a counter-petition demanded the retention of the Duchy court at Westminster, 'that a more remote application may free us from the oppression of neighbours of potency and interest'.[15]

It was altogether a better time for the country gentry, who began to meet again for horse-racing, for convivial gatherings in their mansions, to resume their old habits of hospitality and free spending. Dorothy Osborne wrily observed the return of the old ways at Sir Thomas Peyton's house at Knowlton, Kent, in July 1654: 'We go abroad all day and play all night, and say our prayers when we have time.' In Buckinghamshire the Verneys and their friends were similarly occupied in hunting parties that sometimes attracted the Protector's son Richard, and son-in-law John Claypole. Moderate gentlemen totally unsympathetic to all governments since 1648 ceased their grumbling, and even that unrepentant countryman Sir Roger Burgoyne hoped (perhaps in jest) 'for a place as Groom of the Stole'. Old debts were at last being repaid, houses ruined or neglected during the wars repaired and rebuilt. Even the repressive measures of the summer of 1655, when country gentlemen were rounded up and gaoled in large numbers on suspicion of Royalism, did not altogether destroy the mood, the rediscovery of the bonds of community. At Buckingham assizes, Sir Ralph Verney was told, the high sheriff 'kept a free and noble table for all comers, and wished you heartily at it'. It was, Sir Anthony Ashley Cooper insisted during the 1654 election campaign, a time 'to choose such as were of healing spirits'.[16]

V

Time was quickly to prove, alas, that men of healing spirits might still disagree, and that their disagreement might frustrate further moves towards settlement. This was evident enough in the 1654 Parliament, when many independent country gentry were among those excluded, and many others showed no desire to swallow the 'Instrument of Government' in its entirety. The Norfolk members searched their hearts before they reluctantly agreed to subscribe the 'recognition' that was required before they could take their seats. They did so, they said, 'to preserve the peace of our countries', to which, rather than to any concept of party consistency, they owed their first loyalty.[17] It was also evident that Cromwell's overtures to the Cavaliers – Ludlow asserts that in 1654 the circuit judges were told 'to extend all favour and kindness' to them – had been rebuffed. The official line was that the J.P.s' leniency to disaffected persons had been largely to blame for the Royalist outbreaks, and they were sharply told to execute the laws more conscientiously. Their powers, in any event, were soon to be undermined by the major-generals and their obedient commissioners. Actually the commissioners were generally less severe than their counterparts of the old county committees had been. A Somerset observer was surprised to find that they acted 'very mildly', and asked no awkward questions about the accuracy of particulars of estates submitted for calculation of the new decimation tax. Although in theory the commissioners had little discretion, and could grant no exemptions without order from the Council (they often complained that prominent Royalists could use influence at court to get off), Sir Ralph Verney received similarly moderate treatment in Buckinghamshire.[18]

But whether vindictive or lenient, the major-generals and their underlings were the agents of a very different kind of political community from the one the gentry were used to in the shires. The interest of the 'godly party', the minority of 'Good Old Cause' adherents, was to be preferred above legality, tradition and all else. When Thomas Kelsey, major-general in Kent, called on Cromwell to disregard constitutional restraints and bar from the 1656 Parliament the recently elected moderates (who had almost swept the Kent seats behind the slogan, 'No Swordsman! No Decimator!') he spoke the authentic language of his party. 'Maintain the interest of God's people,' he urged Cromwell, 'which is to be preferred before 1,000 Parliaments.' And his officers saw themselves as the agents of an impersonal national State, the only means of imposing the will of the godly on the recalcitrant counties. 'Was I made a commissioner to do good or favour to my friends?' one of them asked. '. . . I never thought so, but to serve the state.' The sweeping arrests of the summer and autumn of 1655, the careful supervision of the Cavalier gentry's movements by the major-generals, took the country far away from Cromwell's anticipated settlement. 'I love old England very well,' Sir Ralph Verney wrote, 'but as things are carried here the gentry cannot joy much to be in it.' Horse-racing and cock-fighting were prohibited as threats to public order: 'All sports put down, and the gentry not permitted to meet,' Henry Verney complained.[19]

The major-generals, furthermore, ensured that the J.P.s took a tougher line in the reformation of manners and the enforcement of godly reformation. Addressing the Corporation of London in March 1656, Cromwell denounced the 'remissness' of the local magistrates in such matters; in September, at the opening of Parliament, he boasted that the major-generals had been 'more effectual towards the discountenancing of vice and settling religion, than anything done these fifty years'. Even after the system had been abandoned, the Protector still thought the officers more effective than the J.P.s: 'Really a Justice of Peace shall from the most be wondered at as an owl, if he go but one step out of the ordinary course of his fellow justices in the reformation of these things.' The major-generals sought out reliable men for promotion to the bench; they bullied and cajoled the J.P.s into stricter performance of their duties, especially in the regulation of alehouses. And while the major-generals were not themselves responsible, the initiative coming from the Council, during their period of activity there were efforts to improve the local government system itself, in which they played an important part. In January 1656 Cromwell instructed them to appoint the most reliable of the J.P.s to review the freeholders' books, to ensure that only men of 'clearest integrity and prudence' were selected for juries. Attention was also given to the sheriffs: it was recommended that the major-generals should now provide the troop to escort the assize judges, and that sheriffs should no longer be required to undertake the lavish entertainment customary at such times – measures that would open the office to men of lesser means than the rich gentry who normally monopolised it.[20]

VI

The major-generals left bitter memories. The gentry never forgot the interruption of their accustomed authority, the imprisonment of friends and neighbours, the disruption of rural sports and freedom of movement. When Cromwell again embarked on the policy of settlement in 1657 his task was therefore much harder. Yet even so, the atmosphere in the counties changed remarkably. A new generation was growing up. Sons of Royalist fathers might inherit a preference for the old constitution, but they were not themselves technically disqualified from local office. The Protectorate court was a dramatic reminder that a Royalist past was no barrier for those who accepted the new regime: the prominence of Broghil and Fauconberg (who married Cromwell's daughter) demonstrated it. And so in 1657, in the commissions of peace and the assessment commissions, the old families came drifting back, in much larger numbers than before. Among other possible examples from the counties Somerset will serve as a case in point. In March 1657 the commission of the peace was drastically reconstructed. Out went the old Rumpers, out went the men of John Pyne's radical clique. In came men of moderate parliamentarian background, men with more impressive, 'county' names: a Wyndham, a Luttrell, a Rogers. In came young men from Cavalier families: Hugh Smyth, George Norton, George Trevelyan. The assessment commission tells the same story. Besides the new J.P.s, the 1657 commission included William Strode of Barrington (an outspoken Presbyterian, secluded and imprisoned in 1648), back on the commission after an absence of ten years, and his son; a Poulett, a Berkeley, among others from Royalist families; even a kinsman of one of the most notoriously bloodthirsty of the Civil War Cavaliers, the vindictive Sir Francis Dodington.

The same tendency can be observed in Yorkshire, where the 1657 assessment commission excluded old Rumpers like the Darleys, Chaloners and many of their lesser allies, and replaced them by such as William Ayscough (an M.P. who had withdrawn from public affairs after December 1648), Darcy Wentworth and Barrington Bourchier, both moderate parliamentarians of distinguished family. It was so too in Wales, whose historian concludes that the 1657 commission was 'the most representative Wales had had since the war', including many men from old families 'tempted back into political life by the apparent stability of the Protectorate'.[21] Not all of them were enthusiastic: many secretly hankered for the greater security that a Stuart restoration might bring. But Charles II could be restored only through bloodshed and at the cost of further upheaval. So the Protectorate could be accepted as second best. It was moving in the right direction, towards a reunion of the nation and of the local communities of which it was made.

The gentry might not share the Protector's remarkably tolerant attitude to Quakers and other radical sectaries who so often flouted magistracy and made disturbances in church; but the danger from the Puritan Left was another reason for closing ranks. The Quakers were notorious, but even relatively moderate sects like the Baptists could frighten the gentry. The funeral of the Baptist leader, John Pendarves, at Abingdon in September 1656, attracted a large crowd of his followers from all over the country. There were disturbances, violent statements against government and clergy; in the end troops had to be used, leading to some minor bloodshed.[22] In many counties the J.P.s, when not restrained by the major-generals, took a tough line. Often, indeed, the Council had to intervene and reprove them for undue severity. But Cromwell himself was moving away from his old allies among the sects, purging disaffected Baptist officers from the army, and setting his face still more firmly in the direction of moderate settlement.

With the disappearance of the major-generals the country gentry could feel that they were recovering the powers and the local independence that had traditionally been their due. In Hertfordshire in March 1657, they successfully petitioned to be allowed to take over funds remaining in the hands of the now redundant sequestration and militia officials, and use them for 'county' purposes such as the repair of bridges, gaols and houses of correction.[23] Neutral and Royalist gentry might still suffer from occasional fits of severity, such as the widespread arrests of April 1658, but for most the normal round of entertaining and visiting in the country houses went on undisturbed. A moderate parliamentarian, John Fitzjames of Leweston, Dorset, after fuming at the Commonwealth's illegalities, had been happier in the early days of the Protectorate, making up to Richard Cromwell by attending him in New Forest hunting expeditions. Angered by the major-generals and the government's interference with elections, in 1656 he went into opposition. But two years later he was again enjoying the Protectorate's stability, and engaging in friendly correspondence with the government propagandist Marchamont Nedham. He was, he told Nedham, in favour of 'what may be best, according to the present constitution, to settle and consolidate . . . all considerable parties'.[24] Fitzjames's outlook was shared by many for whom the comfortable security of their counties meant more than party politics.

VII

Yet in spite of these hopeful signs, the Protectorate's settlement was never really completed in the counties, and the gentry of the old communities never really united in accepting the regime. Everitt argues, on the evidence of Kent, that this was because the Protectorate, no less than the Commonwealth, represented the 'nation-state', to which the conservative, locally oriented gentry were not yet willing to be assimilated. Kent was therefore governed, as during the Commonwealth, by 'a small clique of newer families who, unlike the older gentry, were intensely puritanical and politically minded'.[25] There is no doubt that this was true of Kent. It was also true of the rest of the country during the major-generals interlude. But English counties differed, as Everitt himself has often insisted, and the Kent example may be misleading for the beginning and end of the Protectorate. Kent was after all a special case. No other county had risen so unanimously in 1648 against domination from London, and had suffered so bitterly in consequence. The Kent gentry were perhaps more totally alienated than those of any other county: it was correspondingly harder for Cromwell to attract them. Over much of the rest of England, the Protectorate seemed rather less the menacing nation-state than its predecessors had been. As the gentry were allowed greater authority and independence, more of them responded with at least outward acceptance of the government. Kent was an extreme case of the Protectorate's failure, but it was hardly typical.

But we should not exaggerate the Protectorate's success even in the other counties. A significant number of moderates, non-party men and even Royalists might be returning to political life; but the personnel of local government still contained a curious blend of older gentry, Commonwealth upstarts and military men, and agile survivors from each earlier stage of the revolution. This was true even of the J.P.s: denunciations of the Protectorate's 'journeymen justices' were not unknown.[26] Some counties, before and after the major-generals, were still controlled by military bosses assisted by a few minor local men. Such was the case in Herefordshire, where the power of the Harleys had been broken in 1648 and replaced by that of the radical Puritan outsider, Wroth Rogers, the military governor. Rogers was suspected to be none too happy about the Protectorate; yet he was its main support in a county which showed its dislike of military interference at both 1654 and 1656 elections by returning moderate Presbyterians and crypto-Royalists.[27]

Less perhaps than the Commonwealth before it, but still to a dangerous degree, the Protectorate did indeed rely heavily on the services of a few key men in the counties. Sometimes, like Sir Richard Onslow in Surrey and Sir John Coplestone in Devon, they were members of old families. But more were military men, often from outside the county, or men recently sprung up from relative obscurity because of their loyalty to the regime: John Blackmore in Devon, John Wade in Gloucestershire, Francis Hacker in Leicestershire and Gilbert Ireland in Lancashire are some examples. In Somerset the older families might be recovering their power as J.P.s, but the Protector's chief political agent was the upstart Colonel John Gorges, a man 'but of yesterday',[28] as an enemy contemptuously described him – though he was in fact a connection of the influential Gorges family of Wraxhall. Gorges's inability to command the confidence of Pyne's old friends among the Puritan gentry may have made him even more willing to seek support among families hitherto generally Cavalier. His active allies were a miscellaneous lot: some none too reliable survivors of the broken Pyne machine, officers of Disbrowe's army of occupation, and a few upstart newcomers. Only the former Royalist Robert Hunt of Speckington and the moderate John Harington of Kelston, son of the county M.P. of 1646, were authentic representatives of the governing families.

Outside the commissions of the peace the Protectorate had great difficulty in finding influential men who were willing to serve. When the new militia was organised in Dorset after Penruddock's rising, one of Disbrowe's officers observed that the men who came forward to volunteer were 'mostly old soldiers', men already committed to the Good Old Cause, and that there were few new recruits. He also noted the obstruction encountered by his officers, 'strangers' in the county, when they sought out disaffected persons; the local rulers dragged their feet and protected them as friends and kinsmen. There was a general lack of enthusiasm for the performance of anything beyond the most routine duties. When in 1655 the government called on the sequestration officials and J.P.s to compile lists of recusants, there was much shuffling and delay. In several counties the J.P.s failed to comply, while the Cornish return, the clerk noted, was 'so very imperfect that no execution can be done on it'.[29] The old committees would have been more energetic.

Local officials who did try to do their jobs were often browbeaten and abused by more powerful neighbours. In Warwickshire the republican Sir Peter Wentworth refused to pay his assessment, and the sub-collector would not take action 'for fear of Sir Peter'. The commissioners bravely distrained Wentworth's goods, but he retaliated by having two of them arrested for illegal entry, and had to be dealt with by the Protector and Council. Reporting on the case, an official stressed the importance of backing up the commissioners and their agents, 'for in these parts, such as are active are few compared with the whole lists'.[30] The few dedicated officials were always liable to be sued in local courts, where juries were only too happy to support their neighbours against them. The constable of Speenhamland, Berkshire, did his duty by conscripting horses for state service during Penruddock's rising, and was successfully sued for his pains. Three years later a J.P. of the same county committed a militia officer for trial at the assizes for nothing worse than disarming an allegedly disaffected person. He was brought before the Council and imprisoned, but further investigation was impeded by a significant dearth of witnesses.[31] The unpopular excisemen were particularly subject to this kind of thing, and J.P.s were reluctant to protect them. One excise officer, Daniel Wise, was sentenced to death at Haverfordwest – convicted by a Welsh jury, 200 miles from home, he complained – for killing a man in the course of his duties. The local major-general got the judges to reprieve him, but Wise still thought it necessary to draw the moral when he applied to the Protector for confirmation of the reprieve: 'Hardly any will gather excise, when country people have such a precedent as this will be.'[32]

Resistance to government, particularly central government and excisemen, was of course endemic in seventeenth-century England. What made it more serious during the Protectorate was the government's inability to call on the loyal support of more than a growing minority of the governing class. The legacy of the Civil War, the fatal division in the political nation, the continued disqualification of former Royalists from office obviously account for much of this. But Cromwell himself was also partly responsible. His reputation as the revolution's strong right arm, as the militant leader of the Puritan Saints; his dependence on a committed minority of zealots in the army: both would have made it difficult to overcome the suspicions of Royalists and neutrals even at the best of times. But his hesitations, his inconsistency in pursuing the settlement which half his mind so strongly yearned for, undermined whatever chance of success the programme would have had. 'I am fully persuaded,' Anthony Nicoll told Secretary Thurloe, 'if you keep quiet above, and grow towards a settlement, the countries will quietly settle.'[33] But instead of growing towards a settlement, Cromwell allowed himself to be stampeded into the disastrous experiment of the major-generals. The renewed bad blood that this engendered meant that far too many of the old county leaders remained unconverted by the new atmosphere of 1657, and continued to look with nostalgia and hope to the exiled Charles II.

For all his moderation, Cromwell was a formidable symbol of the Good Old Cause, and thus himself a major obstacle to settlement. His death and the peaceful accession of Richard gave the Protectorate one more chance of gaining the loyalty of the counties. Through the parliamentary debates of the early months of 1659 can be sensed the gentry's hopes that Richard might succeed where his father had failed, might break the grip of the army and the 'godly party', and return to normal methods of government. Even William Prynne, no friend to the Protectorate, recognised Richard's intentions of rebuilding the links between government and the natural leaders of local society, the country gentry.[34] But the fatal internal contradiction of the Protectorate – its attempt to pursue settlement while depending for its survival on an army dedicated to the Good Old Cause – led instead to Richard's own downfall. Only the legitimate monarchy, it seemed, could really guarantee a stable settlement. The year of anarchy that followed reinforced that conclusion.

8. Last Quests for a Settlement 1657–1660

AUSTIN WOOLRYCH

THERE is a natural temptation to pass over the last years of the Interregnum as a phase of dwindling vitality and interest before the Restoration took its inevitable course. It is commonly assumed, not without reason, that what remained of the Great Rebellion was held together only by the figure of Oliver Cromwell, but that does not imply, as many textbooks have done, that the twenty months which intervened between his death and the return of Charles II are without much significance. We should also be wary of the view, which seems to be gaining currency, that conservative reaction went so far under the Protectorate that the transition from Oliver Protector to Charles Rex did not make so very much difference. We ought to put aside the distorting lens of hindsight and seek to recover the views that contemporaries took of the situation. Was it so unreasonable of them, for instance, to hope that the ship of state might be sailing into calmer waters when the Protectorate was re-established in 1657 on the basis of a constitution framed by Parliament? That frame looked monarchical, certainly, but did the ethos of Cromwell's later government much resemble that of Charles II's? Why did Richard Cromwell's Protectorate fall, and why was the immediate reaction a great surge of optimism among men as diverse as Milton, Harrington, Vane and Lambert?

It is with questions such as these that this chapter is concerned, rather than with the actual narrative of the Interregnum's closing stages, which can be found elsewhere. Its subject is the successive attempts to find a settlement that would avoid both military dictatorship and excessive dependence on one man. It will deal not only with constitutional schemes as such, but with the interests that promoted them and their viability in relation to the social structure and the ingrained political attitudes of seventeenth-century England. Its starting-point is the 'Humble Petition and Advice' – what it offered and why it failed. It will then consider the kinds of political aspiration that were released when Richard's downfall reversed the last six years' trend towards more traditional ways, and compare the radicalism of 1659 with that of a decade or so earlier, when the Levellers, the Diggers and the Fifth Monarchy Men had made their several bids to remodel the state and the social order. It will next review selectively the 'models of a commonwealth' that the various schools of anti-Cromwellians advanced, and suggest why and when they all foundered under an irresistible tide of public opinion in favour of the old monarchy.

There was of course a conservative reaction under the Protectorate, and it did not begin in 1657. But that year it won two notable victories. The first was Parliament's success in ending the rule of the major-generals. At one level, as Professor Roots has pointed out,[1] their regime effected a partial substitution of a local militia for the regular army, which had already been much reduced. But this advantage was more than offset by the major-generals' heavy encroachment on the authority of local magistrates and on the semi-autonomy of the county communities. Their removal raised hopes that the 'natural' rulers of the localities, or as many at least of the nobility and greater gentry as were not proscribed as unrepentant Royalists, would continue to resume their old sway. The second victory was of course the 'Humble Petition and Advice', even though its promoters failed to persuade Cromwell to assume the crown. Not only did it substitute a parliamentary constitution for one imposed by a junto of army officers – even the work of a purged parliament was better than that – but it also secured a number of amendments that were welcome to the uncommitted country gentry who formed the largest single element in every Cromwellian parliament. It brought a new Upper House into being; it ruled that no member might be debarred from sitting except by the judgement of his own House; it required the direct approval of Parliament for all appointments to the Privy Council, as well as to specified offices of state; it encouraged, if it could not enforce, the hereditary principle by empowering Cromwell to name his successor; and it tightened Parliament's control over religion by requiring that the established clergy should conform to a confession of faith (not yet formulated), as well as by defining more strictly the terms on which dissenters from the 'public profession' should be tolerated.[2]

This constitution's chances of lasting naturally depended a great deal on the quality of Cromwell's successor, and no one would discount the political inadequacy of his son Richard, or the lack of statesmanship among Richard's councillors as powerful reasons why it did *not* take root. But as a programme for settlement it deserves to be judged on less personal grounds, and it is worth asking two questions: was it inherently workable, and did it command the broad support of the political nation?

The 'Humble Petition and Advice' is not a well-drafted document, and the republicans probed its loopholes and ambiguities skilfully in Richard's Parliament. It should, for instance, have been much more precise about the functions of the Other House, especially about its right – and the Protector's – to reject or delay bills passed by the Commons. But these and other less basic deficiencies could have been amended by future parliaments. More pregnant with future trouble, perhaps, was Parliament's enhanced control over conciliar appointments, but the extent of the executive's responsibility to the legislature was a constitutional problem that remained unsolved all through the seventeenth century.[3] It must be admitted, too, that the 'Other House' that Cromwell selected carried nothing like the same social weight and respect as the House of Lords, and that it contained too many of his kinsmen, officials and army officers to be acceptable as an impartial arbiter of constitutional or legislative conflicts. But a possible remedy lay in reinforcing it with those of the old peers who had been faithful to the Parliament; that was Monck's advice to Richard, and Richard's Parliament voted independently to bring them back. The religious clauses looked black to the sectaries and to unbending voluntaryists like Milton, but they represented the same kind of compromise as the Rump had been contemplating in its latter days, and while Cromwell lived they do not seem to have reduced in practice the large freedom that all peaceable sects enjoyed. Christopher Hill argues that Cromwell's *via media* in religion, as in politics, became increasingly narrow'. But none of the evidence that he cites shows that the peaceable sects suffered any practical loss of liberty. The state papers reveal Cromwell and the Council continuing to mitigate the letter of the law and the harshness of some local magistrates, although this needs further research. There is no reason to believe that Cromwell significantly changed his views about the need for a broad established church or the extent to which dissenters from it should be tolerated.[4] All in all, the new constitution struck a reasonable balance between the powers of the Protector, the Council and Parliament, and if it had been given time to develop a modicum of working conventions under a firm steersman, it might well have proved less contentious in operation than the thing of shreds and patches with which the Revolution Settlement saddled William III.

G

No constitution would work without a fair degree of acceptance by the men of substance in the counties and the corporations who held local government in their hands and returned their own kind to sit in Parliament. The only durable alternative to governing with their co-operation was to change the whole social basis of political power. Some historians have disparaged the Protectorate because it consolidated the forces that had checked the threat of social revolution in the late 1640s. But much as one may sympathise with those social revolutionaries in their wrongs and their aspirations, they showed very few signs of any capacity to *govern* a country whose ruling class, whether Royalist or parliamentarian, stood solidly against them. The Levellers' ideas, for example, of how executive government should be carried on in the intervals between their brief biennial parliaments were extremely sketchy. Lilburne was no Lenin, and if the Levellers had managed to capture the army, whether in the autumn of 1647 or the spring of 1649, the future of the revolution would probably have been short and bloody.

Perhaps a great opportunity was missed when the Rump quietly shelved the compromise version of the 'Agreement of the People' that the army presented in January 1649, but that was the Rump's fault rather than the army's. When Cromwell became Protector at the end of 1653 his potential competitors for power, apart from the Royalists, were mainly the right-wing parliamentarians whose ideals were limited monarchy and religious authoritarianism, the whiggish politicians of the Rump and the millenarian contenders for a rule of the saints. None of these were notably liberal or democratic, and before condemning the Protectorate for courting the traditional political nation – and a rough wooing it was at times – it is worth remembering how much it preserved of the aims of the 1649 'Agreement of the People'. By 1657 it had progressed a considerable way from military dictatorship towards constitutional rule. The parliamentary constituencies had been reformed, regular elections guaranteed, and the right of elected members to take their seats fully vindicated. Regarding liberty of conscience, the government was still far ahead of public opinion. In other matters such as the reform of the law, the relief of poverty, the increase of educational provision and the general improvement of social justice towards the underprivileged, achievements fell far short of intentions, but the prospects still remained more favourable than they would be for a very long time after the Restoration.

Yet how far did the Protectorate actually succeed in reconciling the political nation? Cromwell opened the gates wider from January 1654

onward by rescinding the Engagement, but how many former opponents of the Commonwealth came in, by serving as magistrates, officials
or commissioners at the county level, is a question well worth the attention of regional historians. The Protectorate's stock of goodwill slumped
under the major-generals, but it probably recovered. It cannot be fairly
gauged by the stormy parliamentary session of January–February
1658, when the return of the embittered republicans coincided with the
translation of so many leading Cromwellians to the Other House. If
Cromwell had lived to meet the Parliament that he intended to call
later in 1658, it might well have been as generally favourable to the
Protectorate as Richard's Parliament was to prove.

At the national level the most significant development of his later
years was the emergence of a party of conservative, mainly civilian
supporters who ranged themselves against the military element in his
counsels, led by Lambert (until July 1657), Fleetwood and Disbrowe.
Their leaders included members of old families such as Edward Montague and Charles Howard, some men of Royalist background like Lord
Broghil, Sir Charles Wolseley and Cromwell's son-in-law Viscount
Fauconberg, and the great lawyer-officials Nathaniel Fiennes, John
Glyn, Bulstrode Whitelocke, Sir Thomas Widdrington and William
Lenthall. John Thurloe, Secretary of State, and from 1657 a privy
councillor, aligned himself with them; so did Henry Cromwell in
Ireland and George Monck in Scotland.[5] It was this party that led the
parliamentary attack on the major-generals and promoted the offer of
the crown. Its policies were not merely opportunist. Its principles were
largely those of prewar Parliamentmen: the supremacy of the common
law; mixed government and a 'balanced polity', against either personal
autocracy or the unlimited sovereignty claimed for Parliament by the
republicans; the old right of the county communities to order their own
affairs; and above all, no military dominance over civil government.
These traditionalist Cromwellians stood for the old social hierarchy and
they were temperamentally opposed to sectarian 'enthusiasm'. They
were not blindly reactionary, but their rising influence was encouraging
to those many country gentry who, while disliking much in Cromwell's
rule, respected it as a bulwark against further social revolution and as a
dispenser of firm government.

It is an over-simplification to call these two main factions the
military and civilian parties, since the former had some support from
civilian councillors like Strickland and Pickering, and the latter included
such officers as Monck, Montague (now an admiral), Howard and

Richard Ingoldsby. Perhaps for convenience we can refer to them as old and new Cromwellians, even though that too is an over-simplification. Cromwell was very careful to hold a balance between them, valuing the one partly for old comradeship's sake, partly because of course he needed the army's loyalty, and the other because it could help him to rally the governing class and strengthen the rule of law. The whole negotiation over the kingship shows him picking his way sensitively between their opposing pressures.

We cannot know how far he could have gone on broadening the social and political bases of his rule, without either compromising the causes for which he truly cared or provoking the army officers to a confrontation. But the calm that followed his dismissal of Lambert in July 1657 and his cashiering of Packer and five captains in February 1658, showed that his grip on the army was still firm. His death, however, weakened the loyalties that restrained both parties and destroyed the balance between them. One of Richard's weaknesses that has often been pointed out was his lack of standing in the army, but another was that he leaned too heavily and obviously upon the new Cromwellians. Among these who were already councillors, Thurloe's influence rose especially rapidly, and outside the Council he was said to confide much in William Pierrepont, Oliver St John, Lord Broghil and Viscount Fauconberg. His accession seems to have been genuinely welcomed through much of the country, and one hostile pamphleteer managed to list ninety-four addresses of loyalty that he received. One of them spoke for over a hundred Independent congregations, while at the other end of the political spectrum the Royalists, according to the French ambassador, were glad enough to have a pretext in Richard's obvious moderation for accommodating themselves to the regime and nursing their estates back to health. The minority of active Royalist conspirators were at a low ebb after the exposure of their plans for a rising in the previous spring, while we have Richard Baxter's testimony that most Presbyterians, who had regarded Oliver as a traitorous hypocrite, adjusted their consciences to accepting this guileless young man. They told themselves that government was an ordinance of God, and that if he had meant the Stuart line to be restored he would have moved ere now.[6]

But the tendencies that commended Richard's regime to the moderate gentry of most shades only alienated the army. The 'grandees' who foregathered at Wallingford House, Fleetwood's London residence, resented the fact that 'courtiers' whose aims they distrusted were elbowing them out of the political influence that they had taken as their right since they had first erected the Protectorate. A deeper swell of discontent was rising among the mass of junior officers, many of them radical Independents or sectaries with republican leanings, who had always been strangers to the court. During the later months of 1658 Richard managed to fend off a number of challenging demands from the assembled officers, but as Thurloe wrote at the end of the year, 'things seem sometimes to be skinned over, but break out again'. Ugly disputes erupted in the Privy Council itself between the old and new Cromwellians, beginning probably with an abortive attempt by Richard to add Broghil and Fauconberg to it. In December, Disbrowe openly accused Admiral Montague in Richard's presence of conspiring with Fauconberg and Ingoldsby to seize himself and Fleetwood and confine them in Windsor Castle.[7]

Yet the main danger to Richard came not so much from the senior officers at Wallingford House as from their more radical subordinates. Fleetwood was Richard's brother-in-law, Disbrowe, his uncle by marriage; their loyalty was strained but not yet broken, and their hopes lay in re-establishing their old ascendancy within the framework of the Protectorate rather in overthrowing it. Large numbers of junior officers, however, felt no such ties. They had resented the growing rift between themselves and the grandees, and the monarchical trappings of the Cromwellian court offended them. Their sympathies lay with old leaders whom Oliver had dismissed for their republican convictions, such as Okey, Alured, Saunders, Overton, Ludlow and Packer, and they took their cue from Commonwealthsmen still in service, such as Colonel Robert Lilburne and Lieutenant-Colonels Ashfield, Mason and Moss. The many religious radicals among them probably took note of Richard's preference for moderate Presbyterian divines, and they knew him to be a total stranger to their own visions of a new Jerusalem. His good relations with the old nobility and gentry further alienated them, and they were even more suspicious than the grandees of his intimacy with men with a Royalist past.[8]

This current of disaffection in the army could become really menacing if the republican politicians succeeded in harnessing it to their own purpose. They had tried to do so before. Sir Henry Vane's pamphlet, *A Healing Question*, had launched one such effort in 1656, and they had really shaken the government with the mass City petition that prompted Oliver to dissolve his last Parliament in February 1658. Soon after Richard's Parliament met that same petition was revived, and on 15

February it was presented to the Commons with 20,000 or more signatures to it.[9] It struck at the whole protectoral system with its call to re-establish the supreme authority of the people's representatives and its artful appeals to the interests of soldiers, sectaries and Commonwealthsmen. But although one after another of the republican leaders supported it, the House gave it a cold answer. The republicans indeed were having much less success than when they had sat in strength in September 1654 and January–February 1658. They assailed the 'Humble Petition and Advice' at one point after another, but they found that the majority of the members, who were not Commonwealthsmen or courtiers or crypto-Royalists but unattached, conservative country gentlemen, obstinately inclined to maintain it in principle. They could find support for defining the Protector's authority more closely, especially regarding his power of veto and his disposal of the armed forces, and even more for their attacks on the 'swordsmen' in the Other House. Nevertheless the Commons recognised Richard as chief magistrate, agreed to transact with the Other House as a House of Parliament (at the same time saving the right of the faithful old peers to sit in it), and endorsed the Privy Council's conduct of foreign policy. The republicans were reduced to spinning out time by filibusters, procedural wrangles and every kind of obstruction, and the House often became very irritated with them.[10]

But if they could not get their way in the Parliament, they could still build up the pressure from outside it. This was what made time worth winning, and their success was dramatic. Agitation rose again in the army in February, and then after a brief lull, climbed to a peak in April. It was fomented by a spate of pamphlets and sermons that appealed to the soldiers, the gathered churches and the populace at large in the name of the Good Old Cause.[11] Few of them specified just what the cause was. In essence it was not a programme but a call to repentance for the 'backsliding' that had promoted the Protectorate, under whose cover a power-hungry faction was said to be turning the revolution back into the bad old channels of king, lords and commons. It aroused a powerful nostalgia for the 'halcyon days' of the past, 'those virgin days' when the Lord's presence had constantly been with them, and Parliament and army had pulled together in winning his battles. Sometimes the call for unity with the men of the old Parliament was explicit; more often the message was wrapped in a haze of moral exhortation, scriptural prophecies and heady allusions to the fortunes of an earlier chosen people.[12] Some of these tracts were strongly millenarian, associating Richard's supporters with 'the spirit of the Beast and false prophet in the former and present monarchs of this and other nations', and identifying the Good Old Cause with the imminent kingdom of Christ.[13] Much of this propaganda was indeed sectarian rather than republican in inspiration, and although we can see the republicans' hands in a number of tracts and petitions during February and March they capitalised on the Good Old Cause much more in April, when the army had already been brought to the pitch of action. But long before then this harking back to old hopes of a new Jerusalem was doing their work by bringing together what William Prynne called 'the confederated triumvirate of republicans, sectaries and soldiers',[14] which was soon to overthrow the Protectorate.

Meanwhile the conservative majority in Richard's Parliament was unwittingly playing into their hands. It added fuel to the flames of agitation by its nagging anti-militarism, its hostility towards the sects, its evident intention to draw the bounds of the established church much tighter, its speeches and votes in favour of the old peerage, and the open predilection of at least a few members for monarchy itself. Had Oliver been still alive he might have been relied upon to check the tide of reaction, but the army had no such confidence in Richard. Although the House tried to ban the reporting of its debates they were widely discussed in the army, and strongly resented. There had been a crop of rumours that this Parliament would make Richard king, and some officers suspected that 'this gentleman, who they would have made so much haste to dress and set on horseback, was but to warm the saddle for another whom they better loved and liked.' They feared 'that the Protector did intend to cast them out of their places, and put the army into the hands of the nobility and gentry of the nation, thereby to bring in the king'.[15]

These army Commonwealthsmen might yet have been held in check if Fleetwood, Disbrowe and the other chief officers had firmly discountenanced them and maintained their allegiance to Richard. But the Wallingford House grandees wavered disastrously. They were moved not only by their own thwarted ambitions and their own dislike of Richard's counsellors but by fears that their authority over the army would crumble unless they aligned themselves to some extent with their unruly subordinates. Fauconberg was sure that Lambert was covertly fanning the junior officers' unrest, and in Parliament he was in full and open alliance with the republican leaders. Under these strains Fleetwood and his *confrères* gave way. Towards the end of March they made secret overtures to the republicans through ex-Major-General Ludlow. Hesilrige and Vane made a very guarded response and declined to go to Wallingford House, but they must have felt immensely strengthened. There was no real commitment on either side, but Fleetwood and Disbrowe were now lost, and Richard with them. Early in April they did Richard a further mischief by reviving the General Council of Officers, and from then on the army and the Parliament set themselves on a collision course that ended in the grandees' naked coercion of the Protector on the night of 21 April and the dissolution of Parliament next day.[16]

The army commanders certainly intended then to preserve Richard as Protector, if only as a figurehead. They apparently hoped that the republicans would join them in a coalition to bring his government under their combined dominance. But the republicans would neither accept a mere partnership nor tolerate even a nominal continuance of Richard's authority, and they had the bulk of the army behind them. The vociferous junior officers utterly rejected the grandees' endeavours 'to piece and mend up that cracked government';[17] nothing would content them now but the re-establishment of the Commonwealth and the restoration of the Rump to the full authority that it had wielded before Cromwell ejected it in April 1653. In case they were not already sufficiently determined, a flood of pamphlets, petitions and broadsides poured from the presses to persuade them. Between the coup on 21 April and the Rump's return on 7 May, the bookseller Thomason collected twenty-eight separate publications bearing on the Good Old Cause, and the great majority of them urged the recall of the Rump. Some of them deliberately incited the army to root out the officers who remained loyal to Richard, attacking them as 'court-parasites and apostates', 'camp-court creatures' and 'prostituted parasites'.[18] It was a striking achievement of republican propaganda to identify the Good Old Cause with 'the good old Parliament', as nearly 400 men of Goffe's regiment did in a remonstrance that they published after defying their colonel on 21 April, when he tried to bring them to Richard's support.[19] After all, this was much the same army that had turned the Rump out six years earlier, and in all this literature the republicans made very few pledges as to what they would do when they got back. Such was the pressure from below, however, that the grandees were not even able to negotiate any conditions before they invited the Rumpers to return to their trust. The Protectorate was over, and Richard shortly signed a declaration acknowledging it.

Some regimes perish from causes that can reasonably be called inevitable: for instance, because they obstruct intolerably the interests of the dominant social and economic groups in the country, or because their political structures breed irresolvable conflicts, or because they become incurably bankrupt. Others fall victim to more contingent weaknesses, such as the folly or inadequacy of the men who operate their institutions. Richard's Protectorate surely belongs to the latter category. There was nothing grandly inevitable about Fleetwood's fatal ambivalence towards the agitation in the army, or the lack of a firm body of government spokesmen to lead Parliament's debates and curb its reactionary tendencies, or Richard's failure to reassure the 'people of God' that his government was not being infiltrated by crypto-Royalists and that he would not suffer liberty of conscience to be impaired. What *is* tolerably certain is that with his fall the opponents of Stuart monarchy lost their last chance of basing a settlement on adequate social foundations. The Protectorate was brought down by a coalition of forces – army malcontents, republican politicians and sectarian enthusiasts – each of which spoke for a small minority of the people of Britain and was repugnant to most of the men of substance who constituted the political nation. Moreover its destroyers had planned no viable constitution to take its place.

The main burden naturally fell on the Rump, but before describing the schemes for a settlement that it discussed during the summer it is worth giving a brief hearing to some voices from a more radical past that joined the chorus of the Good Old Cause, both before and after the Rump's return. Among them were some echoes of the Leveller movement, though some of the old Levellers were still pursuing their fruitless approaches to the exiled royal court.[20] Several anti-Protectorate tracts revived the idea of an Agreement of the People, though they usually invoked it rather to remind the army of its republican pledges in 1649 than to advocate a specifically Leveller programme. A pamphlet called *The Leveller* that was published in February, probably by John Wildman,[21] had more of Harrington's *Oceana* in it than of Lilburne, Overton or Walwyn. But *The Humble Desires of a Free Subject*[22] revived the central Leveller doctrine that the sovereign people should reserve certain 'fundamentals' from the powers that they entrust to their governors, and demanded a reapportionment of taxation so that the rich should pay more. *The Honest Design: or the True Commonwealthsman*[23] called for the reform of the law, the decentralisation of justice and the abolition of copyholds; it appealed for a self-denying 'representative of the people' that would feel for the burdens of smaller men and 'sift away the Levellers' bran and dross from those finer parts of righteousness' that they had upheld. 'We are your principals, and you our agents,' another pamphleteer told the newly restored Rump, and he called upon all noble spirits to meet at Lilburne's tomb each week 'in order to concord and unity'.[24] The author of *Englands Safety in the Laws Supremacy* advocated annual parliaments, the abolition of imprisonment for debt, and the popular election of all justices and sheriffs,[25] while Samuel Duncon wanted the constitution to be defined by an 'Agreement of the People', to be subscribed by all citizens of the Commonwealth within six months.[26] But though these tracts revived various bits and pieces of the old Leveller programme, and very occasionally invoked the charisma of the old Leveller leaders, none of them restated that programme in anything like its entirety. The old coherence was gone, as was the organisation that had once made the Levellers a formidable movement.

These radical tracts showed curiously little interest in the franchise. The only one, so far as I can discover, that even raised the issue of manhood suffrage was *Speculum Libertatis Angliae Re Restitutae*.[27] Its anonymous author would have restricted voting rights to those who subscribed a new Great Charter under which England, Scotland and Ireland were to be unified and their constitution defined, but otherwise he would have excluded none but the dissolute and such as were notoriously disaffected to the Commonwealth. A pamphlet suggestively called *Lilburns Ghost*, on the other hand, would have given the vote only to such 'as have made contribution of their purses, strength and counsels, to manage the cause for the liberty and freedom of the people',[28] while the author of *Chaos*, although he echoed a number of typical Leveller demands, advocated an elaborate system of indirect elections with the basic franchise set at £5 a year in land or £100 in cash.[29] But the franchise makes a very small appearance in this radical literature compared, for example, with pleas for the abolition of the law's mysteries and the provision of cheap and speedy justice in every county or hundred. Perhaps the experience of the last decade had dampened people's faith in direct political action; perhaps, also, 'the industrious sort' were less exercised about the franchise, even in the Levellers' heyday, than historians have been. Most of them probably regarded political participation chiefly as a means to the main ends of equitable dealing in tenurial, commercial and fiscal matters, and their protection in these by a law that they could understand and afford.

Another strain of radicalism lay in the Fifth Monarchy movement, which had kept up its militancy, though probably not its numbers, throughout the Protectorate. The Fifth Monarchists gave their own twist to the Good Old Cause. In *The Cause of God and of These Nations* it meant 'the bringing of all things in earth to answer the mind of God'. 'How God will do it I know not, but by *His own appearing*; it is the day of His power, the day of the Spirit, that is to have its turn next.'[30] Christopher Feake was his old fulminating self in *A Beam of Light*,[31] proclaiming 'the name and interest of the approaching king of saints', denouncing the Rump and the Protectorate alike, and rallying the 'faithful remnant' to await the Messiah's imminent command 'to execute the vengeance written against Babylon'. John Rogers on the other hand supported the republicans in Richard's Parliament, reconciling the advancement of Christ's kingdom with 'parliamentary government rightly stated', and in July he expressly rejected his old fellow-prisoner Feake's claim that the saints should bear rule without regard to the people's right to elect their governors.[32] John Canne, another prominent Fifth Monarchist, gave the restored Rump a more qualified welcome than Rogers did, but he took service as its official newswriter.[33] During the brief interregnum between the dissolution of Richard's Parliament and the Rump's return to power, some Fifth Monarchist congregations canvassed the junior officers in their meetings at St James's in favour of a sanhedrin of seventy godly men, such as had been agitated in 1653, but the officers cried it down as utterly impracticable.[34] In June that curious figure Dr Peter Chamberlen, who inherited the family secret of the obstetrical forceps and became physician to Charles II in 1660, advocated a parliament elected solely by the gathered churches and proclaimed that 'Jesus Christ is the only one law-giver'.[35] A few more calls for a rule of the saints were raised during the summer and autumn,[36] but time was sorting out the lunatic fringe of the Fifth Monarchy movement from the more sober millenarians who accepted that the saints had no divine mandate to seize political power.

The Rump approached the problem of settlement in a very different spirit from these radical pamphleteers. It had to face the dilemma that had dogged every government in the last decade; it had, that is, to reconcile the principle that it had so boldly enunciated on 4 January 1649, that all just power derives from the people and is to be wielded by their representatives, with the fact that most of the people did not want a commonwealth at all and would reject most of its present rulers if given the choice. Very few congratulatory addresses greeted its return to power. 'There is a strange contempt and hatred through the nation of this present Parliament,' sighed a member of the Council of State in July, and Harrington in the same month wrote that the Rump was more hated throughout the counties than the Protectorate had been.[37] One reason lay in the many changes that it made among county justices and officials, beginning with a large purge of the militia commissioners and officers. Sir George Booth particularly referred to this when he raised the standard of revolt in Cheshire on 1 August, ostensibly for a full and free Parliament, though really for Charles II. The Rump, he wrote, was 'subjecting us under the meanest and fanatic spirits of the nation . . . a mean and schismatical party must depress the nobility, and understanding commons'.[38] This of course was the exaggeration of propaganda, but it seems true that the social basis of the Commonwealth's support was already almost fatally narrow.

The only chance of broadening it lay in reassuring the county and borough communities that the country would indeed be governed by their chosen representatives, regularly and freely elected. The Rump voted that it would not sit beyond 7 May 1660, and then settled down to debate how on earth it could provide for a successor which could be trusted to maintain the republican cause. It spent every Wednesday in grand committee on that question, without reaching any constructive conclusion.[39] Many members could think no further than the well-worn proposal, dating back at least to the 'Agreement of the People' of January 1649, for a regular succession of sovereign single-chamber parliaments, each electing a Council of State to wield executive authority until the next one met. Apparently they trusted that stringent qualifications and engagements would suffice to keep out men who hankered for monarchy or a House of Lords. This was very doubtful – and what if the next Parliament should relax or repeal the qualifications? Hesilrige evidently sensed the danger; influenced no doubt by Harrington, he toyed with the idea of keeping Parliament perpetually in being, with a third of the members retiring each year and with a very restrictive two-stage process of election to the places thus left vacant.[40]

The army leaders pressed a different solution. They wanted the legislative power to be shared between a 'representative of the people', elected at regular intervals, and 'a select Senate, co-ordinate in power, of able and faithful persons, eminent for godliness, and such as continue adhering to this cause'.[41] They did not state how this Senate should be chosen or whether its members should serve for life, but its obvious role was to prevent the people's representatives from transgressing any of 'the fundamentals of our good old cause' set down in this same 'Humble Petition and Address', which Lambert and others presented to the Rump on 13 May. Equally obviously the chief officers expected to become senators themselves. This would compensate them for the loss of their places in the vanished Other House, and safeguard the army from being treated as Parliament had threatened to treat it in 1647, in 1653 and in recent months.

Hesilrige and the dominant faction in the Rump would never tolerate such a curb as a Senate, but Sir Henry Vane and his supporters were more sympathetic. Vane had adumbrated the notion of a Senate three years earlier in the 'standing council' that he proposed in *A Healing Question*, and in May 1659 he expanded it in *A Needful Corrective or Ballance in Popular Government*.[42] He gave it a different emphasis from that of the officers. For him the central problem was 'how the depraved, corrupted, and self-interested will of man, in the great body, which we call the people' could be held on the right course by 'the balancing and ruling motion of God's spirit'. He therefore proposed that the Senate or 'Body of Elders' should be elected only by those whom the spirit of God had regenerated or whom the Commonwealth trusted to bear arms in its defence. It should wield full executive authority, but it should share the legislative function with successive parliaments elected 'by the people's suffrage', whose role was apparently to be that of consent only. Vane's advocacy of a senate split the Rump and divided his following more and more from that of Hesilrige, which was much the larger. The chief officers remained wedded to the idea of a Senate, which received its fullest and most sophisticated exposition in October, from Vane's young protégé Henry Stubbe.[43] Stubbe openly stated what Vane and the officers had only implied, namely that the senators were to serve for life. The fatal snag in any such scheme was that an elected parliament was no more likely to recognise a senate's authority than the parliament of 1654 had been to accept the Instrument of Government as binding.

The Rump considered other devices for safeguarding the 'fundamentals' of a commonwealth, including 'a select number of men in the nature of the Lacedemonian Ephori'[44] – presumably rather like the 'Conservators of Liberty' whom Ludlow was to propose in December. More adventurously, Henry Neville led a very small lobby in favour of the elaborate constitution which his friend James Harrington had expounded in *Oceana* in 1656 and in several shorter works since. Harrington was the most discussed political philosopher of these years. Seeing a chance at last of getting his model of a commonwealth adopted, he launched a veritable campaign of pamphlets and petitions in 1659, and promoted it further through a club that functioned in Bow Street in the summer and developed into the famous Rota in the autumn.[45] Harrington's basic tenet was that the distribution of property ultimately determines whether government shall be monarchical, aristocratic or republican, and he believed that the ownership of land had become so dispersed under the Tudors that England could only settle under a commonwealth. To keep it so, there must be an 'agrarian law' to prevent the concentration of very large estates. But it was equally important that the 'superstructures' should fit the foundations, and in Harrington's view a sovereign single-chamber legislature was totally unfit, for it must inevitably fall a prey to factions and interest-groups. The way to avoid this, he believed, was to divide the supreme legislative authority between two assemblies, both elected by the people: a senate of about 300, representing the 'wisdom' of the Commonwealth and empowered only to debate and propose laws, and an assembly of over 1000 representing the various 'interests' of the people, which was only to ballot for and against the Senate's proposals. (With the additional Scottish and Irish members proposed in *Oceana*, the Senate and the 'representative' assembly would have numbered 360 and 1410 respectively.) Wisdom was apparently a concomitant of property, for the Senate was to be elected from and by men worth over £100 a year, and the popular assembly was to be balanced above and below this figure in the ratio of three to four. 'Servants' were to be excluded from the franchise. Both Senate and popular assembly were to be subject to the annual rotation of a third of their number, those retiring being disqualified from immediate re-election. The various executive councils and officers of state were to be elected by and from the Senate, mostly on an annual basis. The ballot was to be used in all voting, whether in elections or in the popular assembly.

Harrington's model is immensely intriguing; his advocacy of it was often brilliant, and nearly all serious political writers in 1659–60 paid him the compliment of joining in argument with him. But there are at least three reasons why it would not have worked. In the first place he was far too sanguine in his belief that exquisitely ordered institutions would *of themselves* – for he would allow no exclusion of any party, even the Cavaliers – guarantee the Commonwealth's survival against men intent on bringing back the king. Secondly, England's 'natural' rulers were not in the least likely to submit to the rigid rotation that he demanded. Thirdly, it was utterly unrealistic to expect an assembly of over 1000 to come to Westminster merely to vote in silence for or against the Senate's proposals, or as Milton put it 'to convey each man his bean or ballot into the box, without reason shown or common deliberation; incontinent of secrets, if any be imparted to them, emulous and always jarring with the other Senate'.[46]

The constitutional debates in the Rump became more and more sterile as the summer progressed, partly because the members disagreed so much among themselves and partly because they rashly provoked the army that had restored them to power. The quarrel was held in check by the knowledge that the Royalists were again planning a national rising, but that threat lifted in August when Booth's forlorn attempt in Cheshire and Lancashire was crushed with ease by Lambert. The whole sad affair seemed to show that the Royalist activists were incompetent conspirators, that there was not much love lost between the old Cavaliers and the Presbyterians or 'new Royalists', and that most gentlemen who would have liked the king back preferred to wait and see how the first round went before risking their lives and estates. But it bred a false confidence in both the Parliament and the army. We need not follow the petty occasions that heightened their mutual distrust during September, or the series of reckless provocations on both sides that culminated in the army's second interruption of the Rump on 13 October. The result was that the whole question of a settlement was thrown wide open again, and the burden fell back upon the men who had first established and finally broken the Protectorate.

It was Hesilrige more than any other one man (even Lambert) who had pushed the quarrel to an open breach, and in doing so he had fallen out completely with Vane, who had done his best to keep on terms with the army.[47] There was probably very little ground for the suspicion of Hesilrige's party that Lambert was aiming to become generalissimo or even head of state. The army showed not the slightest idea what to do with the power that it had seized, and a whole fortnight went by before the leading officers clothed that power with even a fig-leaf of respectability. This they did on 27 October by associating a few civilians with themselves in a Committee of Safety, and declaring their intention (just like the republicans!) to settle the constitution without a single person, kingship or a House of Lords. Their first plan, it seems, was to establish a senate of around fifty to seventy members and then to readmit the Rump to sit in conjunction with it until some provision for 'successive' parliaments could be enacted.[48] But the complete refusal of Hesilrige and his colleagues to compromise, and the difficulty that the officers had in scraping together even the twenty-three members of their Committee of Safety, soon ruled out this solution. The Rumpers were fortified by a promise from General Monck to bring his army in Scotland to their support if necessary, and Lambert soon had to march north to counter this threat. The Committee therefore had to wrestle with the problems of settlement under the threat of civil war, knowing that many of the officers in England too remained loyal at heart to the Rump.

On 1 November it appointed a sub-committee 'to prepare a form of government', on which the chief non-military members were Vane, Ludlow, the perennial Whitelocke and the Scotsman Johnston of Wariston. They considered going back to the 'Agreement of the People' of January 1649, but their disagreements ran deep. Rumours came through of several schemes for securing a compliant legislature by various combinations of nomination and election, but nothing was published.[49] Then on 15 November a draft treaty was patched up between commissioners of the opposed armies of England and Scotland. Its main provision, quite contrary to Monck's instructions, was that a Parliament was to be summoned as soon as possible, in a manner and form to be determined by a General Council of Officers representing every regiment in England, Scotland and Ireland, and also the fleet. On 6 December this General Council actually met, though in a very truncated form and without any representatives from Scotland or Ireland. Despite strenuous pleas by Ludlow and Colonel Rich for the recall of the Rump, it agreed that a new Parliament should be called and that it should consist of two Houses, one of them evidently in the nature of a senate. Ludlow feared that either it would be the officers' mere creature or they would dissolve it like its predecessors. He therefore urged those present in the General Council that they should first define the inviolable essentials of the common cause, and set up twenty-one 'conservators of liberty' with power to determine any differences that might develop over them between the Parliament and the army. They agreed; but when they proceeded to elect a succession of Wallingford House men in place of Hesilrige and other leading republicans whom he had proposed, Ludlow walked out in dudgeon. Nevertheless the General Council published the names of the 'conservators', and also 'seven principles and unalterable fundamentals', of which the last was 'that both the assemblies of the Parliament shall be elected by the people of this Commonwealth duly qualified'.[50]

By 13 December, however, when these fundamentals were agreed, the Committee of Safety was already tottering. That day Vice-Admiral

Lawson's fleet in the Downs and the army in Ireland both declared for the Rump; Portsmouth had been seized by Hesilrige and some fellow-republicans ten days earlier. For the last six weeks the country, and especially the capital, had been drifting towards anarchy. The judges had ceased to hold their courts at Westminster because their parliamentary commissions had run out; clashes between the citizens and the soldiery multiplied, culminating in a violent riot and a minor Peterloo on 5 December; the goldsmiths were moving their stocks out of town, the apprentices were on the rampage, and even the cautious city fathers were on the point of defiance. 'We are here in great disorder, and expect to be in blood every hour,' wrote a newswriter to Monck on the thirteenth, after a republican plot to seize the Tower had just been foiled. 'The city lies under the highest discontents that ever I knew it,' wrote another, 'shops shut up, trade gone, fears and jealousies multiply.' The morale of Fleetwood's forces was cracking, and soldiers were saying they would make a ring for their officers to fight in.[51] Shortly after the General Council had voted its fundamentals, Disbrowe privately proposed to Ludlow that sixty of the Rump should immediately be constituted as the Senate, with a veto over the proceedings of the new 'representative'. Whitelocke's advice to Fleetwood was perhaps more realistic; it was to get in ahead of Monck and offer his services to the king.[52]

The collapse of order, intensifying as it did the already acute depression of trade, was building up a tremendous pressure of opinion in favour of restoring the old monarchy, as the only possible guarantor now of the rule of law. The contrast between the tepid response to the Royalist call to arms in August and the enthusiasm at the end of the year is very striking. Everywhere the popular cry was for a full and free Parliament, which meant either a new one, elected without restrictive qualifications, or the readmission to the old one of the 'secluded members' whom Colonel Pride had kept out in 1648. Either course could be relied upon eventually to bring back the king. Associations sprang up in a number of counties to refuse all taxes until they were represented in a full and free Parliament, and London's Common Council, swung heavily towards monarchy by the annual elections on 21 December, showed strong signs of moving the same way. Fleetwood, no longer able to command his own forces, resigned his authority over them to the speaker of the Parliament on the twenty-fourth, lamenting that 'the Lord had spit in their faces'. Two evenings later, Speaker Lenthall led about forty Rumpers back to the Parliament House, carefully taking back streets lest the secluded members should try to enter with them.

But the Rump was only one degree less unpopular now than the Committee of Safety, and the threats of a tax strike continued. Monck marched into England, even though his demand for the Parliament's return had been met. During January and early February 1660 the Rump made provisions to fill up its shrunken numbers to 400 with by-elections – a curious and suspect course in view of its pledge to dissolve by 7 May. We need not retell the story of how Monck gave it a last chance to effect a settlement – or enough rope to hang itself – before he himself readmitted the secluded members on 21 February. That made the Restoration inevitable, for these members who had refused to give up negotiating with Charles I in 1648 were almost unanimously for Charles II in 1660. They had been meeting and organising for some time, confident of massive support from most of the peers and gentry who had sided with Parliament in the Civil War. The rest is familiar: the self-dissolution of the Long Parliament on 16 March, the full tide of anti-republican reaction in the elections to the Convention, that body's acceptance of the Declaration of Breda and its proclamation of the king on 8 May.

The Rump and the army had in turn demonstrated their political bankruptcy. During the last autumn and winter of the revolution, pamphleteers continued to offer schemes for a settlement and models of a commonwealth, but those that were not merely quaint were mostly variations on old themes. One last great voice raised itself when most others took fright or gave up hope. It was John Milton's. Gone now was his early confidence that a regenerate nation could soon be trusted to elect governors worthy of it; and Cromwell's Protectorate, which he had eulogised in 1654, now seemed to him a lapse from which the Commonwealth must painfully recover. He dictated *The Ready and Easy Way to Establish a Free Commonwealth* in February 1660, when the way was already far from easy. He knew how the tide of popular feeling was running, but he utterly denied the right of the majority to enslave (under monarchy) the minority that would be free: 'More just it is doubtless, if it come to force, that a less number compel a greater to retain, which can be no wrong to them, their liberty, than that a greater number, for the pleasure of their baseness, compel a less most injuriously to be their fellow slaves.'[53] It was a dangerous doctrine, but the situation was desperate.

He had already outlined his recipe for saving the Commonwealth in two short unpublished pieces in the previous autumn, but he now gave it to an incredulous world for the first time. He proposed that the Rump, reinforced by the by-elections that it was planning, should be erected into a Senate or Grand Council, and that its members should serve for life unless they betrayed their trust. (Unfortunately for Milton, Monck readmitted the secluded members just as his work was ready for the press, but that did not deter him from publishing it.) If perpetual membership should be thought intolerable, Milton would concede a system of rotation, though only very reluctantly. The Grand Council should control the armed forces, conduct foreign relations, raise and manage the revenue, and exercise most other branches of sovereignty; but there should also be a standing council in each county, and the Grand Council must obtain the assent of the majority of these to any national legislation that it proposed. The local councils were also to have large powers to make bye-laws, hold courts of justice, and maintain schools and academies. Milton claimed that they would introduce a more than sufficient element of democracy to temper the oligarchy of the Grand Council, and some commentators have agreed with him. Yet if one looks closely at his picture of the nobility and chief gentry making the county towns into flourishing capitals by building themselves *palazzi* in them, appointing judges to execute their local laws without appeal and maintaining academies to bring up their children in 'all learning and noble education', what it seems to portray is a kind of English equivalent of the regent class in Holland – except that here the qualifications are to be not mere wealth but adherence to the principles of a Miltonic commonwealth.[54] It is a picture of a central oligarchy uneasily balanced by local oligarchies, and a one-party state is a one-party state, however decentralised. As Harrington put it, more convincingly in an age when governments still largely lacked the instruments of mass coercion that they possess today, 'A commonwealth consisting of a party will be in perpetual labour of her own destruction.'[55]

Within weeks of the Restoration Milton risked his liberty, his unfinished *Paradise Lost* and quite possibly his life by publishing a second, much enlarged edition of *The Ready and Easy Way*. He now proposed that the new Parliament – the Convention in process of being elected – should assume the role of perpetual General Council. Nothing was more improbable, and in his heart he knew it. His whole scheme was so contrary to what Englishmen would stand for, and so full of potential conflicts and dangers of its own, that as a serious political proposal it may seem little more than a curiosity. But it is in fact much more than that. Milton's deeper purpose in that second edition was to celebrate for posterity the ideals of a republic governed by an aristocracy of virtue, and to contrast them with the servitude and corruption that he foresaw in a return to Stuart monarchy. 'What I have spoken,' he wrote in his moving peroration, 'is the language of that which is not called amiss *the good old cause*.'[56] This was the very last quest for a settlement before the Restoration ordered things otherwise, and with all its incongruences between noble ends and dubious means it makes a fitting close to the post-Cromwellian Commonwealth's vain search for firm foundations.

LIST OF ABBREVIATIONS IN BIBLIOGRAPHY
AND REFERENCES

Abbott, *Writings & Speeches*
      The Writings and Speeches of Oliver Cromwell, ed. W. C. Abbott,
      4 vols, Cambridge, Mass. 1937–47
Bodl.   Bodleian Library
BM   British Museum
Burton, *Diary* *Diary of Thomas Burton, Esq. M.P. . . . from 1656 to 1659 . . .*
      with . . . an account of the Parliament of 1654 from the Journal
      of Guibon Goddard, Esq. M.P. . . ., ed. J. T. Rutt, 4 vols, 1828
C CAM   *Calendar of the Committee for the Advance of Money,* ed.
      M. A. E. Green, 3 vols, one pagination, 1888
CCC   *Calendar of the Committee for Compounding,* ed. M. A. E. Green,
      5 vols, one pagination, 1889–92
CHJ   *Cambridge Historical Journal*
CSPD   *Calendar of State Papers, Domestic: Charles I,* 1858–97; *The*
      Commonwealth, 1875–86; *Charles II,* 1860–1947; volumes are
      normally designated according to the years covered
CJ   *Journals of the House of Commons* fol., n.d.
DNB   *Dictionary of National Biography,* 22 vols, Oxford 1908–9
EHR   *English Historical Review*
ECHR   *Economic History Review*
Firth & Rait *Acts and Ordinances of the Interregnum, 1642–1660,* ed. C. H.
      Firth and R. S. Rait, 3 vols, 1911
HJ   *Historical Journal*
HMC   Historical Manuscripts Commission (designated by the number
      of the *Report* or the name of the collection calendared)
JBS   *Journal of British Studies*
Lomas, *Letters & Speeches*
      T. Carlyle, *Oliver Cromwell's Letters and Speeches, with*
      elucidations, ed. S. C. Lomas, 3 vols, 1904
LJ   *Journals of the House of Lords* fol., n.d.
P&P   *Past and Present*
PRO   Public Record Office, London
SP   State Papers (when cited direct from manuscripts and not
      from printed *Calendars*)
TSP   *A Collection of the State Papers of John Thurloe, Esq. . . .,* ed.
      Thomas Birch, 7 vols fol., 1742
TRHS   *Transactions of the Royal Historical Society*

Other abbreviations: titles of books and articles have usually been shortened
after their first citation

Bibliography

GENERAL

NB Items that are relevant for more than one chapter, or that are cited in the editor's Introduction, are listed here and full publication details are not repeated subsequently. Place of publication is London unless specified otherwise.

W. C. Abbott (ed.), *The Writings and Speeches of Oliver Cromwell* 4 vols (Cambridge, Mass. 1937–47).

M. Ashley, *The Greatness of Oliver Cromwell* (paperback repr. 1957).

H. N. Brailsford, *The Levellers and the English Revolution*, ed. C. Hill (1961).

D. Brunton and D. H. Pennington, *Members of the Long Parliament* (1954).

G. Davies, *The Restoration of Charles II, 1658–1660* (San Marino, Cal. 1955; repr. Oxford 1969).

A. Everitt, *The Community of Kent and the Great Rebellion, 1640–60* (Leicester 1966).

—— *Change in the Provinces: the seventeenth century* (Dept. of English Local History, Occasional Papers, 2nd ser., i, 1969).

—— *The Local Community and the Great Rebellion* (Historical Association pamphlet G.70., 1969).

—— *Suffolk and the Great Rebellion, 1640–1660* (Suffolk Rec. Soc., iii, 1960).

C. H. Firth, *The Last Years of the Protectorate, 1656–1658*, 2 vols (1909; repr. New York 1964).

—— *Oliver Cromwell and the Rule of the Puritans in England* (1901; repr. Oxford, 'World Classics' ser.).

F. J. Fisher (ed.), *Essays in the Economic and Social History of Tudor and Stuart England: in honour of R. H. Tawney* (Cambridge 1961).

S. R. Gardiner, *The History of the Great Civil War, 1642–1649* 3 vols (1886–91); 2nd edn 4 vols (1893).

—— *History of the Commonwealth and Protectorate* 3 vols (1894–1901); 2nd edn 4 vols (1903).

—— (ed.), *The Constitutional Documents of the Puritan Revolution, 1625–1660* 3rd edn (Oxford 1906).

C. Hill, *The Century of Revolution, 1603–1714* (Edinburgh 1961; repr. 1970).

—— *Intellectual Origins of the English Revolution* (Oxford 1965).

—— *God's Englishman: Oliver Cromwell and the English Revolution* (1970).

R. Howell, *Newcastle-upon-Tyne and the Puritan Revolution: a study of the Civil War in North England* (Oxford 1967).

J. P. Kenyon (ed.), *The Stuart Constitution, 1603–1688* (Cambridge 1966).

W. Lamont, *Godly Rule. Politics and Religion, 1603–1660* (1969).

C. B. Macpherson, *The Political Thought of Possessive Individualism* (Oxford 1962).

R. S. Paul, *The Lord Protector: Religion and Politics in the life of Oliver Cromwell* (1955).

V. Pearl, *London and the Outbreak of the Puritan Revolution 1625–1643* (Oxford 1961).

I. Roots, *The Great Rebellion 1642–1660* (1966).

W. A. Shaw, *A History of the English Church during the Civil Wars and under the Commonwealth 1640–1660* 2 vols (1900).

L. Stone, *Crisis of the Aristocracy 1558–1641* (Oxford 1965).

—— (ed.), *Social Change and Revolution in England 1540–1640* (*Problems and Perspectives* ser. 1965).

H. Trevor-Roper, *Historical Essays* (1957).

—— *Religion, the Reformation and Social Change* (1967).

—— *The Gentry 1540–1640* (Econ. Hist. Soc., supplmts, i, 1953).

D. Underdown, *Royalist Conspiracy in England 1649–1660* (New Haven 1960).

—— *Pride's Purge: Politics in the Puritan Revolution* (Oxford 1971).

C. V. Wedgwood, *The King's Peace 1637–1641* (1955)

—— *The King's War 1641–1647* (1958), parts i and ii of 'The Great Rebellion'.

—— *The Trial of Charles I* (1964); also published as *A Coffin for King Charles* (New York).

C. Wilson, *England's Apprenticeship 1603–1763* (An economic and social history of England) (1965).

P. Zagorin, *The Court and the Country: the beginning of the English Revolution* (1969).

—— *History of Political Thought in the English Revolution* (1954; repr. New York 1966).

1. LONDON'S COUNTER-REVOLUTION

Besides the standard account in Gardiner's *Great Civil War*, now greatly in need of replacement by a fresh synthesis, and other works cited in the General Bibliography, see:

1. Valerie Pearl, 'London Puritans and Scotch Fifth Columnists: a Mid-Seventeenth Century Phenomenon', in *Essays on London History presented to P. E. Jones*, ed. A. E. J. Hollaender and William Kellaway (1969).

2. Lawrence Kaplan, 'Presbyterians and Independents in 1643', EHR, lxxxiv (1969).

3. David Underdown, 'The Independents Again', JBS, viii (1968).

4. George Yule, 'Independents and Revolutionaries', JBS, vii (1968).

5. Valerie Pearl, 'The Royal Independents in the English Civil War', TRHS, 5th ser., xviii (1968).

6. Valerie Pearl, 'Oliver St John and the Middle Group in the Long Parliament', EHR, lxxxi (1966).

7. David Underdown, 'The Independents Reconsidered', JBS, iii (1964).

8. J. H. Hexter, *Re-appraisals in History* (1960): 'The problem of the Presbyterian Independents'.

9. J. H. Hexter, *The Reign of King Pym* (Cambridge, Mass. 1941).

2. THE LEVELLERS AND THE FRANCHISE

The most important Leveller writings have been collected in *Tracts on Liberty in the Puritan Revolution*, ed. William Haller (New York 1933–4; reprinted 1965); *Leveller Manifestoes of the Puritan Revolution*, ed. Don M. Wolfe (New York 1944; repr. 1967); *The Leveller Tracts, 1647–1653*, ed. William Haller and Godfrey Davies (New York 1944; repr. Gloucester, Mass. 1964).

The text of the Putney Debates was printed by C. H. Firth in vol. i of *The Clarke Papers* (Camden Soc. 1891–1901). It was re-edited by A. S. P. Woodhouse in *Puritanism and Liberty* (1938).

The best modern accounts of the Leveller movement are Joseph Frank, *The Levellers* (Cambridge, Mass. 1955) and Brailsford (the most detailed treatment so far). Theodore Calvin Pease, *The Leveller Movement* (Washington, D.C. 1916; repr. Gloucester, Mass. 1965) is still strong on the constitutional aspects. Valuable studies of Leveller thought can also be found in W. Schenk, *The Concern for Social Justice in the Puritan Revolution* (1948); D. B. Robertson, *The Religious Foundations of Leveller Democracy* (New York 1951); Zagorin, *Political Thought*; Christopher Hill, 'The Norman Yoke', in *Puritanism and Revolution* (1958); Pauline Gregg, *Free-born John. A Biography of John Lilburne* (1961). Howard Shaw, *The Levellers* (1968) is a recent summary.

Professor C. B. Macpherson's interpretation of the Levellers comes in his *The Political Theory of Possessive Individualism* (Oxford 1962) pp. 107–59. His arguments have been endorsed by Hill, 'Pottage for Freeborn Englishmen: Attitudes to Wage Labour in the sixteenth and seventeenth centuries', in *Socialism, Capitalism and Economic Growth*, ed. C. H. Feinstein (Cambridge 1967). They have been criticised by A. L. Merson, 'Problems of the English bourgeois revolution', in *Marxism Today*, vii (1963); Peter Laslett, 'Market society and political theory', HJ, vii (1964), pp. 150–4; J. C. Davis, 'The Levellers and Democracy', P&P, xl (1968); and Roger Howell, Jr and David E. Brewster, 'Reconsidering the Levellers: the evidence of *The Moderate*', P&P, xlvi (1970). The most thorough-going critique is A. L. Morton, *Leveller Democracy – Fact or Myth?* (*Our History*, pamphlet no. 51, 1968; repr. in his book, *The World of the Ranters* [1970]).

The following articles are also relevant: G. E. Aylmer, 'Gentlemen Levellers?', P&P, xlix (1970); R. L. Bushman, 'English franchise reform in the seventeenth century', JBS, iii (1963); J. H. Plumb, 'The Growth of the Electorate in England from 1600 to 1715', P&P, xlv (1969); V. F. Snow, 'Parliamentary re-apportionment proposals in the Puritan Revolution', EHR, lxxiv (1959).

3. CONQUEST AND CONSENT

Zagorin provides the best introductory sketch of political theory under the Commonwealth. See also the Introductions to the first four volumes of *The Complete Prose Works of John Milton* (New Haven 1953–66) under the general editorship of Don M. Wolfe.

The best general account of the engagement controversy is John M. Wallace, *Destiny his Choice: The Loyalism of Andrew Marvell* (Cambridge 1968), ch. 1. The best account of the relations between historical and political thinking during the revolution is J. G. A. Pocock, *The Ancient Constitution and the Feudal Law* (Cambridge 1957). The relations between the historical and political views of the *de facto* theorists are discussed in Quentin Skinner, 'History and Ideology in the English Revolution', HJ, viii (1965), 151–78. The relations between *de facto* writings and Hobbes's political theory are further pursued in Quentin Skinner, 'The Ideological Context of Hobbes's Political Thought', HJ ix (1966), 286–317. Among the *de facto* theorists only Ascham, Dury and Nedham have been separately studied. There is as yet no modern edition of Ascham, but there is now a critical edition of Marchamont Nedham, *The Case of the Commonwealth of England, Stated*, ed. Philip A. Knachel (Charlottesville 1969), with a valuable Introduction on Nedham as a political writer. Ascham is discussed in Irene Coltman, *Private Men and Public Causes* (1964) (mainly a biographical account) and in J. A. W. Gunn, *Politics and the Public Interest in the Seventeenth Century* (1969) (a brief paraphrase). Coltman's interpretation is convincingly challenged by John M. Wallace, 'The Cause too Good', *Journal of the History of Ideas*, xxiv (1963), 150–4. Dury is discussed in G. H. Turnbull, *Hartlib, Dury and Comenius* (Liverpool 1947) and in J. M. Batten, *John Dury* (Chicago 1944).

The literature on Hobbes is of course vast. The fullest recent checklist of secondary authorities has been compiled by Arrigo Pacchi, and published in *Rivista Critica di Storia della Filosofia*, xvii (1962), 528–47. See also H. Macdonald and M. Hargreaves, *Thomas Hobbes: A Bibliography* (1953). The best biography will always be the account given by John Aubrey, even though many of its details must remain doubtful. A paperback edition of Aubrey's *Brief Lives*, ed. Oliver Lawson Dick (1969) is available. The fullest analysis of Hobbes's contemporary reputation is contained in Samuel I. Mintz, *The Hunting of Leviathan* (1962). See also the important essay on the context of Hobbes's thought by Keith Thomas, 'The Social Origins of Hobbes's Political Thought', in *Hobbes Studies*, ed. K. C. Brown (1965), a brilliant and learned critique of C. B. Macpherson's remarkable attempt to present Hobbes as the original apologist of 'bourgeois' and 'market' values in politics (in *The Political Theory of Possessive Individualism: Hobbes to Locke* [1962]). The best recent general accounts of Hobbes's political system are M. M. Goldsmith, *Hobbes's Science of Politics* (New York 1967) and J. W. N. Watkins, *Hobbes's System of Ideas* (1965). The major concern of recent commentators has been Hobbes's theory of obligation. A very subtle general account is given by Michael Oakeshott in the Introduction to his edition of *Leviathan* (Oxford 1946). An attempt to assimilate Hobbes's theory of obligation to the Christian natural law tradition is made by H. Warrender, *The Political Philosophy of Hobbes* (Oxford 1957). For criticisms see the important essay by Stuart M. Brown, 'The Taylor Thesis: Some Objections', and other contributions in *Hobbes Studies*. The most extreme such interpretation is F. C. Hood, *The Divine Politics of Thomas Hobbes* (Oxford 1964). For criticism, see Quentin Skinner, 'Hobbes's *Leviathan*', HJ, vii (1964), 321–33. For a valuable and less contentious recent account of Hobbes's views about the state of nature and natural law see F. S. McNeilly, *The Anatomy of Leviathan* (1968).

4. THE CHURCH IN ENGLAND 1646–1660

J. Stoughton, *Ecclesiastical History of England from the Opening of the Long Parliament to the Death of Oliver Cromwell*, 2 vols (1867) is old-fashioned, but readable and contains ideas still worth developing. Shaw, *A History of the English Church* is invaluable as a work of reference but somewhat indigestible as a narrative; he concentrated almost exclusively on the national church, and hardly considered the separatist churches at all.

Among the many books on the growth of Puritanism in seventeenth-century England the most illuminating are W. Haller, *The Rise of Puritanism* (New York 1938) and *Liberty and Reformation in the Puritan Revolution* (New York 1955); and Hill, *Puritanism and Revolution* (1958) and *Society and Puritanism in Pre-Revolutionary England* (1964). Three other books contain valuable detail on religious thought from 1640 to 1660: W. K. Jordan, *The Development of Religious Toleration in England from the Convention of the Long Parliament to the Restoration 1640–1660*, 2 vols (Boston, Mass. and London 1938–40) – much wider in scope than the title may suggest; on the chaplains of the New Model Army see L. F. Solt, *Saints in Arms, Puritanism and Democracy in Cromwell's Army* (1959); for the idea of the millennium in the first half of the seventeenth century see Lamont, *Godly Rule*. Among biographies of Cromwell note especially R. S. Paul, *The Lord Protector: Religion and Politics in the Life of Oliver Cromwell* (1955).

G. F. Nuttall, in his pioneering studies, *The Holy Spirit in Puritan Faith and Experience* (Oxford 1946) and *Visible Saints: the Congregational Way, 1640–1660* (Oxford 1957) successfully transcends denominationalism. R. W. Dale, *History of English Congregationalism* (1907), gives a more traditional account of Independency. A. C. Underwood, *A History of English Baptists* (1947) is a more readable account of Baptist history than W. T. Whitley, *History of British Baptists* (1923), although the latter is still useful. W. C. Braithwaite, *Beginnings of Quakerism* (2nd edn, Cambridge 1955) is the standard work, but see the vigorous, recent study by H. Barbour, *The Quakers in Puritan England* (New Haven 1964). For the prelatical Anglicans who refused to compromise see R. S. Bosher, *The Making of the Restoration Settlement: the Influence of the Laudians 1649–1662* (1951). G. B. Tatham, *The Puritans in Power* (Cambridge 1913), is limited to the effect of the Puritan Revolution on the Church of England. G. R. Abernathy, 'The English Presbyterians and the Stuart Restoration 1648–1663', *Transactions of the American Philosophical Society*, New Series, vol. lv, part 11 (1965) concentrates on the period 1659 to 1663. All who work on church history between 1642 and 1662 are indebted to A. G. Matthews for his biographical reference books on the clergy of both sides who were ejected from their livings: *Calamy Revised: being a revision of Edmund Calamy's Account of the ministers and others ejected and silenced 1660–2* (Oxford 1934), and *Walker Revised: being a revision of John Walker's Sufferings of the clergy during the Grand Rebellion 1642–60* (Oxford 1948). There are numerous articles in the *Journal of Ecclesiastical History*, *Church History* and such denominational journals as *Transactions of the Congregational Historical Society*, *Transactions of the Baptist Historical Society* (now continued in the *Baptist Quarterly*), *Journal of the Presbyterian Historical Society of England* and the *Journal of the Friends Historical Society*.

For the localities see Howell, *Newcastle* and Everitt, *Kent*. H. Smith, *The Ecclesiastical History of Essex under the Long Parliament and Commonwealth* (Colchester 1933) is a source book rather than a coherent narrative but it is useful as a guide to what material may be available nationally and locally.

Lastly there are the primary records. The period abounds in diaries: among some of perhaps the most enjoyable and easily accessible diaries and personal narratives are R. Baxter, *Autobiography* (1931); L. Hutchinson, *Memoirs of Col. Hutchinson* (1965); *Diary of John Evelyn*, ed. E. S. De Beer, 6 vols (Oxford 1955); *The Diary of the Rev. Ralph Josselin 1616–1683*, ed. E. Hockcliffe, (Camden Society, 3rd ser. xv, 1908). The records of the national and the gathered churches are well worth sampling. Presbyterian *classes* can be seen in action in *Register-Booke of the Fourth London Classis in the Province of London*, ed. C. E. Surman, (Harleian Society, nos. 82 and 83, 1953), or W. A. Shaw, *Minutes of Bury Presbyterian Classis* (Chetham Society, 150, 1896). The minute book of the London provincial assembly is in Syon College, London: MS.L.40. 2/E17 (t.s. version by C. E. Surman, Dr Williams's Library). The Directory of Worship is printed in full in *Reliquiae Liturgicae*, ed. P. Hall, iii (Bath 1847). The separatist churches spring excitingly to life in *Records of a Church of Christ meeting in Broadmead, Bristol, 1640–1687*, ed. E. B. Underhill (Hanserd Knollys Society, 1847), an account of the founding of a church written by a member a generation later, and *Records of the Church of Christ gathered at Fenstanton, Warboys and Hexham, 1644–1720*, ed. E. B. Underhill (Hanserd Knollys Society, 1851), the minute books of three different Baptist churches.

5. SOCIAL AND ECONOMIC POLICIES UNDER THE COMMONWEALTH

Slingsby Bethel's attack on the Protectorate's commercial and foreign policies and panegyric on the Rump's in *The World's Mistake in Oliver Cromwell* (1668, repr. *Harleian Miscellany*, i) reproduced the arguments of the republicans in the Commons' debates in 1659. Roger Coke in *A Detection of the Court and State of England* (1694) attacked the Navigation Acts of 1651 and 1660 and the main policies of the 1650s and 1660s. A. Anderson's influential *An Historical and Chronological Deduction of the Origins of Commerce* (1764) praised the Rump for its Navigation Act and for reducing the rate of interest and denounced Cromwell's war with Spain. Adam Smith shared Anderson's enthusiasm for the 1651 act and exaggerated his tendency to see the act of 1660 as merely a re-enactment. J. R. Seeley, *The Expansion of England* (1883) (pp. 110–17) saw the Protectorate as a decisive new beginning in commercial and colonial policies, breaking with those of the early Stuarts. A much more evolutionary view of these developments, though still assigning importance to the Protectorate, was taken in two detailed studies by Americans, G. L. Beer, *The Origins of the British Colonial System 1578–1660* (New York 1908) and C. M. Andrews, *British Committees, Commissions and Councils of Trade and Plantations* (Baltimore 1908). Meanwhile W. Cunningham, *Growth of English Industry and Commerce* (1st edn 1882, 6th edn 1920) had revived both Bethel's disparaging of Cromwell and Coke's attack on the results of the 1651 act. While emphasising difficulties in enforcing the later Navigation Acts, Cunningham put the decisive creative developments after 1660. His most important influence was in postulating a decisive break in paternalistic social and economic regulation at home after 1640 (see above p. 121). He was followed in this by G. Unwin, in his *Industrial Organisation in the sixteenth and seventeenth centuries* (Oxford 1904), and by R. H. Tawney, in *The Agrarian Problem in the sixteenth century* (1912). The same general thesis received detailed illustration in E. Lipson, *Economic History of England* ii, iii, *The Age of Mercantilism* (1st edn 1931, 6th edn 1956) and explicitly expressed in *The Growth of English Society* (1949). Of the two most detailed studies of the Interregnum, M. Ashley, *The Financial and Commercial Policies of the Cromwellian Protectorate* (1934, 2nd edn 1962) took a less gloomy view than Cunningham, but saw them 'as a gradual return to old ways'. The other, M. James, *Social Problems and Policy during the Puritan Revolution 1640–1660* (1930) tended to reinforce Cunningham's thesis of a decisive break in economic regulation due to the Civil War (see above pp. 122–3), although J. U. Nef's *Industry and Government in France and England 1540–1640* (Philadelphia 1940) suggested that government control had never been as effective in England. More recently these assumptions about economic regulation have been further modified by work such as M. G. Davies, *The Enforcement of English Apprenticeship 1563–1642* (Harvard 1956) while those about the poor law were damagingly criticised by W. K. Jordan, *Philanthropy in England 1480–1660* (1959), ch. v. Recent work has clarified changes in the structure of overseas trade in the seventeenth century and is ably summarised in W. E. Minchinton's introduction as editor to *The Growth of English Overseas Trade in the Seventeenth and Eighteenth Centuries* (1969) and more briefly by R. Davis in *A Commercial Revolution* (Historical Association, 1967). The latter's *Rise of the English Shipping Industry* (1962) illuminates a basic aspect of Anglo-Dutch rivalry, of which C. H. Wilson, *Profit and Power* (1957) gives a general account. In addition to recent works cited in the text, J. E. Farnell, 'The Navigation Act of 1651, the first Dutch War and the London Merchant Community', ECHR, 2nd ser., xvi (1964) is of particular interest. Firth, Tawney and Unwin all believed that the Civil War caused considerable transfers of land which were responsible for social and economic changes, but H. J. Habakkuk has shown that transfers and their consequences were less revolutionary than has often been supposed ('Public Finance and the Sale of Confiscated Property during the Interregnum', ECHR xv [1962–3]; 'Landowners and the Civil War', *Ibid.*, xviii [1965]; cf. J. Thirsk, 'The Restoration Land Settlement', *Journal of Modern History*, xxvi [1954]). Nevertheless agricultural improvements were much canvassed in the 1650s and were being applied, though E. Kerridge, *The Agricultural Revolution* (1967) may exaggerate their extent. Of the two most recent general economic histories, the interpretation of C. Hill, *Reformation to Industrial Revolution* (1967; Pelican edn 1969) synthesises recent work, republican apologetics and that part of Cunningham's legacy that stressed the end of regulation to see the Commonwealth as a period of decisive innovation (see also pp. 121–3 above), while C. H. Wilson, *England's Apprenticeship 1603–1763* (1965) offers a much more evolutionary interpretation of the 1650s and, following another of Cunningham's leads, tends to find the most positive developments after 1660.

6. CROMWELL'S ORDINANCES: THE EARLY LEGISLATION OF THE PROTECTORATE

Besides the standard works by Gardiner, Firth and Abbott, and the recent biographies of Cromwell by Paul and Hill, information on other members of the Council of State can be found in the DNB, supplemented for the military men by M. P. Ashley, *Cromwell's Generals* (1954). W. H. Dawson's pedestrian *Cromwell's Understudy* (1938) is the only life of Lambert. There is as yet no satisfactory study of Thurloe.

C. H. Firth and R. S. Rait, *Acts and Ordinances of the Interregnum, 1642–1660*, 3 vols (1911), though superseding H. Scobell, *A Collection of Acts and Ordinances* (1658), is incomplete and was rather hastily edited. A collection of documents on the law and working of the constitution during the Interregnum is in preparation by D. H. Pennington and I. Roots. The legal ordinances are considered in D. Veall, *The Popular Movement for Law Reform 1640–1660* (Oxford 1970). See also S. E. Prall, *The Agitation for Law Reform during the Puritan Revolution* (The Hague 1966). Informed discussion of other ordinances, including investigation of their implementation or lack of it in the localities, has hardly been attempted, though Matthews and Shaw are useful on ecclesiastical arrangements. Knowledge of the administrative history of the Protectorate, to which a number of the 1653–4 ordinances contribute, will be enhanced when the results of Professor G. E. Aylmer's researches, continuing *The King's Servants* (1961), are published.

'Cromwell and his Parliaments' are brusquely handled by H. R. Trevor-Roper in *Essays Presented to Sir Lewis Namier*, ed. R. Pares and A. J. P. Taylor (1956); revised version in *Religion, the Reformation and Social Change* (1967). (Some of its conclusions are challenged in two articles by P. J. Pinckney, mentioned in note 32 to this chapter.)

7. SETTLEMENT IN THE COUNTIES 1653–1658

The essays by Roots, Everitt and Pennington in *The English Revolution, 1600–1660*, ed. E. W. Ives (1968) together provide a brief, general introduction to the relationship between the State and the local communities during the Civil War. The outstanding work is Everitt's *Community of Kent*, though its coverage of the Protectorate is disappointing. Everitt's other works (see note 2 to this chapter) should also be consulted. A. H. Dodd, *Studies in Stuart Wales* (Cardiff 1952) includes a valuable discussion of the Welsh committees. David Underdown, *Pride's Purge: Politics in the Puritan Revolution* (Oxford 1971) has two chapters on the revolution and the localities. Older county histories offer little guidance, though Mary Coate, *Cornwall in the Great Civil War and Interregnum* (Oxford 1933) and Alfred C. Wood, *Nottinghamshire in the Civil War* (Oxford 1937) are suggestive.

F. P. and M. M. Verney, *Memoirs of the Verney Family* (1892–9), iii, in spite of naïve and chaotic editing, is still the best source for the day-to-day life of the Cavalier and non-partisan gentry. Paul H. Hardacre, *The Royalists during the Puritan Revolution* (The Hague 1956) surveys all but the Royalists' conspiratorial activities. The major-generals' system is examined in detail by D. W. Rannie, 'Cromwell's Major-Generals', EHR, x (1895), 471–506. See also the chapter by Roots in *The English Civil War and After, 1642–1658*, ed. R. H. Parry (1970). Paul J. Pinckney, 'The Cheshire Election of 1656', *Bulletin of the John Rylands Library*, xlix (1967), 387–426, throws interesting light on the state of gentry opinion at this time.

Abbot, *Writings and Speeches* contains many basic documents. Quarter sessions records where published often provide fascinating illustrations of local government at work. On the poor law and other social problems, see above Chapter 5, and the further reading suggested there.

8. LAST QUESTS FOR SETTLEMENT 1657–1660

The closing stages of Cromwell's rule are treated in masterly fashion by Firth in his *Last Years*. Godfrey Davies continues the political narrative on the same scale in *The Restoration of Charles II*; he is generally accurate but rather meagre in interpretation. There are good briefer accounts of these years in Roots, *Great Rebellion*, and in Davies, *The Early Stuarts* (*Oxford History of England*, 2nd edn 1959). Firth also contributed an excellent chapter on 'Anarchy and the Restoration' to the old *Cambridge Modern History*, iv (1906). There is special emphasis on quests for a settlement in my introduction to *The Complete Prose of John Milton*, vii (Yale), now in the press. Articles that bear on the subject include Woolrych, 'The Good Old Cause and the Fall of the Protectorate', CHJ, xiii (1957) and 'The Collapse of the Great Rebellion', in *Conflicts in Tudor and Stuart England*, ed. Ivan Roots (Edinburgh 1967). A vivid account of these years by a contemporary with a strong republican bias is in *The Memoirs of Edmund Ludlow*, ed. C. H. Firth, ii (Oxford 1894).

REFERENCES AND NOTES ON TEXT

INTRODUCTION: THE QUEST FOR SETTLEMENT   *G. E. Aylmer*

1. L. Stone, 'The Educational Revolution in England, 1560–1640', P&P, xxviii (1964), and 'Social Mobility in England, 1500–1700', P&P, xxxiii (1966); G. R. Elton, a review (kindly but rightly critical) of the present editor's textbook, *The Struggle for the Constitution*, in the Italian journal *Annali della Fondazione italiana per la storia amministrativa*, ii (1965), 759–66 (in English) (see also Elton's paper 'A High Road to Civil War?', on the Commons' Apology of 1604, in *From Renaissance to Counter-Reformation Essays in honour of Garrett Mattingly*, ed. C. H. Carter (1966); compare Stone, 'Theories of Revolution', *World Politics*, xviii (1966), 159–76; P. Laslett, *The World We have Lost* (1965), p. 4 (see also ch. 7, 'Social Change and Revolution in the Traditional World', esp. pp. 150–1, 158, 160–2, 164).

2. See L. Stone, *The Crisis of the Aristocracy 1558–1641* (Oxford 1965), esp. pp. 9–10, 15–17, 746–53, as well as Stone, *Social Change and Revolution* and 'Social Mobility'.

3. See D. Brunton and D. H. Pennington, *Members of the Long Parliament* (1954), ch. 2; and an important article, D. Underdown, 'Party management in the recruiter elections, 1645–1648', EHR, lxxxiii (1968), 235–64; DNB, John Swinfen (1612–94), M.P. for Stafford.

4. For a comparison of the Propositions with the Heads, see *Constitutional Documents of the Puritan Revolution 1625–1660*, ed. S. R. Gardiner (3rd edn Oxford 1906 and reprinted), nos, 66 and 71.

5. A full bibliography is not possible here. The following may be suggested as a beginning: A. R. Hall, *The Scientific Revolution 1500–1800* (1954) and *From Galileo to Newton* (*Rise of Modern Science ser.* iii) (1963), ch. v; articles by C. Hill, H. F. Kearney, T. K. Rabb, G. Whittredge and B. J. Schapiro in P&P, xxvii–xxxiii (1964–6) and xl (1968), the last with excellent bibliographical footnotes; M. Purver, *The Royal Society: Concept and Creation* (1967); Hill, 'Newton and his Society', *Texas Quarterly*, autumn 1967, and 'Intellectual Origins of the Royal Society–London or Oxford?', *Notes & Records of the Royal Society*, xxiii (1968); articles by P. M. Rattansi and C. Webster in the history of science journal *Ambix*, xi and xiv (1965 and 1968), and by Hall and Webster in *History of Science*, ii and vi (1963 and 1967); Kearney, *Science and Change* (1971). On the related, if only less controversial, question of educational change in relation to politics and religion, the best discussion is now *Samuel Hartlib and the advancement of learning* ed. C. Webster (Cambridge 1970), esp. pp. 38–72; this may be followed up with W. A. L. Vincent, *The State and School Education in England and Wales 1640–60* (1950).

6. According to another calculation, in King's notebooks, those in receipt of alms totalled between about a quarter and a fifth of the whole population (J. P. Cooper, 'The Social Distribution of Land and Men in England 1436–1700', ECHR, 2nd ser. xx (1967), App. II, p. 440).

7. The best account of this is now H. J. Habakkuk, 'The Parliamentary Army and the Crown Lands', *Welsh Hist. Rev.*, iii (1967); see also I. Gentles, 'The Management of the Crown Lands, 1649–60', *Agricultural History Review*, xix (1971).

8. See H. R. Trevor-Roper, 'Three Foreigners: the Philosophers of the English Revolution' and 'Cromwell and his Parliaments', in his *Religion, the*

Reformation and Social Change (1967); W. M. Lamont, *Godly Rule* (1969); A. Woolrych, 'The Calling of Barebone's Parliament', EHR, lxxx (1965); J. E. Farnell, 'The Usurpation of Honest London Householders: Barebone's Parliament', EHR, lxxxii (1967); Woolrych, 'Cromwell and the Saints' in *The English Civil War and After 1642–58*, ed. G. B. Parry (1970); also Tai Liu, 'The Calling of the Barebone's Parliament Reconsidered', *Journal of Ecclesiastical History*, xxii (1971); *Puritans, the Millennium and the future of Israel: Puritan Eschatology 1600 to 1660*, ed. P. Toon (1970), ch. by B. S. Capp; A. L. Morton, *The World of the Ranters* (1970); H. Barbour, *The Quakers in Puritan England* (New Haven 1964); A. Cole, 'The Quakers and the English Revolution', P&P, x (1956), repr. in *Crisis in Europe 1560–1660*, ed. T. Aston (1965; paperback edn 1970); Cole, 'Social Origins of the early Friends', *Journal of the Friends' Hist. Soc.*, xlviii (1957); R. T. Vann, *The Social Development of English Quakerism 1655–1755* (Cambridge, Mass. 1969); Vann, 'Quakerism and the Social Structure in the Interregnum', P&P, xliii (1969); Judith J. Hurwich, 'The Social Origins of the early Quakers'; and Vann, 'Rejoinder', in P&P, xlviii (1970). There is also much valuable material about the radical sectaries of the Interregnum in Keith Thomas, *Religion and the Decline of Magic* (1971).

9. I owe this concept to the conclusion of a course of lectures given by Professor Trevor-Roper, in Oxford, over twenty years ago; I am not aware that it has been formulated in precisely this way in any published work.

10. By Mr Blair Worden of Pembroke College, Cambridge.

11. This is discussed at length in my forthcoming book, *The State's Servants* ch. 3, ss. viii–ix.

12. See Clayton Roberts, *The Growth of Responsible Government in Stuart England* (Cambridge 1966), ch. 4, esp. pp. 144–53; and M. J. C. Vile, *Constitutionalism and the Separation of Powers* (Oxford 1967), chs II and III, esp. pp. 32–57; also Aylmer, 'Place Bills and the Separation of Powers: some seventeenth century origins of the "Non-Political" Civil Service', TRHS, 5th ser. xv (1965), 45–69; W. B. Gwyn, *The Meaning of the Separation of Powers* (Tulane Studies in Political Science. ix. 1965), esp. ch. IV.

13. C. V. Wedgwood, *The Trial of Charles I* (1964; published in America as *A Coffin for King Charles*), p. 88.

14. See Gardiner, *Constnl. Docs.*, no. 81; *Leveller Manifestoes of the Puritan Revolution*, ed. Don M. Wolfe (New York 1944 and repr. London 1967), pp. 293–303 and 333–54.

15. Worden, 'Cromwell and the Dissolution of the Rump', EHR, lxxxvi (1971).

16. See the refs, cited in note 8 above.

17. See M. Ashley, *Financial and Commercial Policy under the Cromwellian Protectorate* (Oxford 1934), esp. introduction to the repr. edn (1962); G. D. Ramsay, 'Industrial Laissez-Faire and the Policy of Oliver Cromwell', ECHR, old ser. xvi (1946); M. Prestwich, 'Diplomacy and Trade in the Protectorate', *Journ. Mod. Hist.*, xxii (1950); M. Roberts, 'Cromwell and the Baltic', EHR, lxxvi (1961); many of the other works cited in Mr Cooper's chapter are also relevant here.

18. For Ireland, J. C. Beckett, *The Making of Modern Ireland 1603–1923* (revised and paperback edn 1966) is the best general account; see also *Irish Historical Studies* (Dublin 1937–) for articles and valuable bibliographical information; a large-scale, collaborative *New History of Ireland* is now in progress. For Scotland the best general account is G. Donaldson, *Scotland: James V to VII* (Edinburgh 1965); note also the brilliant synthesis of T. C. Smout, *History of the Scottish People 1560–1830* (1969). Neither has a great deal about

the years to English occupation and the forced Union (1654–60), on which see H. R. Trevor-Roper, 'Scotland and the Puritan Revolution', in *Historical Essays 1600–1750: presented to David Ogg*, ed. H. Bell and R. Ollard (1963), and repr. in Trevor-Roper, *Religion, the Reformation and Social Change* (1967). An important Glasgow Ph.D. thesis by D. Stevenson (1970) will shed additional light on Anglo-Scottish relations from 1637 to 1651 when it is published.

19. The forthcoming edn of James Harrington's *Oceana* and his other writings by Professor J. G. A. Pocock is likely to be of especial value; see also references in Mr Skinner's chapter and his articles already published in the *Historical Journal* and elsewhere.

20. V. Pearl, *London and the Outbreak of the Puritan Revolution 1625–1643* (Oxford 1961); see also R. Ashton, 'Charles I and the City of London', in *Essays in the Economic and Social History of Tudor and Stuart England: In honour of R. H. Tawney*, ed. F. J. Fisher (Cambridge 1961).

21. This is established in H. J. Habakkuk, 'Landowners and the Civil War', ECHR, 2nd ser. xviii (1965).

22. See B. S. Manning: 'The Nobles, the People and the Constitution', P&P, ix (1956), repr. in *Crisis in Europe*, ed. Aston; 'The Outbreak of the English Civil War', in *The English Civil War and After*, ed. Parry, and 'The Levellers', in *The English Revolution 1600–1660*, ed. E. W. Ives (1968).

23. The tendency towards the restoration of the old-established county families under the Protectorate, which is also supported for Wales by the evidence in A. H. Dodd, *Studies in Stuart Wales* (Cardiff 1952), ch. IV, 'Nerth y Committee', should not be confused with the thorough-going aristocratic reaction after 1660, particularly as exercised through the office of Lord Lieutenant.

24. W. K. Jordan, *Development of Religious Toleration in England*, (1938 and repr. Gloucester, Mass. 1965), iii, 357, 456–7; C. H. Firth, *Cromwell's Army* (3rd edn 1921), ch. III, pp. 34–5; Firth and G. Davies, *Regimental History of Cromwell's Army*, 2 vols (Oxford 1940), i, Introduction, pp. xvii–xxvii.

I. LONDON'S COUNTER-REVOLUTION   *Valerie Pearl*

1. Vestry Minute Book, St Stephen's Coleman Street, Guildhall MSS 4458/1, pp. 125, 135, 147, 161–2; *To the Right Worshipful, The Aldermen and Common Counsellmen of the Ward of Farringdon Within, at their Ward-Mote, 22 December 1645* [Thomason Tracts 669, f. 10 (41)]; Corporation of London Record Office, Journal of the Common Council, 40, f. 161; 'The Records of the Provincial Assembly of London, 1647–1660', ed. C. E. Surman (1957, typescript in Dr Williams's Library), ii, 295; Pearl, *London and the Outbreak of the Puritan Revolution*, pp. 167, 326.

2. Guildhall MSS 3016/1, 3570/2, 3570/2 f. 52v; 4458/1 p. 147 (records of various London parishes).

3. Cyprian Blagden, *The Stationers' Company* (1960), pp. 133, 135, 137; Leona Rostenberg, *Publishing, Printing and Bookselling in England 1551–1700* (New York 1965); Pearl, *London*, pp. 137, 253. I.P. [John Price], *The City-Remonstrance Remonstrated* (1646), p. 19.

4. J.Co.Co., 40, ff. 151v–153v; BM, Add. MS 18, 780 (Walter Yonge's diary) ff. 123–123v, 167v–169v.

5. J.Co.Co., 40, ff. 148–148v, 176, 186v, 199; 'Records of the London Provincial Assembly', ed. Surman, *passim*; CJ, v, 316, 324; J. Rushworth, *Historical Collections* (1701) part I, iv, 788; *Moderate Intelligencer*, no. 132, p. 1286, no. 133, p. 1299.

6. PRO, Commonwealth Exchequer Papers, SP 28/162; A. B. Beaven, *Aldermen of London*, 2 vols (1908–13).

7. Maurice Gethin was a woollen-draper: CSPD, 1625–49; J. R. Woodhead, *The Rulers of London 1660–1689* (1965), p. 76. So also were Aldermen Thomas Cullum and Thomas Adams. Laurence Bromfield was a cutler and swordmaker who supplied the parliamentary army: C. Welch, *History of the Cutlers* (1923), ii, 3; PRO Commonwealth Exchequer Papers SP 28/162 (unnumbered). John Gase supplied the parliamentary armies with bandoliers and spades: CSPD, 1645–7, p. 290; CSPD, 1650, p. 579. Colonel Edward Hooker was described as a distiller of Thames Street. There was a strong party of Presbyterians among booksellers: John Bellamy, George Thomason, Samuel and Thomas Gellibrand Thomas Underhill and Christopher Meredith. Lieutenant-Colonel Jeremy Baynes and Daniel Sowton were Southwark brewers. Colonel Joseph Vaughan was described as a leatherseller in Cornhill, but both he and Alderman Bunce may have been of the Company rather than of the trade. Colonel Thomas Gower is the only name appearing among leading Common Councilmen on the Committee of Militia who was primarily an overseas merchant, his particular trading area being the West Indian and American.

8. Aldermen Gibbs, Wollaston and Vyner were goldsmiths. For Adams and Cullum, see note 7. George Witham was of the Leathersellers' Company and John Bride of the Brewers'; this does not tell us their trade but neither was prominent in overseas trading companies: A. B. Beaven, *Aldermen of the City of London* (1908), ii, 67. Prominent merchants among the Presbyterian Party were Christopher Packe and Samuel Avery of the Merchant Adventurers' Company and Simon Edwards, who traded in the Levant.

9. J.Co.Co., 40, f. 151v *seq.*, 160v, 174–174v; BM, Add. MSS 31, 116 (Whittacre's diary) ff. 259v–260; CJ, iv, 479; R. Baillie, *Letters and Journals*, ed. David Laing (Edinburgh 1841), ii, 366.

10. *Certain Considerations and Cautions agreed upon by the Ministers of London, According to which they resolve to put the Presbyteriall Government in execution upon the Ordinances of Parliament* (June 1646); *Vindiciae Veritatis* (1654), part I, 38 *seq.*; Baillie, *Letters*, ii, 358.

11. *Ibid.*, ii, 365, 372.

12. J.Co.Co., 40, ff. 178v–181; also *The Humble Remonstrance and Petition of the Lord Mayor, Aldermen and Common Council, May 26 1646*.

13. *A Justification of the City Remonstrance ... 1646*; Baillie, *Letters*, ii, 368; I.P. [John Price] *The City-Remonstrance Remonstrated* (1646), p. 7.

14. *A Petition of Citizens of London. Presented to the Common Councell for their Concurrence with, and thankfulness and submission to the Parliament; and that nothing may be done, tending to disturb the Parliament*, delivered 22 May 1646; *The Humble Acknowledgement and Petition of Divers Inhabitants, 2 June 1646*; *The Humble Petition of divers well-affected Citizens and Freemen of London* (1646).

15. LJ, viii, 331–4; *The City's Remonstrance*.

16. BM, Add. MS 37, 344 (Bulstrode Whitelocke, 'Annals', ff. 52v–53).

17. Baillie, *Letters*, ii, 400.

18. Henry Burton, *Conformitie's Deformity* (1646).

19. CCAM, pp. 3–4, 18, 25, 31, 567; BM, Thomason Tracts, 669, f. 5 (134); J.Co.Co., 40 f. 148v; CJ, iv, 445; *Mercurius Civicus*, no. 143.

20. *Moderate Intelligencer*, no. 92; *The Weekly Account*, no. 52; *A Perfect Diurnal*, no. 175; CJ, v, 17; *The diplomatic correspondence of Jean de Montereul*, ed. J. G. Fotheringham (Edinburgh 1893), i, 354; J.Co.Co., 40, ff. 203, 174v.

21. *An Humble Representation of the pressing grievances, and important desires of the well-affected Freemen, and Covenant-engaged Citizens ...* (1646); *The*

H

Humble Petition of the Lord Mayor, Aldermen and Common Council of the City of London (1646); *The Humble Petition of many well-affected Freemen of the City of London* (1646/7); *To the Parliament: the petition of the Lord Mayor and Common Councell,* 17 March 1646 (1646–7); *Correspondence of Sir Edward Nicholas,* ed. G. F. Warner (Camden Soc., 1886), i, 81; J.Co.Co., 40, ff. 199v–200v, 204, 207.

22. J.Co.Co., 40, f. 204v; *The Humble Petition of many well-affected Freemen; Perfect Occurrences,* no. 5.

23. CJ, vi, 12, 15–17.

24. Whitelocke, Annals (BM, Add. MS 37, 344 f. 74v); CJ, v, 88–9, 91, 92–3; Whittacre's diary (BM, Add. MSS 31, 116 f. 302); *The Weekly Account,* no. 7, 15 Feb. 1647; *Moderate Intelligencer,* no. 102, 15–16 Feb. 1647; *Kingdomes Weekly Intelligencer,* no. 188.

25. Montereul, *Letters,* i, 430–1, ii, 44, 74; LJ, viii, 712; *Perfect Occurrences,* no. 6; *To the Parliament: the Petition of the Lord Mayor and Common Councell, 17 March 1646* (1646–7).

26. HMC, Portland MSS, part I, 447; LJ, ix, 115.

27. J.Co.Co. 40 f. 215v; Firth & Rait, i, 928, 990; CJ, v. 160–1, 188, 189, 203, 207; Harington's diary (BM, Add. MS 10, 114 f. 25); Firth, *Cromwell's Army,* p. 17; *Perfect Occurrences,* nos. 22, 23, 24; *Clarke Papers,* ed. C. H. Firth (Camden Soc., 1891), i, 152–6; *The Perfect Weekly Account,* 27 May 1647.

28. Firth & Rait, i, 928–935; CJ, v, 197, 205; *A Perfect Diurnal,* no. 201; *Perfect Occurrences,* no. 23.

29. CJ, v, 207, 199, 201, 197; LJ, ix, 245, 255, 248; Rushworth, *Hist. Colls.,* part I, iv, 553; Harington's diary (BM, Add. MS 10, 114 f. 25); Whittacre's diary (BM, Add. MS 31, 116 f. 312); Bodl., MS Clarendon 29, ff. 240, 236; Whitelocke, Annals (BM, Add. MS 37, 344 f. 91v).

30. J.Co.Co., 40, ff. 219–221v, 222–222v; CJ, v, 217, 214; D. Holles, *Memoirs* (1699), p. 161.

31. J.Co.Co., 40, f. 220v; Rushworth, *Hist. Colls.,* part IV, i, 558.

32. CJ, v, 238, 248–9, 253; BM, Egerton MS 1048 ff. 57–8; *A particular charge of Impeachment . . . 6 July 1647* (1647).

33. Whitelocke, Annals (BM, Add. MS 37, 344 f. 99); CJ, v, 252, 254–5; LJ, ix, 354; *A Perfect Diurnal,* no. 207; *A Petition from the City of London with a Covenant* (1647); *The Arraignment and Impeachment of Major Generall Massie* (1647).

34. CJ, v, 256; Firth & Rait, i, 928, 990; J.Co.Co., 40, ff. 238–240v; Whitelocke, Annals (BM, Add. MS 37, 344 ff. 100–100v); HMC, *Viscount de Lisle and Dudley MSS,* vi (1966) 569; Rushworth, *Hist. Colls.,* part IV, i, p. 747; *A Declaration of William Lenthal* (1647); *A Perfect Summary,* no. 2; *Clarke Papers,* i, 218; Stephen Marshall, *A Sermon preached to the two Houses of Parliament* (12 August 1647), p. 19; Harington's diary, (BM, Add. MS 10, 114 f. 25v).

35. Sir William Waller, *Vindication of the Character and Conduct of Sir William Waller* (1793), p. 183; Holles, *Memoirs,* p. 145; HMC, *de Lisle and Dudley,* vi, 569.

36. *A continuation of Certaine speciall and Remarkable Passages* (28 July 1647).

37. *A Perfect Diurnal,* 26 July–2 August 1647; Rushworth, *Hist. Colls.,* part IV, i, 646.

38. Waller, *Vindication,* pp. 105, 102, 104; Holles, *Memoirs,* pp. 153–4; Whitelocke, Annals (BM, Add. MS 37, 344 f. 101).

39. Whitelocke, Annals, f. 103; *The Memoirs of Edmund Ludlow,* ed. C. H. Firth (Oxford 1894), i, p. 164; *A Perfect Diurnal,* no. 210.

40. C. B. [Cornelius Burgess], *Sion College what it is, and doeth* (1648), pp. 22–3; Baillie, *Letters*, iii, 17.

41. *A Paire of Spectacles for the Citie* ('1648'), ['4 Dec. 1647': Thomason inscription], p. 6.

42. Waller, *Vindication*, pp. 188, 189; *A Copie of a Letter . . . 1647*.

43. Rushworth, *Hist. Colls.*, part IV, ii, 788, 792, 821, 828, 1126; Surman, *Records*, ii, 227, 241, 249, 281, 290; PRO, SP 16/539/201; HMC, *Seventh Report*, Appendix, pp. 686–7; CJ, v, 283; J.Co.Co., 40, f. 241; LJ, ix, 357.

44. Baillie, *Letters*, ii, 400; *Mr Love's Case*; G. R. Abernathy, *The English Presbyterians and the Stuart Restoration 1648–1663* (*Trans. Amer. Phil. Soc.*, 1965, lv, new ser., part II), pp. 17, 32, 49.

45. PRO, Commonwealth Exchequer Papers, SP/28/237; LJ, ix, 233.

46. *A word for the Armie*, p. 6; *A short Plea for the Commonwealth* (1651), p. 12.

47. LJ, ix, 282, 284–5; G. G. Harris, *The Trinity House of Deptford 1514–1660* (1969), pp. 34–9; H. Humpherus, *History of the Origin and Progress of the Company of Watermen and Lightermen of the river Thames* (1859), i, 234–6; *The Tower of London Letter-Book of Sir Lewis Dyve*, ed. H. G. Tibbutt, Bedfordshire Rec. Soc., xxxviii–xxix (1958–9), 75; *Persecutio Undecima* (1648), p. 68.

2. THE LEVELLERS AND THE FRANCHISE   *Keith Thomas*

This chapter is a revised version of a paper read originally to an Oxford seminar in 1963. I am grateful to Mr J. P. Cooper for much help on that occasion and to Mr A. L. Merson and Professor W. E. Minchinton for subsequent advice. I also owe a general debt to those writers (see Bibliography to this chapter, pp. 207–8 above) who first formulated in print many of the arguments restated in this chapter.

1. *The Clarke Papers*, ed. C. H. Firth (Camden Soc., 1891–1901), i, 328.

2. Macpherson, *Possessive Individualism*, pp. 294–6; but see also Richard B. Morris, *Government and Labor in Early America* (1946; reprinted New York 1965), p. 504 n. 15; and Pauline Gregg, *Free-born John* (1961), pp. 221–2, both of whom stress that the Levellers never wanted universal suffrage.

3. Warren O. Ault, 'Some early village by-laws', EHR, xlv (1930); 'Village by-laws by common consent', *Speculum*, xxix (1954); C. Bridenbaugh, *Vexed and Troubled Englishmen, 1590–1642* (Oxford 1968), p. 242; C. Gross, 'The early history of the ballot in England', *American Historical Review*, iii (1897–8), 462; Peter Laslett and John Harrison, 'Clayworth and Cogenhoe', in *Historical Essays, 1600–1750, presented to David Ogg*, ed. H. E. Bell and R. L. Ollard (1963), p. 158; G. R. Lewis, *The Stannaries* (1908; reprinted Truro 1965), p. 126.

4. Brian Manning, ECHR, 2nd ser., xxii (1969), 132.

5. G. D. Owen, *Elizabethan Wales* (Cardiff 1962), p. 233; Macpherson, *Possessive Individualism*, p. 112; Edward and Annie G. Porritt, *The Unreformed House of Commons* (Cambridge 1903).

6. Porritt, *Unreformed Commons*, i, 10.

7. John Glanville, *Reports of Certain Cases, Determined and Adjudged by the Commons in Parliament in the Twenty-First and Twenty-Second years of the Reign of King James the First* (1775), pp. 141–2; CJ, i, 893; R. L. Bushman, 'English franchise reform in the seventeenth century', JBS, iii (1963); J. H. Plumb, 'The Growth of the Electorate in England from 1600 to 1715', P&P, xlv (1969).

8. *Commons Debates, 1621*, ed. Wallace Notestein, Frances Helen Relf and

Hartley Simpson (New Haven 1935), iv, 421–2; Bushman, 'English Franchise Reform . . .'. appendix.

9. Mary Frear Keeler, *The Long Parliament, 1640–1641* (Amer. Phil. Soc., Philadelphia 1954), p. 8.

10. *The Journal of Sir Simonds D'Ewes*, ed. Wallace Notestein (New Haven 1923), p. 43; BM, Harleian MS 162, f. 377: D'Ewes's journal, 30 March 1641, cited by G. P. Gooch, *The History of English Democratic Ideas in the Seventeenth Century* (Cambridge 1898), p. 154n, where 'men resiants' was misread as 'non-vagrants'; CJ, ii, 114, 120, 129 (cf. p. 333).

11. Plumb, 'The growth of the electorate . . .', pp. 109, 108.

12. *Commons Debates, 1621*, iv, 22; *Journal of Sir Simonds D'Ewes*, ed. Notestein, p. 431; William Prynne, *Brevia Parliamentaria Rediviva* (1662), p. 187; John Cartwright, *The Legislative Rights of the Commonalty Vindicated: or, Take Your Choice!* (2nd edn, 1777), pp. 122–3.

13. John Lilburne, *Londons Liberty in Chains discovered* (1646), pp. 53–4; *Clarke Papers*, i, 316; *Leveller Manifestoes of the Puritan Revolution*, ed. Don M. Wolfe (New York 1967), p. 269.

14. Mary Reno Frear, 'The election at Great Marlow in 1640', *Journal of Modern History*, xiv (1942), 435n; *Verney Papers. Notes of Proceedings in the Long Parliament*, ed. John Bruce (Camden Soc., 1845), pp. 3–4; Keeler, *The Long Parliament*, p. 33; Bodl., Rawlinson MS C 949; William Bohun, *A Collection . . . touching the Right of Electing Members to serve in Parliament* (1702), esp. p. 257; (Thomas Carew), *A Historical Account of the Rights of Elections* (1745); T. Cunningham, *An Historical Account of the Rights of Election* (1783); CJ, viii, 351; xvi, 454; (James Burgh), *Political Disquisitions* (1774–5), i, 37.

15. R. N. Kershaw, 'The elections for the Long Parliament, 1640', EHR, xxxviii (1923), 502; T. H. B. Oldfield, *The Representative History of Great Britain and Ireland* (1816), iii, 197, 308; v, 231, 466; HMC, *Various Collections*, ii, 319; Bohun, *A Collection*, p. 257; Charles M. Andrews, *The Colonial Period of American History* (New Haven 1964), i, 180, 184; Wesley Frank Craven, *Dissolution of the Virginia Company* (Gloucester, Mass. 1964), pp. 277–8; A. G. Dickens, *The English Reformation* (revised edn, 1967), p. 399.

16. *The Works of Gerrard Winstanley*, ed. George H. Sabine (Ithaca, N.Y. 1941), p. 542; B. S. Capp, 'The Fifth Monarchy Men. An Analysis of their origins, activities, ideas and composition' (Oxford D.Phil. thesis, 1969), pp. 101–2; 'Laophilus Misotyrannus', *Mene Tekel: or the Downfal of Tyranny* (1663), p. 16.

17. *Clarke Papers*, i, 342, 301, 304.

18. *Clarke Papers*, i, 331, 338, 339–40, 315–16; Macpherson's description of Rainsborough's garbled reply as 'a fairly clear rejection of Rich's imputation' (p. 128) seems very unconvincing.

19. '*Brief Lives*' . . . *by John Aubrey*, ed. Andrew Clark (Oxford 1898), i, 290; Petty was, however, still a prominent Leveller in 1649 (C. H. Firth, 'Thomas Scot's account of his actions as intelligencer during the Commonwealth', EHR, xii [1897], 118); *The Memoirs of Edmund Ludlow*, ed. C. H. Firth (Oxford 1894), i, 166.

20. *Puritanism and Liberty*, ed. A. S. P. Woodhouse (1938), p. 452.

21. *The Case of the Army soberly discussed* (1647), p. 6; *Leveller Manifestoes*, p. 212.

22. *Canadian Journal of Economics and Political Science*, xi (1945), 635.

23. *Leveller Manifestoes*, pp. 217, 403. The punctuation of *The Case of the Army* is too erratic to allow the position of the commas to be taken as a guide to the authors' meaning.

24. *Puritanism and Liberty*, p. 357; *Leveller Manifestoes*, pp. 402–3, 269; John Wildman, *Truths Triumph* (1648), p. 4; *The Remonstrance of Many Thousands of the Free People of England* (1649), p. 4; Macpherson, *Possessive Individualism*, p. 118n.

25. 'Sirrahniho' (John Harris), *The Grande Designe* (1647), sig. B3ᵛ; *Leveller Manifestoes*, p. 269; Marchamont Nedham, *The Case of the Commonwealth of England, Stated*, ed. Philip A. Knachel (Charlottesville, Va. 1969), p. 98; *Clarke Papers*, i, 342; Davis, 'The Levellers and Democracy', p. 179; Oldfield, *Representative History*, iii, 20; iv, 278, 281–2, 436.

26. D. E. Underdown, 'The Parliamentary Diary of John Boys, 1647–8', *Bulletin of the Institute of Historical Research*, xxxix (1966), 152; Macpherson, *Possessive Individualism*, p. 147; *Leveller Manifestoes*, p. 270; Charles Herbert Mayo, *A Historic Guide to the Almshouses of St John Baptist and St John the Evangelist, Sherborne* (Oxford 1933), p. 44.

27. J. P. Cooper, The Social Distribution of Land and Men in England, 1436–1700', ECHR, 2nd ser., xx (1967), 437–40.

28. Mayo, *A Present for Servants*, p. 3.

29. E.g. 20 Geo. ii, c. xix (1747); William Gouge, *Of Domesticall Duties* (3rd edn, 1634), p. 695; Richard Baxter, *Chapters from A Christian Directory*, ed. Jeannette Tawney (1925), p. 27; Thomas Fuller, *The Holy State* (2nd edn, Cambridge 1648), p. 112; Edward Chamberlayne, *Angliae Notitia* (1669), p. 513.

30. 6 & 7 Gul. & Mar., c. 6; *London Inhabitants within the Walls*, (London Rec. Soc., 1966), introduction by D. V. Glass, p. xx.

31. R. B. Schlatter, *The Social Ideas of Religious Leaders, 1660–1668* (1940), pp. 81–3.

32. *The Works of John Whitgift*, ed. John Ayre (Parker Soc., 1851–3), i, 456; Firth & Rait, i, 835; John Eliot, *The Christian Commonwealth* (1659), pp. 5–6; Gordon J. Schochet, 'Patriarchalism, politics and mass attitudes in Stuart England', HJ, xii (1969), 423n.

33. *The Inhabitants of Bristol in 1696*, ed. Elizabeth Ralph and Mary E. Williams (Bristol Rec. Soc., 1968), pp. xxiii–iv (Cf. Laslett and Harrison 'Clayworth and Cogenhoe', pp. 178–9); Peter Laslett 'Size and Structure of the Household in England over three centuries', *Population Studies*, xxiii (1969), 219; Macpherson, *Possessive Individualism*, p. 285.

34. C. Hill, 'Pottage for Freeborn Englishmen', in *Socialism, Capitalism and Economic Growth*, ed. C. H. Feinstein (Cambridge 1967), p. 343; St John's College, Oxford, MS 319, f. 46v; Eric Kerridge, *Agrarian Problems in the Sixteenth Century and after* (1969), pp. 90–1; *Clarke Papers*, i, 316; *L. Colonel John Lilburne his Apologetical Narration* (Amsterdam 1652), p. 32, citing a legal case of 11 Eliz.; William Harrison, *The Description of England*, ed. Georges Edelen (Ithaca, N.Y. 1968), p. 118; Chamberlayne, *Angliae Notitia*, p. 514. Cf. Chief Justice Holt: 'One may be a villein in England, but not a slave' (William Salkeld, *Reports of Cases* (4th edn, 1742–3), ii, 666).

35. See Felix Raab, *The English Face of Machiavelli* (1964), p. 170n.

36. *Regall Tyranny Discovered* (1647), p. 11 (quoted in Pease, *The Leveller Movement* (Gloucester, Mass. 1965), p. 143).

37. William J. Blake, 'Hooker's Synopsis Chorographical of Devonshire', *Report and Transactions of the Devonshire Association*, xlvii (1915), 342; Sir Thomas Smith, *De Republica Anglorum*, ed. L. Alston (Cambridge 1906), p. 138; Lilburne, *Londons Liberty in Chains*, p. 38; *Vox Plebis*, pp. 10, 11; *Leveller Manifestoes*, pp. 11–12.

38. *A Declaration of Some Proceedings of Lt. Col. Iohn Lilburn* (1648), p. 37;

Roger Coke, *A Survey of the Politicks of Mr Thomas White, Thomas Hobbs, and Hugo Grotius* (1662), p. 109; Lilburne, *Londons Liberty in Chains*, p. 10; *Leveller Manifestoes*, p. 370; [Richard Overton], *A Defiance against all Arbitrary Usurpations* (1646), p. 7.

39. *Clarke Papers*, i, 300, 342.

40. Lilburne, *The Oppressed Mans Oppressions declared* (1647), p. 2; *Leveller Manifestoes*, pp. 193, 178; *Tracts on Liberty in the Puritan Revolution, 1638–1647*, ed. William Haller (New York 1965), iii, 270.

41. Smith, *De Republica Anglorum*, p. 137; Chamberlayne, *Angliae Notitia*, p. 516 (and cf. pp. 479–80); *Clarke Papers*, i, 342; Lilburne, *The Free-mans Freedome vindicated* (1646), p. 10; *Leveller Manifestoes*, p. 106n.; Aylmer, 'Gentlemen Levellers?'.

42. Overton, *A Defiance against all Arbitrary Usurpations*, p. 14.

43. *The Case of the Army soberly discussed*, p. 6; *A Letter sent from several Agitators of the Army* (1647), in *Puritanism and Liberty*, ed. Woodhouse, p. 452; *Leveller Manifestoes*, p. 152; *Patriarcha and other Political Works of Sir Robert Filmer*, ed. Peter Laslett (Oxford 1949), p. 287. Cf. Macpherson, *Possessive Individualism*, pp. 143, 296.

44. Harris, *The Grand Designe*, sig. B3. Cf. *Tracts on Liberty*, ed. Haller, iii, 291–2; *The Armies Petition* (1648), pp. 5–6.

45. Jacob Viner, '"Possessive Individualism" as original sin', *Canadian Journal of Economics and Political Science*, xxix (1963), 549–50. Cf. *Leveller Manifestoes*, p. 194.

46. *Leveller Manifestoes*, pp. 124, 136–7, 193, 200, 215, 268, 288, 194, 216, 270, 391; *The Representative of Divers Well-affected Persons* (1649), p. 15; Zagorin, *History of Political Thought*, p. 18; *Speculum Libertatis Angliae Re Restitutae* (1659), p. 6.

3. CONQUEST AND CONSENT *Quentin Skinner*

In citing from Hobbes, I have tried wherever possible to make use of the most accessible modern editions. In each case, however, I have added references in parentheses to *The English Works of Thomas Hobbes*, ed. W. Molesworth, 11 vols (1839–45), cited hereafter as EW. The only exception is that any page references referring to Hobbes in the text itself are from *Leviathan*, ed. C. B. Macpherson, (Harmondsworth 1968). All spelling and punctuation modernised.

1. *A Declaration of the Parliament of England* (1649); *The Complete Prose Works of John Milton*, ed. Don. M. Wolfe *et al.* (New Haven 1962), iii, 190–258.

2. For the earliest modern discussion of them, see Perez Zagorin, *A History of Political Thought in the English Revolution* (1954). The fundamental research on the group has been done by Professor John M. Wallace, in 'The Engagement Controversy, 1649–52, an Annotated List of Pamphlets', *Bulletin of the New York Public Library*, lxviii (1964), 384–405 (hereafter cited as Wallace, Bibliography), and in *Destiny his Choice*. I agree to a great extent with Professor Wallace's conclusions, and it will be clear that I am greatly indebted to his scholarship. I am also most grateful for numerous discussions with him about this chapter.

3. John Dury, *Considerations Concerning the Present Engagement* (1650), p. 10.

4. E.g. John Evelyn to Sir Thomas Browne, in *Sir William Temple upon the Garden of Epicurus with other XVIIth Century Garden Essays*, ed. A. F. Sieveking (1908), pp. 173–182, at p. 176.

5. Anthony Ascham, *The Bounds and Bonds of Public Obedience* (1649),

pp. 36–7 (for attribution, see note 15 below); Nedham, *Case,* ed. Knachel, p. 127; S.W., *The Constant Man's Character* (1650), pp. 71–2. See also the anonymous *Logical Demonstration,* pp. 2–3; and *Memorandums* (1650), p. 7.

6. Thomas Hobbes, *Philosophical Rudiments Concerning Government and Society* in EW, ii, 200–2. (This was Hobbes's own translation of *De Cive.*) See also Hobbes, *The Elements of Law,* ed. Ferdinand Tönnies, 2nd edn, with an Introduction by M. M. Goldsmith (1969), pp. 143, 169 (EW, iv, 168–9 and 202); *Leviathan,* ed. Macpherson, Part II, ch. 29, p. 374–5 (EW, iii, 320–1); EW, ii, 133, 136; and the accounts in *Behemoth,* ed. Ferdinand Tönnies, 2nd edn, with an Introduction by M. M. Goldsmith (1969), pp. 3–4, 22. (EW, vi, 167–8, 191–2); *Leviathan,* Part II, ch. 30, p. 380 (EW, iii, 326).

7. Anonymous, *The Grand Case of Conscience Stated, about submission to the Present Power* (n.p., n.d.), p. 3; *An Enquiry after Further Satisfaction concerning obeying a change of Government believed to be unlawful* (1649), pp. 9–10, and *A Religious Demurrer, concerning submission to the present power* (n.p., n.d.), postscript, p. 8.

8. *The Humble Declaration of John Wenlock of Langham* (1662), p. 80, quoted in Paul H. Hardacre, *The Royalists during the Puritan Revolution* (The Hague 1956), p. 83.

9. See, for example, *The Subject's Sorrow* (attributed by Thomason to Bishop Juxon) of March 1649, and Fabian Phillips, *Charles I No Man of Blood but a Martyr for his People,* June 1649; *Not Guilty,* February 1649, and *Reason against Treason,* an anonymous attack on Bradshaw of June 1649.

10. CJ, vi, 306–7; Firth and Rait, ii, 325–9 (for an abbreviated version, see J. P. Kenyon, *The Stuart Constitution* (1966), pp. 341–2).

11. *Arguments and Reasons to prove the inconvenience and unlawfulness of taking the new Engagement* (n.p., n.d.); *Traitors Deciphered,* May 1650; *An Answer to Mr J. Dury* (n.p., n.d.) of the same year.

12. W. K. Jordan, *Men of Substance* (Chicago 1942), esp. pp. 140–202; Gerrard Winstanley, 'England's Spirit Unfoulded, or an Incouragement to take the Engagement', ed. G. E. Aylmer, P&P, xl (1968), 3–15.

13. For the intellectual origins of conquest theory as expressed by Hobbes and the other *de facto* theorists in 1651, see Wallace, *Destiny his Choice,* esp. pp. 22–7; B. D. Greenslade, 'Clarendon's and Hobbes's *Elements of Law',* *Notes and Queries,* ccii (1957), 150 (cited in Thomas, 'Social Origins', in *Hobbes Studies,* ed. Brown, p. 201n.); J. Sirluck, Introduction to vol. ii of *The Complete Prose Works of John Milton* (New Haven 1959), p. 35.

14. See Zagorin, pp. 64–7, Wallace, pp. 30–68, Gunn, pp. 82–7.

15. I accept the attribution to Ascham argued by Wallace (Bibliography, pp. 390–2).

16. See the *Combat,* pp. 6–7; *Bounds and Bonds,* pp. 2–3, 22–3; *Confusions,* pp. 31, 47, 109–10, 115.

17. Robert Sanderson, *A Resolution of Conscience* (n.p., 1649), p. 6; HMC, Portland MSS, ii, 137–8.

18. See Nedham, *Case,* ed. Knachel, pp. 32, 49; Osborne, *Persuasive,* pp. 6–7; N.W. *A Discourse,* pp. 3–9; *Memorandums,* Sig. A, 2b.

19. The exact date of *Leviathan* is not known, but it was published within the first half of 1651, as the following reference (for which I am indebted to Dr Charles Webster) makes clear: William Rand to Samuel Hartlib, 18 July 1651, from Amsterdam: 'I have a booke entitled Leviathan or of a Commonwealth made by one Hobbs wherein I meet with a world of fine cleare notions, though some things too paradoxicall & savouring of a man passionately addicted to ye royall interest . . .' (Sheffield University Library, Hartlib MSS, Bundle lxii).

20. Ascham, *Confusions*, pp. 119, 121, also pp. 108, 151; Nedham, *Case*, ed. Knachel, pp. 129–30 and 135–9; Albertus Warren, *Eight Reasons Categorical* (1653), p. 5; Francis Osborne, *A Miscellany* (1659), Sig. A.

21. See Hobbes, *Elements of Law*, ed. Tönnies, pp. 74, 103, 137–8 (EW, iv, 86, 121, 161–2). See also *Leviathan*, part I, ch. 15, pp. 215–17, and part II, ch. 21, p. 268, ch. 27, p. 345, ch. 29, pp. 375–6, ch. 30, p. 380. (EW, iii, 146–7, 203, 288, 322, 326).

22. See *Elements of Law*, ed. Tönnies, esp. ch. 14, pp. 70–4 (EW, iv, 81–6); *Philosophical Rudiments*, (EW, ii, esp. ch. i, pp. 1–13); *Leviathan*, esp. part i, ch. 13, pp. 183–8 (EW, iii, 110–16).

23. *Leviathan*, part II, ch. 17, p. 228, and ch. 20, pp. 251–3 (EW, iii, 158–9 and 185–6).

24. *Leviathan*, part II, ch. 21, pp. 273–4 (EW, iii, 209). See also part II, ch. 20, pp. 254–6 and the Review, pp. 719–21. (EW, iii, 188–9, and 703–5).

25. Hobbes, 'Six Lessons', in EW, vii, 335–6.

26. *Leviathan*, Review, p. 728 (EW, iii, p. 713).

27. *Elements of Law*, ed. Tönnies, p. 126 (EW, iv, p. 148); *Leviathan*, Review, p. 728 (EW, iii, 713).

4. THE CHURCH IN ENGLAND   Claire Cross

1. T. Goodwin, *et al.*, *An Apologeticall Narration* (1643), p. 24.

2. L. Hutchinson, *Memoirs of Colonel Hutchinson* (Everyman edn, 1965), pp. 178–9.

3. CJ, iii, 626.

4. Parliamentary Propositions of December, 1647 in S. R. Gardiner, *Constitutional Documents of the Puritan Revolution, 1625–1660* (third edn, 1906), p. 345.

5. Lomas, *Letters and Speeches*, ii, 294; Abbott, *Writings and Speeches*, iii, 62.

6. The 'Instrument of Government' (1653) in *The Stuart Constitution 1603–1688*, ed. J. P. Kenyon (Cambridge 1966), p. 347.

7. CJ, vii, 258–9, 269. The Barebone's Parliament took up the same idea (CJ, vii, 361).

8. *The Autobiography of Richard Baxter* (1925), ed. J. M. Lloyd Thomas, pp. 70–1.

9. Kenyon, *Stuart Constitution*, pp. 347, 355.

10. *Records of the Churches of Christ gathered at Fenstanton, Warboys and Hexham 1644–1720* (Hanserd Knollys Soc., 1854), ed. E. B. Underhill, p. 82 (subsequently cited as *Fenstanton Records*).

11. *Autobiography of Richard Baxter*, pp. 77–9; *Oliver Heywood's Autobiography . . .'* i, ed. J. H. Turner (Brighouse 1882), 78–81; *The Diary of the Rev. Ralph Josselin, 1616–1683*, ed. Hockliffe (Camden Soc., 3rd ser. xv, 1908), 80–84.

12. *Life of Adam Martindale* ed. R. Parkinson (Chetham Soc., 1845), iv, 73–4.

13. *The Register-Booke of the Fourth Classis in the Province of London*, ed. C. E. Surman (Harleian Soc., 1953).

14. *Minutes of the Manchester Presbyterian Classis*, ed. W. A. Shaw (Chetham Soc., 1890) cxxxiv; *Minutes of the Bury Presbyterian Classis*, ed. Shaw (Chetham Soc., 1896) cl; *Diaries and Letters of Philip Henry*, ed. M. H. Lee (1882), pp. 34–9; 'Minute Book of the Wirksworth Classis', ed. J. C. Cox, *Journal of the Derbyshire Archaeological and Natural History Society*, ii, 135–222; R. Howell, *Newcastle upon Tyne and the Puritan Revolution* (Oxford 1967), p. 224; H. Smith,

'Presbyterian Organisation in Essex', *Essex Review*, xxviii, 15–17; xxxii, 173–9; B. Dale, 'The History of early Congregationalism in Leeds', *Transactions of the Congregational History Society*, ii, 245 ff.

15. C. G. Bolam, J. Goring, H. L. Short, R. Thomas, *The English Presbyterians* (1968), p. 51.

16. Some 2425 parochial livings were sequestered between 1643 and 1660 on account of the incumbent's hostility to Parliament, popish innovations or devotion to the Prayer Book, his non-residence or pluralism or his moral depravity (A. G. Matthews, *Walker Revised* [Oxford 1947], p. xv). Miss Whiteman, taking the number of parish livings to be approximately 8600, calculated that approximately 30 per cent of livings in England were affected (A. Whiteman, 'The Restoration of the Church of England', in *From Uniformity to Unity, 1662–1962* ed. G. F. Nuttall and O. Chadwick [1962], pp. 34–5). There may, however, have been rather more parish livings than this: a contemporary in 1646 stated that there were 9284 (C. Hill, *Economic Problems of the Church* [Oxford 1956], p. 144).

17. A. T. Russell, *Memorials of the life and works of Thomas Fuller* (1844), pp. 220–1.

18. See A. Everitt, *The Community of Kent and the Great Rebellion, 1640–1660* (Leicester 1966), pp. 53–4.

19. G. F. Nuttall, 'Congregational Commonwealth Incumbents', *Transactions of the Congregational Historical Society*, xiv, 155–67. A. G. Matthews thought 171 of those ejected in 1662 were Independents, but not all of these held parochial livings (Matthews, *Calamy Revised* [Oxford 1934], p. xlii); A. T. Jones, *Notes on the Early Days of Stepney Meeting 1644–1689* (1887); *Vestry Minute Books . . . of St Bartholomew Exchange 1567–1676*, ed. E. Freshfield (1890), pp. xxxii–xxxiii; W. T. Whitley, *A History of British Baptists* (1923), p. 70; T. Crosby, *The History of the English Baptists*, i (1738), 278–97.

20. Whiteman, 'Restoration of the Church of England', in Nuttall and Chadwick, *From Uniformity to Unity*, pp. 37–42.

21. *The Diary of John Evelyn* ed. E. S. De Beer, iii (Oxford 1955), 164, 181.

22. Lomas, *Letters and Speeches*, iii, 6; Abbott, *Writings and Speeches*, iv, 368.

23. *Records of a Church of Christ meeting in Broadmead, Bristol*, ed. E. B. Underhill (Hanserd Knollys Soc. 1847), pp. 17–18; *The Church Book of Bunyan Meeting 1650–1821*, ed. G. B. Harrison (1928), p. 2.

24. 'A True and Short Declaration . . .', ed. C. Burrage, *Transactions of the Baptist Historical Society*, ii, 143–6; Jones, *Early Days of Stepney Meeting*, pp. 16–22; *The Christian Reformer*, x (1824), 6–7; *Fenstanton Records*, pp. 21, 81.

25. *The Minutes of the General Assembly of the General Baptist Churches*, W. T. Whitley, i (1909) 6–8; B. R. White, 'The Organisation of the Particular Baptists 1644–1660', *Journal of Ecclesiastical History*, xvii, 209–66; W. K. Jordan, *Development of Religious Toleration in England*, iii (1938), 452–62.

26. Jones, *Early Days of Stepney Meeting*, pp. 19–22; *Christian Reformer*, x, 52–3.

27. G. F. Nuttall, *Visible Saints* (Oxford 1957), p. 12; Howell, *Newcastle*, pp. 218–73; *Christian Reformer*, x, 3–5; *Autobiography of Richard Baxter*, pp. 135–7; G. F. Nuttall, 'The Worcestershire Association: its Membership', *Journal of Ecclesiastical History*, i, 197–206. There are minutes of the Cornwall and Cambridge Voluntary Associations in Shaw, *Minutes of the Bury Presbyterian Classis*, p. 175 ff. and p. 189 ff. For the minutes of the Exeter Assembly see 'Puritanism in Devon', ed. R. N. Worth, *Report and Transactions of the Devon Association for the Advancement of Science, Literature and Art*, ix, 279 ff.

5. SOCIAL AND ECONOMIC POLICIES *J. P. Cooper*

1. I am deeply indebted to Mr Blair Worden of Pembroke College, Cambridge, for allowing me to read some of his preliminary studies of politics in the Rump.

2. C. Hill, *Reformation to Industrial Revolution* (Pelican edn, 1969), pp. 135–8, 149–50, 155–61, 169–75; *God's Englishman* (1970), pp. 130–1.

3. Burton, *Diary*, i, pp. xxv, xlix.

4. CSP *Venetian 1647–52*, pp. 187–8.

5. *Humble Proposal against Transporting Gold and Silver* (1661), pp. 2, 3.

6. Andrews, *British Committees . . .*, pp. 26–32, restated more fully in the same author's *The Colonial Period of American History*, iv (1938), 'England's Commercial and Colonial Policies', 34–47.

7. S. R. Gardiner, *Constitutional Docs.*, p. 382.

8. W. G. Hoskins, 'Harvest Fluctuations and English Economic History 1620–1759', in *Agricultural History Review*, xvi (1968), 20, 29.

9. B. E. Supple, *Commercial Crisis and Change in England 1600–1642* (Cambridge 1959); J. P. Cooper, 'Economic Regulation and the Cloth Industry in Seventeenth Century England', TRHS, 5th ser. xx (1970); R. Ashton, 'Parliament and Free Trade in 1604', P&P, xxxviii (1967), and 'Jacobean Free Trade Again', P&P, xliii (1969); W. B. Stephens, 'The Cloth Exports of the Provincial Ports 1600–1640', in ECHR, xxii (1969), 241–3.

10. *Briefe Considerations concerning the advancement of Trade and Navigation* (1649), pp. 2–3, 7–8 (Dutch encroachments); cf. B. Worsley, *The Advocate* (1652), reprinted in R. W. K. Hinton, *The Eastland Trade and the Commonwealth* (Cambridge 1959), pp. 208–9; *Leveller Manifestoes* ed. D. M. Wolfe (New York 1944), pp. 136–7, 193, 200, 215, 268 and 288; J. Lilburne, *Charters of London* (1646), for petitions by interlopers; Bodl. MS, Rawlinson D918 f. 184, abstract of excise commissioners' receipts, 1650.

11. G. H. Turnbull, *Hartlib, Dury and Comenius* (Liverpool 1947); C. Webster, *Samuel Hartlib and the Advancement of Learning* (Cambridge 1970); W. K. Jordan, *Men of Substance* (Chicago 1942); I am indebted to Mr Charles Webster of Corpus Christi College, Oxford, for further information about the Hartlib circle.

12. See nos. 26 to 58 of the *Moderate*, from which these instances are taken.

13. *Records of the County of Wiltshire* ed. B. H. Cunnington (Devizes 1932) pp. 182–3, 208; HMC, *Various Collections*, i (1901), 115, 117; PRO, Assizes 24/21, ff. 104, 105, 93, 123, 124, 131V; J. S. Morrill, 'The Government of Cheshire during the Civil Wars and Interregnum' (Oxford D.Phil. thesis, 1971), pp. 335–8; *Quarter Sessions Records for the County of Somerset* (Somerset Rec. Soc., xxviii) pp. iii, 25–7 (January 1647), 51–2, 60–1, 83–4.

14. Firth & Rait, i, 1042; PRO, SP 16/515/140, 139, 128; SP 18/25, nos. 49–50 (cf. P. J. Bowden, *The Wool Trade in Tudor and Stuart England* (1962) p. 178); CJ, vi, 45.

15. *Sergeant Thorpe . . . his Charge . . .* (1649), pp. 10, 21–7; North Riding Rec. Soc., v (1887), *Quarter Sessions Records*, pp. 45, 73, 12, 18, 26, 32, 39, 44.

16. CJ, vi, 137 (10 Feb.), 160 (9 Mar.), 167; PRO, Assizes 24/21, f. 144v; PRO SP 25/62, p. 250 (Ipswich, 2 May 1649); SP 25/94, pp. 451–2, 486 (20 Sept., 13 Oct.) to Mayor of Wycombe; CSPD, *1649–50*, pp. 121, 316, 341, 303 (Lancashire).

17. Firth & Rait, ii, 442, 104, 508–9; Corp. of London Rec. Office, Journal vol. 41ˣ, p. 11, July 1650; CSPD *1652–3*, p. 15; CJ, vi, 329, 357, 416, 439, 441, 485–6, 226, 284, 322, 535, 556; vii, 94; James, *Social Problems . . .* p. 299;

Worcs. Hist. Soc. N.S., ix, *Miscellany*, ii, 83, 'Henry Townshend's Notes . . .'
ed. R. D. Hunt; CSPD, *1650*, pp. 399, 454; PRO E 351/653, 654; W. K. Jordan,
Philanthropy in England, pp. 138–40.

18. See A. L. Beier, 'Poor Relief in Warwickshire 1630–60', in P&P, xxxv
(1966), and for Essex, County Rec. Office, Q/SR 346, nos. 23, 20, 22, 24; Q/SO 1;
Cf. *Kentish Sources*, iv (1964), 'The Poor', ed. E. Melling, pp. 20–2; *V.C.H.
Yorks, East Riding*, i, 163–4; *V.C.H. City of York*, pp. 171–2.

19. *Original Letters and Papers of State* . . ., ed. J. Nickalls (1743), pp.
29–33, 36, 59; CJ, vi, 374, 416; vii, 127, 129, 190, 249, 252, 253, 258–9.

20. BM, Add. MS 21, 427, f. 224 (Leeds); K. J. Allison, 'The Norfolk Worsted
Industry in the Sixteenth and Seventeenth Centuries', part II, *Yorks. Bulletin
of Social and Economic Research*, xli (1961), 73; Essex, PRO SP 18/25, nos.
49–50; D. Masson, *Life of Milton*, iii (1877), 160; CSPD *1649–50*, pp. 270, 277.

21. R. Maddison, *Great Britain's Remembrancer*, (1654); B. E. Supple,
Commercial Crisis . . . pp. 186, 205, 221; see also DNB 'Sir Ralph Maddison';
CSPD *1649–50*, pp. 284, 457, 475, 162; *1651–2*, p. 25; *1650*, pp. 130, 182, 200–1,
281, 483; *1651*, pp. 175, 231–4, 284, 310, 313–15, 401, 460–1, 487–9; *1651–2*,
pp. 23–6, 153–6, 239, 241, 243, 498; *1652–3*, pp. 20, 130, 218, 260, 280, 349, 360;
Firth and Rait, ii, 194 (17 July 1649), 495 (9 Jan. 1651); CJ, vi, 186, 240, 385,
379, 393, 400, 403, 458, 461; vii, 278 (15 April 1653).

22. CSPD, *1649–50*, p. 28; CJ, vi, 162 (12 March 1649); Firth & Rait, ii,
548–50.

23. Thomas Mun, *The Petition and Remonstance of the* . . . *Merchants* . . .
Trading to the East Indies . . . *to* . . . *the House of Commons* . . . (1628) pp.
31–3; T. Violet, *The Advancement of Merchandize* (1651), pp. 5–6; Lewis
Roberts, *Treasure of Traffike* (1641), pp. 32–3, 40, 44–5; Henry Robinson,
England's safety in trades increase (1641), pp. 20–1; PRO SP 105/144, ff. 68–74;
(Walwyn's petition); H. Peter, *Good Work for a Good Magistrate* (1651), pp. 20,
80–1; R. V[aughan], *Certain proposalls in order to the peoples freedome* (1652)
pp. 12, 22; H. Robinson, *England's safety* . . . (1641), p. 19; Violet, *Mysteries of
Trade and Mint Affairs* (1652), pp. 17–18, 5–6; *The Advancement of Merchand-
ise* . . . (1651), pp. 10–11.

24. Journal 41ˣ f. 10, 28 Nov.

25. Abbott, *Writings and Speeches*, iii, 84–5, 106–7, 123–4; TSP, ii, 125.

26. CJ, vi, 575; vii, 79, 85, 147; vi, 336, 346–7, 353, 403, 434, 451; CSPD,
1649–50, pp. 417, 460, 462; Firth & Rait, ii, 403–6.

27. PRO SP 18/16, no. 138 'Narrative of what things have been reported from
the Council of Trade'; CJ, vi, 521–2; W. R. Scott, *The Constitution and Finance
of* . . . *Joint Stock Companies to 1720* (Cambridge 1910) ii, 16, 92–4; Bodl.,
Carte MS 74, ff. 482–3.

28. James, *Social Problems* . . ., App. B, pp. 392–5.

29. CJ, vi, 426; *Milton State Papers*, p. 43; Dr Gourdain (or Guerdain), the
Master of the Mint and Captain Limbrey were added, 11 April 1651 (CJ, vi,
560); Sheffield University Library, Hartlib Papers, Bundle xiii.

30. Turnbull, *Hartlib, Dury and Comenius*, pp. 31, 260–2, 98, 268, 317;
Hartlib Papers, Bundles lxxi/11, lxi/2, xxxiii. For Trenchard, see Keeler,
Members of the Long Parliament (Philadelphia 1954) and for Sadler DNB. Sadler's
nomination to the Council of Trade was rejected (CJ, vi, 426); CSP *Colonial,
1574–1660*, pp. 331–2, 339; Violet, *Mysteries and Secrets of Trade* . . . (1653)
p. 178; CSPD, *1651–2*, pp. 488, 502. I am grateful to Mr Charles Webster, who is
editing Hartlib's *Ephemerides*, for additional references from these.

31. Violet, *The Advancement of Merchandise* . . . (1651); *Mysteries and
Secrets* . . ., *passim*, both dedicated to Bradshaw; CSPD, *1650*, pp. 431, 473, 480;

ibid., 1651, pp. 231–4, 460–1; DNB, 'T. Violet'; TRHS, 5th ser., xx (1970), 89–90; Bodl. MS, Clarendon 75, f. 300v, 8 Nov. 1661 (cf. Hinton, *Eastland Trade* . . . p. 90); L. A. Harper, *The English Navigation Laws* (New York 1939), p. 45.

32. Harper, *Navigation Laws*, pp. 39–48; C. H. Wilson, *Economic History and the Historian* (1969), p. 146; Sir George Clark, *History*, n.s., vii, 285; Hinton, *Eastland Trade*, pp. 89–90.

33. Farnell, ECHR, 2nd ser., xvi, 43–6; (CJ, vi, 474, 478); Andrews, *Colonial Period*, iv, 43–4; Harper, *Navigation Laws*, p. 41.

34. Harper, *Navigation Laws*, pp. 42–5, 49; *Acts and Ordinances of the Eastland Company*, ed. M. Sellars (Camden Soc. 3rd ser., xi), 76; *Cambridge History of the British Empire*, i (Cambridge 1929), 215–17.

35. BM, Add. MS 5138, ff. 145–67 (copies of this committee's papers); Hinton, *Eastland Trade* . . ., pp. 93–4; 213–8; ECHR, 2nd ser., xvi, 447–8; EHR, lxxxii (1967), 38; A. B. Beaven, *Aldermen of London*, ii (1913), 69, 83, 89; London RO, Journal 41ˣ, 9 Dec. 1651.

36. BM, Add. MS 5138, f. 144–8v, opinions of unnamed merchants, 26 May 1651, and not a report of the Council of Trade as in Andrews, *Colonial Period*, iv, 42.

37. V. A. Rowe, *Sir Henry Vane the Younger* (1970), pp. 147–8; R. Maddison, *Great Britain's Remembrancer*, pp. 38–9; 'Narrative' (above note 27); CJ, vii, 21.

38. Journal 41ˣ ff. 76, 76v, 80v, 81, 57, 66; *Records of the Merchant Adventurers of Newcastle-upon-Tyne* (Surtees Soc. xciii, 1895), i, 164–8; Hartlib Papers, Bundle liii, 11.

39. Howell, *Newcastle*, pp. 300–11; R. Gardner, *Englands Grievance Discovered* . . . (1655), pp. 58–60.

40. Surtees Soc., xciii, 173–9; BM, Add. MS 5138, ff. 165–6; Ashley, *Financial* . . . *Policy* . . ., pp. 60–1.

41. R. Davis, *Rise of the English Shipping Industry* (1962) pp. 50–3; CSPD, *1651–2*, p. 433; *1652–3*, p. 45; Ashley, *Financial* . . . *Policy*, p. 57; Journal 41ˣ, f. 89, 24 Oct. 1653.

42. CSPD, *1651–2*, pp. 114, 119, 125, 130, 195, 210–11, 215, 238, 240, 241, 211, 469, 479–82; CJ, vii, 119; PRO SP 18/25, nos. 51, 52 (n.d., probably late 1652); cf. CSPD, *1652–3*, pp. 230, 270.

43. *Ibid.*, pp. 18, 82, 102, 116, 125, 140, 90, 136; CJ, vii, 190, 246, 253, 255, 257–8, 259, 252, 307.

44. PRO SP 18/74, no. 37, ii, July 1654; Firth & Rait, ii, 1006–7, 451–5, 697–8; B. Whitelocke, *Memorials*, (4 vols, Oxford 1853) iii, 446; CSPD, *1651*, pp. 460–1, 487–9; *1651–2*, pp. 153–6, 212; *1650*, p. 149; CJ, vi, 240, 378, 380, 383, 393, 526; vii, 144, 233; *A Word to the Army* . . . (1653), pp. 6–7; Violet, *Proposals Humbly Presented* . . . (1656), pp. 17–18, 39–40, 111–12.

45. J. Cook, *Unum Necessarium* (1648), pp. 2, 7.

46. F. G. Emmison, *Elizabethan Life: Disorder* (Chelmsford 1970), chap. 2; compare Essex Quarter Session Rolls 1649–52, Q/SR 338–54.

47. H. C. Darby, *The Draining of the Fens* (Cambridge 1940), pp. 64–82; *Foedera*, ed. Rymer, xvii, 413; *Old and Scarce Tracts on Money*, ed. J. R. McCulloch (1933), pp. 145–53; Firth & Rait, ii, 571; Violet, *Proposals* . . . (1656), Sig. Fv.

48. See G. D. Ramsay, 'Industrial *laissez-faire* and the policy of Cromwell', ECHR, xvi (1946).

6. CROMWELL'S ORDINANCES   *Ivan Roots*

1. Burton, *Diary*, iii, 99–100; TSP, i, 637, 610, 612, 621, 632, 648; speech of 4 September 1654 (Lomas, *Letters and Speeches*, ii, 339–59, esp. 342–6; Abbott, *Writings and Speeches*, iii, 434–43); the 'Instrument' of resignation is printed in *A True State of the Case of the Commonwealth* (1654), p. 22, attributed to Marchamont Nedham; Gardiner, *Commonwealth and Protectorate* (4 vols, 1903), ii, 319–41; [Anon.], *The Protector Unveiled* (1655), p. 12; CSPD, *1653–4*, p. 309; G. D. Heath III, 'Making the Instrument of Government', JBS, vi (1967).

2. *Essays Presented to Sir Lewis Namier*, pp. 181–3, and *Religion, the Reformation and Social Change*, p. 374.

3. Gardiner, *Constitutional Documents*, pp. 405–17; Kenyon, *Stuart Constitution*, pp. 342–8; and *The Puritan Revolution*, ed. S. Prall (1969), pp. 250–62.

4. CSPD, *1653–4*, pp. 299–301.

5. Gardiner, *Commonwealth and Protectorate*, iii, 3; *A True State*, p. 46.

6. CSPD, *1653–4*, pp. 297–8; St J. D. Seymour, *The Puritans in Ireland, 1647–1661* (Oxford 1912, repr. 1969), p. 83; Edmund Ludlow, *Memoirs*, ed. C. H. Firth (2 vols, Oxford 1894), i, 373–8, 542–3; TSP, ii, 163; *The Cromwellian Union*, ed. C. S. Terry (Scottish History Soc., xl, 1902), pp. li–lii; TSP, ii, 18; *Scotland and the Protectorate*, ed. C. H. Firth (Scottish History Soc., xxxi, 1899), p. 95; and TSP, ii, 1–2, for the colonies; CSPD, *1653–4*, p. 298.

7. CSPD, *1653–4*, pp. 360, 299, 386–7, 300–1, 310. See also F. M. G. Evans, *The Principal Secretary of State 1558–1670* (Manchester 1932), chap. VI, 'John Thurloe', esp. p. 111 ff.; F. A. Inderwick, *The Interregnum* (1891), pp. 187, 285; J. C. Farnell, 'The Usurpation of Honest London Householders: Barebone's Parliament'; EHR, lxxxii (1967), 24–5; Firth & Rait, ii, 824. (Cf. Firth & Rait, ii, 367; CJ, vii, 99, 231.)

8. CSPD, *1653–4*, p. 301; Firth & Rait, ii, 824. For fees and probate records see CSPD, *1653–4* and *1654*, *passim*.

9. Lomas, *Letters and Speeches*, ii, 350; Abbott, *Writings and Speeches*, iii, 438.

10. E.g. Skippon (Burton, *Diary*, i, 50).

11. For the religious ordinances see Firth & Rait, ii, 855, 922, 968, 1000.

12. Abbott, *Writings and Speeches*, iv, 366; Lomas, *Letters and Speeches*, iii, 20.

13. See D. Veall, *The Popular Movement for Law Reform 1640–1660* (Oxford 1970), esp. p. 151; CSPD, *1654*, p. 202; Firth & Rait, ii, 911.

14. See CSPD, *1653–4* and *1654*.

15. For the attendances of councillors see CSPD, *1653–4* and *1654*, 'Prefaces'; CSPD, *1654*, p. 215 (for standing committees); K. H. D. Haley, *The First Earl of Shaftesbury* (Oxford 1968), pp. 77–81; Dawson, *Cromwell's Understudy*, pp. 190–4.

16. CSPD, *1654*, pp. 202, 206, 67; CSPD, *1653–4*, p. 397.

17. CSPD, *1653–4*, p. 358; CSPD, *1654*, pp. 253, 362, 303; Firth & Rait, ii, 1000–1029, esp. 1013.

18. CSPD, *1654*, pp. 65–7, 174, 190, 245, 246; Firth & Rait, ii, 858, 854.

19. Eg. Firth & Rait, ii, 918, 1016, 861, 922, 937, 941, 1007; see below, and note 11 above.

20. See e.g. E. Littleton, *A Proposal for the Maintenance and Repairing the Highways* (1692), quoted in S. and B. Webb, *Story of the King's Highway* (1963 reprint), pp. 20–1. For the post office see C. H. Firth, 'Thurloe and the Post Office', EHR, xii (1897), 527–33.

21. TSP, ii, 148, 195; Firth & Rait, ii, 855, 861, 897.

22. Firth & Rait, ii, 774, 830, 831; CSPD, *1653–4*, p. 316.

23. Firth & Rait, ii, 949, 21 Aug. 1654.

24. See M. Cotterell, 'Interregnum Law Reform: The Hale Commission of 1652', EHR, lxxxiii (1968); G. B. Nourse, 'Law Reform under the Commonwealth and Protectorate', *Law Quarterly Review*, lxxv (1959); S. E. Prall, 'Chancery Reform and the Puritan Revolution', *American Journal of Legal History*, vi (1962); and Veall, *Popular Movement for Law Reform*; for the Barebone's debates on Chancery see CJ., vii.

25. CSPD, *1654*, pp. 202, 252, 262, 267, 281, 303, 318.

26. TSP, ii, 445.

27. P. Geyl, *Orange and Stuart* (1969), pp. 116–25.

28. P. Hardacre, *The Royalists during the Puritan Revolution* (The Hague 1956), chap. VI; Underdown, *Royalist Conspiracy*, chap. 6, especially pp. 97–106; CSPD, *1654*, pp. 233–40, especially p. 235.

29. See C. H. Firth, *Scotland and the Commonwealth* (Scottish History Soc., xviii, 1895), pp. 71–308; *Scotland and the Protectorate*, pp. 8–89; Terry, *Cromwellian Union*, pp. l–lii; Seymour, *Puritans in Ireland*, passim.

30. Terry, *Cromwellian Union*, pp. xvi–xlviii; CJ, vi, 329, 333, 335, 339–40, 355; CSPD, *1653–4*, pp. 310, 311, 364, 365, 382; CSPD, *1654*, pp. 90–1, 113.

31. Firth & Rait, ii, 930, 932, 942, 1015; Seymour, *Puritans in Ireland*, p. 87 ff.

32. For the elections see CSPD, *1654*, pp. ix–xiv; Gardiner, *Commonwealth and Protectorate*, iii, 170–8; Roots, *Great Rebellion*, p. 184; Trevor-Roper, *Religion, the Reformation and Social Change*, pp. 371–5; also P. J. Pinckney, 'The Scottish Representation', *Scottish Historical Review*, xlvi (1967), 96–7, and 'The Cheshire Election of 1656', *Bulletin of the John Rylands Library*, (1967), 49; Haley, *Shaftesbury*, pp. 81–3.

33. Abbott, *Writings and Speeches*, iii, 434–43; Lomas, *Letters and Speeches*, ii, 339–59.

34. Firth & Rait, ii, 1006, 1007, 1026, 1019; CJ, vii, 368; Gardiner, *Constitutional Documents*, pp. 427–47.

35. Burton, *Diary*, i, pp. xii, xlviii, xlix, xc, xci, xcvi.

36. CSPD, *1655–8*, passim, For Cromwell's proclamations; Firth & Rait, ii, 1029, 1035.

37. B. Whitelocke, *Memorials of the English Affairs* (1722), pp. 621–7; Inderwick, *Interregnum*, pp. 227–30; Prall, 'Chancery Reform', pp. 43–4; Veall, *Popular Movement*, pp. 182–3.

38. CSPD, *1655*, pp. 297, 300; TSP, iii, 359, 385; Inderwick, *Interregnum*, pp. 198–200; Gardiner, *Commonwealth and Protectorate*, iii, 300; M. Ashley, *Financial and Commercial Policy Under the Cromwellian Protectorate* (Oxford 1934 and repr. London, 1962), pp. 55, 67; Abbott, *Writings and Speeches*, iii, 498–9, 719, 733, 740. See also G. Selwood, *A Narrative of the Proceedings of the . . . case of Mr George Cony, Merchant* (1655), pp. 25, 26. (The italics in the quotations are Selwood's.)

39. Firth & Rait, ii, 1131–42.

40. Burton, *Diary*, i, 5–6, 11, 38.

41. *Ibid.*, 47, 48; Inderwick, *Interregnum*, pp. 229–30.

42. Burton, *Diary*, ii, 48, 50, 39–40, 41; i, 281–2.

43. *Ibid.*, ii, 40, 42–3.

44. *Ibid.*, 50, 51, 54.

45. *Ibid.*, 60, 61–2; Firth & Rait, ii, 1019–25.

46. Burton, *Diary*, 212; Firth & Rait, iii, pp. x–xiii (and for the bibliography of acts and ordinances, iii, 'Introduction', passim).

7. SETTLEMENT IN THE COUNTIES *David Underdown*

1. Thomas G. Barnes, *Somerset, 1625–1640* (London and Cambridge, Mass. 1961). J. T. Cliffe, *The Yorkshire Gentry From the Reformation to the Civil War* (1969).

2. See also Everitt, *Suffolk and the Great Rebellion, 1640–1660* (Suffolk RS, iii, 1960); *The Local Community and the Great Rebellion* (Hist. Assoc. pamphlet G 70, 1969).

3. Everitt, *Community of Kent*, pp. 13, 16–17.

4. *Ibid.*, chaps V, VI. A. H. Dodd, *Studies in Stuart Wales* (Cardiff 1952) chap iv. For Pyne's role see my forthcoming study of Civil-War Somerset.

5. This paragraph is based on records of changes in the commissions of the peace (IBM cards at History of Parliament Trust). See also Underdown, *Pride's Purge*, chaps X, XI, esp. pp. 299–302, 309–12, 340–1.

6. Underdown, *Pride's Purge*, pp. 148–50, 166–72, 183–4, but cf. C. V. Wedgwood, *The Trial of Charles I* (1964) pp. 76–80; Abbott, *Writings and Speeches*, iv, 485.

7. *Ibid.*, iii, 435, 461; iv, 470 (and cf. iii, 607); iii, 457, 593.

8. *Ibid.*, iii, 145, 573, 400. Contrast Ashley, *Oliver Cromwell: the Conservative Dictator* (1937) with his *The Greatness of Oliver Cromwell* (1957).

9. *Memoirs of Edmund Ludlow*, ed. C. H. Firth (Oxford 1894), ii, 18; Burton, *Diary*, ii, 409; i, 310–20.

10. Abbot, *Writings and Speeches*, iii, 142–3, 166; Firth & Rait, ii, 830–1.

11. CSPD, *1654*, pp. 211–12, 229–30, 395, 344; *1655*, pp. 100, 201–2, 46, 62, 262, 398; *1655–6*, pp. 194, 374; TSP, ii, 120, 124; iii, 227, 140; for Livesey, see scattered evidence in TSP and CSPD (Everitt misses this point); for Pyne see above, note 4.

12. CSPD, *1655*, pp. 92–3.

13. A. H. Woolrych, *Penruddock's Rising, 1655* (Hist. Assoc. pamphlet G 29, 1955) p. 21.

14. CCC, Pref. pp. xx–xxii; CCAM, Pref. p. xiv.

15. CSPD, *1654*, pp. 294–5; *1655–6*, p. 19.

16. *The Letters of Dorothy Osborne to William Temple*, ed. G. C. Moore Smith (Oxford 1928) p. 177; F. P. and M. M. Verney, *Memoirs of the Verney Family* (1892–9), iii, 219–20, 227, 244, 255; Ludlow, *Memoirs*, i, 389.

17. Goddard's Journal (Burton, *Diary*, i, Intro. p. xxvi). In seventeenth-century usage the term 'country' usually means 'county' or 'local community'. Cf. also HMC, *Buccleuch*, i, 311.

18. Ludlow, *Memoirs*, i, 380; CSPD, *1655*, pp. 92–4; HMC, *Bath*, iv, 281; *Verney Memoirs*, iii, 271–3. See also Paul H. Hardacre, *The Royalists during the Puritan Revolution* (The Hague 1956), p. 128.

19. CSPD, *1655–6*, pp. 87–8; Everitt, *Community of Kent*, p. 298; *Verney Memoirs*, iii, 219, 262. See also Hardacre, *Royalists*, pp. 125–30; and Underdown, *Royalist Conspiracy*, pp. 161–7.

20. Abbott, *Writings and Speeches*, iv, 112, 274, 494, 87–8; *Norfolk Quarter Sessions Order Book, 1650–1657*, ed. D. E. Howell James (Norfolk RS, xxvi, 1955), pp. 16, 86, 82, 84; CSPD, *1655–6*, p. 175.

21. Dodd, *Stuart Wales*, pp. 154–7; for Yorkshire see Firth & Rait.

22. James Townsend, *History of Abingdon* (1910), pp. 133–5.

23. CSPD, *1656–7*, p. 316.

24. Duke of Northumberland MSS 551–2 (BM, Microfilm 331): Fitzjames letter books, v, ff. 21v, 27, 89v–95v; vi, ff. 4–28.

25. Everitt, *Community of Kent*, p. 16 and cf. pp. 294–301.

26. TSP, iii, 155–6.

27. *Ibid.*, ii, 501; iii, 147; CSPD, *1654*, pp. 297, 311–12, 319–20; HMC, *Portland*, iii, 208.

28. TSP, iii, 238.

29. CSPD, *1655*, p. 244, and see also pp. 234–5, 249–50; PRO SP 18/126, ff. 22–7; certificates of recusants by J.P.s; CCC, pp. 727–36.

30. CSPD, *1655*, pp. 296–7, 300. For Wentworth's submission see also Ludlow, *Memoirs*, i, 414.

31. CSPD, *1656–7*, pp. 149–50; *1657–8*, p. 315; *1658–9*, pp. 15, 23, 92.

32. *Ibid.*, *1656–7*, p. 56. For Council orders to J.P.s to assist the excisemen see *ibid.*, *1657–8*, pp. 155–6, 293, 321–3; *1658–9*, pp. 76, 107, 127.

33. TSP, iii, 227.

34. William Prynne, *The Re-publicans and others spurious Good Old Cause, briefly and truly Anatomized* (1659), p. 3.

8. LAST QUESTS FOR SETTLEMENT *Austin Woolrych*

1. Ivan Roots, 'Swordsmen and Decimators', in *The English Civil War and After*, ed. R. H. Parry (1970), p. 80.

2. Text in *Constitutional Documents of the Puritan Revolution*, ed. S. R. Gardiner (3rd edn, Oxford 1906), pp. 447–59 and – with some abbreviations – in *The Stuart Constitution 1603–1688*, ed. J. P. Kenyon (Cambridge 1966), pp. 350–7.

3. See Clayton Roberts, *The Growth of Responsible Government in Stuart England* (Cambridge 1966).

4. Hill, *God's Englishman*, pp. 187–90.

5. TSP, vii, 387–8.

6. *State Papers Collected by Edward Earl of Clarendon* (3 vols, Oxford 1767–86; hereafter *Clarendon* SP), iii, 421, 423, 441; *Calendar of the Clarendon State Papers* (4 vols, Oxford 1869–1932; hereafter *Clarendon Calendar*), iv, 111, 118; F. P. G. Guizot, *History of Richard Cromwell*, trans. A. R. Scoble (2 vols, 1856), i, 248, 234; TSP, vii, 437–38; *A True Catalogue* (28 Sept. 1659), BM, E999 (12); Underdown, *Royalist Conspiracy*, pp. 214–32; *Reliquiae Baxterianae*, ed. Matthew Sylvester (1696), part i, 100 (cf. Guizot, i, 252–53).

7. TSP, vii, 581 (on the army's unrest during the autumn see Davies, *Restoration*, chap III); Davies, *Restoration*, pp. 29–33; Guizot, i, 271, 274; *Clarendon Calendar*, iv, 118.

8. *Register of the Consultations of the Ministers of Edinburgh*, ed. W. Stephen (2 vols, Edinburgh 1921–30), ii, 252–3; *Reliquiae Baxterianae*, part i, 101; Prynne, *The Re-publicans* (13 May 1659), BM, E983(6), p. 3; Guizot, i, 252–3.

9. Guizot, i, 302; TSP, vii, 617; *Clarendon Calendar*, iv, 148. See also Firth, *Last Years*, ii, 30–4, and Davies, *Restoration*, pp. 57–8. Text in BM, E936(5), 11 Mar. 1658, and E968(6*), 15 Feb. 1659; it has never been reprinted.

10. For the debates see Burton, *Diary*, iii and iv; they are adequately summarised in Davies, *Restoration*, chaps IV and V.

11. See Woolrych, 'The Good Old Cause and the fall of the Protectorate', CHJ, xiii (1957), 133–61.

12. *A Call to the Officers of the Army* (26 Feb. 1659), BM, E968(8); R. Fitz-Brian, *The Good Old Cause Dress'd in it's Primitive Lustre* (16 Feb. 1659), BM, E968(6), p. 5; *XXV Queries* (16 Feb. 1659), BM, E968(5), pp. 5–6 (repr. in *Harleian Miscellany*, ed. T. Park [10 vols, 1808–13], ix, 424 ff).

13. *A Second Narrative of the Late Parliament* (new edn., 29 Apr. 1659)

BM, E977(3), pp. 39–40; Fitz-Brian, *Good Old Cause Dress'd*; *The Cause of God and of These Nations* (2 Mar. 1659), BM, E968(11).

14. Prynne, *The Re-publicans*, p. 1.

15. TSP, vii, 627, 634; Burton, *Diary*, iv, 223; *Clarendon Calendar*, iv, 140–3, 176; HMC, *10th Report*, App. vi, 194; *XXV Queries*, pp. 5–7; *Clarke Papers*, ed. C. H. Firth (4 vols, Camden Ser., 1891–1901), iii, 211; Sir Richard Baker, *Chronicle of the Kings of England*, continued by Edward Phillips (1670), p. 659. (The quotations in the text paragraph relate to the last two sources.)

16. TSP, vii, 612; Ludlow, *Memoirs*, ii, 63–65; Davies, *Restoration*, pp. 75–85; CHJ, xiii, 146–50.

17. *Clarke Papers*, iv, 213.

18. *Some Reasons Humbly Proposed to the Officers* (28 Apr. 1659), BM, E979(8); *A Perambutory Word* (4 May 1659), E980(15), p. 5; *An Invocation to the Officers* (20 Apr. 1659), E979(1); see also *A Seasonable Word* (5 May 1659), E980(17).

19. *The Humble Remonstrance . . . of Major General Goffs Regiment* (26 Apr. 1659), BM, E979(6).

20. See *Clarendon* SP., iii, 430–2; *cf.* *Clarendon Calendar*, iv, 158.

21. BM, E968(3), 16 Feb. 1659; repr. in *Harleian Miscellany*, iv, 543–50. See Ashley, *John Wildman, Plotter and Postmaster* (1947), pp. 136–7.

22. BM, E980(8), 2 May 1659.

23. BM, E980(11), 2 May 1659.

24. 'H.N.', *An Observation and Comparison* (25 May 1659), BM, E983(29), pp. 5, 9.

25. BM, E988(13), 23 June 1659, pp. 12–13.

26. Samuel Duncon, *Several Proposals* (6 July 1659), BM, E989(9).

27. BM, E989(19), 13 July 1659, pp. 7, 18–19.

28. BM, E988(9), 22 June 1659, p. 5. Despite its title, the Leveller content of this piece is slight.

29. *Chaos* (18 July 1659), BM, E989(27), pp. 38 ff.

30. *The Cause of God*, pref. (unpaginated) and p. 27; see also pp. 19–20.

31. BM, E980(5), 2 May 1659, esp. pref. and pp. 47–48, 51–53, 58–59.

32. *The Plain Case of the Common-Weal* (3 Mar. 1659), BM, E972(5), pp. 31 ff. Rogers acknowledged his authorship of this tract in his Διαπολιτεια (dated by Thomason 20 Sep. 1659 but completed in July; see p. 124), BM, E995(25), p. 69; see *ibid.*, pp. 59 ff., 76–7 for his repudiation of Feake and the militant Fifth Monarchists.

33. J. Canne, *A Seasonable Word to the Parliament-Men* (10 May 1659), BM, E983(1); CJ, vii, 652.

34. *Clarke Papers*, iv, 21.

35. Peter Chamberlen, *The Declaration and Proclamation of the Army of God* (2nd edn, 9 June 1659), BM, E985(26); *A Scourge for a Denn of Thieves* (16 June 1659), BM, E986(23), p. 3.

36. Most notably in *The Fifth Monarchy . . . Asserted* (23 Aug. 1659), BM, E993(31).

37. *Diary of Sir Archibald Johnston of Wariston* (3 vols, Scottish Historical Soc., Edinburgh 1911–40), iii, 124; J. Harrington, *A Discourse, Shewing that the Spirit of Parliaments . . .* (28 July 1659), BM, E993(9), p. 5 (confirmed by the French ambassador and the Venetian resident: Guizot, i, 385–6, 431, 479; CSP, *Venetian, 1659–61*, pp. 37–8, 47–8, 50–2).

38. *A Letter from Sir George Booth* (2 Aug. 1659), 669f21(66).

39. No diary of its debates survives, but Ludlow outlines the schemes that it discussed in *Memoirs*, ii, 98–100.

40. Wariston, *Diary*, iii, 125. Wariston records a conversation with Hesilrige, but his language is far from clear.

41. 'The Humble Petition and Address of the Officers of the Army'; text in *Parliamentary or Constitutional History of England* (24 vols, 1751–62), xxi, 400–5. The chief officers had pressed for a senate in conferences with the republicans just before their readmission of the Rump; see Ludlow, *Memoirs*, ii, 74–7.

42. Bodl. C.13.6(16) Linc, esp. p. 6; not in Thomason. For evidence of authorship and date see CHJ, xiii, 154.

43. Wariston, *Diary*, iii, 119–21, 125; Guizot, i, 424, 426–7; *Clarendon Calendar*, iv, 250; TSP, vii, 704; H. Stubbe, *A Letter to an Officer of the Army Concerning a Select Senate* (26 Oct. 1659), BM, E1001(8).

44. Ludlow, *Memoirs*, ii, 99.

45. Harrington published nine pieces of his own during 1659, ranging from the substantial *Art of Lawgiving* down to brief letters, and various of his supporters published at least half a dozen more. Professor J. G. A. Pocock is preparing a modern edition of his works. For the Bow Street club and the Rota, see John Aubrey, *Brief Lives* (various editions); H. F. Russell Smith, *Harrington and His Oceana* (Cambridge, 1914), pp. 101 ff.; Ashley, *John Wildman*, pp. 142, 145–7; Charles Blitzer, *An Immortal Commonwealth* (New Haven, 1960), pp. 56–61.

46. *The Readie & Easie Way to Establish a Free Commonwealth* (2nd edn, 1660) in *The Works of John Milton* (18 vols, New York, Columbia U.P. edn, 1931–8), vi, 131.

47. Wariston, *Diary*, iii, 135; Ludlow, *Memoirs*, ii, 133–35; Guizot, i, 490–1; ii, 268.

48. Guizot, ii, 267, 272, 277; *Clarendon Calendar*, iv, 415–16, 425–6; *Clarendon* SP, iii, 586.

49. Wariston, *Diary*, iii, 150–2; CSP, *Venetian, 1659–61*, pp. 88–90; Guizot, ii, 286; *Clarendon Calendar*, iv, 428; *A Collection of the State Letters of . . . Roger Boyle*, ed. T. Morrice (2 vols, Dublin, 1743), ii, 248.

50. Ludlow, *Memoirs*, ii, 159–74; the fundamentals are reprinted from *Mercurius Politicus* in a note on p. 171. For the General Council's proceedings see my introduction to *Complete Prose Works of John Milton* (9 vols, New Haven, 1953–), vii (forthcoming).

51. *Clarke Papers*, iv, 186–7, 300 (*cf*. p. 211).

52. Ludlow, *Memoirs*, ii, 182; Bulstrode Whitelocke, *Memorials of the English Affairs* (1682), p. 692.

53. *Works of John Milton* (Columbia edn), vii, 140–1.

54. *Ibid.*, pp. 144–5.

55. *Oceana*, ed. Liljegren, p. 55.

56. *Works* (Columbia edn), vi, 148; italics in original.

NOTES ON CONTRIBUTORS

G. E. AYLMER, Professor of History and head of history department, University of York; graduate of Oxford; formerly visiting fellow at Princeton University, junior research fellow at Balliol College, Oxford and Lecturer in History, University of Manchester. His publications include *The King's Servants: The Civil Service of Charles I, 1625–1642* (1961); and *The Struggle for the Constitution, 1603–1689* (1963) (published in the United States as *A Short History of England in the 17th Century*).

J. P. COOPER, Fellow and Lecturer of Trinity College, Oxford; graduate of Oxford, formerly Assistant Lecturer at Manchester University and Fellow of All Souls College, Oxford; editor of *The New Cambridge Modern History*, iv (1970).

CLAIRE CROSS, Senior Lecturer in History at the University of York; graduate of Cambridge; formerly research scholar at Girton College, Cambridge, visiting international fellow of the American Association of University Women and research fellow at Reading University. Her publications include *The Puritan Earl: The Life of Henry Hastings, Third Earl of Huntingdon* (1966); *The Royal Supremacy in the Elizabethan Church* (1969); and *The Letters of Sir Francis Hastings* (1969).

VALERIE PEARL, Reader in the History of London, University College, London; graduate of Oxford; formerly lecturer and research fellow of Somerville College, Oxford. Her publications include *London and The Outbreak of the Puritan Revolution: City Government and National Politics 1625–43* (1961).

IVAN ROOTS, Professor of History, University of Exeter; graduate of Oxford; formerly senior lecturer at University College, Cardiff. His publications include *The Committee at Stafford, 1643–1645* (with D. H. Pennington, 1957); and *The Great Rebellion, 1642–1660* (1966).

QUENTIN SKINNER, Fellow of Christ's College, Cambridge; graduate of Cambridge; Lecturer in History, University of Cambridge. His publications include a sequence of articles on Hobbes in the *Historical Journal*, and articles in other scholarly periodicals on philosophical topics and on the history of political ideas.

KEITH THOMAS, Fellow and Tutor of St John's College, Oxford; graduate of Oxford; formerly Fellow of All Souls College, Oxford. His publications include *Religion and the Decline of Magic* (1971); contributions to *Crisis in Europe* (1965), *Hobbes Studies* (1965), *Ideas in Cultural Perspective* (1962); and articles in *Past and Present* and other historical journals.

DAVID UNDERDOWN, Professor of History, Brown University, Providence, Rhode Island; graduate of Oxford; formerly tutorial research fellow, Royal Holloway College, University of London, and Associate Professor of History, University of the South and University of Virginia. His publications include *Royalist Conspiracy in England, 1649–1660* (1960), and *Pride's Purge: Politics in the Puritan Revolution* (1971).

AUSTIN WOOLRYCH, Professor of History and head of history department, University of Lancaster; graduate of Oxford; formerly Senior Lecturer in History, University of Leeds. His publications include *Battles in the English Civil War* (1961), and *Oliver Cromwell* (1964).

Index

Abbot, W. C., 171
Abingdon (Berkshire), 178
Act, Artificers (1563), 71; Bullion (1650), 132; against Catholics (1657), 115; Church attendance, 103; to regulate cloth (1649), 129; constituting Council of State (1649), 123; on corn and meal trade (1650), 128; for Council of Trade (1650), 131–2; on debtors (1653), 148; fiscal (1694), 72–3; for fen drainage (1649), 141; for franchise in the counties (1430), 64; lowering interest-rates (1624 and 1651), 129–30; Navigation (1651), 121, 134–8, 141; religious relief (1650), 103; reviewing Ordinances (1657), 161, 163–4; for trade with colonies (1650), 135
Act, Uniformity (1559), 103
Acts, 145, 159, 161–2, 164
Acts, Restoration Navigation, 135, 141
Acts draft, 139
Adams, Ald. Thomas, 55, 217
Administration (see also Bureaucracy; Committees; Officials), 25
Administrative efficiency, 150
Admiralty, Court of, 163
Advance of Money (see also Haberdashers' Hall), 35
Advocate, The, 134
Africa(n), 135
Agitators, 8, 49, 57, 67, 70
Agrarian reforms, 125
Agreement(s) of the People, 57–8, 193–4
Agreement of the People, abortive compromise, 58; first Leveller, 58; second Leveller, 59, 67, 68, 73; third and final Leveller, 59, 68–9, 73; Officers', 15, 17, 26, 143, 186, 196, 200
Agriculture, 121–2
Aldermen (of London), *and* Court of, 30, 33, 55–6
Alehouses, 126, 171, 176
Algiers, 146
Aliens, 130, 142
Alms-takers, *or* receivers of alms, 58–60, 64–6, 68–70, 75–8, 214
Alured, Col., 189
American trade, 217
Anabaptists, *see* Baptists
Andrews, C. M., 123, 134
Andrews, Thomas, 32
Anglican(s), Anglicanism (*see also* Church; Royalists), 5, 19, 111, 120
Anonymous pamphlets, *see under titles;* for others *see under authors*
Anti-Cromwellians, 184
Anti-Presbyterians, 125
Anti-Republicans, 202
Apologeticall Narration, An, 101

Apostolic Succession, 113
Apprentice(s), Apprenticeship, 64, 66, 68, 73, 75–8, 127, 137, 139–40, 201
Approvers, *see* Tryers
Argyll, Marquis of, 5
Armed Forces (*see also* Army; Navy), 141, 144, 160, 190, 203
Arminian(s) (*see also* Laudian), 100, 105, 117
Army (*see also* General Council; New Model; Soldiers), 8, 12, 15, 21, 27, 42–7, 54, 56–8, 102–3, 105, 126, 139, 159, 171, 178, 180–2, 184, 186–93, 199–202, 232
Army leaders (*see also* Grandees), 59, 196–7, 199
Army officers (*see also* Colonels), 16, 57, 144, 178, 184, 185, 188–9, 191–2, 195, 197, 199–200, 234
Artificers (*see also* Acts), 127
Ascham, Anthony, 82, 87–95
Ash, John, 133
Ashe, Simeon, 51
Ashfield, Lt.-Col., 189
Ashley, M. P., 1, 21
Ashton, R., 22
Assemblies (schemes for), 198–9
Assembly of Divines, the, 29, 34, 52, 100–2
Assessment, the monthly (*see also* Commissions; Committees), 26, 125, 159, 169, 180
Assizes and Assize Judges, 126–8, 171, 176, 181
Associations (Baptist), 118; (Voluntary), 119, 225; (County), 201
Astley, Jacob, Lord, 2, 4
Atlantic, 121
Attorney-General, 127
Audley, Capt., 66
Aulnage, 139
Ault, W. O., 61
Avery, Samuel, 217
Ayres, William, 6
Ayscough, William, 177

Badgers (of corn), 126
Baillie, Robert, 33, 35, 38, 41, 52–3, 55, 101
Balance of Trade, 129, 131
Ballot, 61, 198–9, 219
Baltic, 123, 134, 138, 141
Baptists, the, 11, 27, 104–6, 112, 117–20, 173, 178; General, 118–19; Particular, 118–19
Barebone's, the, *see* Parliament
Barley, 126
Barnes, T. G., 166
Barrington (Somerset), 177

Barton, Col. William, 41
Baxter, Richard, 105–6, 110, 112, 119–20, 188
Baynes, Lt.-Col. Jeremy, 217
Bays, 132
Bedford, 65, 116, 118
Bedford, Earl of, 5
Bedfordshire, 117
Beggars (see also Vagrants), 58, 67, 68–70, 73, 77
Behemoth, the, see Hobbes
Bell Tavern, King St (Westminster), 52
Bellamy, John, 33, 37, 50, 217
Bengal, 12
Berkeley, family, 177
Berkshire, 118, 181
Bethel, Slingsby, 122
Bewdley (Worcestershire), 112
Bible, The, 13, 110, 117
Bill(s), for Anglo-Irish Union, 161; for Anglo-Scottish Union, 156, 161; on Chancery, 153; for creditors, 161; for delinquents' tenants, 139; for highways, 161; Militia, 49; for the poor, 129, 139; for the poor prisoners, 161; for the Public Faith, 139; draft, 149
Billeting, 125
Billingsgate (London), 108
Birthright, 59, 63–4, 73–6, 78
Bishops (see also Episcopacy; Lands), 99–100, 109, 113, 120
Bishops' lands (see also Land Sales), 43
Blackmore, John, 180
Bletchingley (Surrey), 62
Bocking (Essex), 128
Bolsheviks, 18, 165
Bolton (Lancashire), 107
Bolton, Edmund, 76
Bondmen, bond slaves, 74–6
Book of Common Prayer, The, 107, 110, 113, 114, 116
Book of Discipline, The, 65, 107
Book-printing, 140
Booksellers, Bookselling (and Printing), 29, 34, 217
Boon, Thomas, 133
Booth, Sir George, 173, 196, 199
Boroughs (see also Corporations; Local Communities; Local Authorities; Towns, etc.), 62, 63, 64, 77, 142, 146, 157, 196
Boston (Lincolnshire), 62
Bounds and Bonds of Public Obedience, The (see also Ascham), 87–8
Bourchier, Barrington, 177
Bourgeois, see Capitalist; see also Citizens; Merchants
Bow St, London, 198
Boys, John, 70
Bradshaw, Ld. President, 134, 223
Bramber (Sussex), 65
Breda, Declaration of, 202
Brewers' Co., 217
Bride, John, 217
Bridenbaugh, C., 61
Bridge, William, 101
Briscow, Col., 162
Bristol, 73, 102, 116, 118, 124, 132, 139

British Isles, 10, 147–8, 150, 156
British Museum, 29
Broadmead (Bristol), 116, 120
Broggers (see also Badgers; Middlemen), 127, 133
Broghill, Lord, 177, 187–9
Bromfield, Col. Lawrence, 45, 54–5, 217
Browne, Mrs Mary, 117
Browne, Sir Richard, 113
Brownrig, Ralph, 113
Buckingham, Duke of, 92
Buckingham(shire), 174–5
Bullion, 129, 131–2, 138, 142
Bunce, Ald. James, 32, 45–6, 55, 217
Bunyan, John, 11
Bureaucracy (see also Administration; Committees; Officials), 174
Burford (Oxfordshire), 4
Burgage, 62
Burges, Anthony, 51
Burgoyne, Sir Roger, 174
Burroughs, Jeremiah, 101
Burton, Henry, 38, 41
Bury (Lancashire), 108–9
Butler, Samuel, 11
By-elections, 202–3, 214

Calamy, Edmund, 51–2
Calvin, John, 81, 107
Calvinism, Calvinist(s), 89, 101, 105, 107, 112, 118–19
Cambridge, 113
Cambridgeshire, 106, 117, 119, 225
Campfield, Col. Nathaniel, 50
Canne, John, 195
Capital, the, see London
Capitalism, Capitalist(s) (see also Revolution), 3, 22–6, 77
Captains, 188
Cartwright, Major John, 64
Cartwright, Thomas, 72
Cary, John, 71
Case of the Army truly Stated, The, 67–8
Cathedrals, 104, 113, 128
Catholicism, Catholic(s) (see also Papists; Popery), 100, 114–15
Cause of God, The, 195
Cavalier(s) (see also Royalists), 2, 25, 172, 175–7, 180, 198–9
Challoner, Thomas, 133
Chaloner family, 177
Chamberlayne, Edward, 69
Chamberlen, Dr Peter, 116–17, 128, 195
Chancery, Court of, 145, 147, 161; reform of, 153–4, 159–60
Channel, English, 138–9
Chaos, 194
Charge of High Treason against Oliver Cromwell, A, 69
Charles I (see also King), 4, 5, 7, 22, 26, 29, 38, 44, 56, 85, 100, 103, 132, 168, 202
Charles I, trial and execution of, 58, 80
Charles II (see also King; Restoration), 19, 26, 54, 99, 106, 110–11, 113, 122, 170, 177, 182, 183, 195–6, 202
Cheshire, 126, 173, 196, 199
Chidley, Samuel, 128

Chiverton, Mr, 136
Christchurch, Newgate (London), 55–6
Christmas, 114
Church, Anglican, 2, 5; the English (*and* of England; National or State-Church), 25, 31, 42, 101, 103–4, 106, 110–16, 119–20, 147, 151, 167, 171, 173, 185, 191
Church, Commonwealth, 110, 118; Cromwellian, 99, 105–6, 112–13; Presbyterian, 29–30, 35, 55, 102, 106, 110
Church(es), *see also* Clergy; Congregations; Gathered Churches
Churches, Reformed, 111
Church government, 7, 21, 31, 72, 100–1
Circuit(s), *see* Assizes; Judges
Cirencester (Gloucestershire), 62
Cities, 61, 146
Citizens, 122
Citizens (of London), 31–4, 37, 56, 201
City, the (*see also* London), 14, 23, 29, 33–56, 112, 134, 138, 155, 160, 189
Civil War(s), 1–3, 24–5, 30, 40, 42, 60, 70, 99, 100, 104, 107, 110, 111, 113, 116, 123, 132, 152, 165–7, 174, 177, 181, 200, 202
Clarendon, Edward Hyde, later Earl of, 1, 3, 25–6, 30, 36
Clarke, Capt., 66
Classis, Classes (Presbyterian), 34, 54, 108–9
Claypole, John, 174
Clergy (*or* Ministers), Clerical Party, 29–32, 34, 99, 101, 104–5, 106–7, 109, 111–15, 143, 157, 163, 184
Clientage, 77
Cliffe, J. T., 166
Cloth, Clothiers, Clothing Industry *and* Trade, 123–4, 126–7, 129, 133, 137–40, 142
Clothworkers' Co., 133
Clotworthy, Sir John, 52
Coal, 127–8
Cobbett, William, 40
Cockermouth (Cumberland), 117–20
Cock-fighting, 149, 151, 176
Coggeshall (Essex), 139
Coin and Coinage, 129, 131, 139
Coke, Roger, 75
Colchester (Essex), 132
Colleges, 112
Colonels (*see also under individuals*), 6, 23
Colonies, Colonial System (*see also* Trade), 10, 121, 123, 130–2, 135, 146
Combat Between Two Seconds, A, 87–8
Comenius, John Amos, 125
Commander-in-Chief, Scotland, 157
Commission(s), for the Assessment, 177, 181; for the Church, 173; ecclesiastical (*see also* High Commission), 163; Hale, 153; local, 159; of Oyer and Terminer, 173; of the Peace, 169, 171, 177, 231; of 1622, 131
Commissioners (*see also* Council of Trade; Great Seal; Treasury); County, 187; Militia, 196; for securing the peace, 172, 175
Committees, 21, 40, 45, 131

Committee(s), Admiralty, 134; Army, 146, 168; of the Assembly of Divines, 102; of Assessment, 169; of the Council of State, 139, 148–9, 153–4, 157, 229; of the Council of Trade, 135–6; County, 42, 141, 168–9, 172, 175, 180; County militia, 169; Financial, 35, 38; Goldsmiths' Hall, 169; of the House of Commons, 15, 62, 100, 105, 125, 127–8, 148, 159, 161, 196; Irish Affairs, 46; London militia, 44–7, 51–2, 54–5, 217; Navy, 131; for Plundered Ministers, 104; of Safety (1647), 46–7; of Safety (1659), 199–200, 202
Common Council of London, 30, 32–4, 41, 47, 50–2, 55, 127–8, 137, 155, 201, 217
Common Prayer, *see Book of*
Commonalty, 62
Commons, House of (*see also* Parliament), 5, 7, 9, 15–17, 29, 35–9, 43–4, 46, 48, 50, 62, 65, 70, 100–2, 125, 127, 141, 143, 148, 157–8, 162, 168, 184–5, 190–1
Common Lands, Commons, 77
Commonwealth, a, 184, 195, 197–8, 202–3
Commonwealth, the, 9, 10, 12–16, 20, 79, 80–2, 84–6, 90, 93, 104, 108–110, 112, 114–15, 121–3, 125, 127–9, 131, 137, 141–2, 144, 146, 168–9, 173–4, 178–9, 187, 192, 194, 196–8, 200, 202, 204
Commonwealthsmen, 122, 142, 189–91, 193
Communities, *see* Local
Companies, chartered *or* trading, 121, 123–4, 131–3, 135–7, 139–40; (London livery), 133
Confession of Faith, 184
Congregationalism, Congregationalist(s) (*see also* Independency), 10, 15, 25, 27
Congregations (Sectarian), or Gathered Churches (*see also* Puritans, Sects), 26, 65, 99, 103, 105, 108, 195
Conquest Theory, 223
Conservators of Liberty, 197, 200
Constitution, the, Constitutions, 3, 19, 24, 57, 158, 172, 184–6
Convention, *see* Parliament
Cony, George, 160
Cook, John, 127, 140
Cooper, Sir Anthony Ashley, 23, 143, 145, 147, 149, 151, 156, 174
Cooper, J. P., 10, 15, 20, 219
Cooper, Samuel, 11
Coplestone, Sir John, 179
Copyhold(s) *and* Copyholders, 63, 193
Corkbush Field (Hertfordshire), 4
Corn *and* Corn Trade, 121, 126–8, 140–1
Cornhill (London), 108, 217
Cornwall *and* Cornish, 119, 126, 171, 173, 180, 225
Corporation(s) (*see also* City *and* London), 62, 113, 130, 138, 141–2, 186
Corporation of London, 174
Corruption, 14, 62
Cosin, John, 113
Council, 167
Council, Irish, 151; of officers, *see* General Council; royal (*see also* Privy Council),

150; of State (*see also* Committees), of the Commonwealth, 9, 79, 121, 127–9, 131–2, 134, 136, 139, 196, 198; of State, Barebones, 143; of State, Protector's, 144–6, 147–9, 152–62, 173, 175–6, 178, 180–81, 185, 188; of Trade, 121, 123, 131–40, 142; of State, Clerk of, 148; President of (*see also* Bradshaw, Lawrence), 148–9

Councillors, Richard Cromwell's, 184, 188, 191; of State, 229

Counsel learned (in the law), 148–9, 151

Counter-rebellion (Catholic), 114

Counter-revolution, 2

County, Counties (*see also* Local), 61–3, 77, 125, 157, 166–71, 175, 177–9, 181–2, 184, 186–7, 194, 196, 201, 203, 231

Country, the, 25–6, 231

Country gentlemen, see Gentry; Landowners

Court, the, 25–6, 113, 167, 177, 189

Court, royal, 193

Courteen, Sir William, 135

Courtiers, 158, 161, 188, 190

Courts, 201, 203

Covenant, Solemn League and, 5, 41, 44, 49, 72, 80–1, 83, 100, 106

Cowley, Abraham, 81

Cowling, Commissary-General, 64, 74

Creditors, 149

Criminals (*see also* Delinquents), 64, 66, 68

Crises, Crisis, see Depression; Economic crisis

Cromwell, Henry, 187

Cromwell, Oliver (*see also* Protector), 2, 4, 6, 9, 12, 16–23, 27, 40, 44, 47, 57, 66, 69, 99–100, 102–5, 111, 113–15, 119–20, 128, 130, 142, 143–4, 146–50, 153–5, 160–1, 164, 166–8, 170–9, 181–2, 183, 185–9, 191–2, 202

Cromwell, Richard (*see also* Protector), 27, 105, 174, 178, 182, 183–5, 187–93, 195

Cromwell, Thomas, 1

Cromwellian(s), Cromwellian Party, 16, 19, 21, 187

Cromwellians, old and new, 188–9

Cross, M. C., 2, 10, 21, 25

Crown (*see also* King; Monarchy), 100, 135, 184, 187

Cullum, Ald. Thomas, 217

Culpepper, Sir Cheney, 125, 133

Cumberland, 118–19, 126

Cunningham, Archdeacon W., 121–3

Customs (duties *and* revenues), 124, 131, 136, 138, 160; Farmers, 147

Danzig, 141

Darley family, 177

Dartmouth (Devon), 133

Davenant, William, 11

Davis, J. C., 69

Day-labourers, 71–2

Dean and Chapter Lands, 104

Dearth, 125–8, 140–1

Debt(s), Debtors, 24, 148, 174, 194

Decimation Tax, 159, 161, 172, 175

Declaration (of the Council of State), 79

De Facto government and *De Facto* theorists, 79–80, 82, 87, 90, 93–8

De Gaulle, General, 3

Delinquent(s) *and* Delinquency, 35, 66–8, 76, 139–40

Denne, Henry, 66, 117, 119

Depression (trade), 123, 125, 136, 139–41, 201

Deptford (Kent), 111

Derbyshire, 108–9

Dering, Sir Edward, 111

Devon(shire), 61, 74, 119, 126, 167, 173, 179–80

D'Ewes, Sir Simonds, 63–4

Digger(s), 8–10, 22, 66, 86, 184

Directory of Worship, The, 106–8

Disbrowe, John, 53, 145, 147, 153–4, 161, 172, 180, 187, 189, 191–2, 201

Discipline (ecclesiastical), 106–7, 110

Discourse concerning the Engagement, A, 90–3

Dissenters (*see also* Non-Conformists), 184–5

Dodington, Sir Francis, 177

Dornix-weaving, 132

Dorset, 119, 125, 133, 178, 180

Doubling, 41–2

Dover, 130

Downs, the, 201

Draperies, new, 124; old and new, 126–7, 139

Drax, James, 134

Drew, John, 91–2

Drunkenness, see Alehouses

Duchy (of Lancaster) Court, 174

Dunbar, 137

Duncan, Samuel, 194

Duncon, Brian, 113

Duppa, Brian, 113

Durham, 109

Dury, John, 81, 89, 125, 133

Dutch, 122–5, 129–30, 133–8; peace with, 155, 158; offer of union to, 130–1, 136–7; War with, 14, 131, 138, 140–1, 155

Dyeing, 132

Dyve, Sir Lewis, 56

Earls Colne, Essex, 104, 107

Earnest Petition, The, 64, 68–70, 75

East Anglia, 168

East Coast, 138

East India Co., 131–3, 135–6

East Indies, 121

Eastcheap (London), 108

Easter, 114

Eastern Association, 168

Eastern Counties, the, 112

Eastland Co., 131–2, 134–6, 141

Economic Crisis, Crises (*see also* Dearth, Depression), 123–5

Economy, the, 11, 22, 130

Edmonds, Simon, 34

Education, *and* Learning; Teaching, 77, 111, 112–13, 186, 214

Edwards, Simon, 217

Edwards, Thomas, 31, 45, 51

Efficiency, administrative, 150

Eikon Basilike, The, 85

Ejectors, the, 104–5, 151, 163, 173
Elders, lay, *see* Laity
Eleazer Bar Ishai, 116
Elections, Electorate, Electors, 61–3, 66, 69, 154–5, 157, 174, 178, 186, 194, 196, 200–3, 214, 230
Eliot, John, 72
Elizabeth I, 114
Elton, G. R., 1, 24
Ely, Isle of, 117, 171
Embassies, foreign, 115
Emigration, 130
Engagement(s), Engagers, 80, 83, 86–7, 90, 93–7, 196
'Engagement', 'The', 85, 91, 141, 152, 169, 172, 187
Engagement Vindicated, The, 86
England's Safety, 194
Engrossers, 126–8, 140
Entrepôt *and* Entrepôt Trade, 130, 135–6, 138
Episcopacy, Episcopalian(s), Episco-palianism, 10, 49, 99, 110, 111–14, 120
Erastian, Erastianism, 10, 100
Essex, 104, 107, 109, 119, 125, 129, 139–42, 168
Essex, earl of, 5, 29, 35, 38
Estwick, John, 44, 55
Europe (*see also* Southern; Western Europe), 130
Evelyn, Sir John, 43
Evelyn, John, 111, 113, 114
Everitt, A. M., 4, 21, 25, 166, 179, 231
Ewin (Mr), 117
Exchange, *see* Foreign Exchange(s)
Excise, the, 39–40, 43, 56, 123, 125, 131, 139, 160, 181
Exchequer, Court of, 150
Excommunication, 118
Exeter, 124, 138–9, 225
Exeter House, 114
Exhortation to Catechising, An, 110
Exports (*see also* Trade, Foreign), 123, 126, 129, 131, 141–2
Extra-European goods, 134

Fairfax, Sir Thomas, *later* lord, 6, 23, 47, 49, 52–3, 54
Farnell, J. E., 121–3, 134, 136
Farringdon Within (London), 39
Fauconberg, Lord, 177, 187–9, 191
Feake, Christopher, 195, 233
Fees, 154
Fens, Fenland, 141
Fenstanton (Huntingdon), 117
Feudal, 25
Fiennes, Nathaniel, 145, 153, 187
Fifth Monarchist(s), Fifth Monarchy Men, 11, 13, 43, 66, 105, 163, 171, 173, 184, 195, 233
Filmer, Robert, 76
Finance (*see also* Committees; Revenue; Taxation), 150
Firmin, Thomas, 71
Firth, C. H., 1, 21, 26, 151
FitzJames, John, 178
Fleet, the (*see also* Navy), 200–1

Fleetwood, Lt.-Gen. Charles, 145, 151, 154, 187–9, 191–3, 201
Food (*see also* Prices), 151
Food Riots, 12
Foreign Affairs, Policy, Relations, Situa-tion, 20, 122, 155–6, 190, 203
Foreign Exchange(s), 129, 131
Forest(s), 147
Forestallers, 126
Fowke *or* Fowks, Ald. John, 31, 35, 44, 48, 55, 133
Fowles, John, 133
Fox, George, 11, 13
France, French, 110, 123, 138–9, 155; Ambassador, 188, 233
Franchise, the parliamentary (*see also* Manhood Suffrage), 17, 57–78, 155, 194
Frankfurt, 65
Freeborn, the, *or* Freeborn People, 64, 66, 68, 73–4, 76, 78
Freeholders, 61, 176
Free Ports, 130, 135–7, 141
Free Quarter, 125, 171
'Free State', A, 9–10, 79
Free Trade, Traders *and* Freedom of Trade, 124, 131–2, 134–6
Fuller, Thomas, 110–11
Fundamentals (*see also* Law), 193, 197, 200, 234

Gangraena, The, *see* Edwards
Gardiner, S. R., 1, 6, 25–6, 29, 126, 145, 160, 165
Gase, John, 217
Gathered Churches (*see also* Congrega-tions; Separated *and* Separatist Churches), 102, 112–13, 115–16, 119, 190
Gayre, Sir John, 38, 55
Gellibrand, Samuel, 217
Gellibrand, Thomas, 217
General Council of the Army, 7, 67
General Council of Officers, 49, 143, 192, 200–1
Generals, *see under* individuals' names
Gentry (*see also* landowners), 25, 30, 121–2, 144, 166–70, 172–6, 178–80, 182, 184, 187–9, 191, 202–3
Gerard, John, 155
Germany, 110, 123
Gethin, Maurice, 217
Gibbs, Ald., 48, 217
Gloucestershire, 173, 180
Glyde, Richard, 45
Glyn, John, 187
Goddard, Guibon, 121, 231
Godly Party, the (*see also* Puritans; Saints), 175, 182
Goffe, Col., *later* Maj.-Gen. William, 192
Goldsmiths, 201, 217
Goldsmiths' Hall, 169
'Good Old Cause', 'The', 175, 180, 182, 190–3, 195, 204
Goodwin, John, 31, 117, 119
Goodwin, Thomas, 101
Gorges family, 180
Gorges, John, 173, 180

Gospel, Propagators *and* Propagating of, 140, 173
Gourdain, Dr, 227
Governing Class, *see* Ruling Class; *also* Gentry; Local
Government(s) (during the Interregnum), 115, 121, 127, 144, 147, 152, 157, 161–2, 164, 174, 178, 181–2, 187, 189, 192–3, 195
Government(s) (in the abstract), 122, 186–7, 195, 198, 200, 203; English, 140, 152, 181; Lawfulness of *and* Obedience owed to, 79–88, 91–3, 96
Gower, Col. Thomas, 217
Grain Trade, 123, 126, 129, 141
Grand Case of Conscience Stated, The, 84
Grand Council, *see* Senate
Grandees, Army, 15, 57–9, 188–9, 191–2
Grantham (Lincolnshire), 65
Graves, Col. Richard, 46
Great Charter, a (*see also* Magna Carta), 194
Great Level (of the Fens), 141
Great Marlow (Buckinghamshire), 63–5
Great Rebellion, the, 2, 4, 183
Great Seal, the, 150; Commissioners of the, 130, 159, 162
Greenhill, William, 102, 112, 117
Greenland Co., 132, 137
Greenwood, William, 133
Groom of the Stole, 174
Grotius, Hugo, 87
Guerdain, *see* Gourdain
Guildhall, 29, 51
Guinea Co., 132, 135
Guizot, F. P. G., 1, 25

Habeas Corpus, 160
Haberdashers' Hall, 35, 39, 42
Hacker, Francis, 180
Hackney-coaches, 151
Hale, Sir Matthew, 153
Hall, Joseph, 113
Hamburg, 129, 135–6, 138–9
Hamilton, Duke of, 6
Hamiltonian(s), 5
Hammond, Lieut.-Gen. Thomas, 6
Hampden, John, 5
Hampshire, 119, 168
Hampton Court Proposals, 7
Hardwicke, Col. John, 53
Harington, John, 43, 46, 50–1, 180
Harington, John, jr., 180
Harlestone, Northants., 61
Harley family, 179
Harper, L. W., 134
Harriman, Ann, 116
Harrington, James, 67, 183, 193, 196–8, 203, 216, 234
Harris, John, 69, 77
Harrison, Maj.-Gen. Thomas, 16, 18, 23
Harrisonians, 18, 24
Hartlib, Samuel, 125, 131, 133–4, 223, 226–7
Harvests, 123, 139
Haverfordwest, 181
Hazzard, Matthew, 116

Heads of Proposals, The, 6–7, 26, 43, 49, 102, 143
'Healing Spirits', 174
Henry VII, 150
Hereditary principle, 184
Herefordshire, 112, 179
Hertfordshire, 178
Hesilrige, Sir Arthur, 6, 16, 23, 143, 192, 196–7, 199–201, 234
Hewson, Col., 163
Heywood, Oliver, 107
Hickman, William, 128
High-Church, 113
High Commission, 167
High Court of Justice, 151–2, 155, 173
High Presbyterians, H.P. Party, 32–3, 35–6, 38, 40–1, 44–5, 52, 54–5
High-Ways, 152
High Wycombe (Bucks.), 127
Hill, J. E. C., 1, 3, 4, 12, 21–2, 24–5, 74, 121–3, 185
Hinton, R. W. K., 134–6
Hobbes, Thomas, 25, 37, 47, 56, 80–2, 94–8
Holland (*see also* Dutch; Netherlands), 101, 133, 203
Holles, Denzil, 5, 7, 29, 35, 38, 42–4, 46–9, 52–3
Holy Communion, 107
Honest Design, The, 193
Honeywood, Lady, 133–4
Honeywood, Sir Robert, 133
Honiton (Devon), 65
Hooker, Col. Edward, 217
Hooker, John, 74
Horse-racing, 151, 174, 176
House, the, *see* Commons; *also* Lords
House(s) of Parliament, 190, 200
Howard, Charles, 187
Howell, R., 21
Hull (Kingston-upon-Hull), 124, 126, 137
Humble Desires of a Free Subject, The, 193
Humble Petition and Address, 197
Humble Petition and Advice, 18–19, 22, 27, 105, 114, 122, 152, 160–1, 163, 172, 183–4, 185, 190
Humble Petition of the Citizens, 49
Humble Petition and Remonstrance, 36
Hume, David, 1
Hundred(s), 194
Hunt, Robert, 180
Huntingdon(shire), 117, 170
Hutchinson, Col. John, 102

Immigration, 130, 142
Imports (*see also* Trade, Foreign), 129, 134
Independency, Independent Party, Independent(s) (*see also* War Party), 2, 6–7, 10, 22–3, 25, 30–2, 36, 38, 42–4, 46, 52–3, 56, 79–80, 83, 86, 144, 166, 170, 189
Independent clergy, *and* congregations, 101, 104–5, 110, 112, 117–20, 188, 225
Inderwick, F. A., 162
Indians, American, 72, 110
Indies (*see also* East *and* West), 138
Industry, 121–3, 131–2, 142
Ingoldsby, Richard, 188–9

Instrument (of Barebone's authority), 18
Instrument (of Barebone's resignation), 229
Instrument of Government, 18–19, 22, 26, 103, 105, 114, 142, 143–5, 147–50, 155–6, 158–60, 164, 171, 175, 197
Interlopers, 124, 132, 134
Interregnum, The, 24, 121, 128, 166, 183
Ipswich, 127
Ireland, 20, 27, 122, 146, 150–1, 154, 156–8, 187, 194, 200–1, 215
Ireland, Gilbert, 180
Ireton, Henry, 6–7, 15, 17, 23, 27, 66
Irish Adventurers, 157
Irish Gentry, 151
Irish M.P.s, 156, 198
Irish Presbyterians, 110
Irish Rebellion, 114
Irish trade, 124
Irish (voluntary) Association, 118
Iron, 141

Jacobins, 165
James I, 62, 116, 146
James II, 163
James, Margaret, 128
Jenkin, William, 51, 86
Jesuits, 9
Jew(s), 116, 142
Johnson, Edward, 133
Johnston, Archibald, of Wariston, 5, 200
Joint-Stock, see Companies
Jones, Philip, 145, 151
Jordan, W. K., 27
Josselin, Ralph, 104, 107
Joyce, Cornet, 46
Jubbes, Lt.-Col. John, 125
Judges, 160, 175–6, 181, 201
Juries, Jurors, 126, 128, 140, 171, 176, 181
Jus Divinum Ministerii Evangelici, 110
Justice, see Law
J.P.(s), Justice(s) of the Peace (see also Commission), 71, 109, 126–7, 168, 170–1, 173, 175–81, 187, 194, 196
Juxon, Bishop, 223

Keeler, M. F., 63
Kelsey, Thomas, 175
Kelston (Somerset), 180
Kent, 53, 118, 166–8, 173–5, 179
Kenyon, J. P., 3–4
Kidderminster (Worcestershire), 106
King, the (see also Charles I; Charles II); (Charles I), 2, 6, 33, 57–8, 85, 100, 167; (Charles I), trial and execution of, 9, 79, 127, 170; (Charles II), 20, 164, 198–9, 201–2; (in the abstract), 80, 122, 163, 190
King, Gregory, 11, 70–1, 73, 214
King, Henry, 113
Kingship (see also Crown; Monarchy), 163, 188, 199
Kirk, the, 31, 33–4, 41, 55
Knowlton, Kent, 174

Labour Movement, 18
Labourers, 61–2, 71–2, 74
Lacedemonian Ephori, 197

Laissez-Faire, 121–2, 140, 142
Laity and Lay Elders, 107–11, 113, 115
Lambert, Maj.-Gen. John, 7, 22–3, 143, 145, 149, 153, 156, 162, 172, 183, 187–8, 191, 197, 199–200
Lancashire, 108–9, 174, 180, 199
Land Sales and Lands to be sold, 14, 126, 129, 140
Landowners and Landlords, 23–5, 124, 127, 140, 174, 198
Langham, Ald. John, 34, 38, 55
Larkham, George, 119
Laslett, P., 1, 3–4
Laud, Archbishop William, 100–1
Lauderdale, Earl of, 5
Laudians, Laudianism, 113, 115, 120, 165
Law, the and Laws, 57, 74–5, 148, 161, 187–8, 194, 197, 201
Law Reform and Legal Reform, 125, 140, 142, 148, 152–3, 171, 186, 193
Lawmaking and Legislation, 144–5, 148, 150, 152, 159, 161, 196–8, 200
Lawrence, Henry, 146
Lawson, Vice-Admiral, 200–1
Lawyers, 153, 171–2
Leather trades, 127
Leathersellers' Co., 217
Leeds, 109, 129, 137
Leicestershire, 180
Lely, Peter, 11
Lenin, 18, 186
Lenthall, William, 187, 201
Leominster (Herefordshire), 112
Leonard, E. M., 122, 128
Levant Co., 131–2, 134–6
Levant trade, 34, 217
Leveller(s), Leveller Movement or Party, 4, 8–10, 12, 15, 17–19, 22–3, 37–8, 43, 49, 56, 57–61, 63–78, 85, 124–6, 130, 140, 171, 184, 186, 193–4
Leveller, The, 193
Leviathan, The (see Hobbes), date of, 223
Lewes (Sussex), 62
Leweston, Dorset, 178
Liberty of Conscience, see Tender Consciences; Toleration
Lichfield (Staffordshire), 128
Lilburne, John, 8, 18, 20, 38, 64, 67, 74–6, 85, 146, 186, 193–4
Lilburne, Col. Robert, 156, 189
Lilburns Ghost, 194
Limbrey, Captain, 227
Limehouse (East London), 117
Lincolnshire, 171
Lisle, Viscount, 51
Livesey, Sir Michael, 173
Local authorities, government, officials (see also Boroughs; City; Corporations; Counties; J.P.s; Parishes; Towns), 61, 126, 128, 140, 157, 167–70, 172–3, 176, 180–1, 184, 186, 196, 203
Local Communities, 61, 141, 165–6, 177, 179, 182, 196
Local rates, 128
Locke, John, 59
Locke, Matthew, 11
Lodder, John, 112

London (*see also* Citizens; City; Committees; Common Council; Companies; Corporation; Militia), 23, 29–32, 44–5, 47–8, 52–3, 57, 64, 67, 109, 112, 114–16, 118, 122, 125, 127, 143, 168, 188, 201; Baptist Association, 118; business community, 22; *Classes* and Provincial Assembly, 108, 118; Committee office in, 35; Corporation of the Poor, 126, 128; disorder in, 42–3, 201; economic role of, 124, 130–1, 136–8; legislation for, 126, 151; revolution in, 45; rule from, 166–7, 174, 179; social policy in, 128, 137
Londoners (*see also* Citizens), 43, 47–8, 133, 137–8
Longstanton (Cambridgeshire), 117
Lord Lieutenant, 216
Lord President, *see* Bradshaw; Council of State; Lawrence
Lord Protector, *see* Cromwell, Oliver *and* Richard; Protector
Lords, House of (*see also* Peers; Upper House), 2, 5, 7, 9, 14, 16, 24, 36–7, 44, 79, 100, 185, 190, 196, 199
Love, Christopher, 31, 41, 55
Low Countries, *see* Netherlands
Ludlow, Edmund, 1, 6, 156, 172, 189, 192, 197, 200–1
Luttrell family, 177

Macaulay, T. B., 1
Mackworth, Col. Humphrey, 145, 149, 153–4
Macpherson, C. B., 58–60, 64, 66–73, 75–7, 95
Maddison, Sir Ralph, 129, 133, 135
Madrid, 122
Magistrates, *see* J.P.s
Magna Carta, 75
Major-Generals, the, 19, 159, 161, 164, 172, 175–6, 178–9, 181, 184, 187
Maltsters, 126
Malynes, Gerard, 129
Manchester, 108
Manchester, earl of, 2, 5, 168
Manhood Suffrage, 58–9, 66–8, 194
Manners, reformation of, 176
Manning, B. S., 24
Manufactures, Manufacturers (*see also* Industry), 123–5, 131, 133, 137, 139
Marshall, Stephen, 50, 53
Marston Moor, 102
Marten, Henry, 6
Martindale, Adam, 107
Marvell, Andrew, 11, 27
Marxist interpretation, 25
Maryland, 132
Mason, Lt.-Col., 189
Masses, the (*see also* Diggers; Levellers; Mob; Poor; Popular Movement; Riots; Servants; Wage-earners), 22, 28
Massey, Colonel, 53
Master of the Rolls, 163
Maynard, John, 160
Mayo, Richard, 70–1
Mazarin, Cardinal, 115
Meal Trade (*see also* Corn; Grain), 137

Meat, 40, 125
Mediterranean, 138
Members of Parliament, M.P.s (*see also* Rumpers), 5, 15, 26, 29, 37, 43, 49–50, 52, 56, 60, 63, 65, 122, 133, 158, 161–3, 171–2, 175, 177, 180, 186–7, 196, 199, 202
Memorandums, 91–3
Merchant Adventurers *and* Merchant Adventurers' Co., 34, 123–4, 132, 135–7, 217
Merchants (*see also* Capitalists), 34, 37, 56, 122–3, 127, 129, 133, 140–1, 160, 217
Meredith, Christopher, 217
Merson, A. L., 219
Methwold, William, 133
Middle Ages, the, 61, 105
Middle class, 26
Middlemen (*see also* Badgers), 126–7, 139–40
Middlesex Artillery Co., 45
Midland(s), East, 118
Militia, 26, 49–50, 159, 168–9, 172–3, 184, 196; in Berkshire, 181; in Dorset, 180; in Hertfordshire, 178; London, 34, 44–7, 49–52, 54–5, 145
Millenarian(s), Millenarianism, 13, 16, 23, 186, 190–1, 195
Milton, John, 11, 17, 27, 79, 86, 183, 185, 199, 202–4
Minchinton, W. E., 219
Ministers, Ministry, *see* Clergy
Minors, 68
Mint, the, 129, 138, 227
Mint affairs and policies, 133–4
Mob(s), 33, 42, 46, 50–1
Moderate, The, 125–6
Monarchy, Monarchies, 16, 26–8, 82, 127, 165, 170, 173, 182, 184, 186, 191, 193, 196, 201–2, 204
Monck, General George, 27, 106, 156, 185, 187, 200–3
Monetary Policies, 129
Money (*see also* Bullion; Coin), 126, 144
Monopolies (*see also* Companies), 77, 132, 141
Montague, Edward, later earl of Sandwich, 145, 187, 189
Montrose, Marquis of, 5
Morrill, J. S., 126
Morton, Thomas, 113
Moss, Lt.-Col., 189
Moyer, Samuel, 23
Muscovy, *see* Russia

Naseby, 30, 102
Nation, *see* State
Naturalisation, 130–1, 136
Naudin, Brother, 116
Navy, Naval Forces (*see also* Armed Forces; Committees), 20, 159
Navy Treasurer, 146
Nayler, James, 147, 162
Nedham, Marchamont, 69, 82, 91, 93, 95, 145, 178
Nef, J. U., 123
Netherlands (*see also* Dutch; Holland; States), 110, 135, 138

Neutrals, Neutralism, Neutrality, 25, 167–9, 178, 181
Neville, Henry, 122, 197
New England, 101, 110
New Forest, 178
New Model Army, 6, 26, 29, 43–5, 47–8, 51, 60, 166, 168, 170
New Testament, 101
Newcastle, Marquis of, 92; Propositions, 6–7
Newcastle-upon-Tyne, 119, 124, 137–8
Newport (Isle of Wight), Treaty of, 7, 168
Newton, Isaac, 11
Nicoll, Anthony, 56, 173, 181
Nobility, Nobles (see also Peerage, Peers), 122, 184, 189, 191, 203
Noel, Martin, 134
Nominated Assembly, see Parliament, Barebone's
Non-conformists, 120
Norfolk, 132, 140, 158, 173, 175
Norman Conquest, 74
North, the, 126
North Shields, 138
North-West, the, 167
Northamptonshire, 61
Northern Counties, 174
Northumberland, earl of, 5
Norton, George, 177
Norwich, 102, 129, 140
Nottingham, 102
Nottinghamshire, 108–9
Noy, William, 64
Nuttall, G. F., 21, 112
Nye, Philip, 101

Oaths (see also Engagement), and Swearing, 79, 82–3, 95, 171, 172
Obligation, political, 79, 83, 85, 91–2, 94–7
Oceana, The, see Harrington
Officers, see Army
Officers, Offices of State, 184, 198
Officials (civil), 148, 150, 160–1, 185; (local), 178, 180–1, 187
Okey, Col., 189
Onslow, Sir Richard, 179
Orange, House of, 155
Ordinances, 147, 150, 152, 158–9, 161–4; making of, 144–5, 148–9, 155
Ordinance, Chancery (1654), 153–4, 159–60, 162; cock-fighting (1654), 149; for creditors (1654), 149; on debtors (1654), 148; Doubling (1646), 41; financial (1654), 150, 160; on hackney-coaches (1654), 151; on highways (1654), 152; Militia (1647), 50, (1648), 168; for murder in Ireland (1654), 151; for poor in London (1647), 126; for poor prisoners (1654), 149; private (1654), 149, 152, 154, 164; on religion (1654) (see also Ejectors; Tryers), 151, 157; Scottish and Irish (1654), 148, 157; on Security (1654), 151; Self-Denying (1645), 14; Sequestration (1654), 149; Social and economic (1654), 151; Treason (1654), 151, 155–7, 159–60; for union with Scotland (1654), 156; uniting parishes (1654), 105

Ordination, 108–9
Osborne, Dorothy, 174
Osborne, Francis, 91–3, 95
Other House, the, see Upper House
Outports, the, 124, 138
Overseas (see also Colonies, Trade), 27
Overton, Richard, 75–6, 193
Overton, Col. Robert, 189
Owen, John, 119
Oxford, 38, 113

Pack(e), Sir Christopher, 161, 217
Packer, Maj. William, 188–9
Paire of Spectacles for the City, A, 54
Palatine Court, 174
Palgrave, Sir John, 173
Papists, 5, 113, 163
Paris, 4, 35, 113, 143
Parish, Parishes, Parochial Organisation, 31–2, 107–8, 112, 115, 127, 225
Parker, Henry, 86
Parliament(s) (see also Commons, House of), 17, 58, 62–4, 67–8, 83, 85, 144–5, 153–4, 156, 158, 160–1, 163–4, 167, 175, 184–6, 187, 194, 196–7, 200–1
Parliament, Barebone's, 4, 13, 18, 22–3, 103–4, 111, 143, 145–8, 150–1, 153–7, 159, 170; Convention, 202–3; First Protectorate, 121, 145, 148, 150, 154, 158–9, 171–2, 175, 197; Long (see also Rump), 2, 7, 8, 14–15, 17, 26, 29, 35–8, 40, 43–56, 58, 63–4, 80, 83, 99–104, 106, 108–9, 111, 114, 120, 121–2, 124–6, 132, 133–4, 150, 168, 170, 190, 192, 196–7, 199, 201–2
Parliament(s), Protectorate, 103–4, 148, 173, 184; Richard Cromwell's, 105, 185, 187, 189–93, 195; Second Protectorate, 22, 115, 147, 152, 159, 161, 163–4, 172, 175–6, 183–4, 187, 189; Short, 100
Parliament House (see also Westminster; Commons), 201
Parliament Men, see M.P.s
Parliamentarians, 3–5, 21–3, 177, 186
Parliamentary connections, 170
Parliamentary constituencies, 186
Parliamentary debates, 182
Parliamentary management, 155
Parliamentary reform (see also Franchise), 171
Parochial Gentry, 25
Parochial livings, 225
Patents, see Monopolies
Peace, see Commission(s); Dutch
Peace Party, 5–7, 35–6, 38, 42–6, 48–51, 54
Pearl, V., 2, 4, 7–8, 21–3
Peerage, Peers (see also Nobility, Nobles), 185, 191, 202
Pendarves, John, 178
Penington, Ald. Isaac, 31, 41, 44
Pennoyer, William, 134
Penruddock's Rising, 114, 172–3, 180–1
Pepys, Samuel, 145
Peter(s), Hugh, 34, 37, 56, 130, 132
Peterloo, 201
Petty, Maximilian, 66–7, 69, 75–6, 220
Peyton, Sir Thomas, 174
Pickering, Sir Gilbert, 23, 143, 187

Pierrepont, William, 188
Plantations, see Colonies
Player, Col., 44, 55
Plumb, J. H., 63
Pocock, J. G. A., 216, 234
Poet(s), poetry, 11, 81–2
Political (and Social), Attitudes, Theory & Thought, 21, 57, 72, 79, 183
Pontefract (Yorkshire), 62
Poor, the (see also Alms-takers; Beggars), 63, 70, 77, 126–8, 140
Poor Law, 128, 139, 151
Poor (or Public) Relief, 78, 121, 128–9, 139–40, 186
Pope, 115
Popery (see also Catholicism), 104
Popular Movement (see also Levellers; Masses; Mob; Riots), 8, 12
Population, 11–12, 28, 59, 70, 73
Ports, English (see also Free Ports; London; Outports), 123
Portsmouth, 201
Post Office, 158
Poulett family, 177
Poverty, see Alms; Beggars; Poor
Powell, Vavasor, 173
Prelacy (see also Episcopacy), 104
Prelatists, 105, 114–15
Presbyterian(s), Presbyterianism (see also Church; Classis; High Presbyterians; Peace Party), 9, 23, 29–56, 79–80, 83–5, 87, 89, 188, 217; (political), 5, 12, 166, 168–70, 173, 177, 179, 199; (religious), 10, 81, 83, 90, 101–4, 108–12, 116, 119–20, 189
Presbyteries, 108
Prices, 11, 33, 40, 123–4, 126–7, 129, 140
Pride, Col., 168, 201
Pride's Purge, 7, 8, 15–16, 58, 80, 110, 125
Priests (Catholic), 114–15
Primogeniture, 77
Privateering, 123
Privy Council (of Protectorate) (see also Council of State), 184, 189–90
Privy Council (royal), 128, 140, 146, 150
Privy Councillors, 187
Prizes, 138–9
Proclamations, 146, 159
Property, Proprietors, Propertied, 37, 48, 59, 73, 75, 77, 143, 147, 157, 170, 198
Protector, the (see also Cromwell, Oliver, and Cromwell, Richard), 27, 185; the (Oliver), 13, 20–1, 103, 144–6, 148–50, 154–6, 158–63, 170–4, 177, 180–1, 183, 186; the (Richard), 190–2
Protectorate, the, 15, 18–19, 24, 104, 106, 108–10, 114–15, 118, 122, 139, 142, 144–5, 151, 154, 166–7, 170–2, 174, 177–82, 183–4, 189–93, 195–6, 199, 202
Protestant(s), Protestantism, 9, 60, 81, 99, 101, 103, 110, 112–15, 120
Provinces (English), 124
Provincial Assembly of London, 34, 54, 55, 108–10
Providence (Divine), 12, 85–8, 90–1, 93–4
Prussia, 123
Prynne, William, 5, 64, 182, 191

Public Faith, the, 38, 139
Public Opinion, 19
Public Record Office, 55
Puritan(s), Puritanism (see also Revolution), 3, 6, 12, 22–3, 32, 101, 106, 114, 120, 165, 167, 170–3, 178–81
Pursuivants, 114
Putney and Putney Debates, 8, 57–9, 64, 66–7, 69, 74–6, 147
Pye, Col. Robert, 46
Pym, John, 5, 39, 145
Pyne, Col. John, 168, 173, 177, 180, 231

Quakers, 13, 105, 117, 119, 177–8
Quarter Sessions, 126, 168, 171
Quartering (see also Free Quarter), 168

Radical(s), Radicalism, 184, 189, 195
Rainsborough, Col. Thomas, 6, 8, 66–7, 220
Rait, R. S., 151
Rand, William, 223
Ranke, L. von, 1
Ranters, 13, 119
Rate of Interest, 129
Rate-payer(s), 59, 62
Reade, Lt.-Col., 76
Rebels, Rebellion, 84–5, 122, 173
'Recognition', The, 158, 175
Recruiters (see also M.P.s), 26
Recusants, 180, 232
Reding, John, 149
Re-exports, re-export trade, 124, 130, 136
Reformadoes, 43–5, 48–9, 54
Reformation, the, 100
Regicide(s), 145
Religion, 12, 99–100, 104, 150, 155, 184
Remonstrance (London), 35–6, 50
Remonstrance of Many Thousand Citizens, 37
Remonstrance of the Free People, 69
Renaissance, the, 165
Rents, 141
'Representative', schemes for a, 194, 196, 198, 201
Republic, the English (see also Commonwealth), 2, 18, 20, 27–8, 204
Republican(s), Republicanism, 3, 10, 15, 19, 21–2, 157–8, 180, 185, 187, 189–93, 199–201, 234
Restoration, the, 4, 12–13, 21–2, 26, 45, 99, 112–13, 120, 145, 152, 164, 166, 177, 183, 186, 202–4
Revenue (see also Finance; Taxation), 150–1, 203
Revolution(s), in agriculture and commerce, 121; capitalist, 4, 10, 21; the (English), 1, 3, 9, 21–2, 24, 79–80, 97, 147, 165, 169–70, 181, 202; of 1641–2, 31; Puritan, 2, 29, 99; Social, 1–2, 26, 56, 186–7; Settlement, 27, 185
Reynell, Thomas, 173
Rich, Col., 66, 200, 220
Right(s), historic and natural, 64
Riots (see also Mob), 12, 125, 127
River Navigation, 131
Robinson, Henry, 86, 124–5, 129–31, 135
Rogers family, 177

Rogers, John, 195, 233
Rogers, Wroth, 179
Roman Catholic, see Catholic; Papist
Rome (see also Popery), Romish, 75, 167
Roots, I. A., 18, 184
Rota Club, 67, 198
Rotation, 198
Rous, Francis, 23, 83–7, 89–90, 92–3, 145
Royal Society, 11
Royalist(s), Royalist Party, Royalism (see
  also Delinquents), 5, 9, 14, 17, 19–20,
  22–4, 30, 36–9, 43, 48, 55, 67, 79–81,
  83, 85, 99, 102, 111, 113–14, 123, 132,
  155, 157, 159–60, 167–70, 172, 174–5,
  177–81, 184, 186–90, 193, 199, 201
Rudé, G., 33
Ruling (or Governing) Class, 181, 186,
  188
Rump, the (see also Parliament, Long),
  9–10, 12–16, 23, 26, 33, 103–4, 121–3,
  125–32, 135, 137–43, 147–8, 151, 153–4,
  156, 161, 169–71, 185–6, 192–7, 199–
  203, 234
Rumpers (see also M.P.s), 157, 177, 200–1
Russia Co., 132, 137
Rye, 126

Sabbath (see also Sunday), 109, 171
Sadler, John, 133
St Albans (Hertfordshire), 65
St Bartholomew's Day, 120
St Bartholomew Exchange (London), 112
St Ewins (Bristol), 116
St Gregory's, London, 114
St James's (Westminster), 195
St James Garlickhithe (London), 39
St John, Oliver, 52, 134, 188
St Margaret's, Fish St (London), 108
St Michael, Crooked Lane (London), 108
St Paul and Pauline injunctions, 80, 83–4,
  86–7, 89
St Stephen's Coleman Street (London), 31
Saints, the, 18, 27, 112, 116, 181, 186, 195
Salt, 125
Salwey, Richard, 133
Sanders, widow, 117
Sanderson, Robert, 90, 92
Sandwich (Kent), 65
Sandwich, earl of, see Montague
Sandys, Sir Edwin, 65
Saunders, Col., 189
Sanhedrin, 195
Savoy Confession, 118
Saye, Lord S. and Sele, 5
Schochet, G., 73
Scientific advances, 11, 214
Scobell, Henry, 148, 151, 164
Scot, Thomas, 122
Scot and Lot, 62–3
Scotland, 5, 20, 27, 100, 150, 154, 156–7,
  168, 187, 194, 200, 215–16
Scot(s), the, Scottish, 5–7, 9, 12, 29, 31,
  33, 35, 43, 44–5, 49, 55, 100–3, 110,
  156, 158, 198, 200
Scriptures, see Bible; New Testament
Seamen, 56, 140
'Secluded Members', 201–2
Second Civil War, 4, 7, 103, 168

Secretary of State, 187
Sect(s), Sectaries (see also Congregations;
  Gathered Churches; Puritans), 25, 31,
  38, 42, 177–8, 185, 189–91, 193
Security, 82, 140–1, 150–1, 156
Self-Denying Ordinance, 14
Self-Denying representative, a, 193–4
Senate, schemes for a, 196–9, 201, 203,
  234
Separated   Churches,   see   Gathered
  Churches
Separation of Powers, 17
Separatists, 105
Sequestration, 149, 169, 174, 178, 180
Serfdom, 74
Sergeant-at-Arms, 146
Sergeantcies (legal), 160
Servants, 58–60, 65–75, 77–8, 198
Settlement, quest for, 1, 5, 6, 8–13, 16–18,
  21, 26–7, 147, 162, 167, 171–2, 175,
  176–7, 181–2, 185, 193, 195, 199, 202,
  204
Sexby, Edward, 76
Shephard, Samuel, 40
Sherborne (Dorset), 70
Sheriffs, 146, 174, 176, 194
Sheriffs of London, 50
Ships and Shipping, 123, 134–6, 141
Shires, see Counties
Shropshire, 109
Silk, 127
Silver, 129
Simpson, John, 118
Simpson, Sidrach, 101
Single person, see King; Monarchy; Pro-
  tector
Sion College (London), 29, 34, 41–2
Skinner, Q., 2, 10, 20, 216
Skinner, Robert, 113
Skinners' Co., 133
Skinners' Hall, 49
Skippon, Philip, 6, 145, 229
Slave(s), Slavery, 74, 221
Slump, see Depression
Smith, Sir Thomas, 60–1, 74
Smithfield (London), 43
Smyth, Hugh, 177
Social and Economic Classes, Groups and
  Structure, 22, 71, 183, 193
Social Policy and Policies, 122
Socinians, 105, 119
Soldiers, Soldiery (and ex-soldiers; see
  also Agitators; Army; Reformadoes),
  12, 33, 37, 43, 48, 58, 70, 76–77,
  102, 126, 139, 158, 178, 180, 190–1,
  201
Solemn Engagement, The, 49–50
Solemn League and Covenant, see
  Covenant
Solicitor-General, 155
Somerset, 119, 126–7, 166, 168, 173, 175,
  177, 180, 231
Southern Europe, 123
Southwark, 53, 217
Sowton, Daniel, 217
Spain, 122
Spaniards, Spanish, 155, 160
Speaker, the, 51, 153, 201

Speckington (Somerset), 180
Speculum Libertatis Angliae, 194
Speenhamland, Berks., 181
Stalin, 4
Stannary Parliament, 61
Staplers (wool), 126–7, 133
Stapleton, Sir Philip, 29, 38
Star Chamber, 167
State, the, *and* Nation-State (*see also* Commonwealth; Government; Protectorate), 147, 165, 167, 175, 179
State Papers, 151, 185
States (States-General of Netherlands), 155
Stationers' Co., 33
Status, social, 26, 60, 66
Statute(s), *see* Act(s); *also* Ordinances
Stepney, 102, 112, 117–18
Stone, L., 1, 3
Stow, John, 48
Straits, the (of Gibraltar), 139
Strickland, Walter, 23, 143, 153, 161, 187
Strode, William, 44, 177
Stuart(s), 27, 120, 152, 155, 166, 188, 193, 204
Stubbe, Henry, 197
Sub-commissioners, for sequestrations, 169
Sub-Committee, of Committee of Safety, 200
Suffolk, 71–2, 132, 158
Suffrage, *see* Franchise; Manhood
Sugar, 124, 141
Sunday(s), 107, 111, 116
'Superstructures', 198
Surman, C. E., 21
Surrey, 179
Sweden, Swedes, Swedish, 141, 162
Swinfen, John, 5
Sydenham, William, 23, 145, 154

Tawney, R. H., 122
Taxation, Taxes, 19–20, 25, 37–40, 100, 125, 160, 166–8, 173, 193, 201–2
Taylor, William, 31
'Tender Consciences' (*see also* Toleration), 31, 82, 102
Theatres, 13
Thermidor, 4
Thomas, K., 8
Thomason, George, 29, 36, 192, 217
Thompson, George, 135
Thompson, Henry, 133, 137
Thompson, Maurice, 133–5
Thorp, Sergeant, 127
Thread, gold and silver, 132
Thurloe, John, 147, 151–2, 154, 162, 181, 187–9
Tichburne, Ald., 146
Tithes, 17, 57, 104, 112, 140, 147, 163
Tobacco, 124, 173
Toleration, religious, *and* Tolerance, 13, 17, 57, 99, 103, 105, 115, 125, 147, 170–1, 184–6, 193
Tombes, John, 112, 119
Tower, the, 53, 201
Towns, 61, 82, 146
Towse, Ald. John, 39

Trade, and Trade Policy (*see also* Re-exports), 20, 125–6, 130–1, 137, 142; colonial, 133, 135, 138, 141; domestic *or* internal, 121, 129, 132; foreign, *or* overseas, 123–4, 133, 138, 141
Traders, Tradesmen, *see* Merchants
Trained Bands (of London), 44–5, 47–8, 50, 54–5
Treason, 151–2
Treasurers-at-War, 146
Treasury, the, 150
Treasury Commissioner, a, 162
Tregony (Cornwall), 65
Trenchard, John, 133
Trevelyan, George, 177
Trevelyan, G. M., 1, 165
Trevor-Roper, H. R., 1, 3, 23–4, 144, 165–6
Trinity House, 134–5
Troops, *see* Soldiers
Trotsky, 4
'True Levellers', 66
Tryers, 104–5, 151, 163, 173
Tudor(s), 141, 165, 198
Turk(s), Turkey, 85, 138
Twisden, Thomas, 160
Tyne, river, 138
Tyranny, Tyrant(s), 84–5

Underdown, D., 8, 14, 18–19, 25
Underhill, Thomas, 217
Unemployment, 125
Union (*see also* British Isles; Dutch), Anglo-Scottish, 156–7
Universities, 158
Unwin, G., 122–3
Upholsterers' Co., 133
Upper Bench, Court of, 161
Upper House, *or* Other House (*see also* Lords, House of), 24, 184–5, 187, 190, 197
Ussher, James, 120

Vagrants (*see also* Beggars), 126, 128
Valor Ecclesiasticus, a new, 105
Vane, Sir Henry, the younger, 6, 15–16, 133–4, 137, 183, 189, 192, 197, 199–200
Vaughan, Henry, 82
Vaughan, Col. Joseph, 217
Veall, D., 148
Venetian ambassador, 122
Venetian resident, 233
Verney family, 174
Verney, Henry, 176
Verney, Sir Ralph, 174–6
Vestry, Vestries, 34
Veto, power of, 190
Village(s), Village Meetings, 61
Villein(s), Villeinage, 74, 221
Vindication of the Presbyteriall Government, A, 110
Viner, *or* Vyner, Ald., 48, 217
Violet, Thomas, 122, 130, 134–6, 140
Virginia, 65, 132–3
Vowell, Peter, 155
Vox Plebis, 74–5

Wade, John, 180

Wage-earners, wage-earning class, 12, 58–60, 65–6, 70–3, 75–7
Wages, 12, 70–1, 73
Wales, and the Welsh, 21, 24, 118, 167, 170, 173, 177, 181, 216
Walker, Clement, 5, 46
Wallace, J. M., 97, 222
Waller, Edmund, 81
Waller, Sir William, 52–4
Wallingford House, 188–9, 191–2, 200
Wallis, John, 96
Walpole, Sir Robert, 40
Walton, Isaac, 82
Walwyn, William, 76, 132, 193
War Finance, 140
War Party (see also Independents), 5–7, 9–10
Wariston, see Johnston
Warner, Ald. John, 31–2, 48
Warner, Samuel, 32
Warren, Albertus, 90, 95
Warwick, earl of, 5
Warwickshire, 180
Watermen's Co., 56
Weavers' Hall, 39, 46
Webster, C., 223, 226–7
Wedgwood, C. V., 1, 15
Weldon, Sir Anthony, 168
Welsh, see Wales
Wenlock, John, 85
Wentworth, Darcy, 177
Wentworth, Sir Peter, 160, 180
West Country, and Western, 110, 118, 139
West Indian trade, 217
West Indies, 121, 132
Western Circuit, 126–7
Western Europe, 123
Western Gentry, 173
Westminster, 45, 49–52, 167–9, 199, 201
Westminster Assembly, see Assembly of Divines
Westminster Confession, The, 106
Westmorland, 119, 126
Whig Tradition, Whig(s), Whiggish, 59, 186

Whitehall, 143
Whitelocke, Bulstrode, 37, 43, 46, 50–2, 159–60, 162, 187, 200–1
Whiteman, A., 225
Whitsun, 114
Widdrington, Sir Thomas, 187
Wigan (Lancashire), 65
Wight, Isle of, 7
Wildman, John, 68, 193
William III, 27, 62, 185
Williamson, J. A., 135
Wills, probate of, 147, 163
Wilson, C. H., 4
Wiltshire, 119, 126
Windsor, 163
Windsor Castle, 189
Wine(s), 160
Winstanley, Gerrard, 9, 86
Wirksworth, Derbyshire, 108–9
Wise, Daniel, 181
Witham, George, 217
Wither, George, 91–3
Wollaston, Ald., 217
Wolseley, Charles, 23, 143, 153–4, 162, 187
Women, 76–7, 116–17
Wool, Wool Trade, Woollens (see also Cloth; Draperies), 124–6, 133, 139
Woolrych, A., 12, 18–19, 21
Wootton Bassett (Wiltshire), 65
Worcester, 14, 128, 170
Worcestershire, 65, 112, 119
Worden, B., 226
Worsley, Benjamin, 133–6
Wraxall (Somerset), 180
Wyndham family, 177

Yarmouth, 102, 119, 133
Yarranton, Andrew, 71
Yonge, Walter, 29
York, 104, 127, 133, 137
Yorkshire, 102, 109, 160, 166–7, 177

Zagorin, P., 3, 165